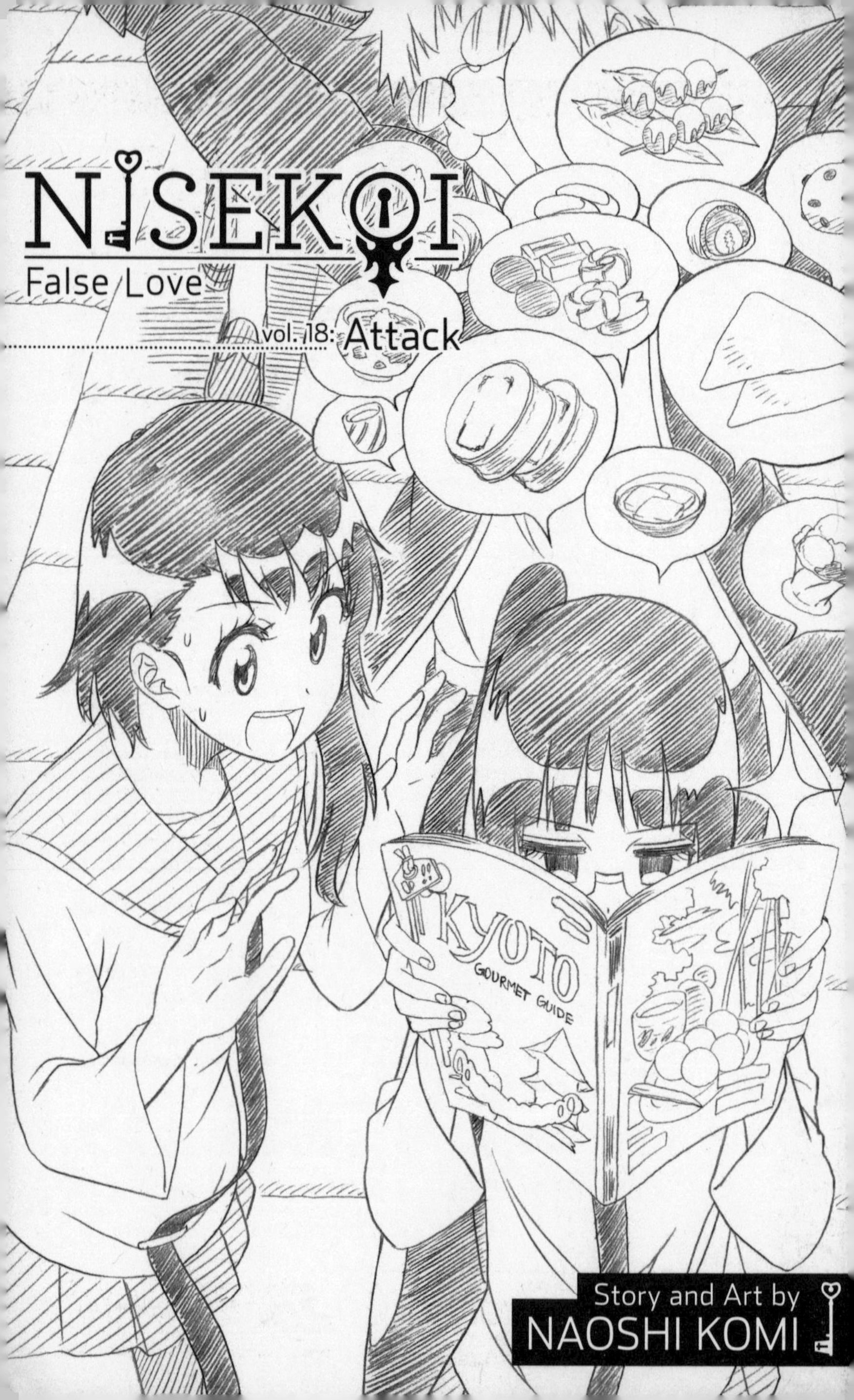
NISEKOI
False Love
vol. 18: Attack
KYOTO
GOURMET GUIDE
Story and Art by
NAOSHI KOMI

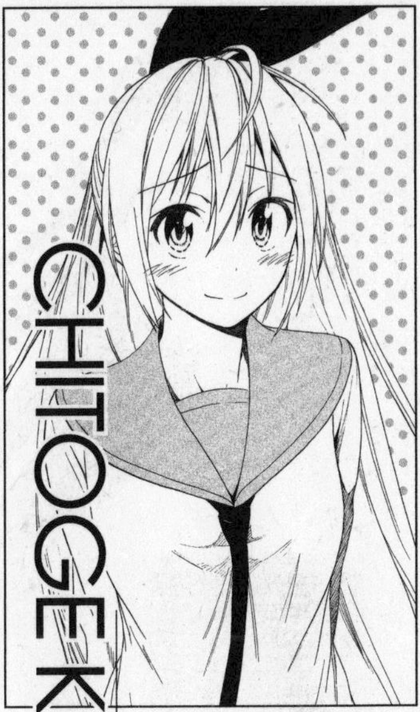

CHITOGE KIRISAKI

A half-Japanese bombshell with stellar athletic abilities. Short-tempered and violent. Comes from a family of gangsters.

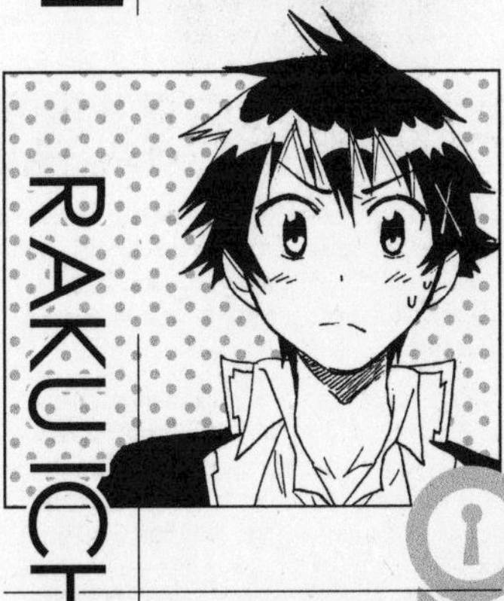

RAKU ICHIJO

A normal teen whose family happens to be yakuza. Cherishes a pendant given to him by a girl he met ten years ago.

KOSAKI ONODERA

A girl Raku has a crush on. Beautiful and sweet, Kosaki has no shortage of admirers. She's a terrible cook but makes food that *looks* amazing.

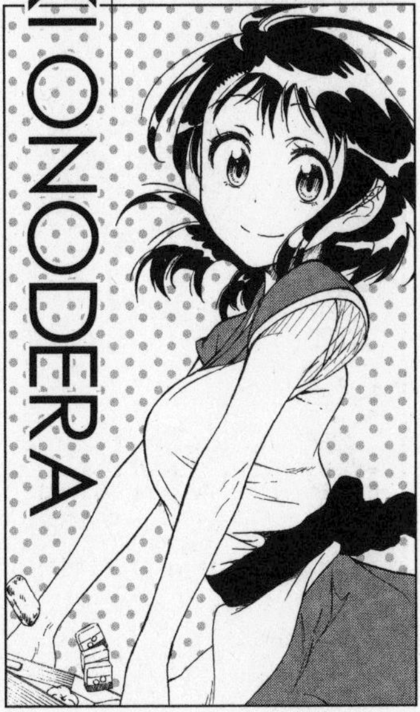

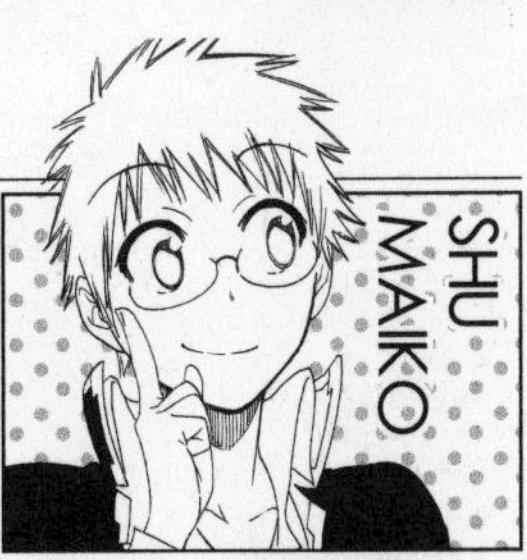

SHU MAIKO

Raku's best friend is outgoing and girl-crazy.

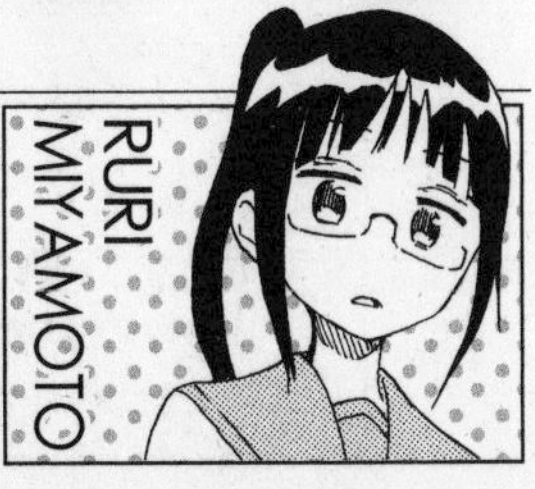

RURI MIYAMOTO

Kosaki's best gal pal. Comes off as aloof, but is actually a devoted and highly intuitive friend.

MARIKA TACHIBANA

Daughter of the chief of police, Marika is Raku's fiancée, according to an agreement made by their fathers—an agreement Marika takes very seriously! Also has a key and remembers making a promise with Raku ten years ago.

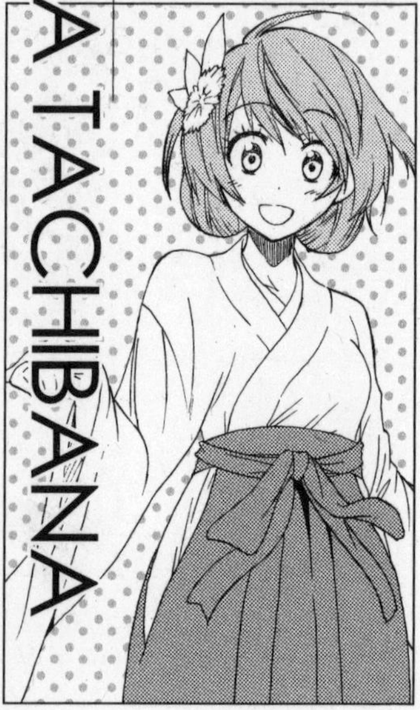

YUI KANAKURA

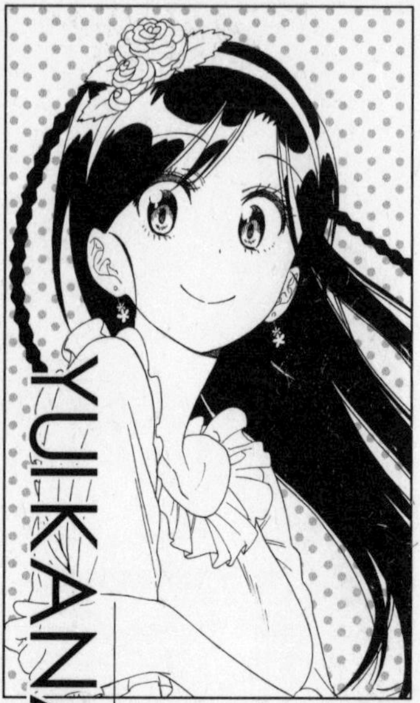

A childhood friend of Raku's, Yui is the head of a Chinese mafia gang and the homeroom teacher of Raku's class at his school. She is currently staying at Raku's house and also has a special key linked to some kind of promise...

CHARACTERS & STORY

Ten years ago, Raku Ichijo made a promise with a girl he loved that they would get married when they met again...and he still treasures the pendant she gave him to seal their pledge.

Thanks to his family's circumstances, Raku has to pretend he's dating Chitoge Kirisaki, the daughter of a rival gangster. Despite their constant spats, Raku and Chitoge manage to fool everyone. Chitoge also has a token from her first love ten years ago—an old key. Meanwhile, Raku's crush, Kosaki, also has a key, as does Marika, the girl Raku's father has arranged for him to marry. Now, Raku's childhood friend Yui has been hired as their homeroom teacher. It turns out that she, too, has a key connected to a special promise. And when the class goes on their school trip, things start to get a little crazy!

SEISHIRO TSUGUMI

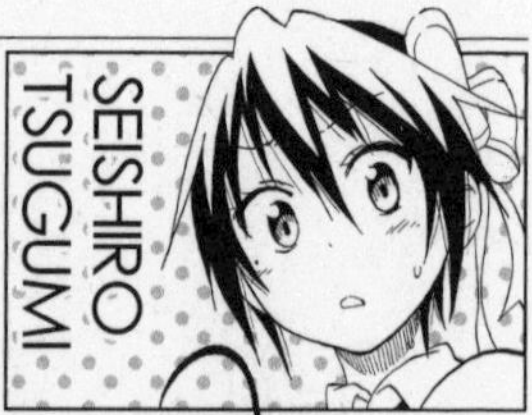

Trained as an assassin in order to protect Chitoge, Tsugumi is often mistaken for a boy.

HARU ONODERA

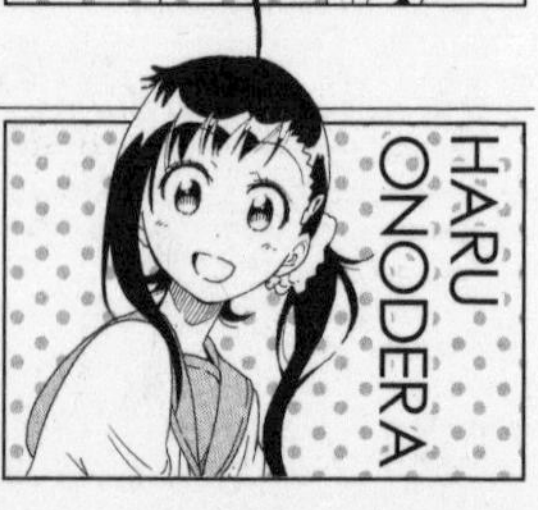

Kosaki's adoring younger sister. Has a low opinion of Raku.

NISEKOI
False Love

vol. 18: Attack

TABLE OF CONTENTS

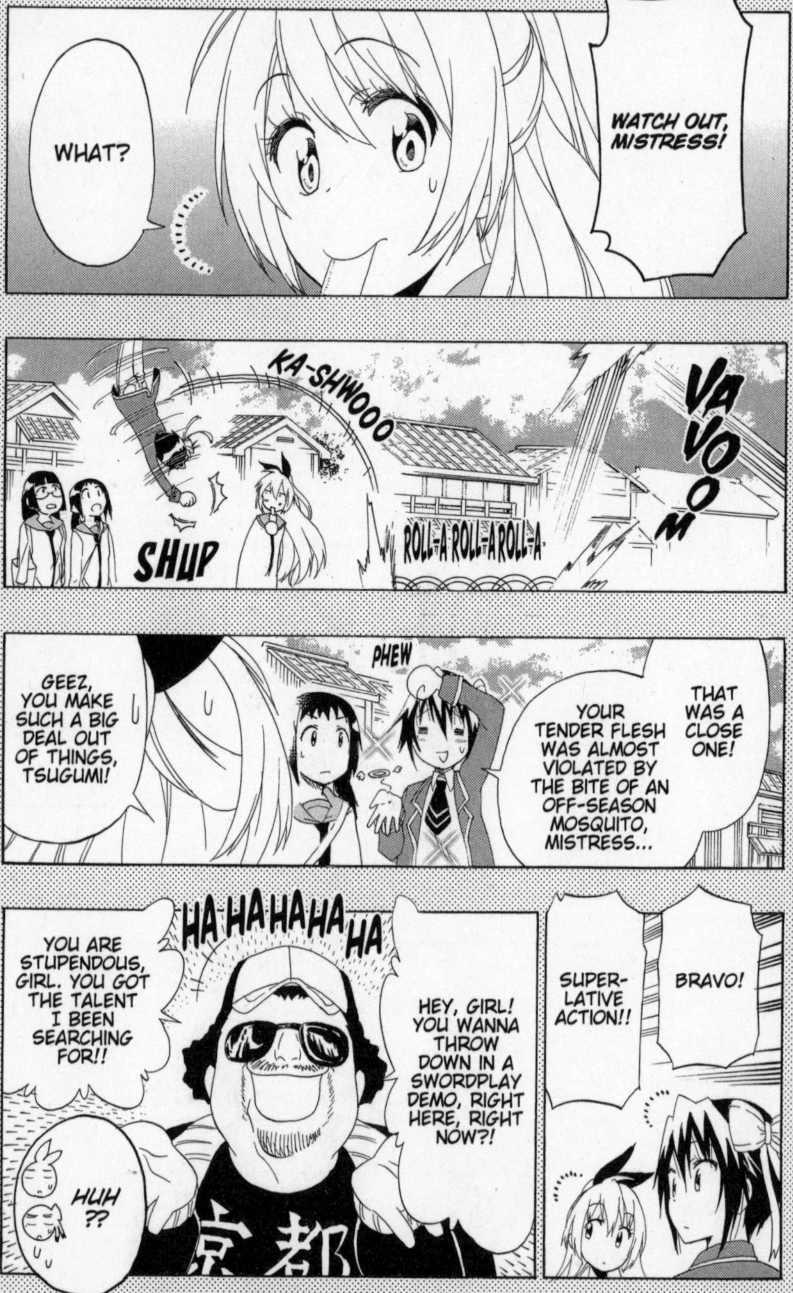
WATCH OUT, MISTRESS!
WHAT?
VAVOOM
ROLL-A ROLL-A ROLL-A
KA-SHWOOO
SHUP
THAT WAS A CLOSE ONE!
YOUR TENDER FLESH WAS ALMOST VIOLATED BY THE BITE OF AN OFF-SEASON MOSQUITO, MISTRESS...
PHEW
GEEZ, YOU MAKE SUCH A BIG DEAL OUT OF THINGS, TSUGUMI!
BRAVO!
SUPER-LATIVE ACTION!!
HA HA HA HA HA
HEY, GIRL! YOU WANNA THROW DOWN IN A SWORDPLAY DEMO, RIGHT HERE, RIGHT NOW?!
YOU ARE STUPENDOUS, GIRL. YOU GOT THE TALENT I BEEN SEARCHING FOR!!
HUH ??

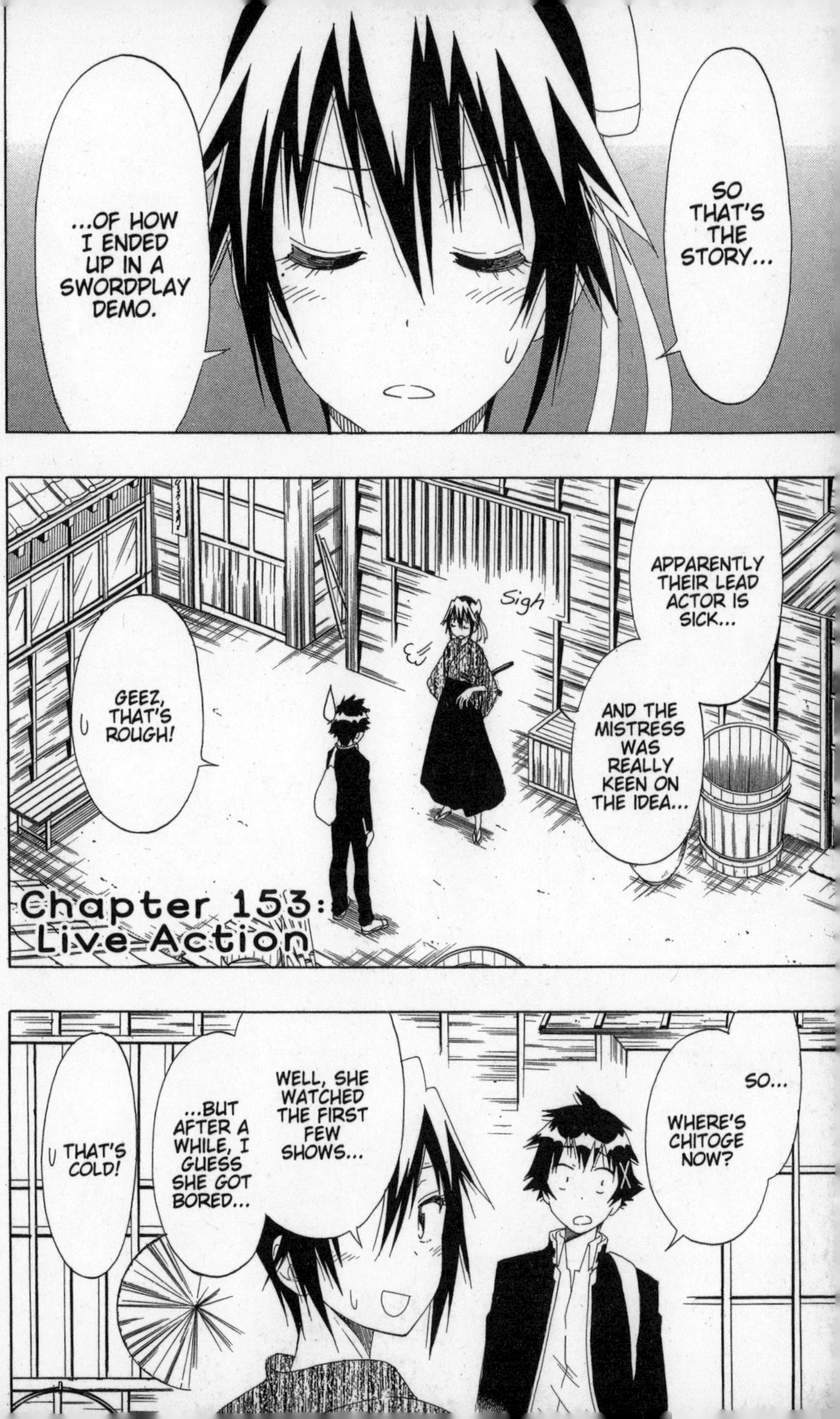
SO THAT'S THE STORY...
...OF HOW I ENDED UP IN A SWORDPLAY DEMO.
APPARENTLY THEIR LEAD ACTOR IS SICK...
AND THE MISTRESS WAS REALLY KEEN ON THE IDEA...
Sigh
GEEZ, THAT'S ROUGH!
Chapter 153: Live Action
SO...
WHERE'S CHITOGE NOW?
WELL, SHE WATCHED THE FIRST FEW SHOWS...
...BUT AFTER A WHILE, I GUESS SHE GOT BORED...
THAT'S COLD!

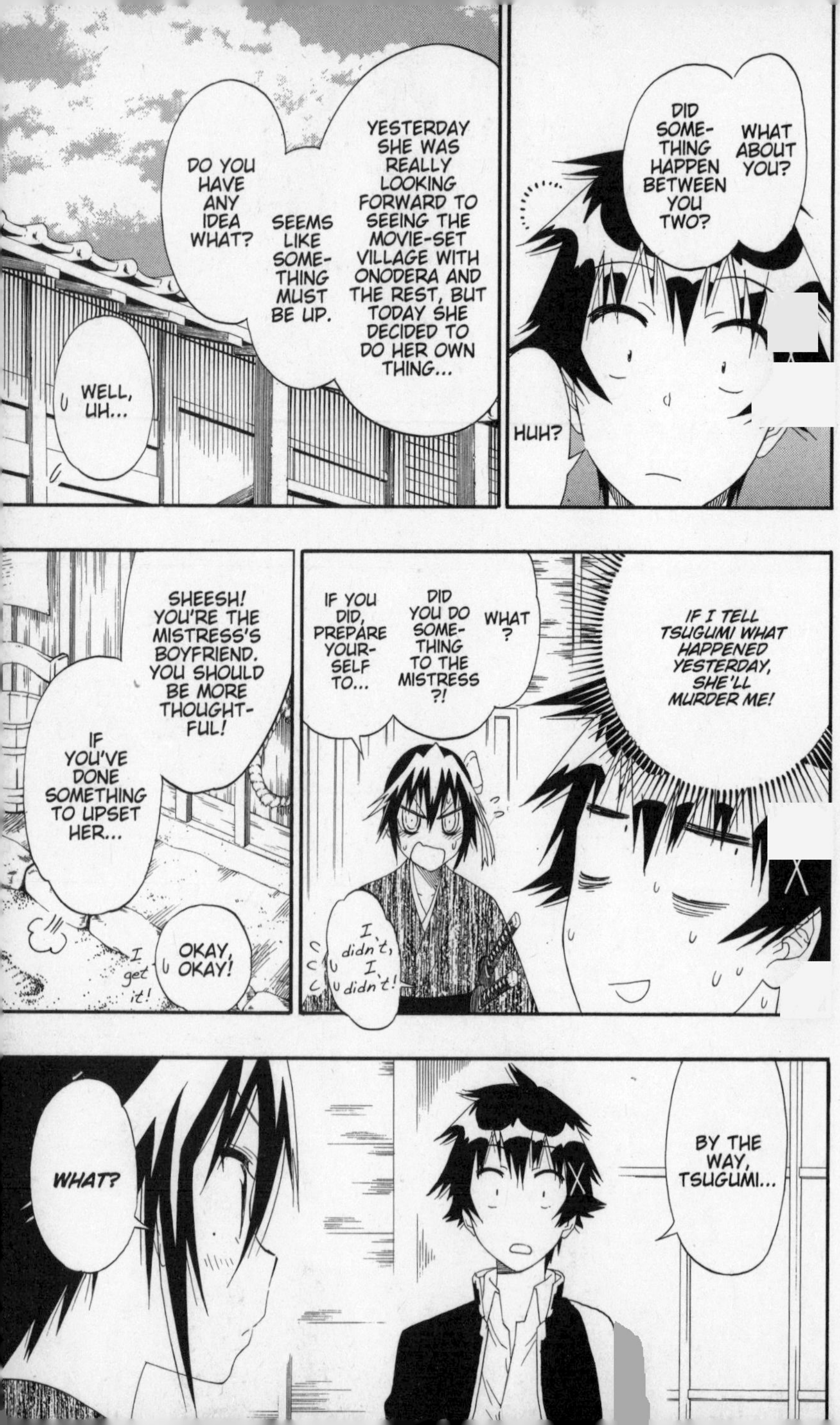

WHAT ABOUT YOU?
DID SOMETHING HAPPEN BETWEEN YOU TWO?
HUH?
YESTERDAY SHE WAS REALLY LOOKING FORWARD TO SEEING THE MOVIE-SET VILLAGE WITH ONODERA AND THE REST, BUT TODAY SHE DECIDED TO DO HER OWN THING...
SEEMS LIKE SOMETHING MUST BE UP.
DO YOU HAVE ANY IDEA WHAT?
WELL, UH...
IF I TELL TSUGUMI WHAT HAPPENED YESTERDAY, SHE'LL MURDER ME!
WHAT?
DID YOU DO SOMETHING TO THE MISTRESS?!
IF YOU DID, PREPARE YOURSELF TO...
I didn't, I didn't!
SHEESH! YOU'RE THE MISTRESS'S BOYFRIEND. YOU SHOULD BE MORE THOUGHTFUL!
IF YOU'VE DONE SOMETHING TO UPSET HER...
OKAY, OKAY!
I get it!
BY THE WAY, TSUGUMI...
WHAT?

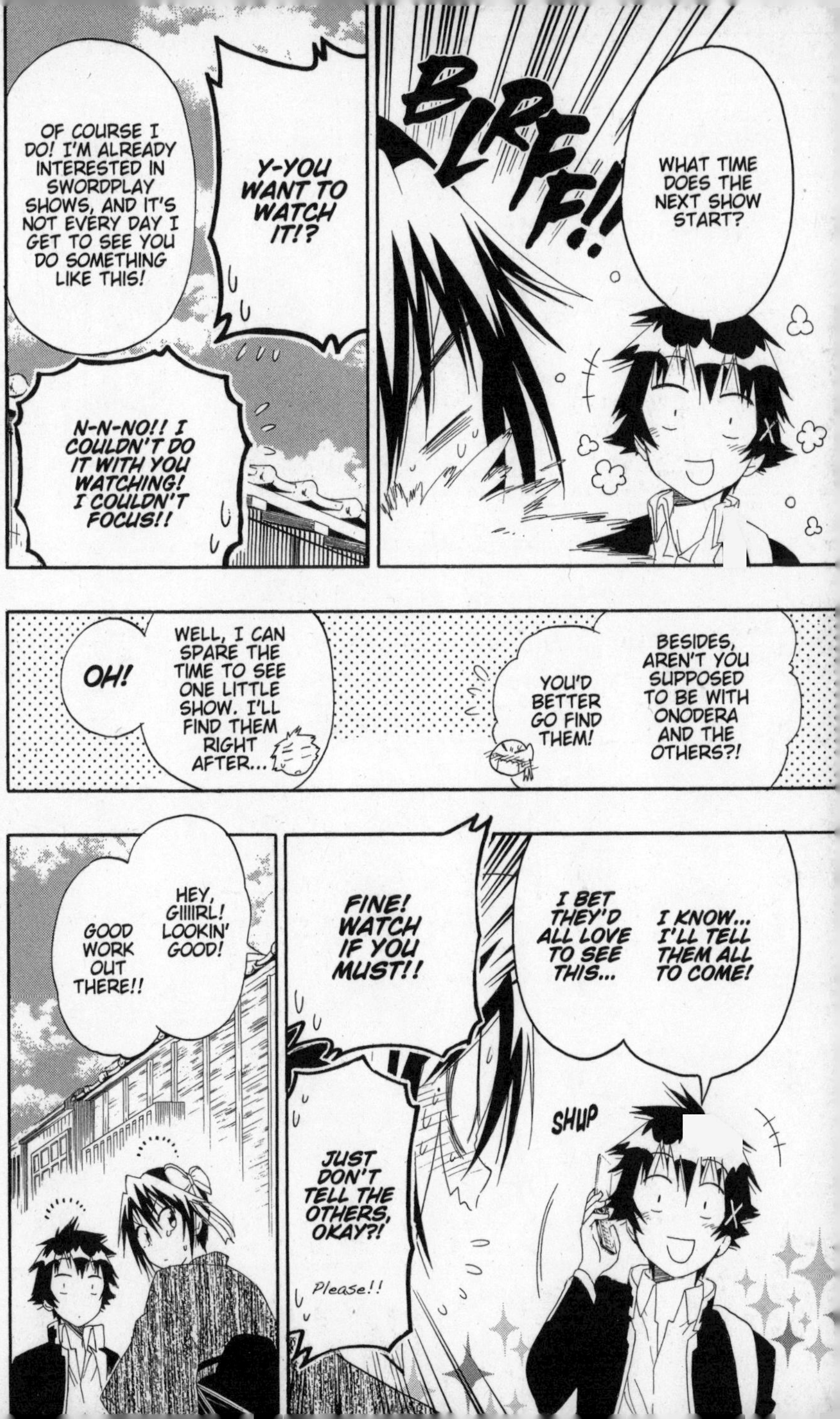
WHAT TIME DOES THE NEXT SHOW START?
BIFF!!
Y-YOU WANT TO WATCH IT!?
OF COURSE I DO! I'M ALREADY INTERESTED IN SWORDPLAY SHOWS, AND IT'S NOT EVERY DAY I GET TO SEE YOU DO SOMETHING LIKE THIS!
N-N-NO!! I COULDN'T DO IT WITH YOU WATCHING! I COULDN'T FOCUS!!
BESIDES, AREN'T YOU SUPPOSED TO BE WITH ONODERA AND THE OTHERS?!
YOU'D BETTER GO FIND THEM!
WELL, I CAN SPARE THE TIME TO SEE ONE LITTLE SHOW. I'LL FIND THEM RIGHT AFTER...
OH!
I KNOW... I'LL TELL THEM ALL TO COME!
I BET THEY'D ALL LOVE TO SEE THIS...
SHUP
FINE! WATCH IF YOU MUST!!
JUST DON'T TELL THE OTHERS, OKAY?!
Please!!
HEY, GIIIRL! LOOKIN' GOOD!
GOOD WORK OUT THERE!!

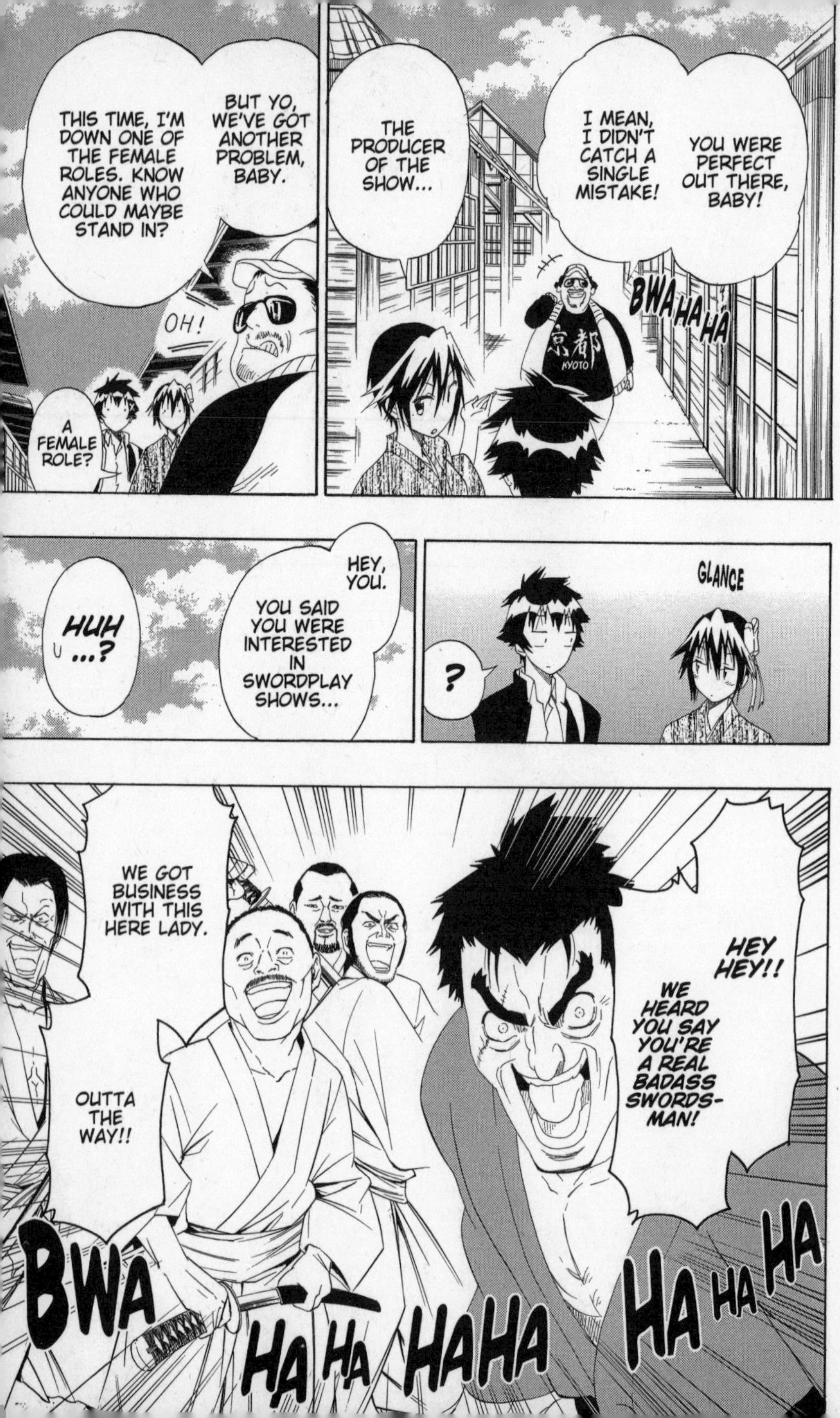
YOU WERE PERFECT OUT THERE, BABY!
I MEAN, I DIDN'T CATCH A SINGLE MISTAKE!
BWA HA HA
THE PRODUCER OF THE SHOW...
BUT YO, WE'VE GOT ANOTHER PROBLEM, BABY.
THIS TIME, I'M DOWN ONE OF THE FEMALE ROLES. KNOW ANYONE WHO COULD MAYBE STAND IN?
OH!
A FEMALE ROLE?
GLANCE
?
HEY, YOU.
YOU SAID YOU WERE INTERESTED IN SWORDPLAY SHOWS...
HUH ...?
HEY HEY!!
WE HEARD YOU SAY YOU'RE A REAL BADASS SWORDS-MAN!
WE GOT BUSINESS WITH THIS HERE LADY.
OUTTA THE WAY!!
BWA HA HA HAHA HA HA HA

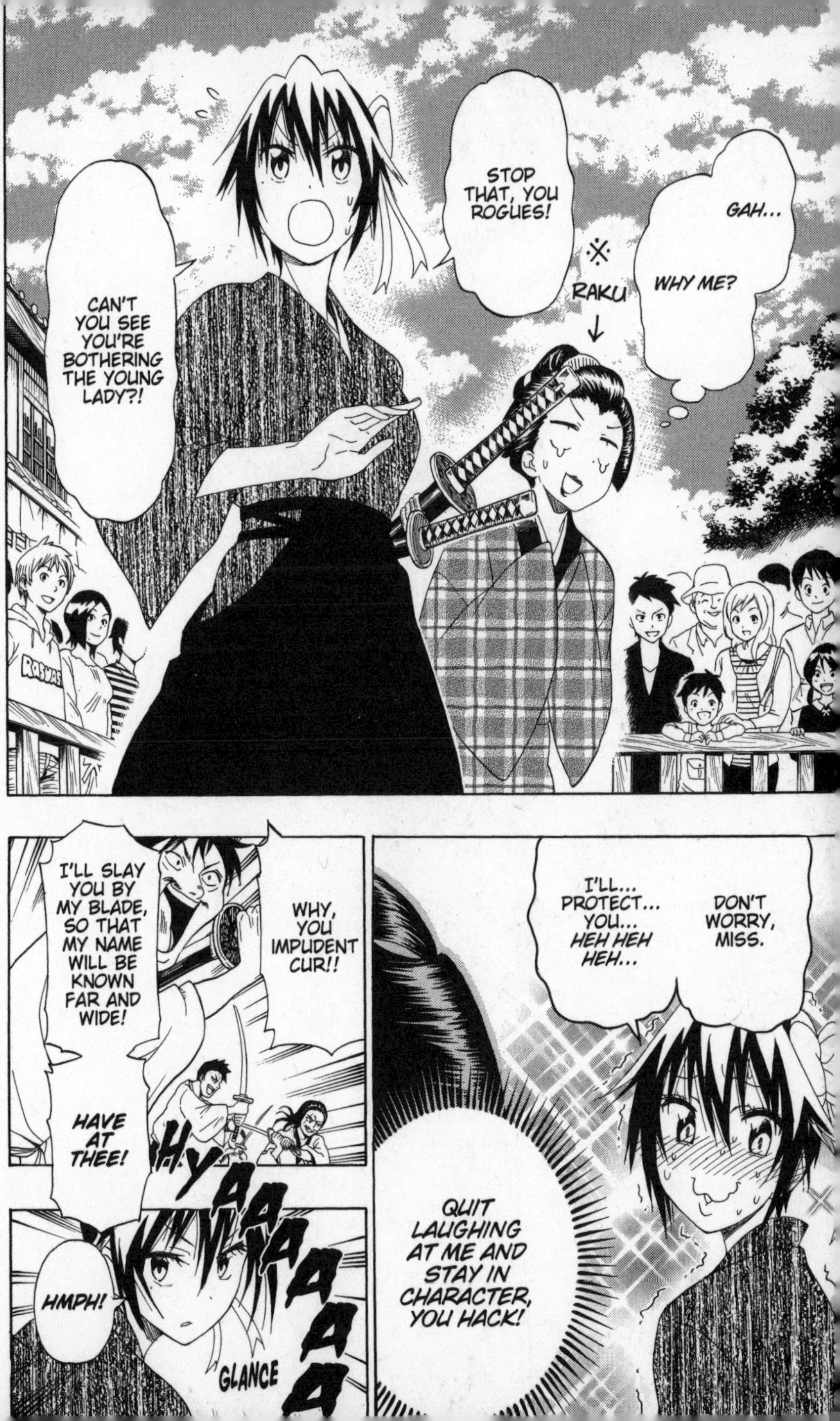
GAH... WHY ME?
※ RAKU
STOP THAT, YOU ROGUES!
CAN'T YOU SEE YOU'RE BOTHERING THE YOUNG LADY?!
DON'T WORRY, MISS.
I'LL... PROTECT... YOU... HEH HEH HEH...
QUIT LAUGHING AT ME AND STAY IN CHARACTER, YOU HACK!
WHY, YOU IMPUDENT CUR!!
I'LL SLAY YOU BY MY BLADE, SO THAT MY NAME WILL BE KNOWN FAR AND WIDE!
HAVE AT THEE!
HYAAAAAAAA
GLANCE
HMPH!

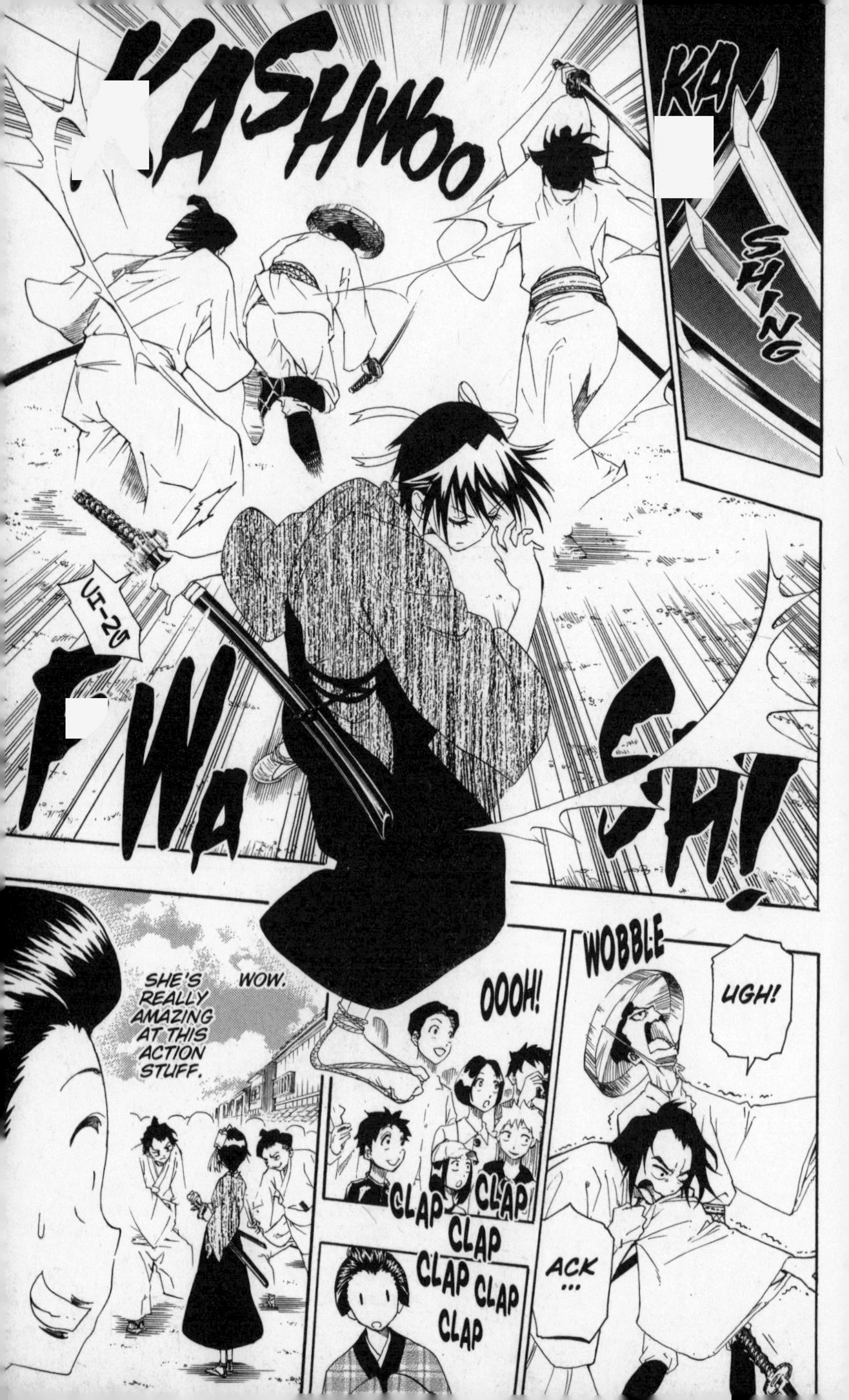

KA
SHING
KASHWOO
UI-ZU
FWaSH!
WOBBLE
UGH!
ACK ...
OOOH!
CLAP CLAP CLAP CLAP CLAP CLAP
WOW.
SHE'S REALLY AMAZING AT THIS ACTION STUFF.

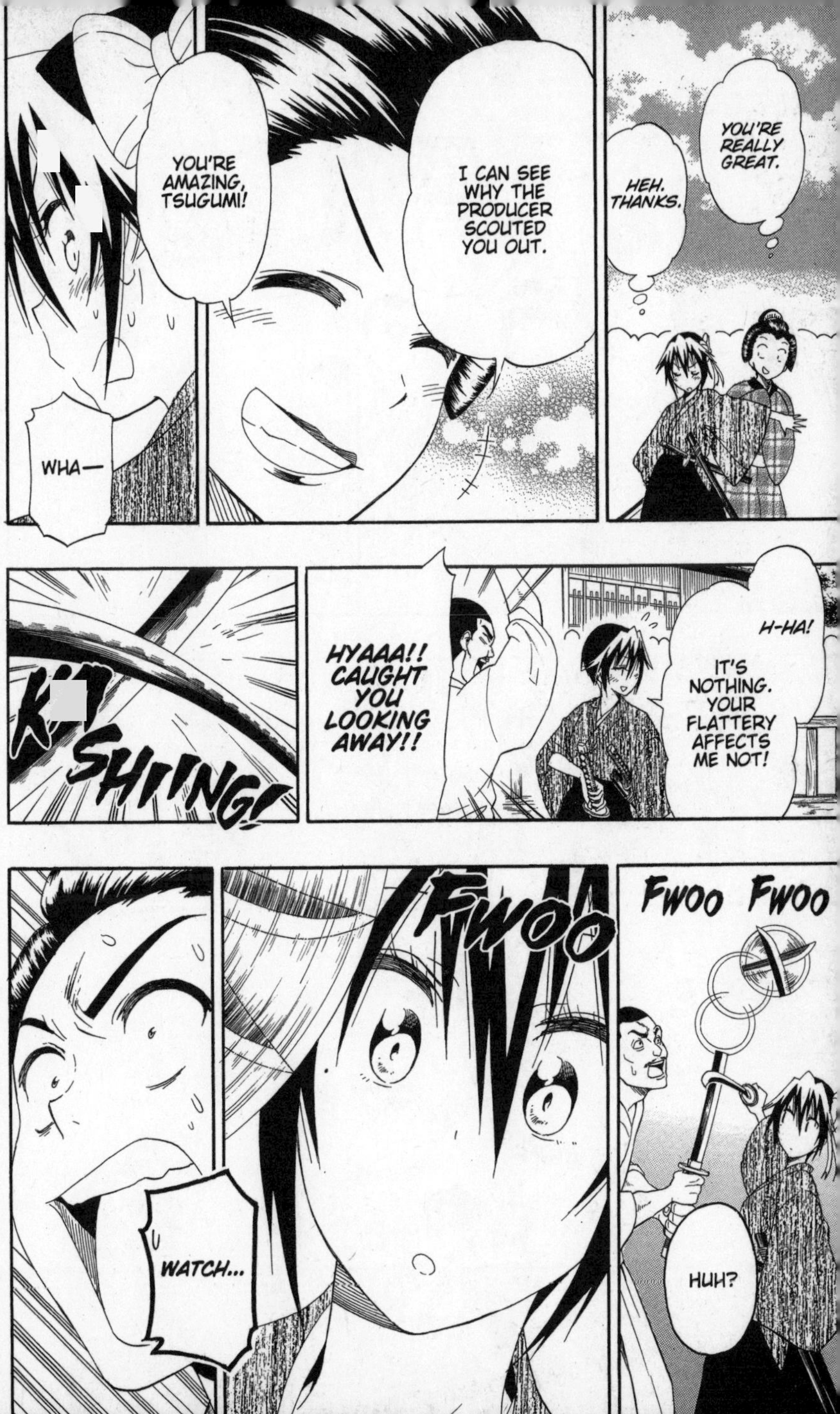
YOU'RE REALLY GREAT.
HEH. THANKS.
YOU'RE AMAZING, TSUGUMI!
I CAN SEE WHY THE PRODUCER SCOUTED YOU OUT.
WHA—
H-HA!
IT'S NOTHING. YOUR FLATTERY AFFECTS ME NOT!
HYAAA!! CAUGHT YOU LOOKING AWAY!!
K SHING!
FWOO FWOO
HUH?
FWOO
WATCH...

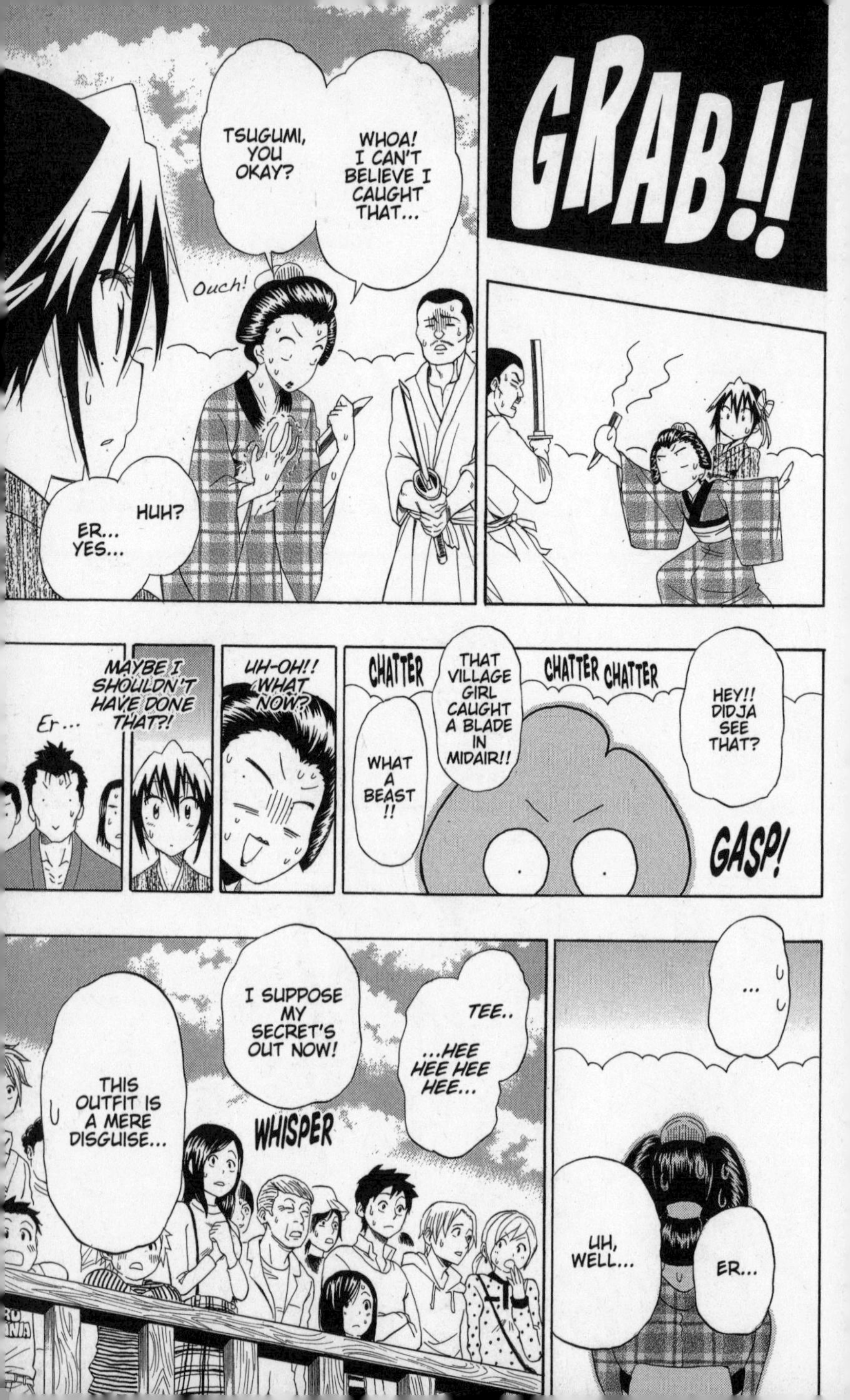
GRAB!!
WHOA! I CAN'T BELIEVE I CAUGHT THAT...
TSUGUMI, YOU OKAY?
Ouch!
HUH?
ER... YES...
HEY!! DIDJA SEE THAT?
GASP!
CHATTER CHATTER
THAT VILLAGE GIRL CAUGHT A BLADE IN MIDAIR!!
CHATTER
WHAT A BEAST!!
UH-OH!! WHAT NOW?
MAYBE I SHOULDN'T HAVE DONE THAT?!
Er...
...
ER...
UH, WELL...
TEE..
...HEE HEE HEE...
I SUPPOSE MY SECRET'S OUT NOW!
WHISPER
THIS OUTFIT IS A MERE DISGUISE...

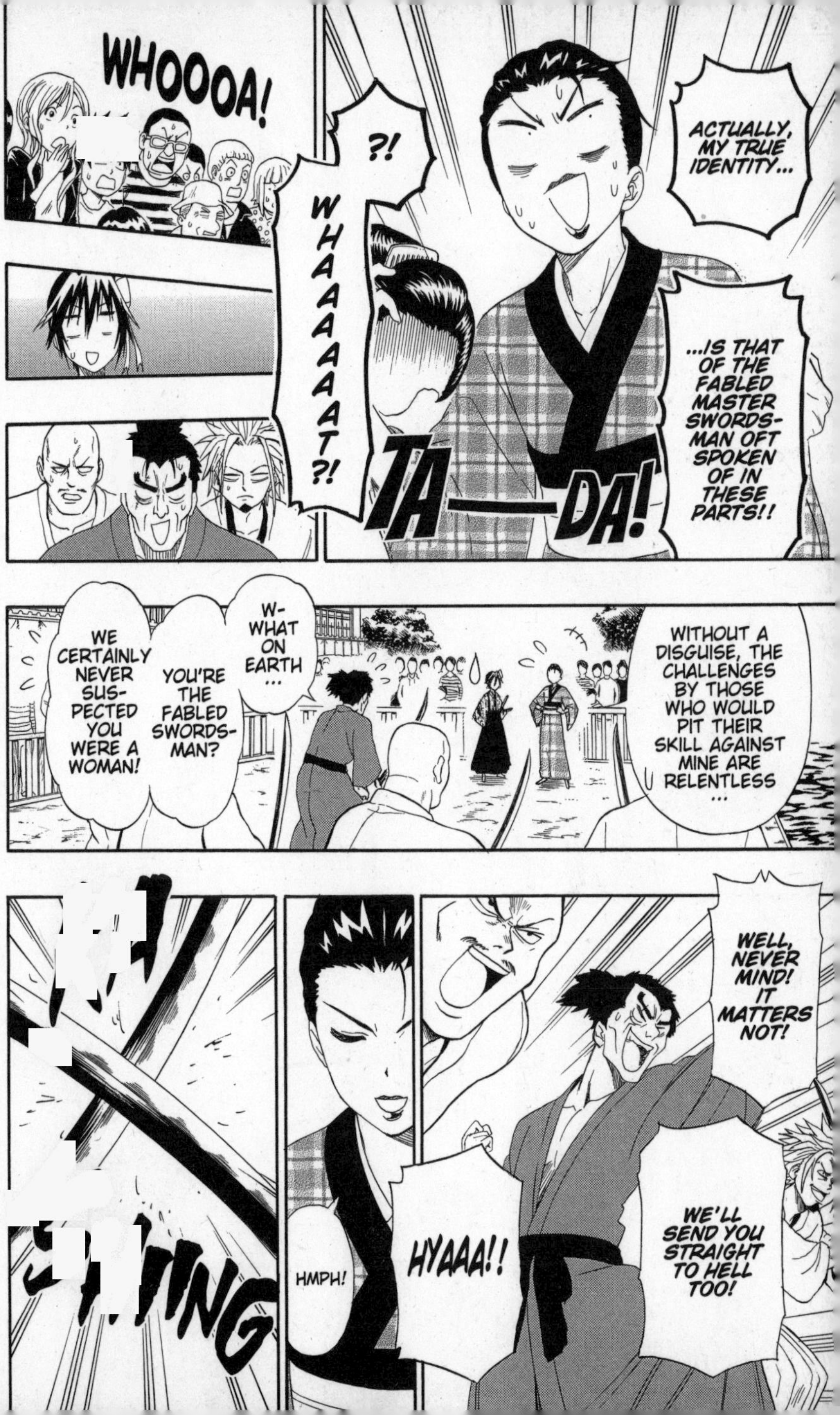

ACTUALLY, MY TRUE IDENTITY...
...IS THAT OF THE FABLED MASTER SWORDS-MAN OFT SPOKEN OF IN THESE PARTS!!
TA—DA!
WHOOOA!
?! WHAAAAAAAT?!
WITHOUT A DISGUISE, THE CHALLENGES BY THOSE WHO WOULD PIT THEIR SKILL AGAINST MINE ARE RELENTLESS...
W-WHAT ON EARTH...
YOU'RE THE FABLED SWORDS-MAN?
WE CERTAINLY NEVER SUS-PECTED YOU WERE A WOMAN!
WELL, NEVER MIND! IT MATTERS NOT!
WE'LL SEND YOU STRAIGHT TO HELL TOO!
HYAAA!!
HMPH!

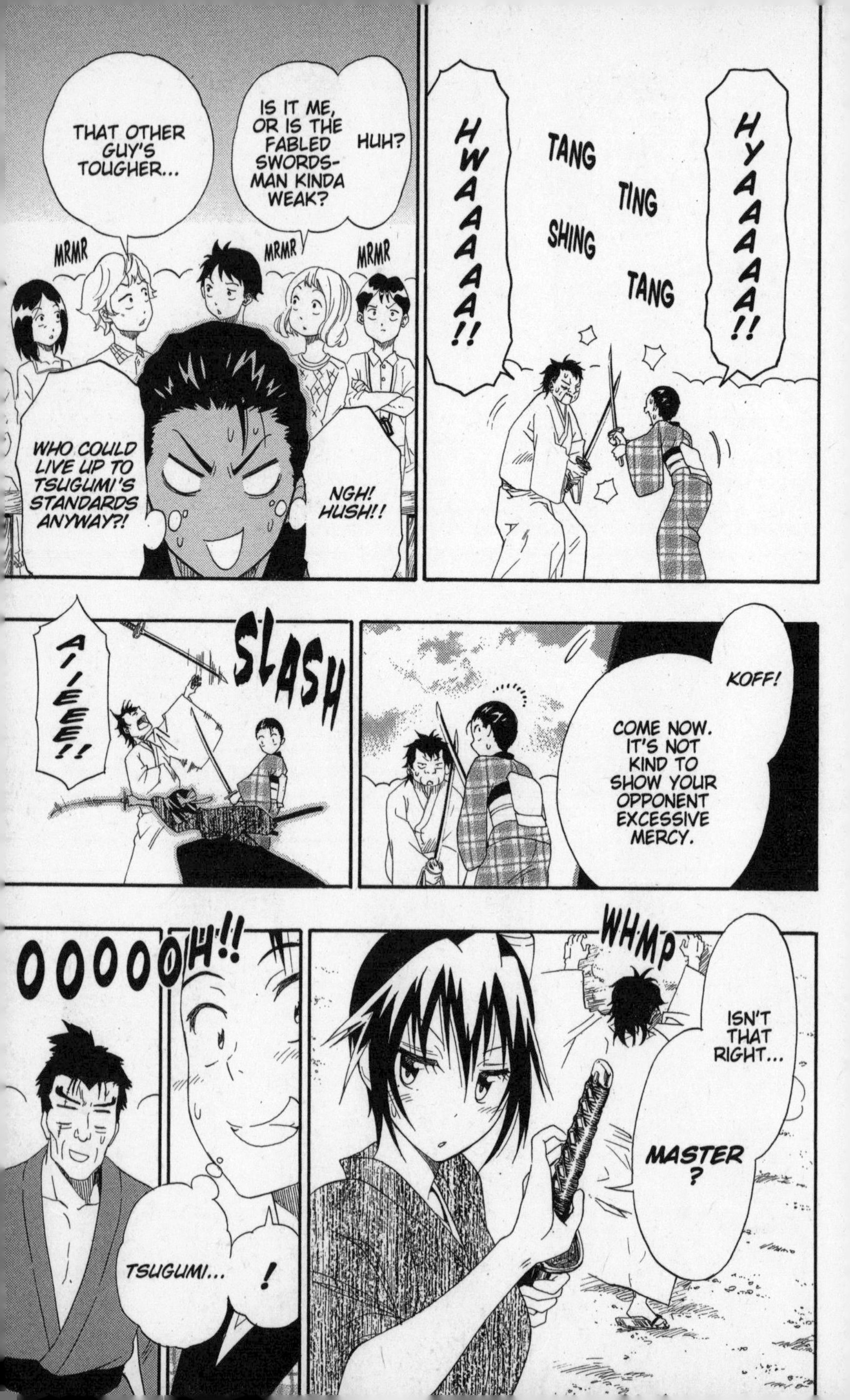
HYAAAAAA!!
TANG
TING
SHING
TANG
HWAAAAAA!!
HUH?
IS IT ME, OR IS THE FABLED SWORDSMAN KINDA WEAK?
THAT OTHER GUY'S TOUGHER...
MRMR
MRMR
MRMR
NGH! HUSH!!
WHO COULD LIVE UP TO TSUGUMI'S STANDARDS ANYWAY?!
KOFF!
COME NOW. IT'S NOT KIND TO SHOW YOUR OPPONENT EXCESSIVE MERCY.
SLASH
AIIEEE!!
WHMP
ISN'T THAT RIGHT...
MASTER?
OOOOOH!!
TSUGUMI... !

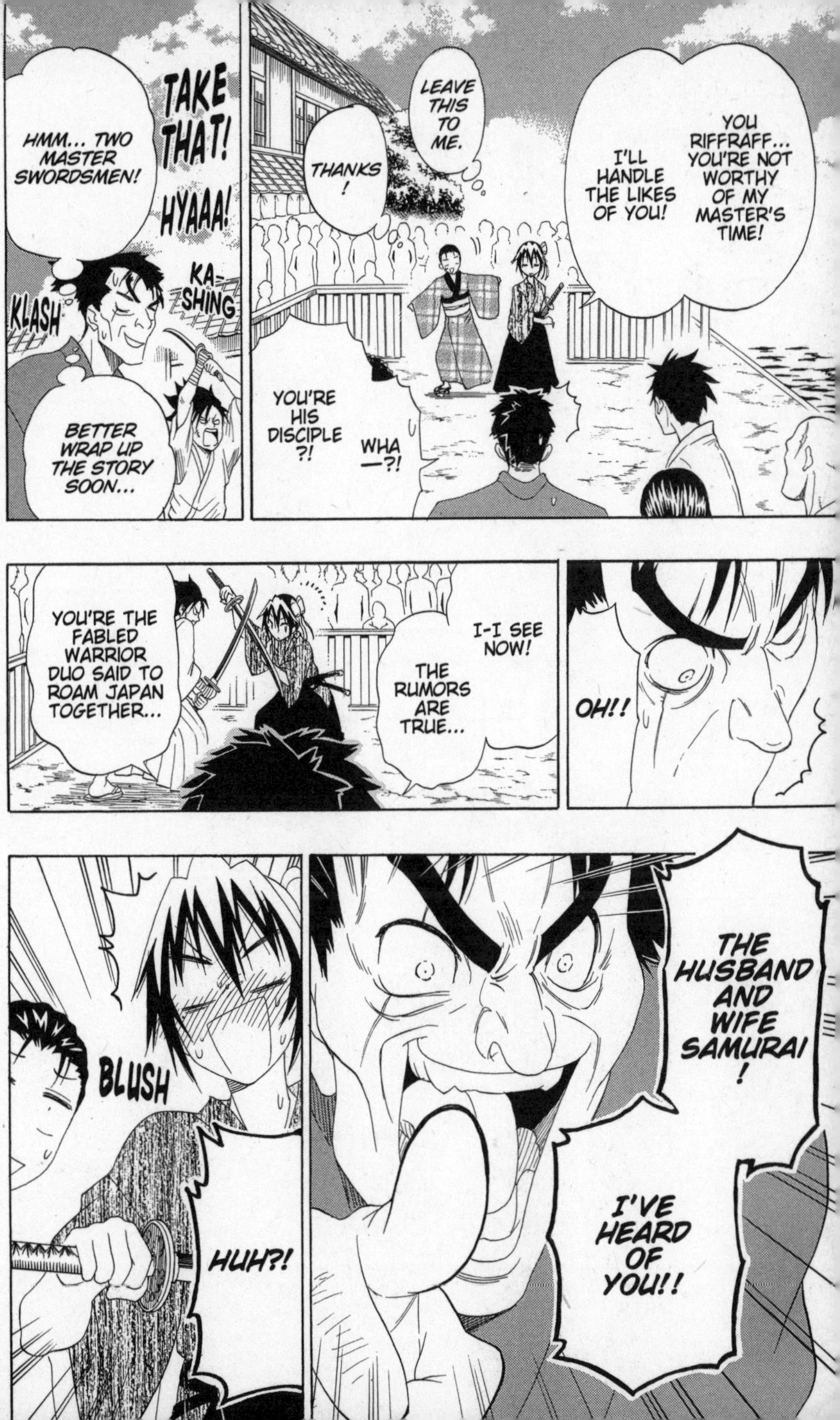
YOU RIFFRAFF... YOU'RE NOT WORTHY OF MY MASTER'S TIME!
I'LL HANDLE THE LIKES OF YOU!
LEAVE THIS TO ME.
THANKS!
WHA—?!
YOU'RE HIS DISCIPLE?!
TAKE THAT!
HYAAA!
HMM... TWO MASTER SWORDSMEN!
KA-SHING
KLASH
BETTER WRAP UP THE STORY SOON...
OH!!
I-I SEE NOW!
THE RUMORS ARE TRUE...
YOU'RE THE FABLED WARRIOR DUO SAID TO ROAM JAPAN TOGETHER...
THE HUSBAND AND WIFE SAMURAI!
I'VE HEARD OF YOU!!
BLUSH
HUH?!

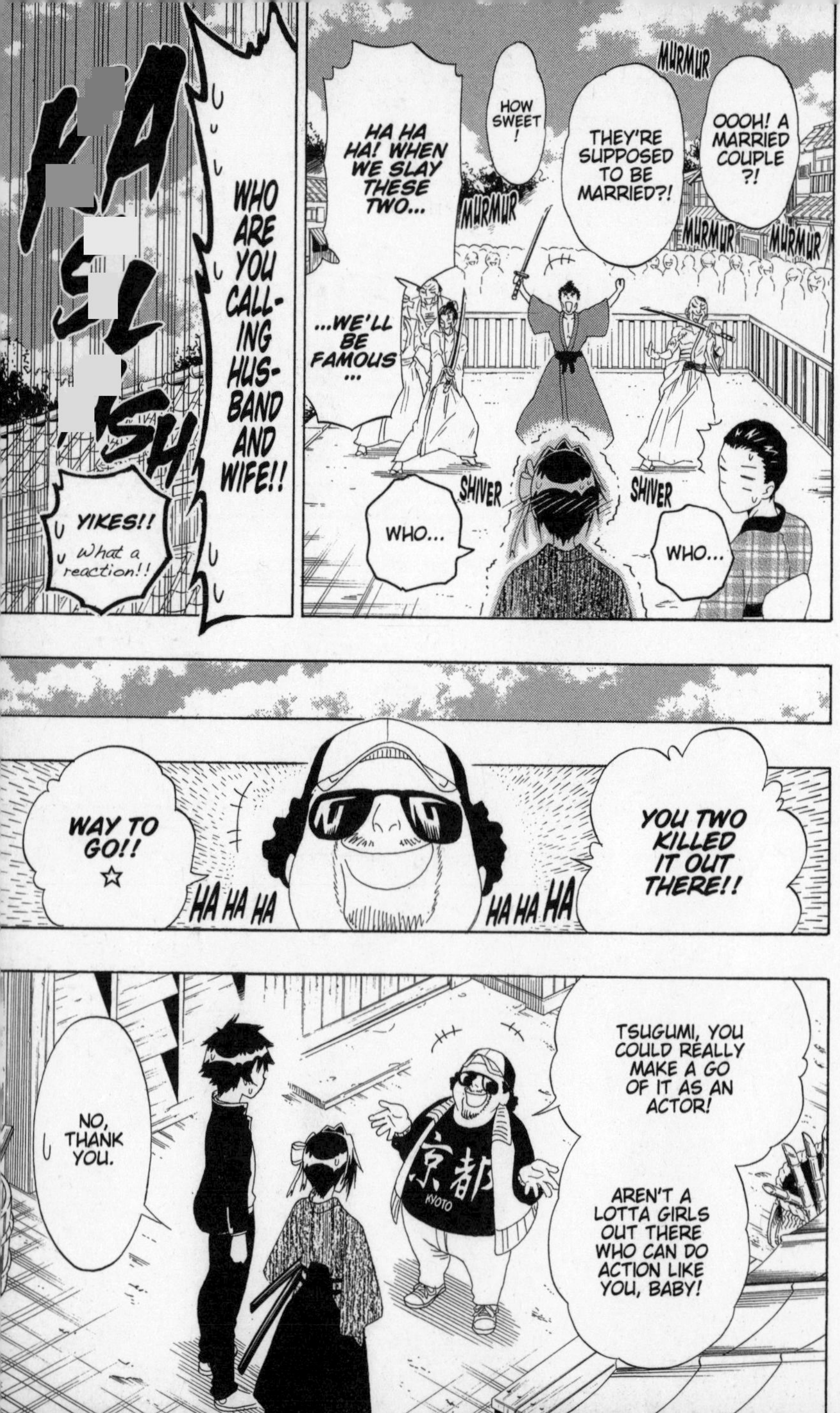
MURMUR
OOOH! A MARRIED COUPLE?!
THEY'RE SUPPOSED TO BE MARRIED?!
MURMUR MURMUR
HOW SWEET!
MURMUR
HA HA HA! WHEN WE SLAY THESE TWO...
...WE'LL BE FAMOUS...
SHIVER
WHO...
SHIVER
WHO...
WHO ARE YOU CALLING HUSBAND AND WIFE!!
YIKES!! What a reaction!!
YOU TWO KILLED IT OUT THERE!!
HA HA HA
HA HA HA
WAY TO GO!! ☆
TSUGUMI, YOU COULD REALLY MAKE A GO OF IT AS AN ACTOR!
AREN'T A LOTTA GIRLS OUT THERE WHO CAN DO ACTION LIKE YOU, BABY!
京都
KYOTO
NO, THANK YOU.

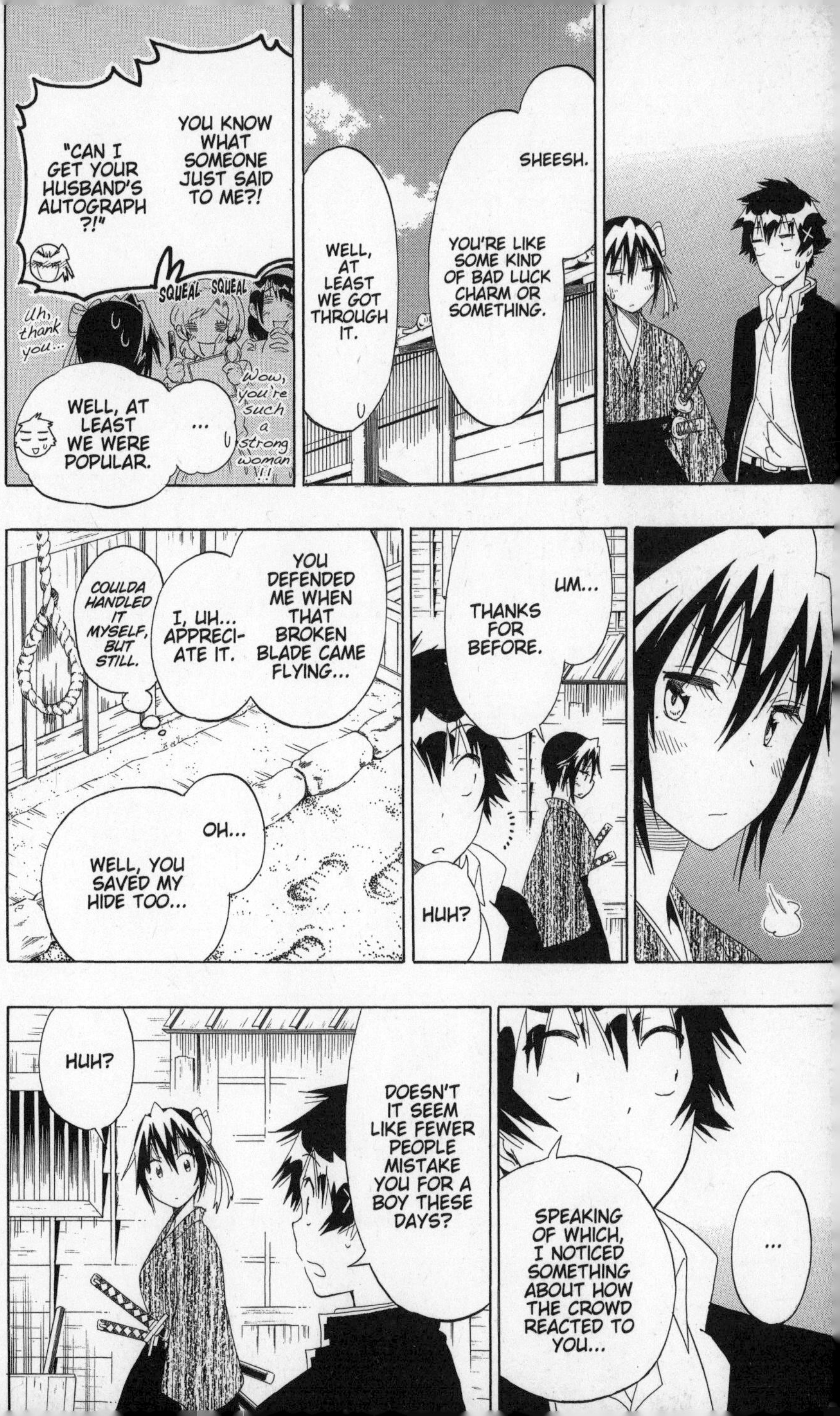
SHEESH.
YOU'RE LIKE SOME KIND OF BAD LUCK CHARM OR SOMETHING.
WELL, AT LEAST WE GOT THROUGH IT.
YOU KNOW WHAT SOMEONE JUST SAID TO ME?!
"CAN I GET YOUR HUSBAND'S AUTOGRAPH?!"
SQUEAL SQUEAL
Uh, thank you...
Wow, you're such a strong woman!!
...
WELL, AT LEAST WE WERE POPULAR.
UM...
THANKS FOR BEFORE.
HUH?
YOU DEFENDED ME WHEN THAT BROKEN BLADE CAME FLYING...
I, UH... APPRECIATE IT.
COULDA HANDLED IT MYSELF, BUT STILL.
OH...
WELL, YOU SAVED MY HIDE TOO...
...
SPEAKING OF WHICH, I NOTICED SOMETHING ABOUT HOW THE CROWD REACTED TO YOU...
DOESN'T IT SEEM LIKE FEWER PEOPLE MISTAKE YOU FOR A BOY THESE DAYS?
HUH?

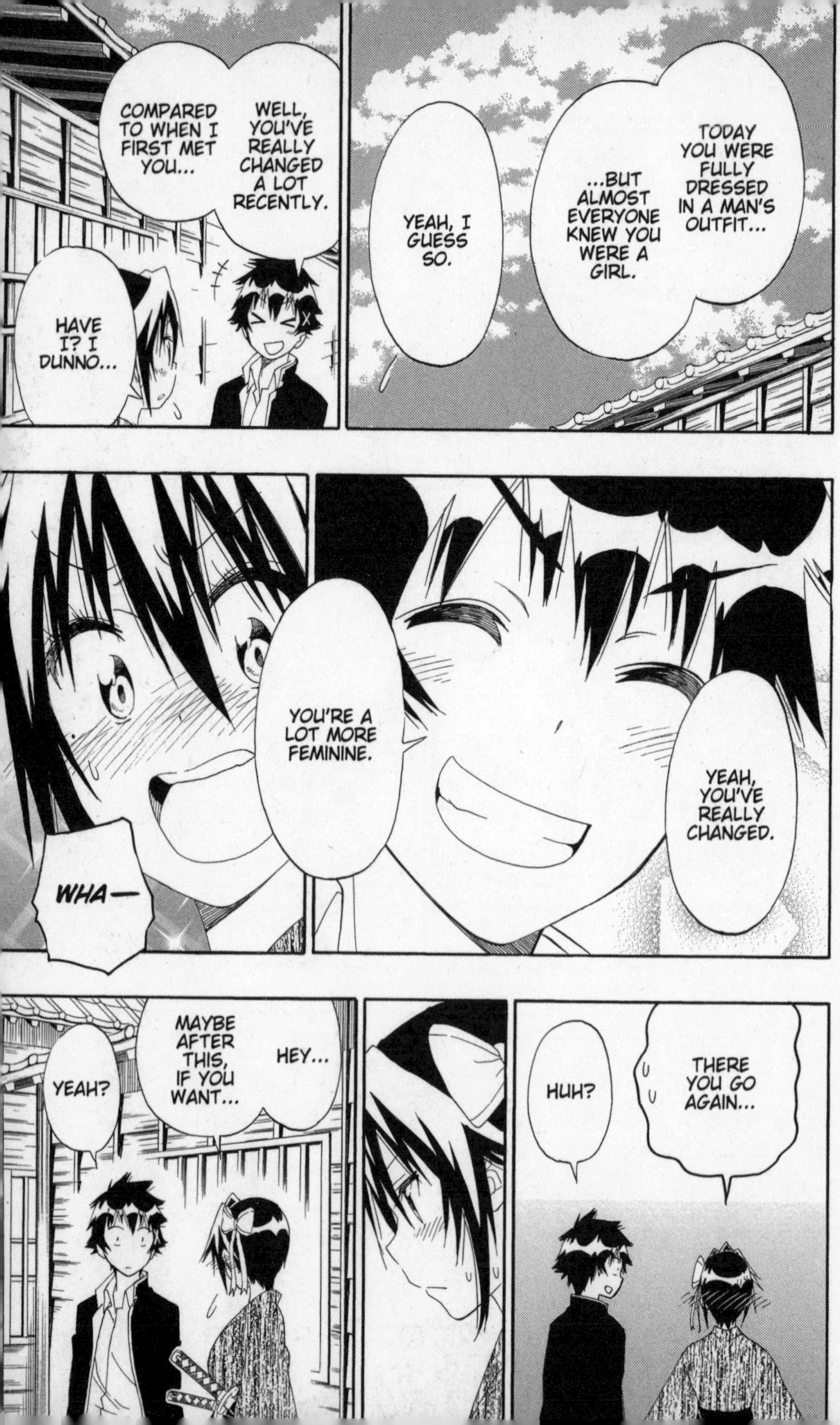
TODAY YOU WERE FULLY DRESSED IN A MAN'S OUTFIT...
...BUT ALMOST EVERYONE KNEW YOU WERE A GIRL.
YEAH, I GUESS SO.
WELL, YOU'VE REALLY CHANGED A LOT RECENTLY.
COMPARED TO WHEN I FIRST MET YOU...
HAVE I? I DUNNO...
YEAH, YOU'VE REALLY CHANGED.
YOU'RE A LOT MORE FEMININE.
WHA—
THERE YOU GO AGAIN...
HUH?
HEY...
MAYBE AFTER THIS, IF YOU WANT...
YEAH?

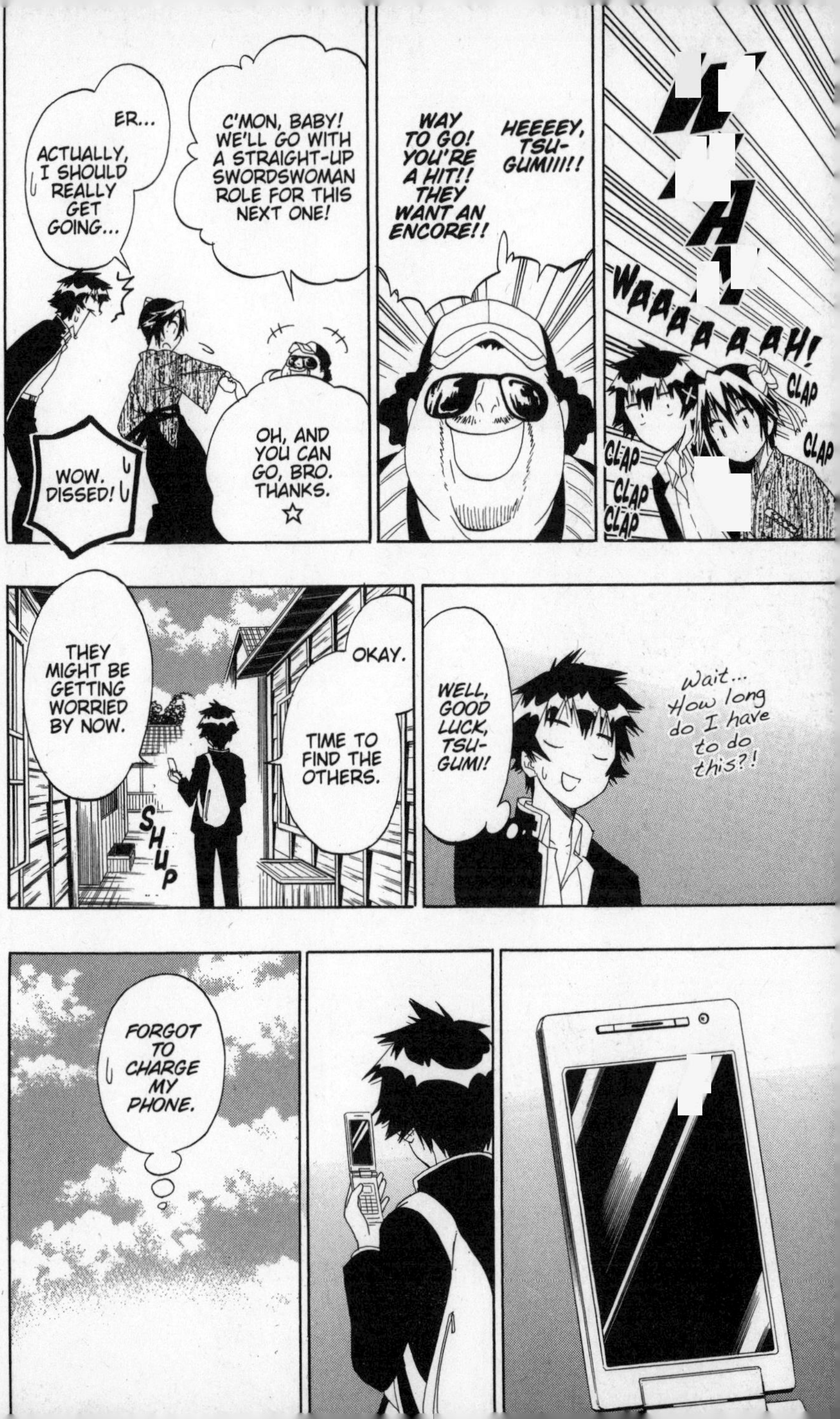

WAAAAAAAH!
CLAP
CLAP
CLAP
CLAP
CLAP
HEEEEY, TSU-GUMI!!!!
WAY TO GO! YOU'RE A HIT!! THEY WANT AN ENCORE!!
C'MON, BABY! WE'LL GO WITH A STRAIGHT-UP SWORDSWOMAN ROLE FOR THIS NEXT ONE!
ER... ACTUALLY, I SHOULD REALLY GET GOING...
OH, AND YOU CAN GO, BRO. THANKS. ☆
WOW. DISSED!
Wait... How long do I have to do this?!
WELL, GOOD LUCK, TSU-GUMI!
OKAY.
TIME TO FIND THE OTHERS.
THEY MIGHT BE GETTING WORRIED BY NOW.
SHUP
FORGOT TO CHARGE MY PHONE.

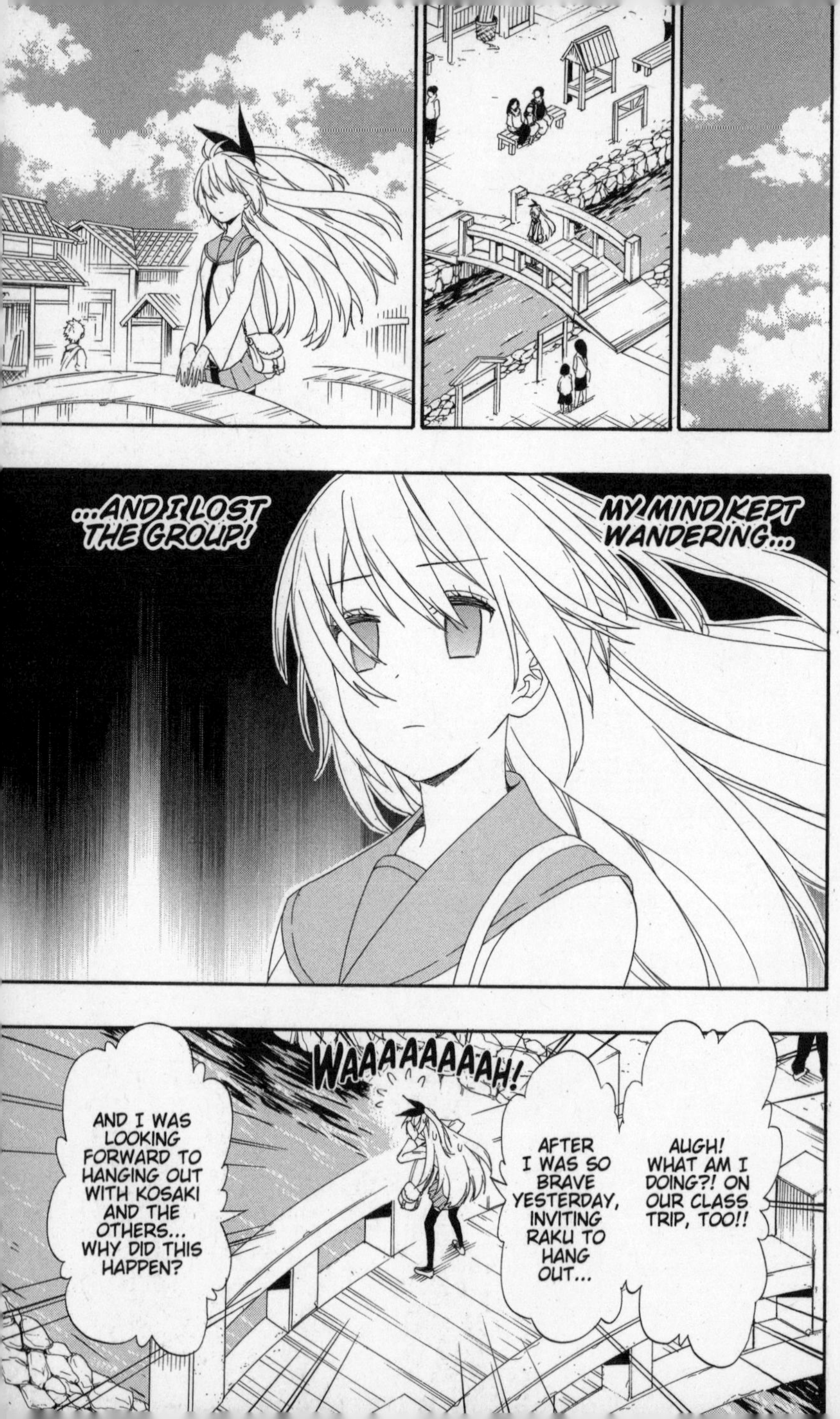
MY MIND KEPT WANDERING...
...AND I LOST THE GROUP!
AUGH! WHAT AM I DOING?! ON OUR CLASS TRIP, TOO!!
WAAAAAAAAH!
AFTER I WAS SO BRAVE YESTERDAY, INVITING RAKU TO HANG OUT...
AND I WAS LOOKING FORWARD TO HANGING OUT WITH KOSAKI AND THE OTHERS... WHY DID THIS HAPPEN?

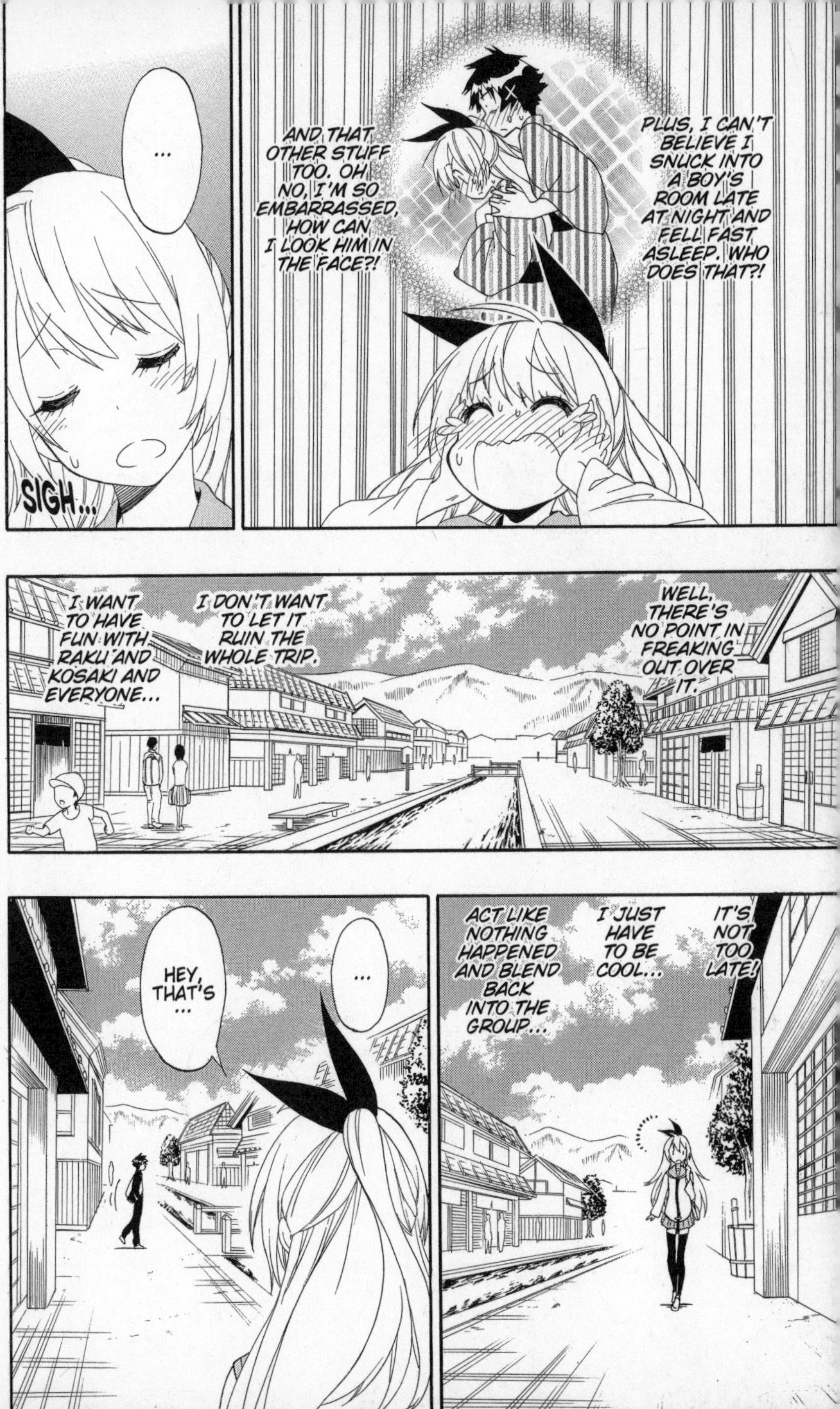
PLUS, I CAN'T BELIEVE I SNUCK INTO A BOY'S ROOM LATE AT NIGHT AND FELL FAST ASLEEP. WHO DOES THAT?!
AND THAT OTHER STUFF TOO. OH NO, I'M SO EMBARRASSED, HOW CAN I LOOK HIM IN THE FACE?!
...
SIGH...
WELL, THERE'S NO POINT IN FREAKING OUT OVER IT.
I DON'T WANT TO LET IT RUIN THE WHOLE TRIP.
I WANT TO HAVE FUN WITH RAKU AND KOSAKI AND EVERYONE...
IT'S NOT TOO LATE!
I JUST HAVE TO BE COOL...
ACT LIKE NOTHING HAPPENED AND BLEND BACK INTO THE GROUP...
...
HEY, THAT'S ...

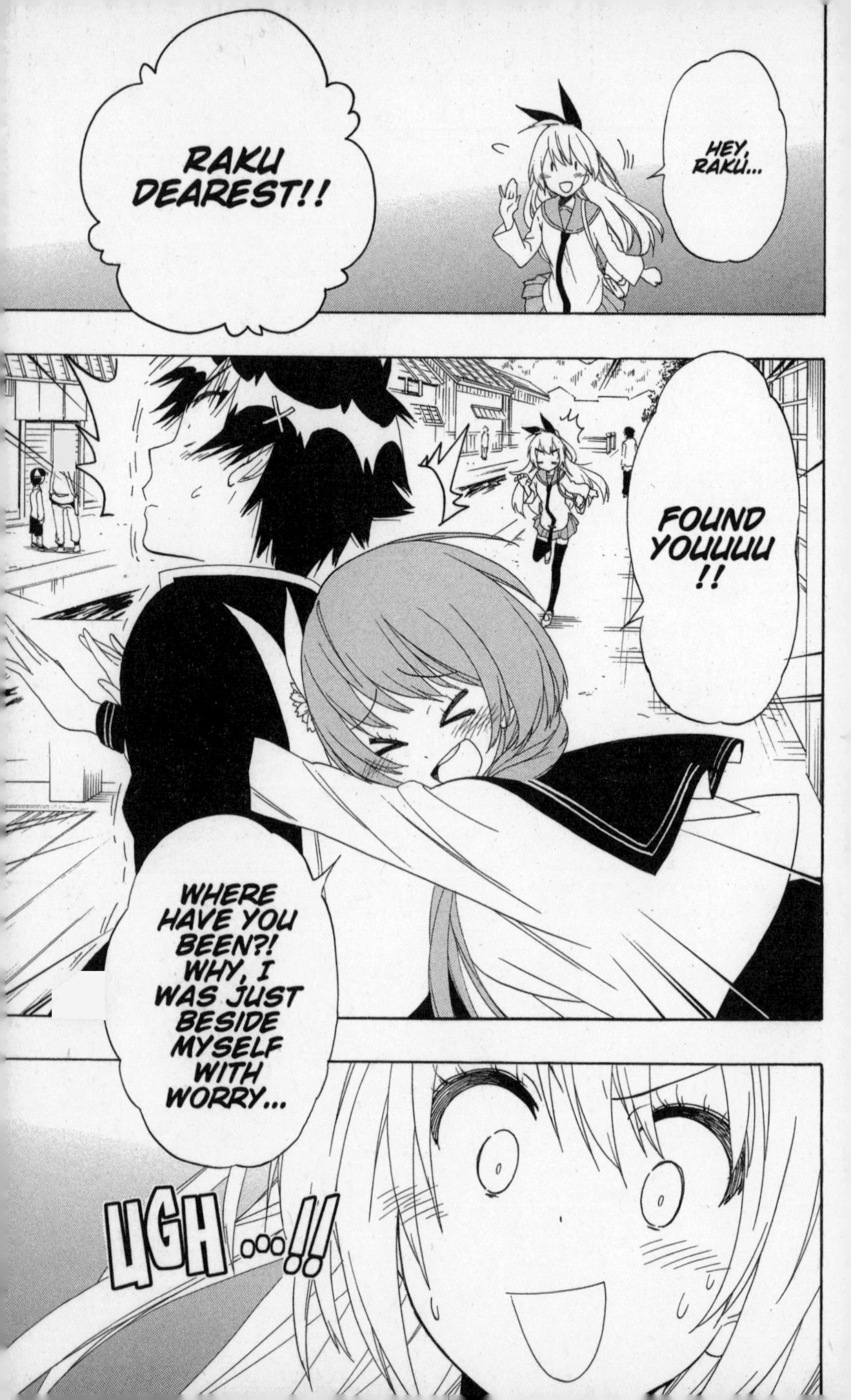
HEY, RAKU...
RAKU DEAREST!!
FOUND YOUUUU!!
WHERE HAVE YOU BEEN?! WHY, I WAS JUST BESIDE MYSELF WITH WORRY...
UGH...!!

SHWOO

VOOSH

BAM

TO BE CONTINUED IN 2 PAGES...

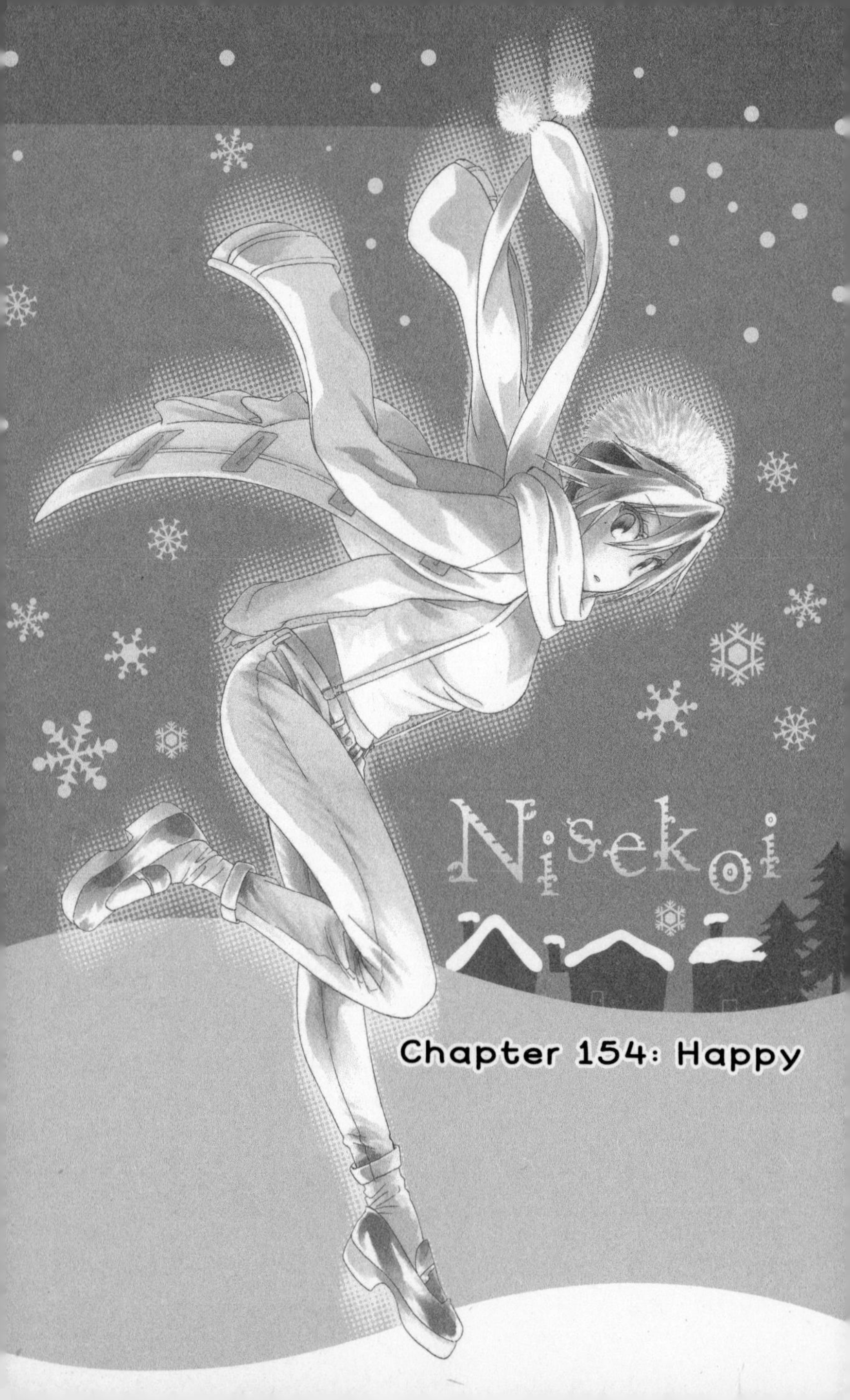
Nisekoi
Chapter 154: Happy

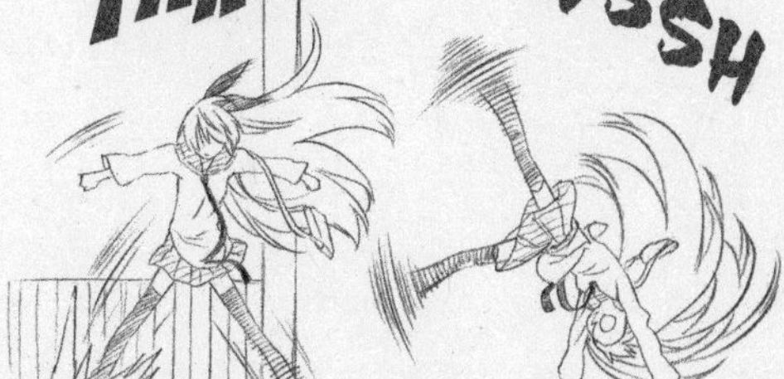
WSSH
TAK!!

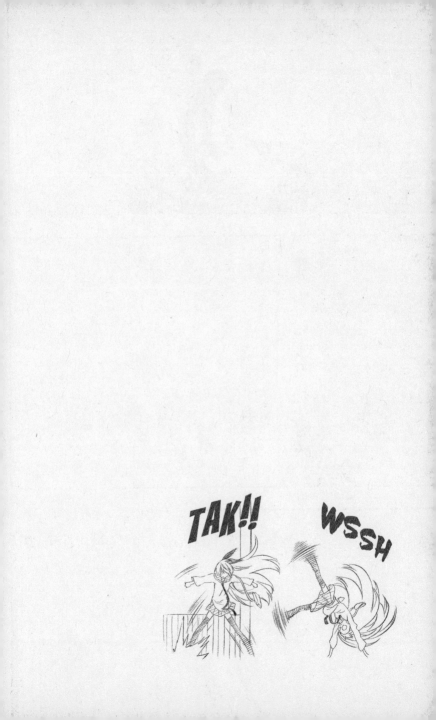

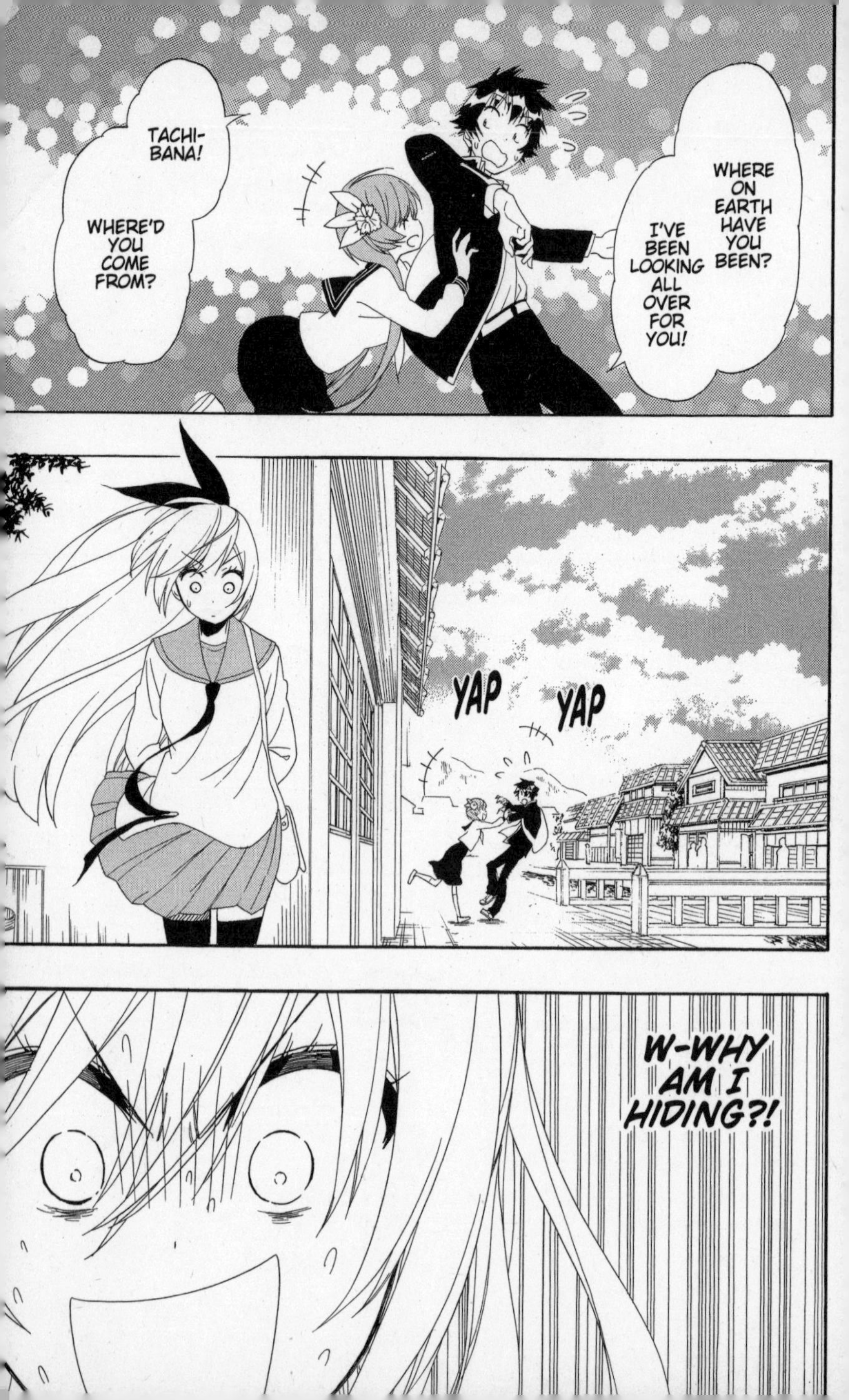
WHERE ON EARTH HAVE YOU BEEN? I'VE BEEN LOOKING ALL OVER FOR YOU!
TACHI-BANA! WHERE'D YOU COME FROM?
YAP YAP
W-WHY AM I HIDING?!

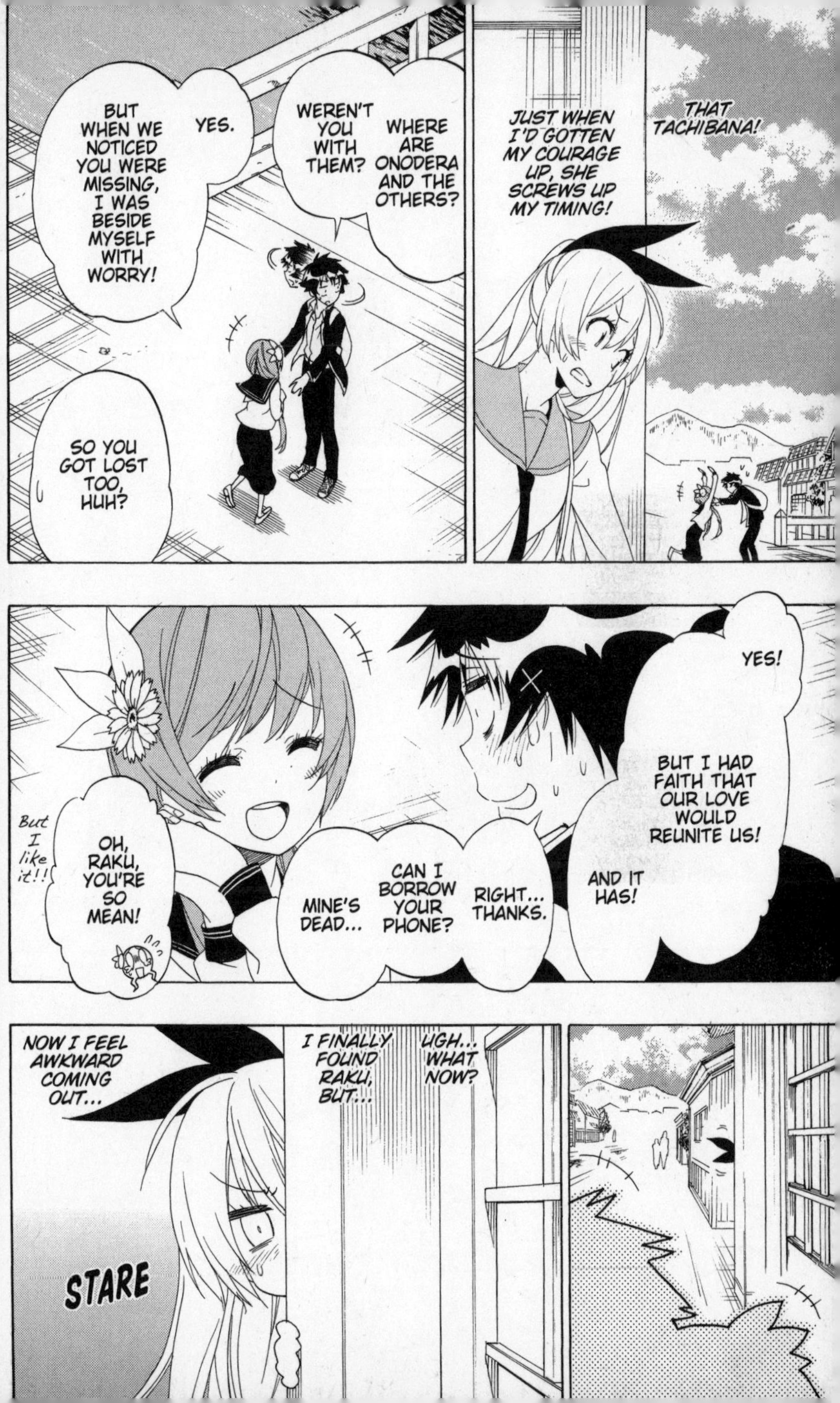
THAT TACHIBANA!
JUST WHEN I'D GOTTEN MY COURAGE UP, SHE SCREWS UP MY TIMING!
WHERE ARE ONODERA AND THE OTHERS?
WEREN'T YOU WITH THEM?
YES.
BUT WHEN WE NOTICED YOU WERE MISSING, I WAS BESIDE MYSELF WITH WORRY!
SO YOU GOT LOST TOO, HUH?
YES!
BUT I HAD FAITH THAT OUR LOVE WOULD REUNITE US!
AND IT HAS!
RIGHT... THANKS.
CAN I BORROW YOUR PHONE?
MINE'S DEAD...
OH, RAKU, YOU'RE SO MEAN!
But I like it!!
UGH... WHAT NOW?
I FINALLY FOUND RAKU, BUT...
NOW I FEEL AWKWARD COMING OUT...
STARE

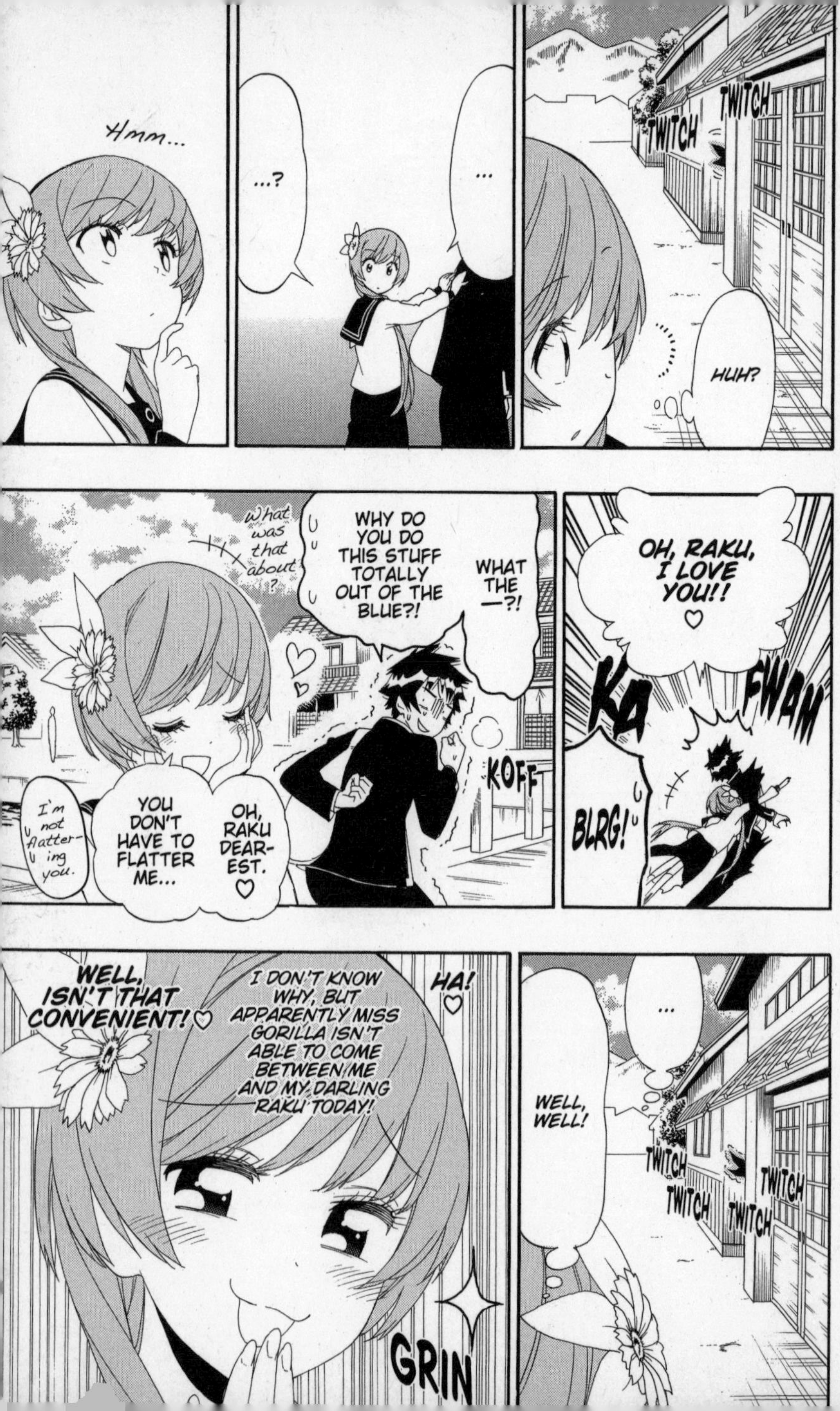
TWITCH
TWITCH
...
HUH?
...
...?
Hmm...
OH, RAKU, I LOVE YOU!! ♡
Ka
FWAM
BLRG!
WHAT THE—?!
WHY DO YOU DO THIS STUFF TOTALLY OUT OF THE BLUE?!
What was that about?
KOFF
OH, RAKU DEAREST. ♡
YOU DON'T HAVE TO FLATTER ME...
I'm not flattering you.
...
WELL, WELL!
TWITCH
TWITCH
TWITCH
TWITCH
HA! ♡
I DON'T KNOW WHY, BUT APPARENTLY MISS GORILLA ISN'T ABLE TO COME BETWEEN ME AND MY DARLING RAKU TODAY!
WELL, ISN'T THAT CONVENIENT! ♡
GRIN

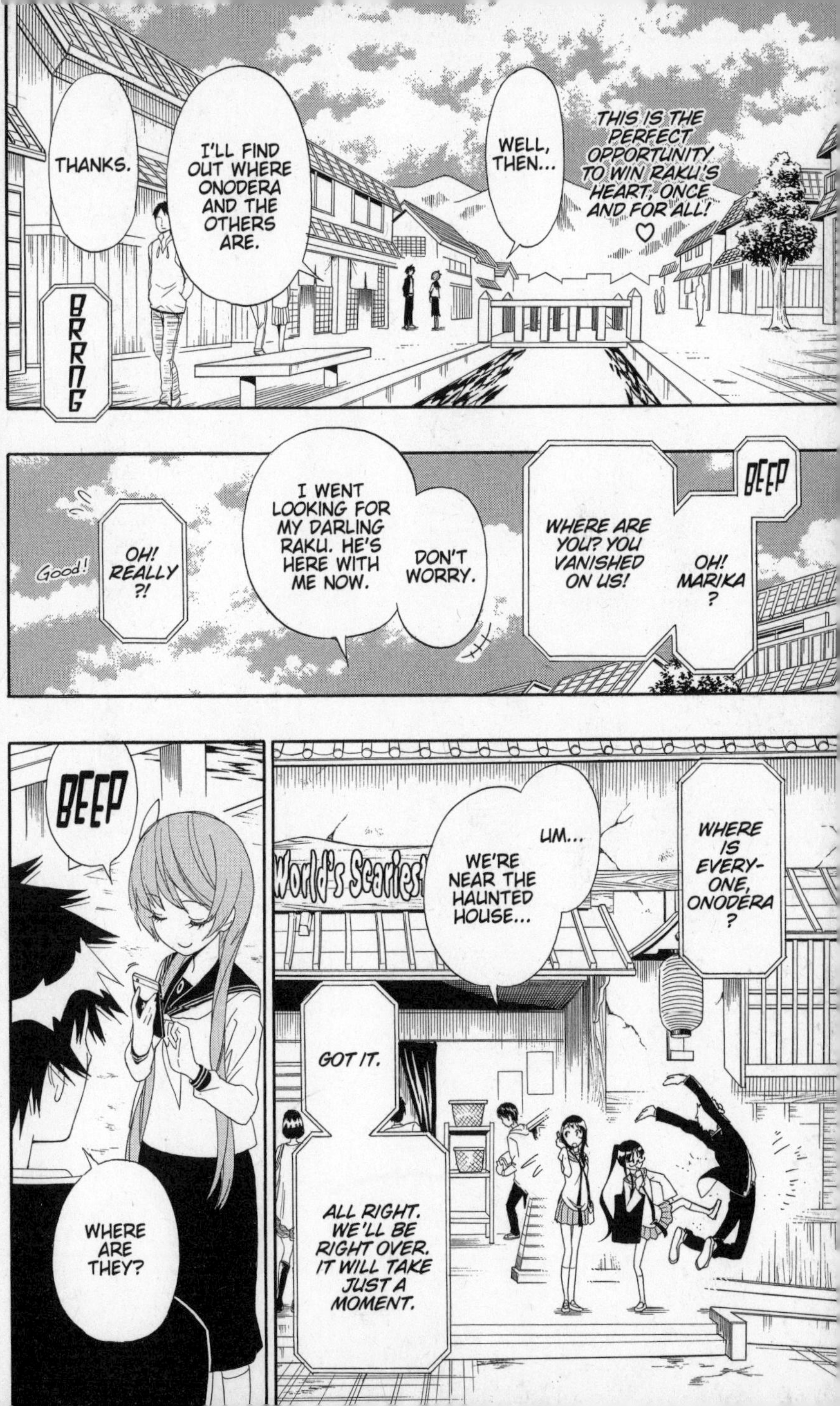
THIS IS THE PERFECT OPPORTUNITY TO WIN RAKU'S HEART, ONCE AND FOR ALL! ♡
WELL, THEN...
I'LL FIND OUT WHERE ONODERA AND THE OTHERS ARE.
THANKS.
BRRRNG
BEEP
OH! MARIKA?
WHERE ARE YOU? YOU VANISHED ON US!
DON'T WORRY.
I WENT LOOKING FOR MY DARLING RAKU. HE'S HERE WITH ME NOW.
OH! REALLY?!
Good!
WHERE IS EVERYONE, ONODERA?
UM...
WE'RE NEAR THE HAUNTED HOUSE...
World's Scariest
GOT IT.
ALL RIGHT. WE'LL BE RIGHT OVER. IT WILL TAKE JUST A MOMENT.
BEEP
WHERE ARE THEY?

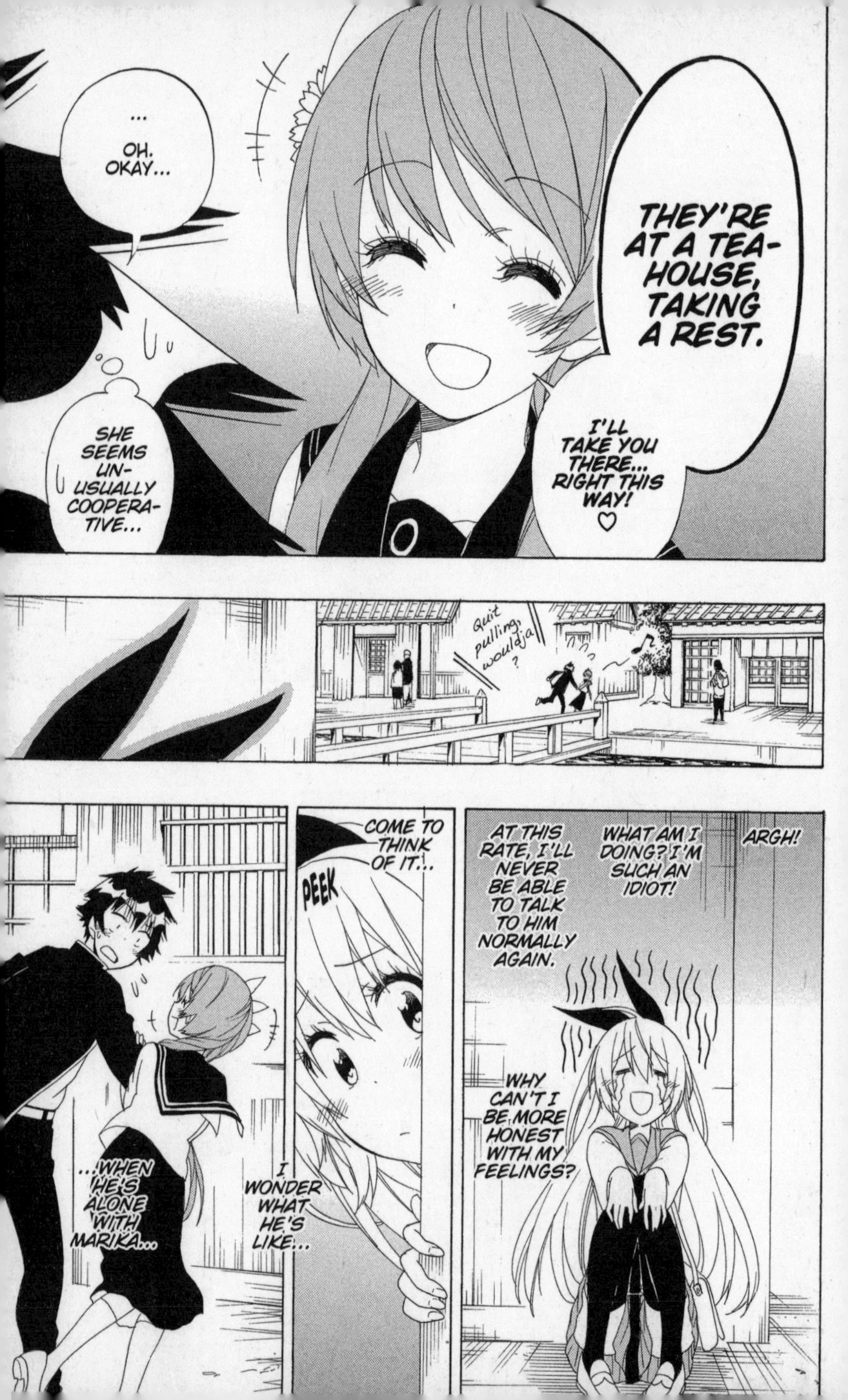
THEY'RE AT A TEA-HOUSE, TAKING A REST.
I'LL TAKE YOU THERE... RIGHT THIS WAY! ♡
... OH. OKAY...
SHE SEEMS UN-USUALLY COOPERA-TIVE...
Quit pulling, wouldja?
ARGH!
WHAT AM I DOING? I'M SUCH AN IDIOT!
AT THIS RATE, I'LL NEVER BE ABLE TO TALK TO HIM NORMALLY AGAIN.
WHY CAN'T I BE MORE HONEST WITH MY FEELINGS?
PEEK
COME TO THINK OF IT...
I WONDER WHAT HE'S LIKE...
...WHEN HE'S ALONE WITH MARIKA...

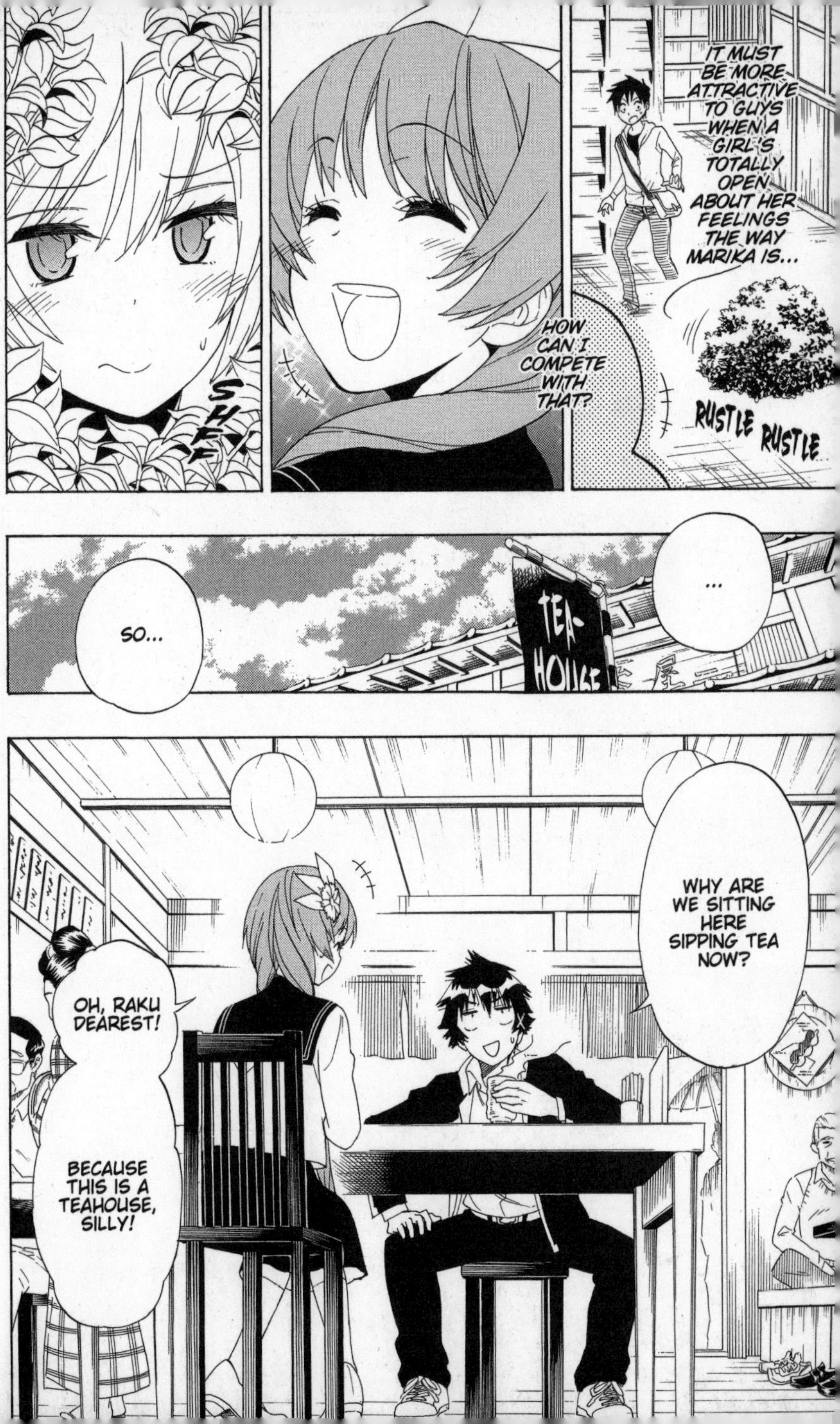
IT MUST BE MORE ATTRACTIVE TO GUYS WHEN A GIRL'S TOTALLY OPEN ABOUT HER FEELINGS THE WAY MARIKA IS...
RUSTLE RUSTLE
HOW CAN I COMPETE WITH THAT?
SHFF
...
SO...
WHY ARE WE SITTING HERE SIPPING TEA NOW?
OH, RAKU DEAREST!
BECAUSE THIS IS A TEAHOUSE, SILLY!

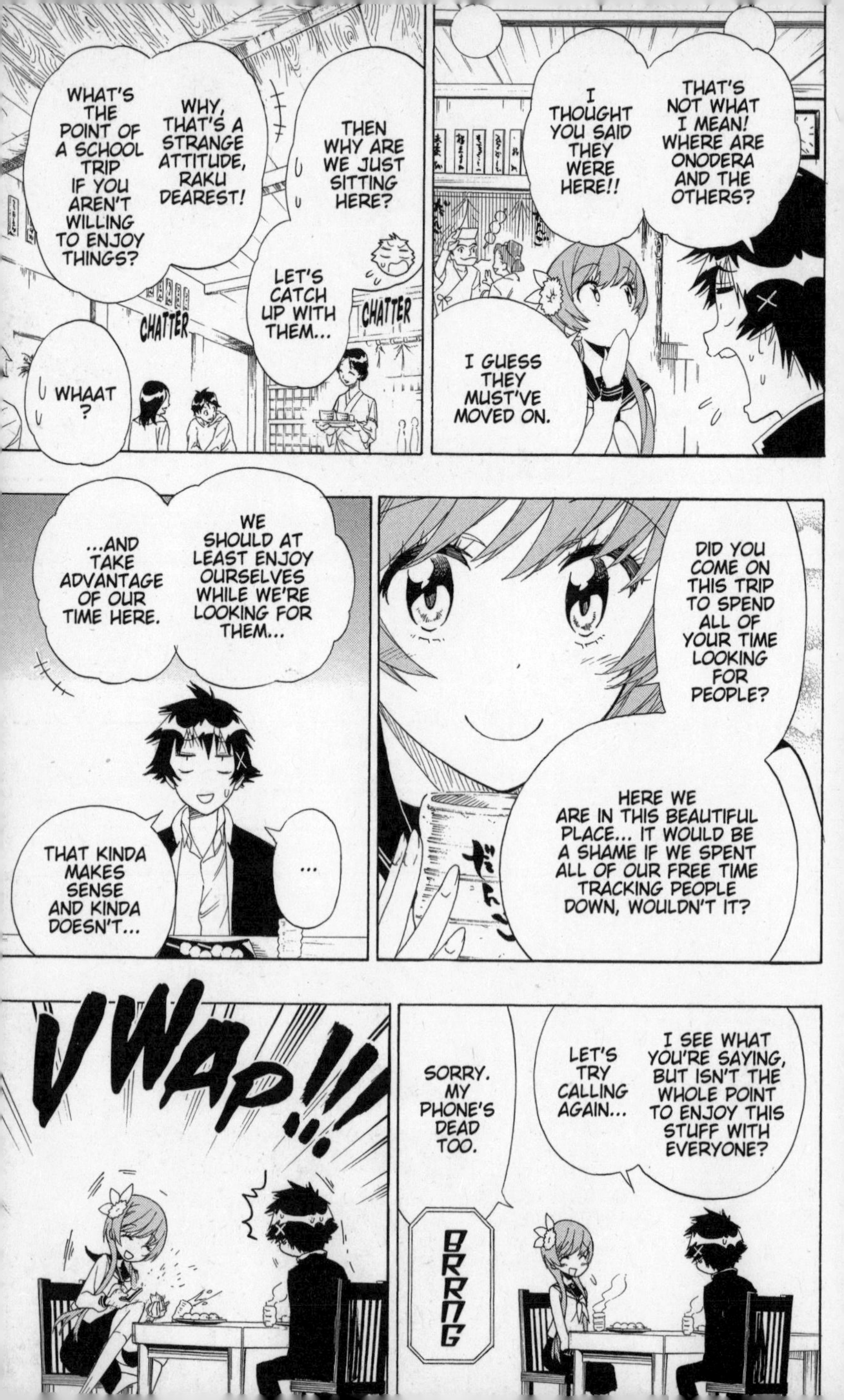
THAT'S NOT WHAT I MEAN! WHERE ARE ONODERA AND THE OTHERS?
I THOUGHT YOU SAID THEY WERE HERE!!
I GUESS THEY MUST'VE MOVED ON.
THEN WHY ARE WE JUST SITTING HERE?
WHY, THAT'S A STRANGE ATTITUDE, RAKU DEAREST!
WHAT'S THE POINT OF A SCHOOL TRIP IF YOU AREN'T WILLING TO ENJOY THINGS?
LET'S CATCH UP WITH THEM...
CHATTER
CHATTER
WHAAT?
DID YOU COME ON THIS TRIP TO SPEND ALL OF YOUR TIME LOOKING FOR PEOPLE?
HERE WE ARE IN THIS BEAUTIFUL PLACE... IT WOULD BE A SHAME IF WE SPENT ALL OF OUR FREE TIME TRACKING PEOPLE DOWN, WOULDN'T IT?
WE SHOULD AT LEAST ENJOY OURSELVES WHILE WE'RE LOOKING FOR THEM...
...AND TAKE ADVANTAGE OF OUR TIME HERE.
...
THAT KINDA MAKES SENSE AND KINDA DOESN'T...
I SEE WHAT YOU'RE SAYING, BUT ISN'T THE WHOLE POINT TO ENJOY THIS STUFF WITH EVERYONE?
LET'S TRY CALLING AGAIN...
SORRY. MY PHONE'S DEAD TOO.
BRRNG
VWAP!!

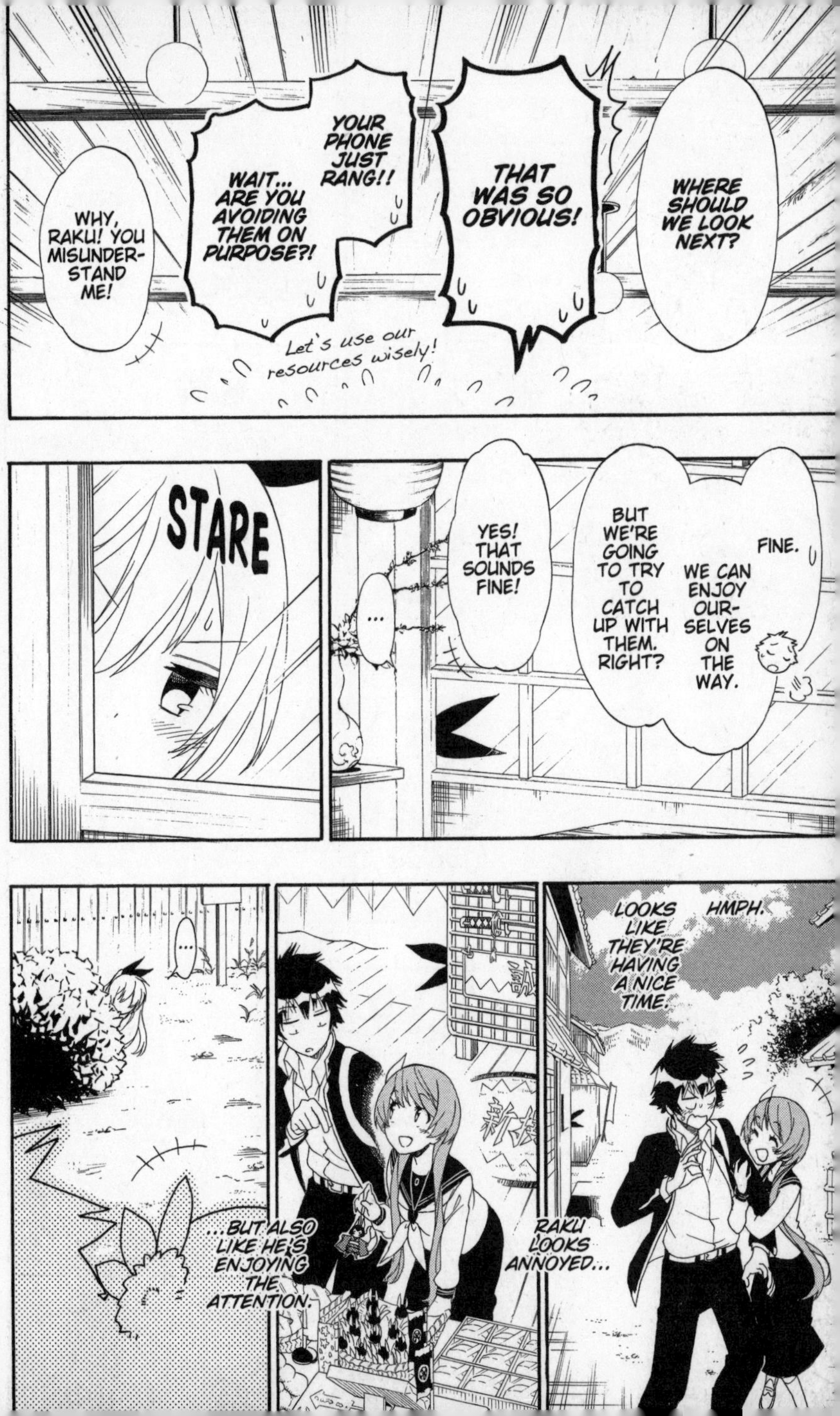
WHERE SHOULD WE LOOK NEXT?
THAT WAS SO OBVIOUS!
YOUR PHONE JUST RANG!!
WAIT... ARE YOU AVOIDING THEM ON PURPOSE?!
Let's use our resources wisely!
WHY, RAKU! YOU MISUNDER-STAND ME!
FINE.
WE CAN ENJOY OUR-SELVES ON THE WAY.
BUT WE'RE GOING TO TRY TO CATCH UP WITH THEM. RIGHT?
YES! THAT SOUNDS FINE!
...
STARE
HMPH.
LOOKS LIKE THEY'RE HAVING A NICE TIME.
RAKU LOOKS ANNOYED...
...BUT ALSO LIKE HE'S ENJOYING THE ATTENTION.
...

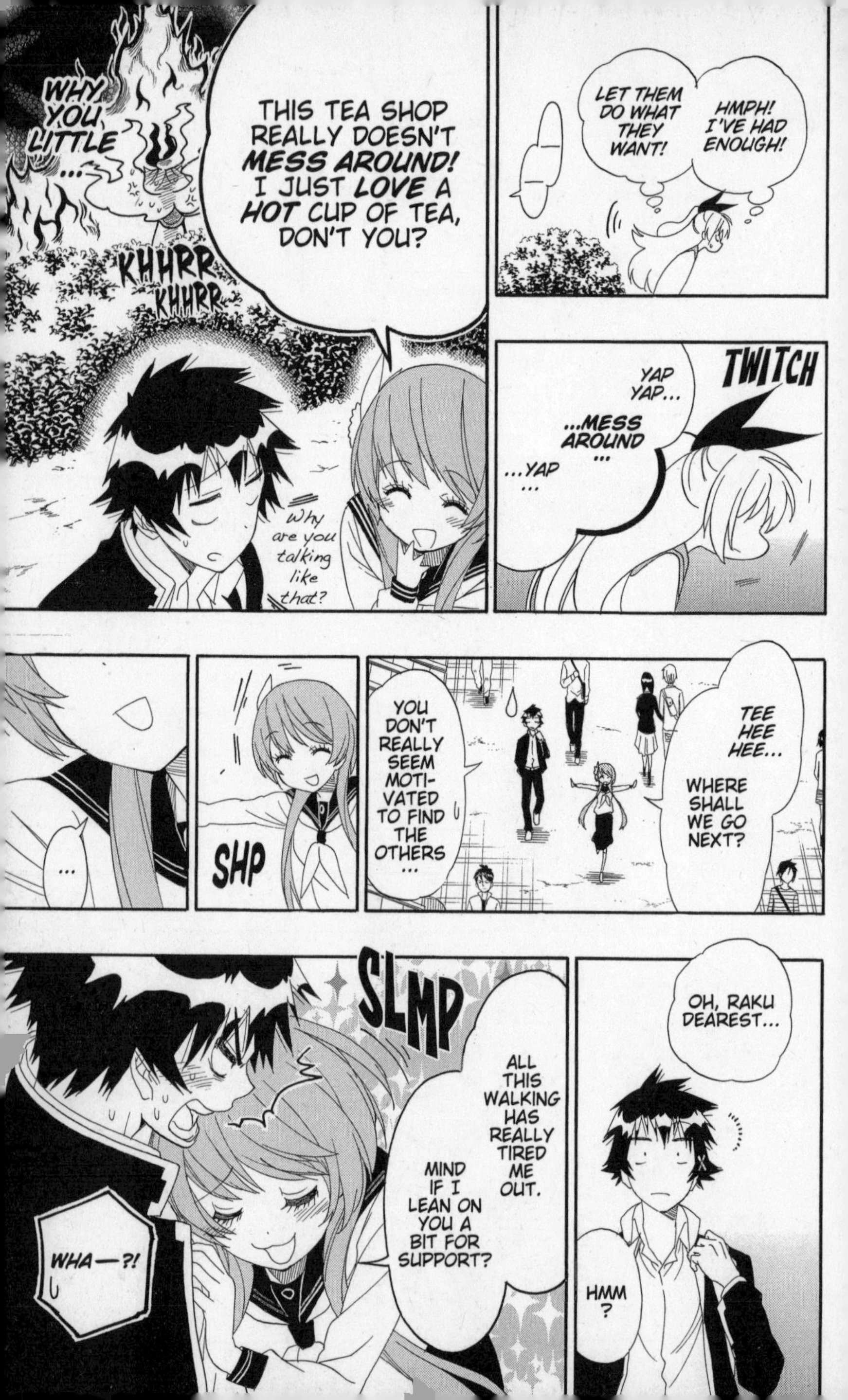
HMPH! I'VE HAD ENOUGH!
LET THEM DO WHAT THEY WANT!
—
TWITCH
YAP YAP...
...MESS AROUND...
...YAP...
THIS TEA SHOP REALLY DOESN'T MESS AROUND! I JUST LOVE A HOT CUP OF TEA, DON'T YOU?
WHY YOU LITTLE...
KHHRR KHHRR
Why are you talking like that?
TEE HEE HEE...
WHERE SHALL WE GO NEXT?
YOU DON'T REALLY SEEM MOTI-VATED TO FIND THE OTHERS...
SHP
...
OH, RAKU DEAREST...
HMM?
SLMP
ALL THIS WALKING HAS REALLY TIRED ME OUT.
MIND IF I LEAN ON YOU A BIT FOR SUPPORT?
WHA—?!

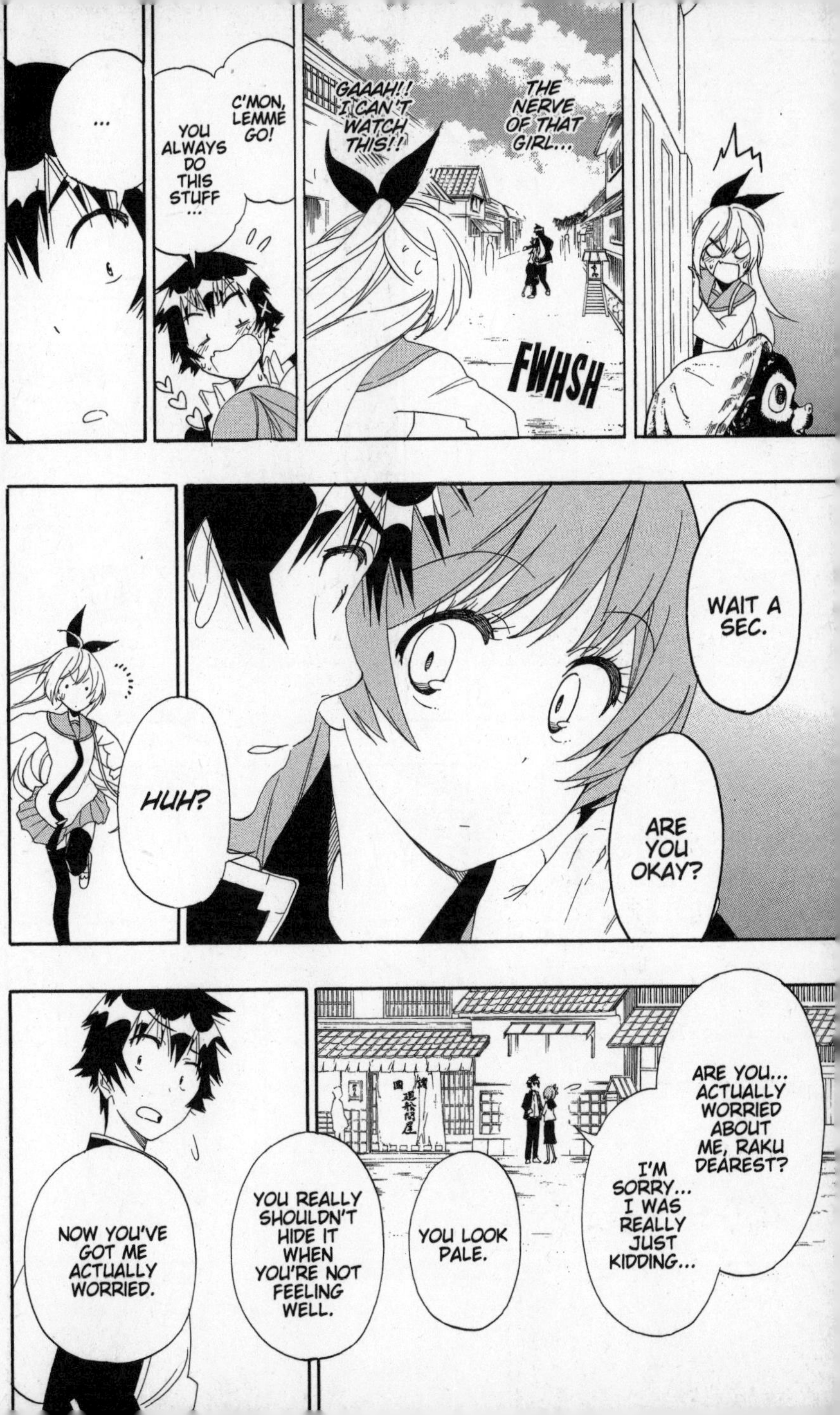
THE NERVE OF THAT GIRL...
GAAAH!! I CAN'T WATCH THIS!!
FWHSH
C'MON, LEMME GO!
YOU ALWAYS DO THIS STUFF...
...
WAIT A SEC.
ARE YOU OKAY?
HUH?
ARE YOU... ACTUALLY WORRIED ABOUT ME, RAKU DEAREST?
I'M SORRY... I WAS REALLY JUST KIDDING...
YOU LOOK PALE.
YOU REALLY SHOULDN'T HIDE IT WHEN YOU'RE NOT FEELING WELL.
NOW YOU'VE GOT ME ACTUALLY WORRIED.

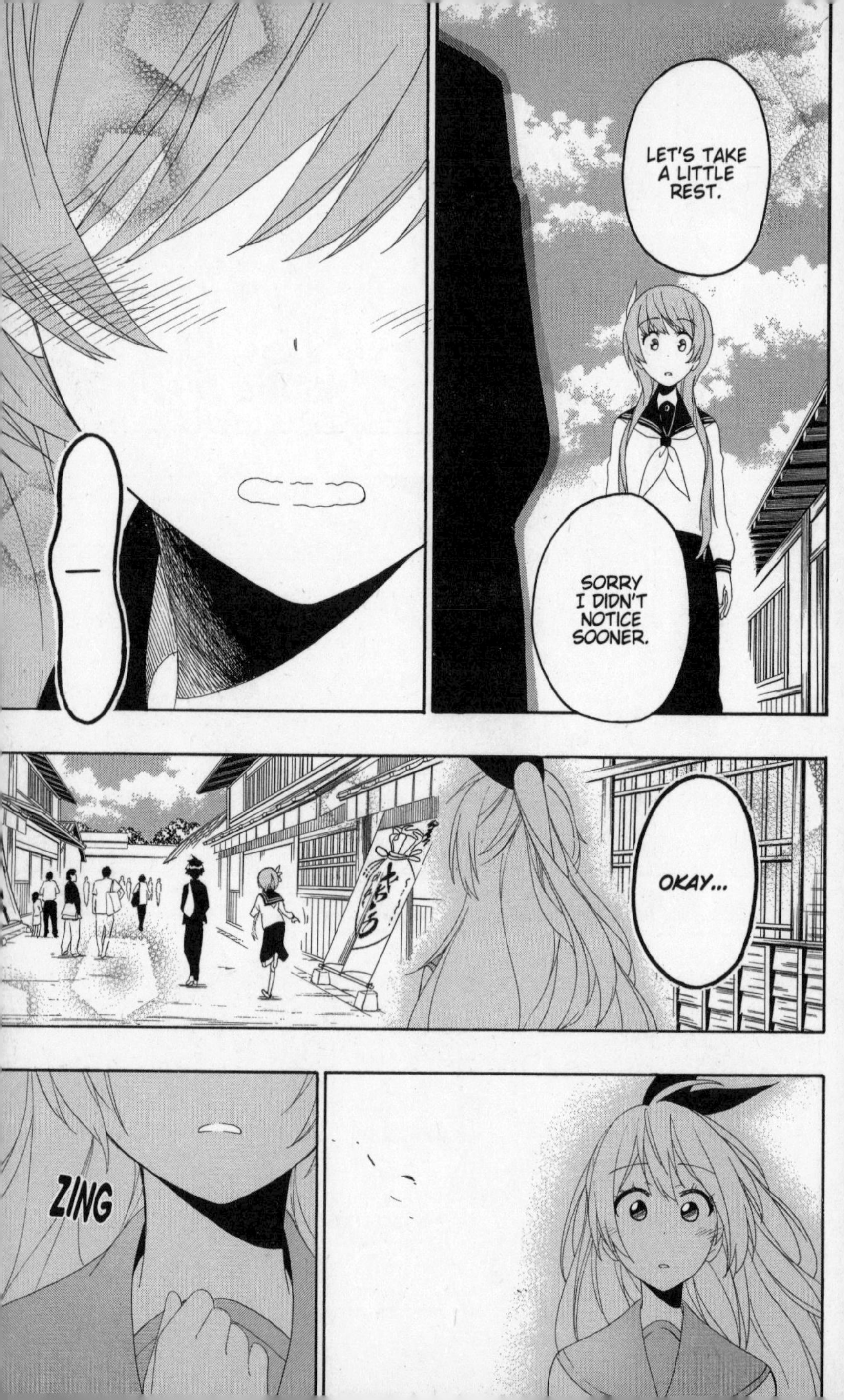
LET'S TAKE A LITTLE REST.
SORRY I DIDN'T NOTICE SOONER.
OKAY...
ZING

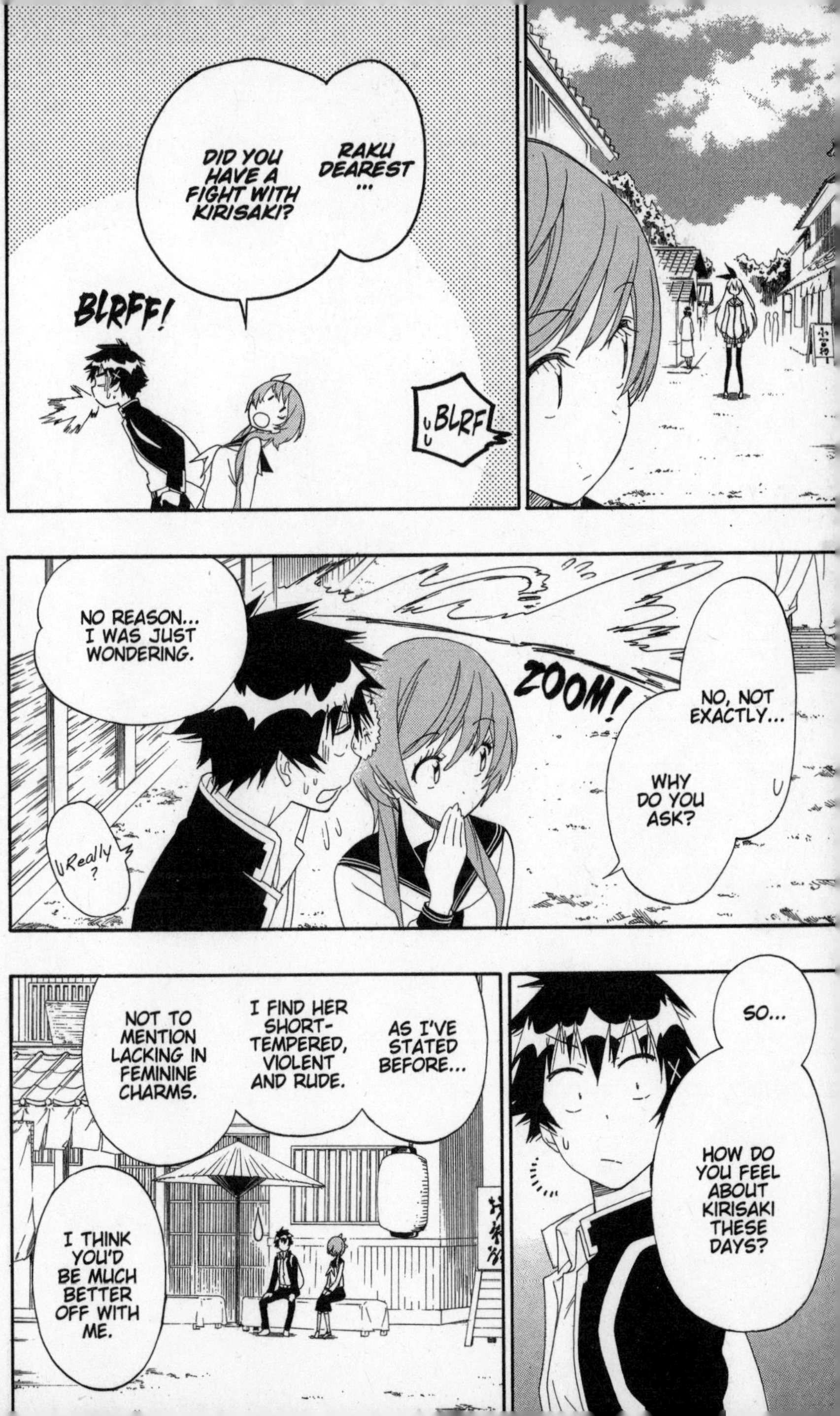
RAKU DEAREST ...
DID YOU HAVE A FIGHT WITH KIRISAKI?
BLRFF!
BLRF
ZOOM!
NO, NOT EXACTLY...
WHY DO YOU ASK?
NO REASON... I WAS JUST WONDERING.
Really?
SO...
HOW DO YOU FEEL ABOUT KIRISAKI THESE DAYS?
AS I'VE STATED BEFORE...
I FIND HER SHORT-TEMPERED, VIOLENT AND RUDE.
NOT TO MENTION LACKING IN FEMININE CHARMS.
I THINK YOU'D BE MUCH BETTER OFF WITH ME.

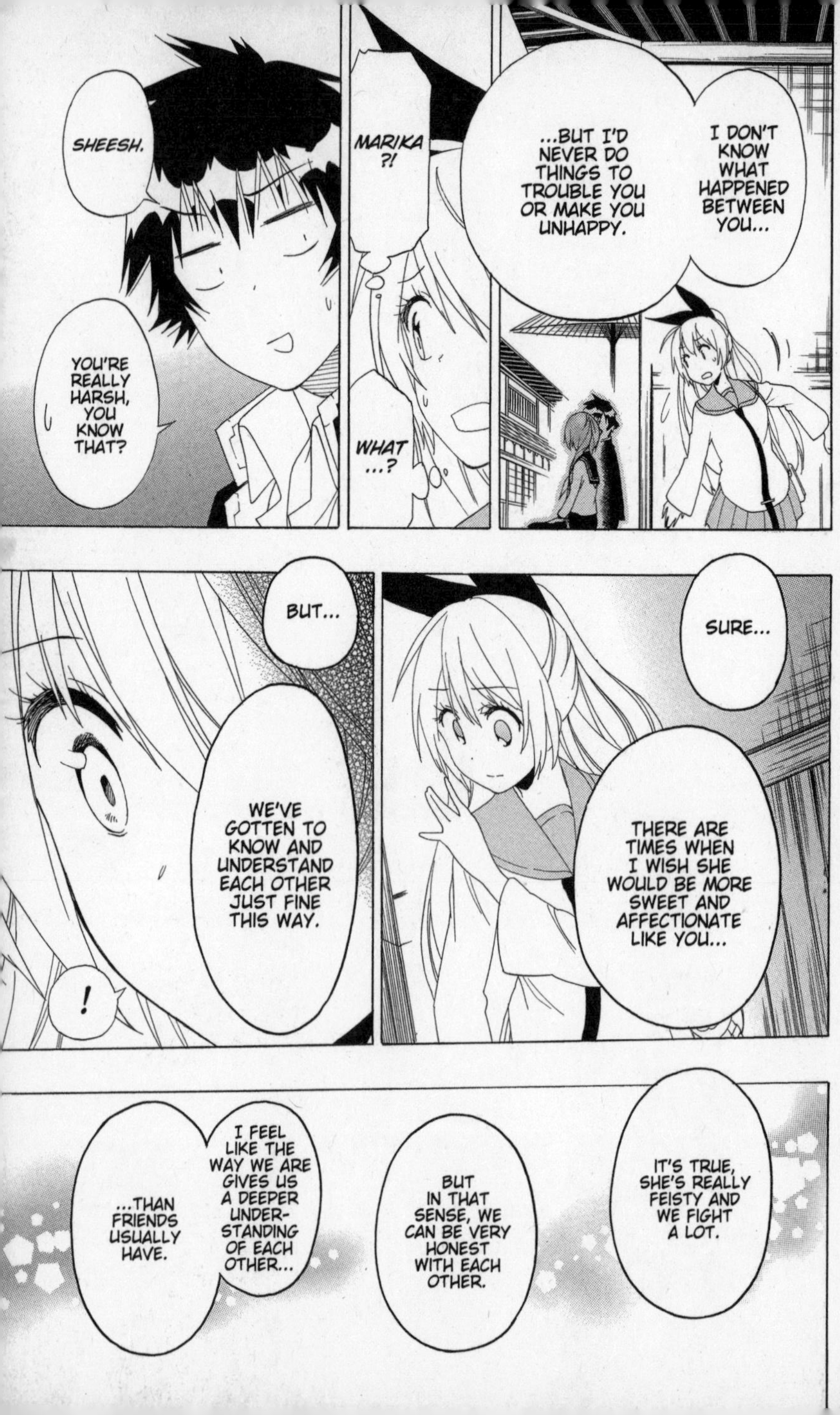
I DON'T KNOW WHAT HAPPENED BETWEEN YOU...
...BUT I'D NEVER DO THINGS TO TROUBLE YOU OR MAKE YOU UNHAPPY.
MARIKA ?!
WHAT ...?
SHEESH.
YOU'RE REALLY HARSH, YOU KNOW THAT?
SURE...
THERE ARE TIMES WHEN I WISH SHE WOULD BE MORE SWEET AND AFFECTIONATE LIKE YOU...
BUT...
WE'VE GOTTEN TO KNOW AND UNDERSTAND EACH OTHER JUST FINE THIS WAY.
!
IT'S TRUE, SHE'S REALLY FEISTY AND WE FIGHT A LOT.
BUT IN THAT SENSE, WE CAN BE VERY HONEST WITH EACH OTHER.
I FEEL LIKE THE WAY WE ARE GIVES US A DEEPER UNDER-STANDING OF EACH OTHER...
...THAN FRIENDS USUALLY HAVE.

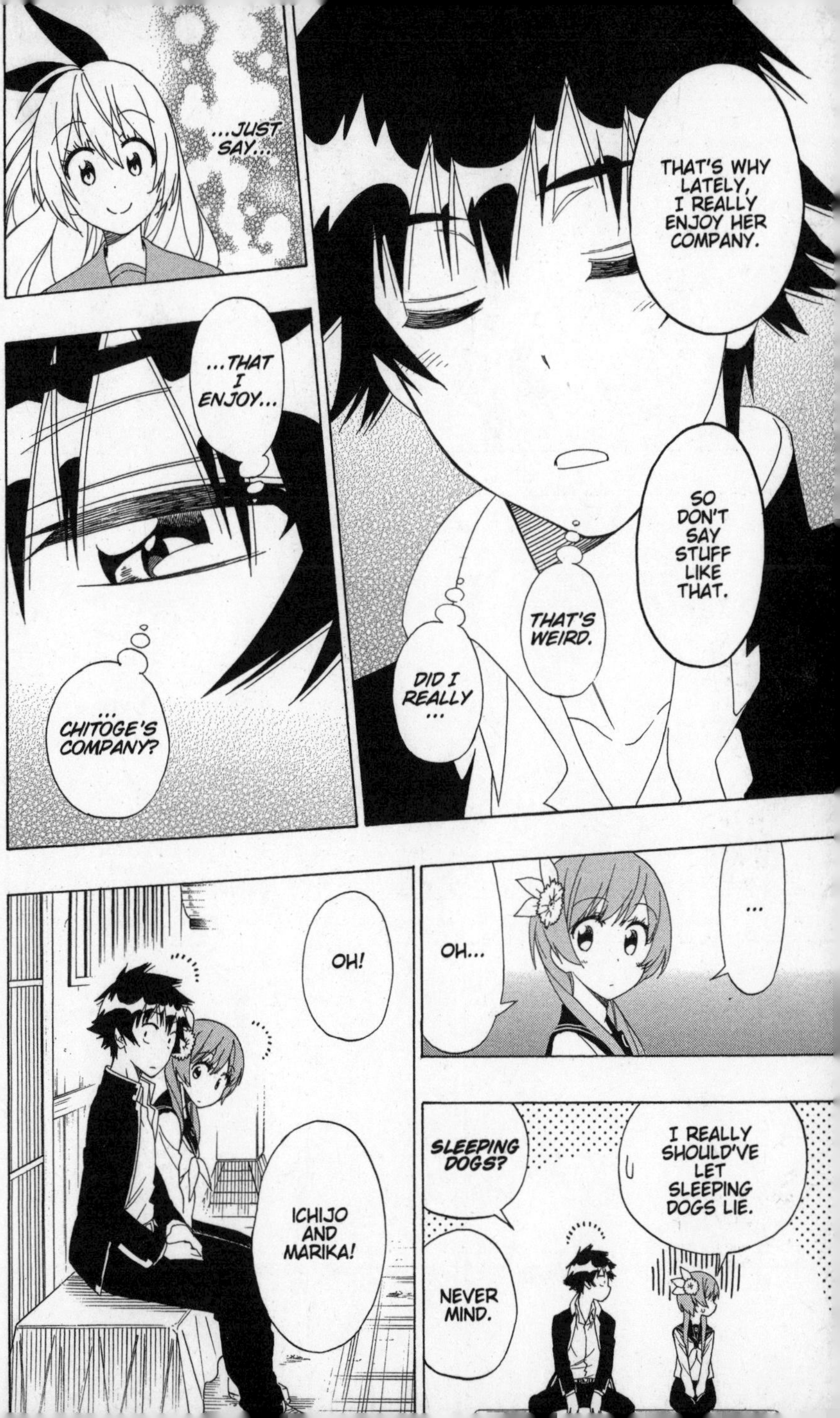

THAT'S WHY LATELY, I REALLY ENJOY HER COMPANY.
SO DON'T SAY STUFF LIKE THAT.
THAT'S WEIRD.
DID I REALLY ...
...JUST SAY...
...THAT I ENJOY...
... CHITOGE'S COMPANY?
...
OH...
I REALLY SHOULD'VE LET SLEEPING DOGS LIE.
SLEEPING DOGS?
NEVER MIND.
OH!
ICHIJO AND MARIKA!

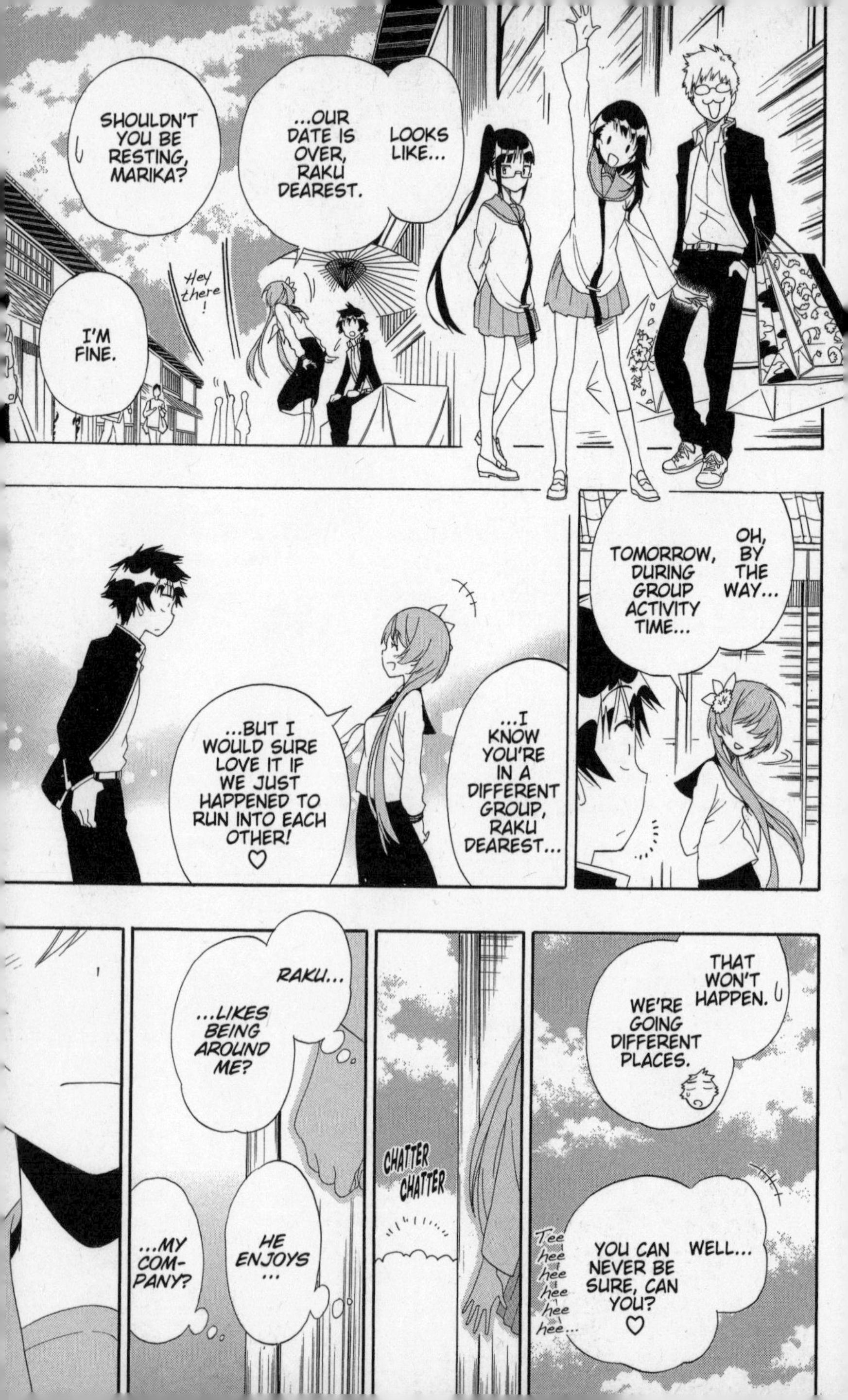
LOOKS LIKE...
...OUR DATE IS OVER, RAKU DEAREST.
Hey there!
SHOULDN'T YOU BE RESTING, MARIKA?
I'M FINE.
OH, BY THE WAY...
TOMORROW, DURING GROUP ACTIVITY TIME...
...I KNOW YOU'RE IN A DIFFERENT GROUP, RAKU DEAREST...
...BUT I WOULD SURE LOVE IT IF WE JUST HAPPENED TO RUN INTO EACH OTHER! ♡
THAT WON'T HAPPEN.
WE'RE GOING DIFFERENT PLACES.
WELL...
YOU CAN NEVER BE SURE, CAN YOU? ♡
Tee hee hee hee hee hee...
CHATTER CHATTER
RAKU...
...LIKES BEING AROUND ME?
HE ENJOYS...
...MY COMPANY?

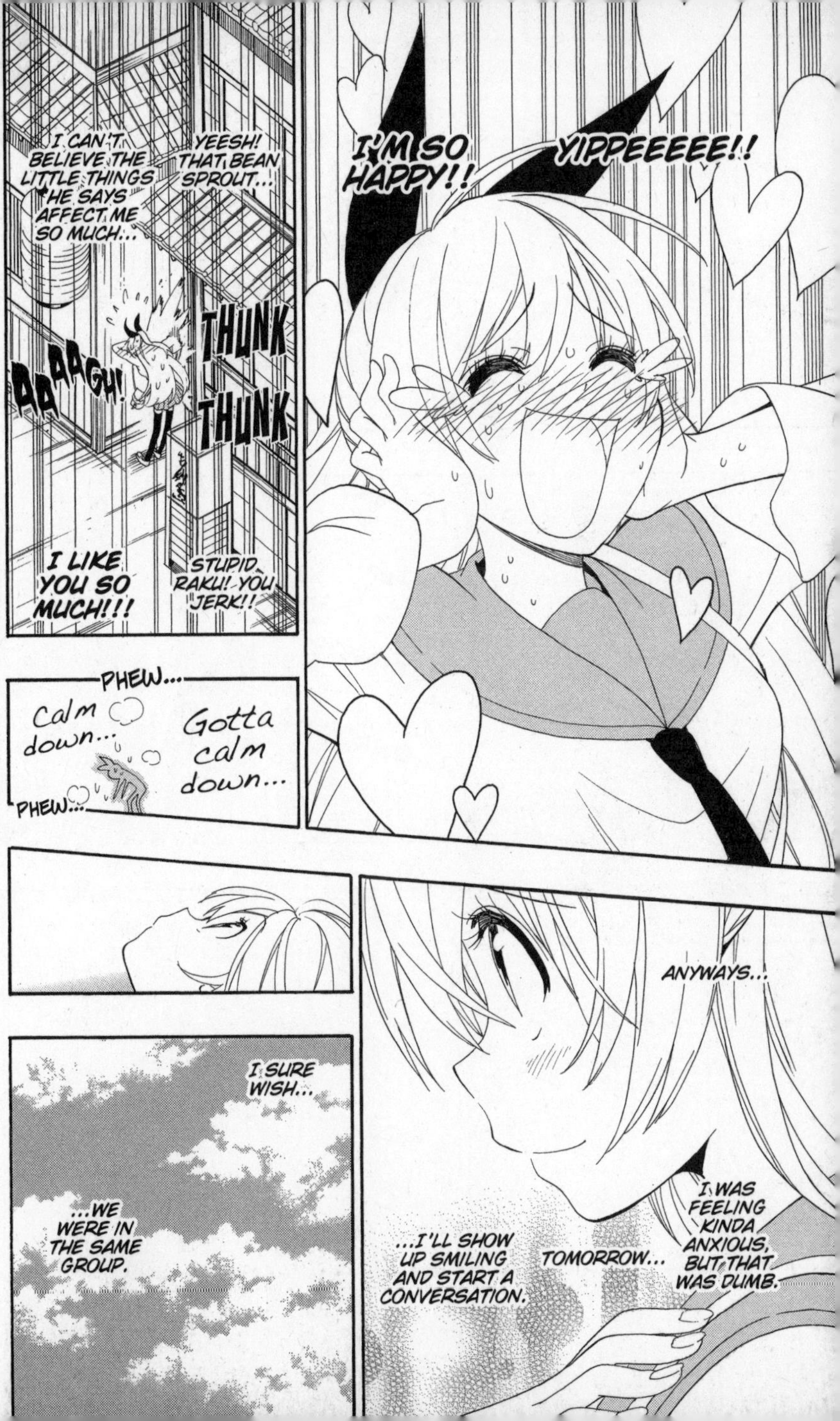
YIPPEEEEEE!!
I'M SO HAPPY!!
YEESH! THAT BEAN SPROUT...
I CAN'T BELIEVE THE LITTLE THINGS HE SAYS AFFECT ME SO MUCH...
THUNK
THUNK
AAAAGH!
STUPID RAKU! YOU JERK!!
I LIKE YOU SO MUCH!!!
PHEW...
Gotta calm down...
Calm down...
PHEW...
ANYWAYS...
I WAS FEELING KINDA ANXIOUS, BUT THAT WAS DUMB.
TOMORROW...
...I'LL SHOW UP SMILING AND START A CONVERSATION.
I SURE WISH...
...WE WERE IN THE SAME GROUP.

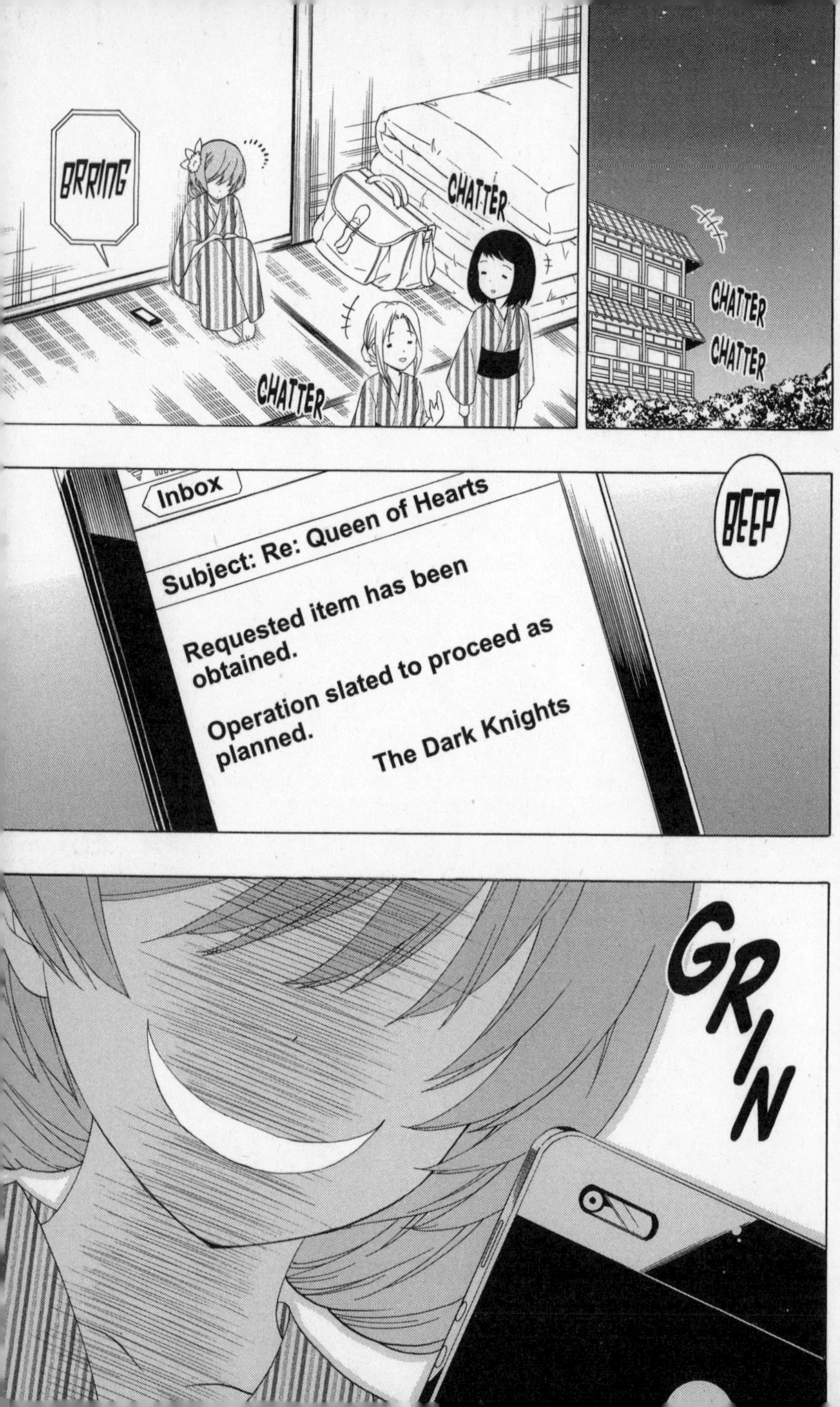
CHATTER
CHATTER
CHATTER
BRRING
CHATTER
BEEP
Inbox
Subject: Re: Queen of Hearts
Requested item has been obtained.
Operation slated to proceed as planned.
The Dark Knights
GRIN

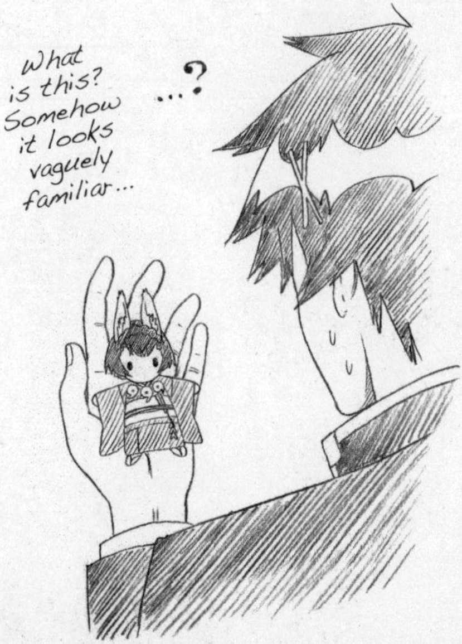
What is this? Somehow it looks vaguely familiar...
...?

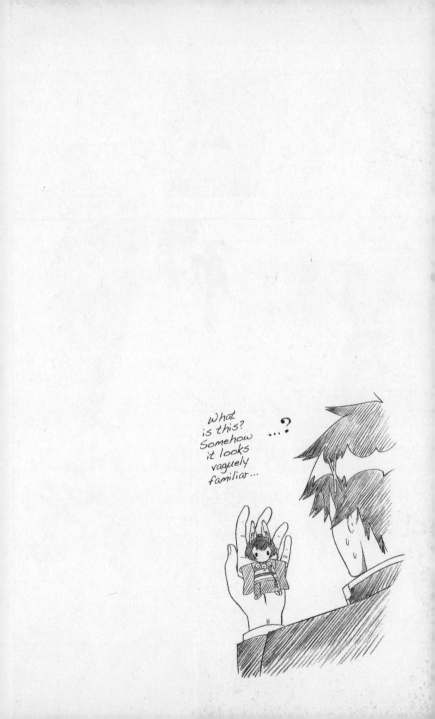

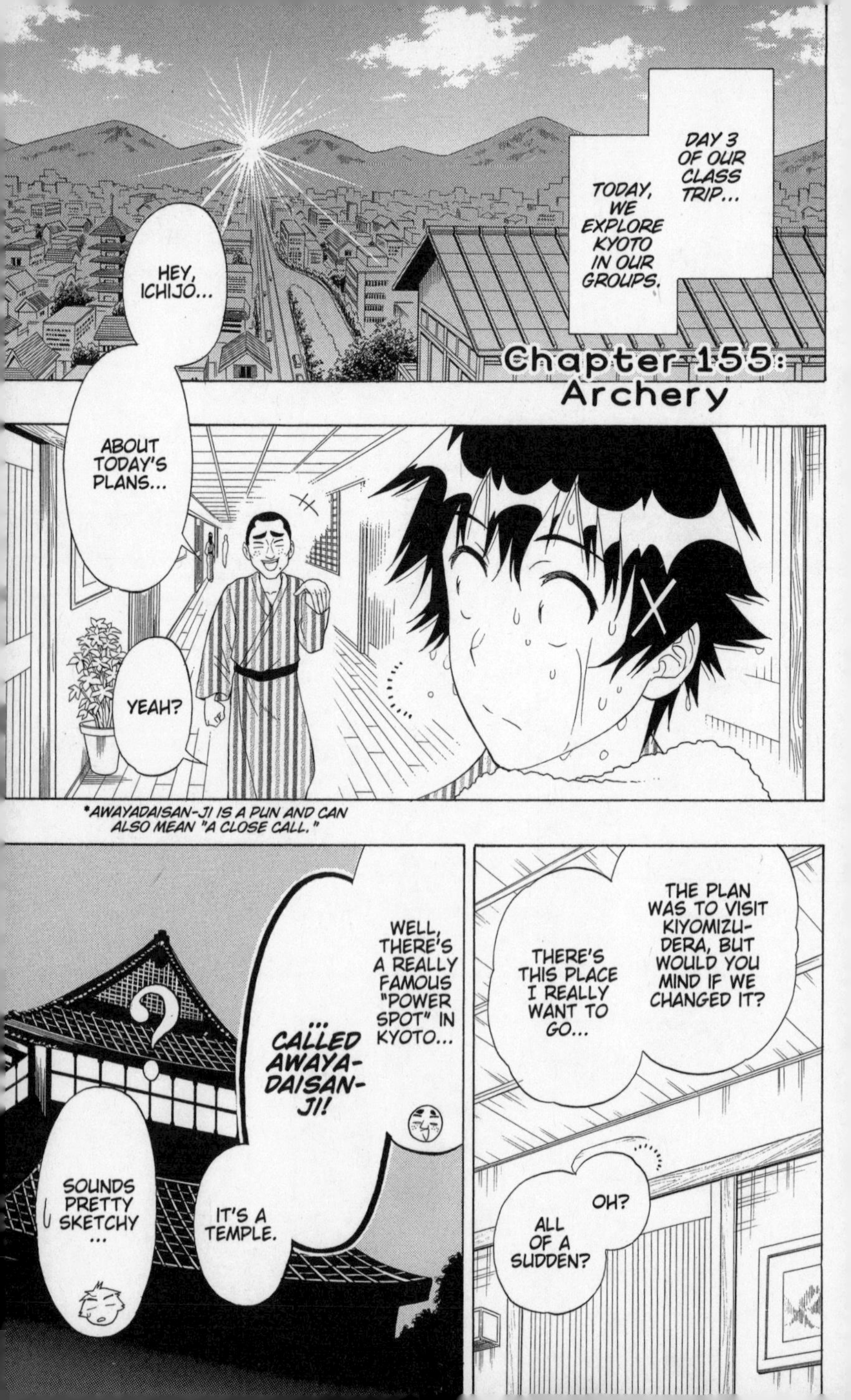
DAY 3 OF OUR CLASS TRIP...
TODAY, WE EXPLORE KYOTO IN OUR GROUPS.
HEY, ICHIJO...
Chapter 155: Archery
ABOUT TODAY'S PLANS...
YEAH?
*AWAYADAISAN-JI IS A PUN AND CAN ALSO MEAN "A CLOSE CALL."
THE PLAN WAS TO VISIT KIYOMIZU-DERA, BUT WOULD YOU MIND IF WE CHANGED IT?
THERE'S THIS PLACE I REALLY WANT TO GO...
OH?
ALL OF A SUDDEN?
WELL, THERE'S A REALLY FAMOUS "POWER SPOT" IN KYOTO...
...CALLED AWAYA-DAISAN-JI!
IT'S A TEMPLE.
SOUNDS PRETTY SKETCHY...

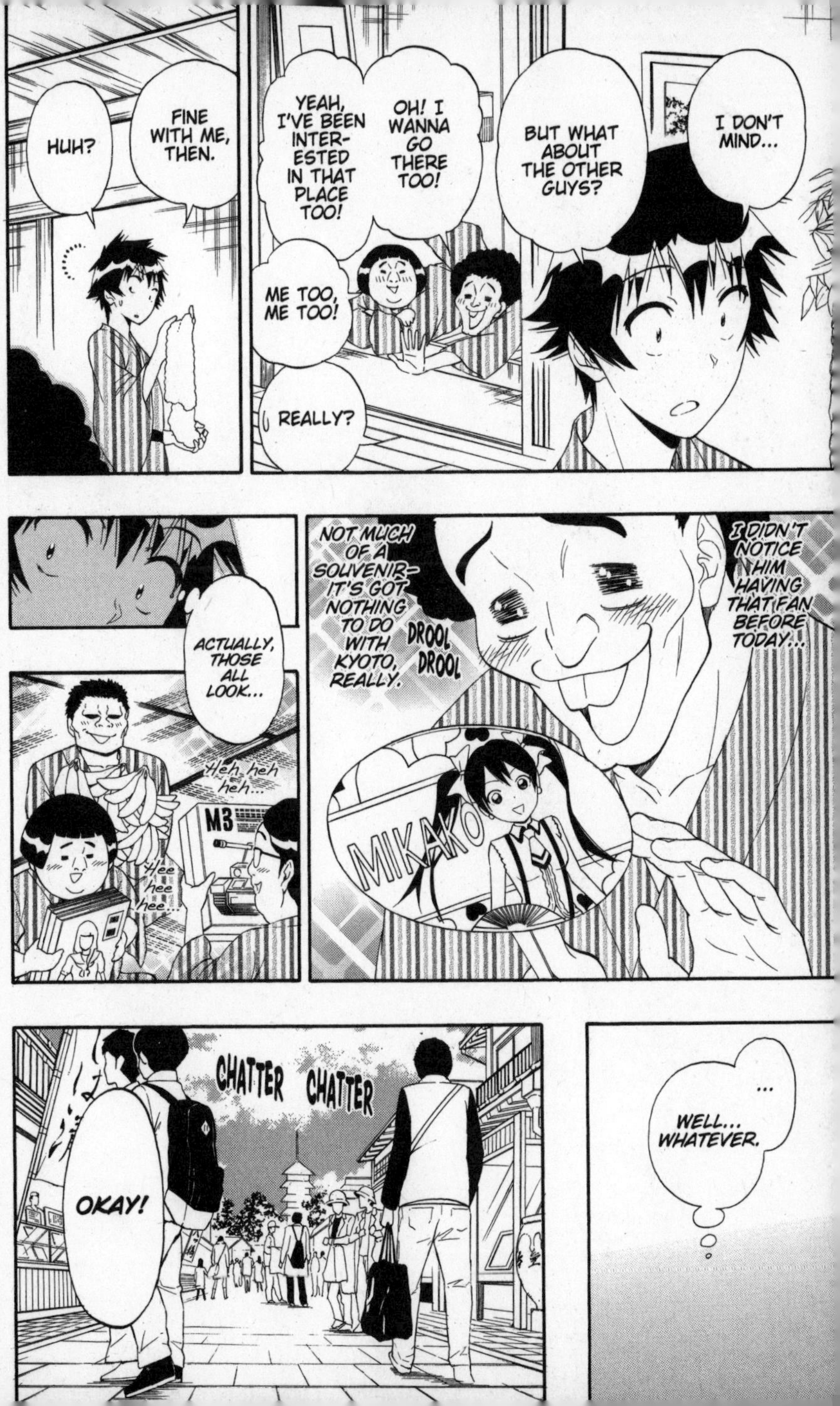
I DON'T MIND...
BUT WHAT ABOUT THE OTHER GUYS?
OH! I WANNA GO THERE TOO!
YEAH, I'VE BEEN INTERESTED IN THAT PLACE TOO!
ME TOO, ME TOO!
REALLY?
FINE WITH ME, THEN.
HUH?
I DIDN'T NOTICE HIM HAVING THAT FAN BEFORE TODAY...
NOT MUCH OF A SOUVENIR—IT'S GOT NOTHING TO DO WITH KYOTO, REALLY.
DROOL DROOL
MIKAKO
ACTUALLY, THOSE ALL LOOK...
Heh heh heh...
M3
Hee hee hee...
... WELL... WHATEVER.
CHATTER CHATTER
OKAY!

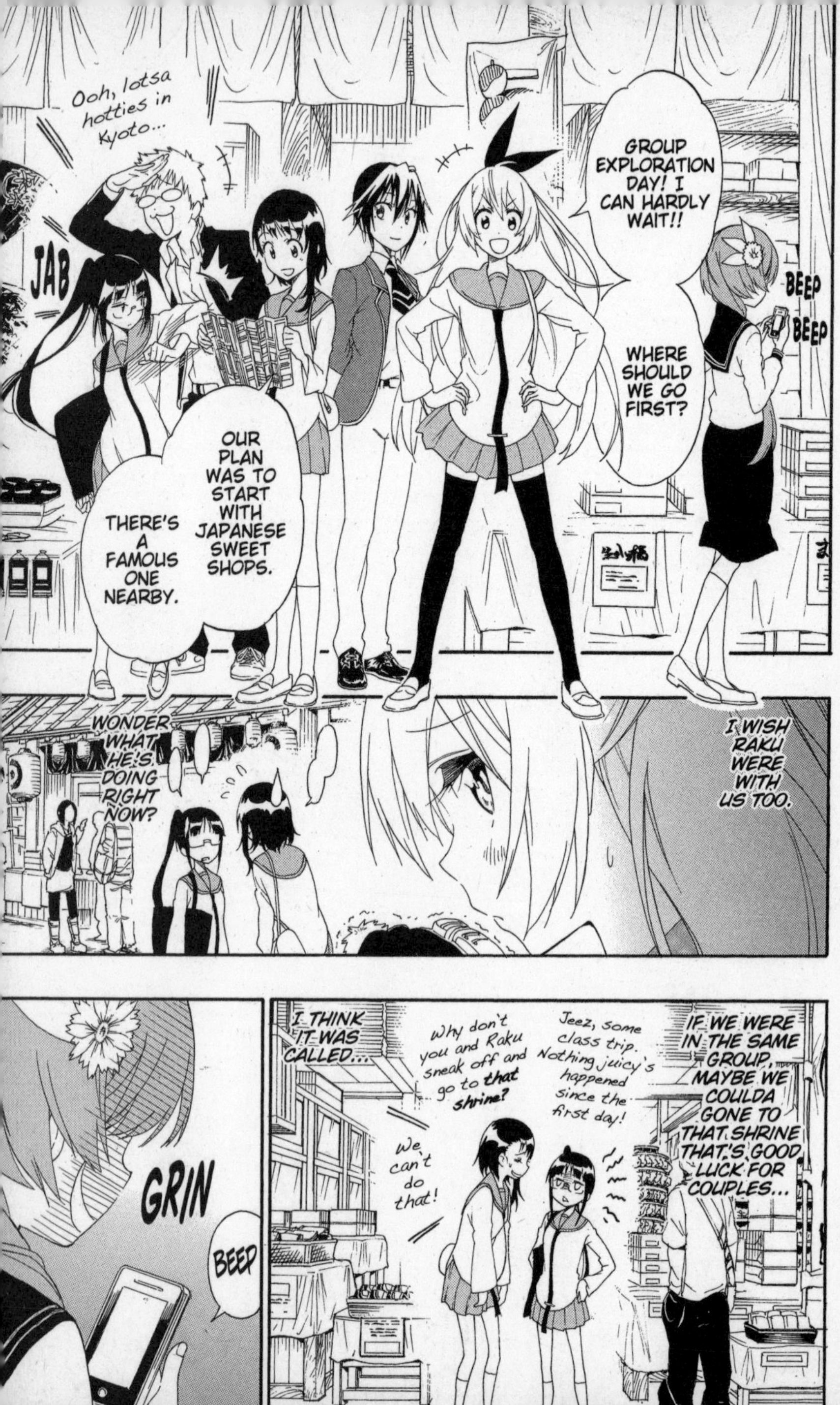
GROUP EXPLORATION DAY! I CAN HARDLY WAIT!!
WHERE SHOULD WE GO FIRST?
BEEP
BEEP
OUR PLAN WAS TO START WITH JAPANESE SWEET SHOPS.
THERE'S A FAMOUS ONE NEARBY.
Ooh, lotsa hotties in Kyoto...
JAB
I WISH RAKU WERE WITH US TOO.
WONDER WHAT HE'S DOING RIGHT NOW?
IF WE WERE IN THE SAME GROUP, MAYBE WE COULDA GONE TO THAT SHRINE THAT'S GOOD LUCK FOR COUPLES...
Jeez, some class trip. Nothing juicy's happened since the first day!
Why don't you and Raku sneak off and go to **that shrine**?
We can't do that!
I THINK IT WAS CALLED...
GRIN
BEEP

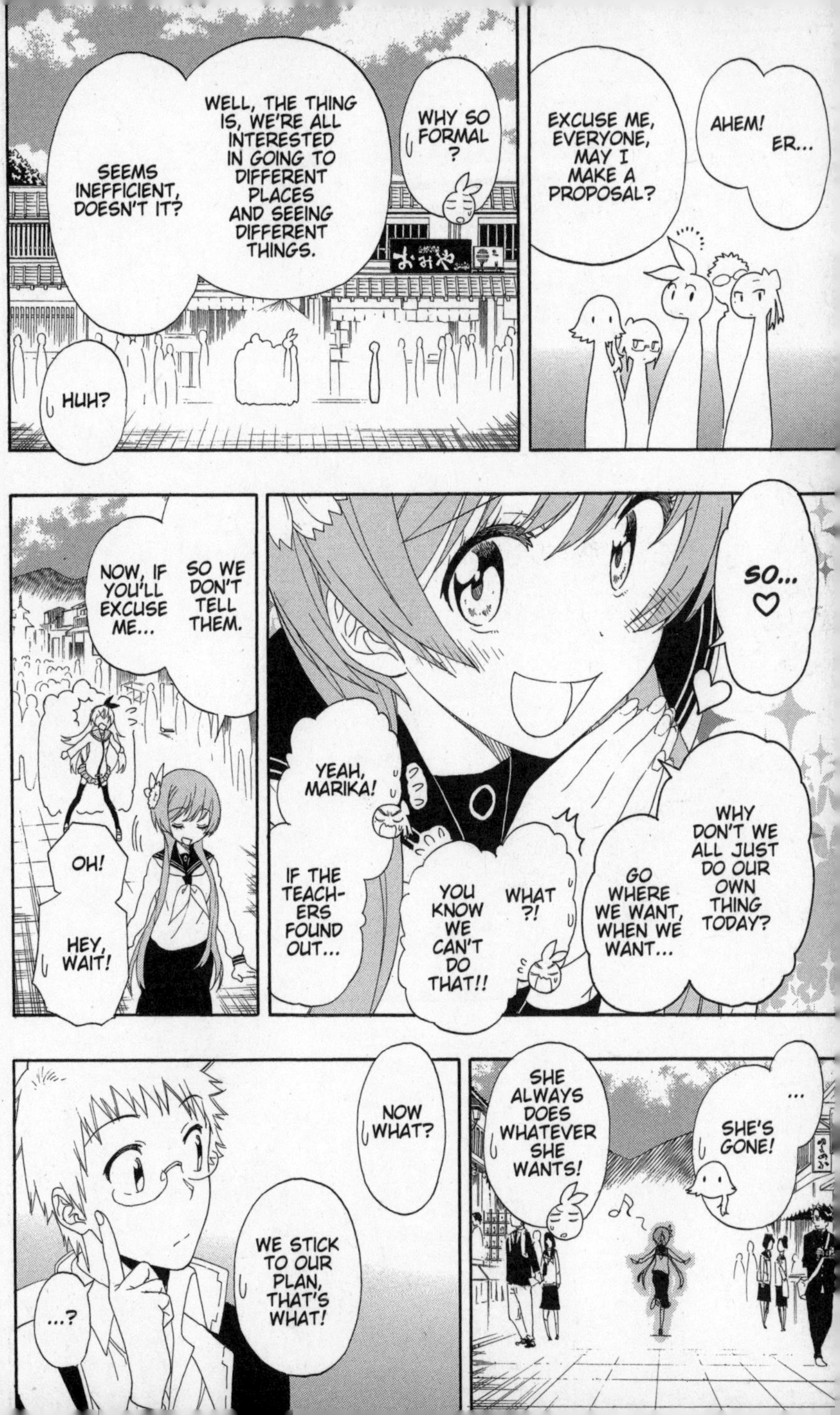
AHEM!
ER...
EXCUSE ME, EVERYONE, MAY I MAKE A PROPOSAL?
WHY SO FORMAL?
WELL, THE THING IS, WE'RE ALL INTERESTED IN GOING TO DIFFERENT PLACES AND SEEING DIFFERENT THINGS.
SEEMS INEFFICIENT, DOESN'T IT?
おみや
HUH?
SO... ♡
WHY DON'T WE ALL JUST DO OUR OWN THING TODAY?
GO WHERE WE WANT, WHEN WE WANT...
WHAT?!
YOU KNOW WE CAN'T DO THAT!!
YEAH, MARIKA!
IF THE TEACHERS FOUND OUT...
SO WE DON'T TELL THEM.
NOW, IF YOU'LL EXCUSE ME...
OH!
HEY, WAIT!
...
SHE'S GONE!
SHE ALWAYS DOES WHATEVER SHE WANTS!
NOW WHAT?
WE STICK TO OUR PLAN, THAT'S WHAT!
...?

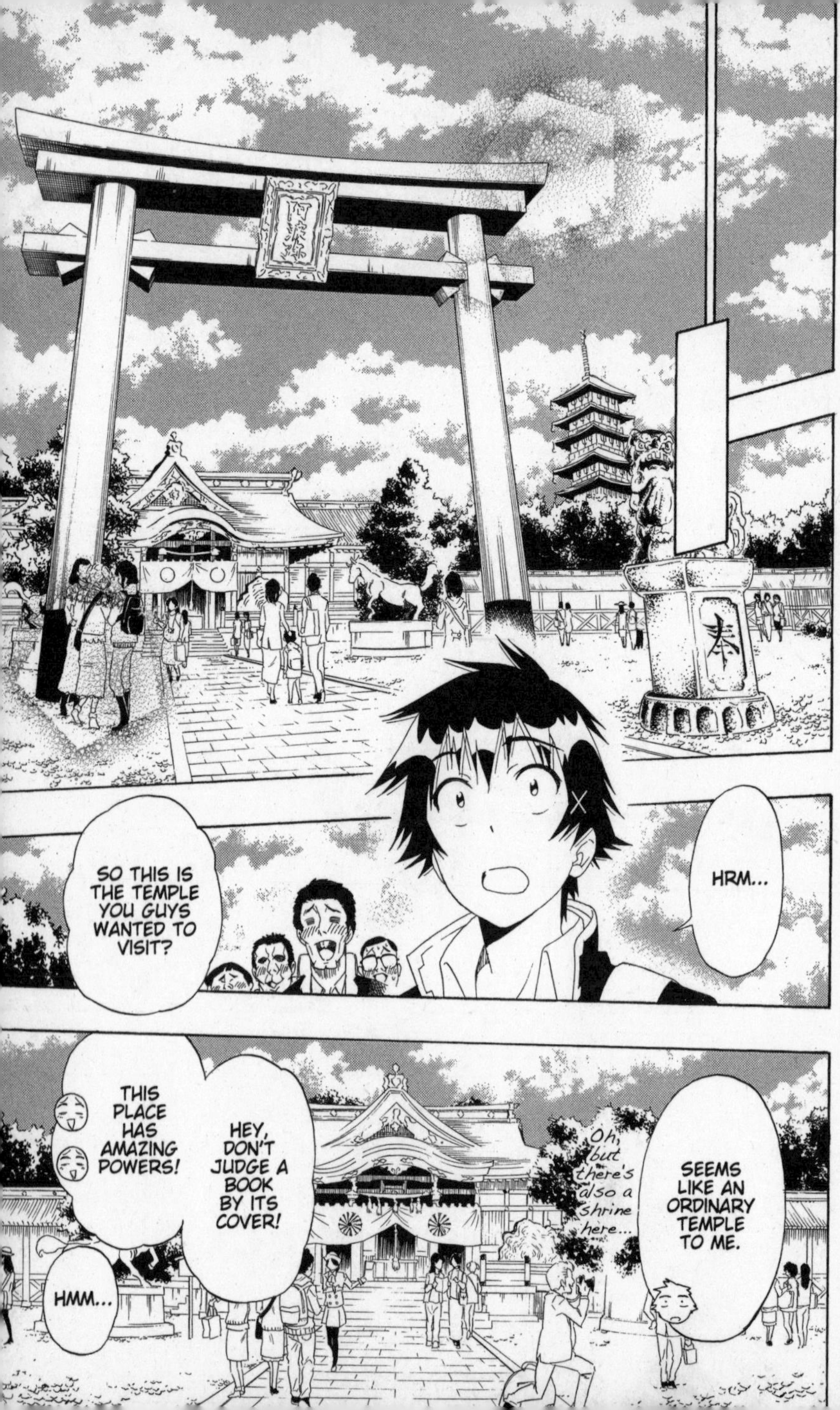
HRM...
SO THIS IS THE TEMPLE YOU GUYS WANTED TO VISIT?
SEEMS LIKE AN ORDINARY TEMPLE TO ME.
Oh, but there's also a shrine here...
HEY, DON'T JUDGE A BOOK BY ITS COVER!
THIS PLACE HAS AMAZING POWERS!
HMM...

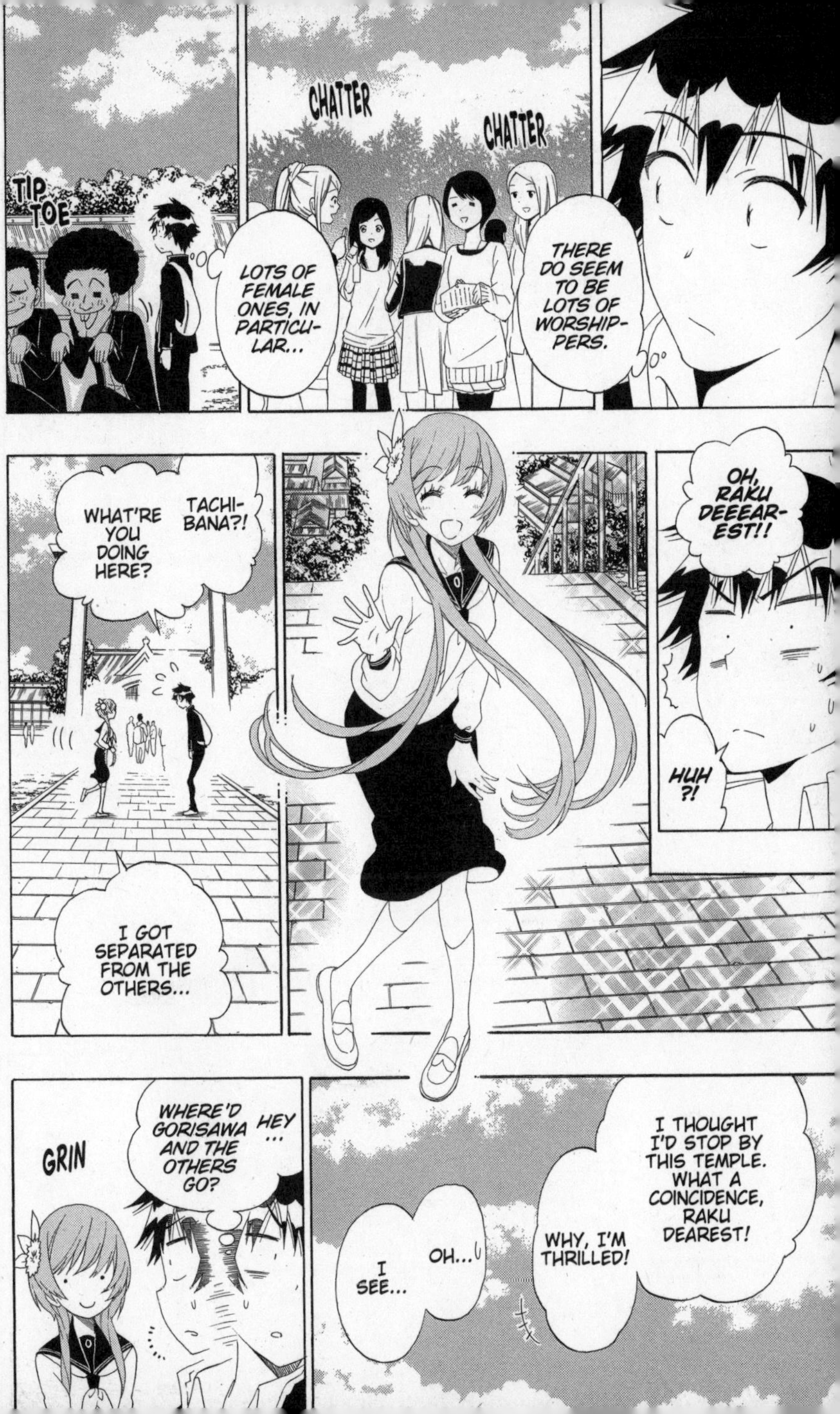
CHATTER
CHATTER
THERE DO SEEM TO BE LOTS OF WORSHIP-PERS.
LOTS OF FEMALE ONES, IN PARTICU-LAR...
TIP TOE
OH, RAKU DEEEAR-EST!!
HUH?!
TACHI-BANA?!
WHAT'RE YOU DOING HERE?
I GOT SEPARATED FROM THE OTHERS...
I THOUGHT I'D STOP BY THIS TEMPLE. WHAT A COINCIDENCE, RAKU DEAREST!
WHY, I'M THRILLED!
OH...
I SEE...
HEY...
WHERE'D GORISAWA AND THE OTHERS GO?
GRIN

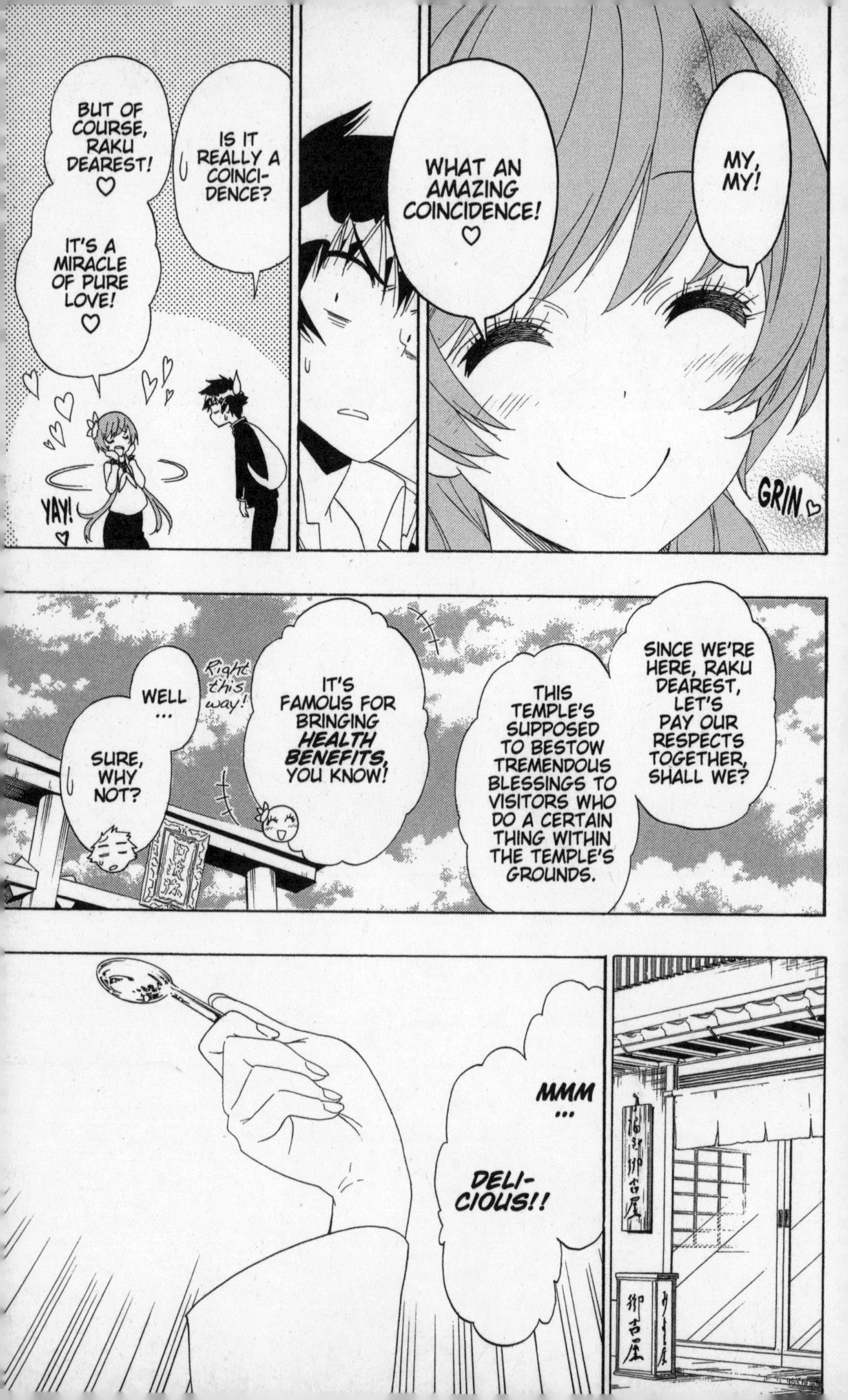
MY, MY!
WHAT AN AMAZING COINCIDENCE! ♡
GRIN ♡
IS IT REALLY A COINCIDENCE?
BUT OF COURSE, RAKU DEAREST! ♡
IT'S A MIRACLE OF PURE LOVE! ♡
YAY! ♡
SINCE WE'RE HERE, RAKU DEAREST, LET'S PAY OUR RESPECTS TOGETHER, SHALL WE?
THIS TEMPLE'S SUPPOSED TO BESTOW TREMENDOUS BLESSINGS TO VISITORS WHO DO A CERTAIN THING WITHIN THE TEMPLE'S GROUNDS.
IT'S FAMOUS FOR BRINGING *HEALTH BENEFITS*, YOU KNOW!
Right this way!
WELL...
SURE, WHY NOT?
MMM...
DELI-CIOUS!!

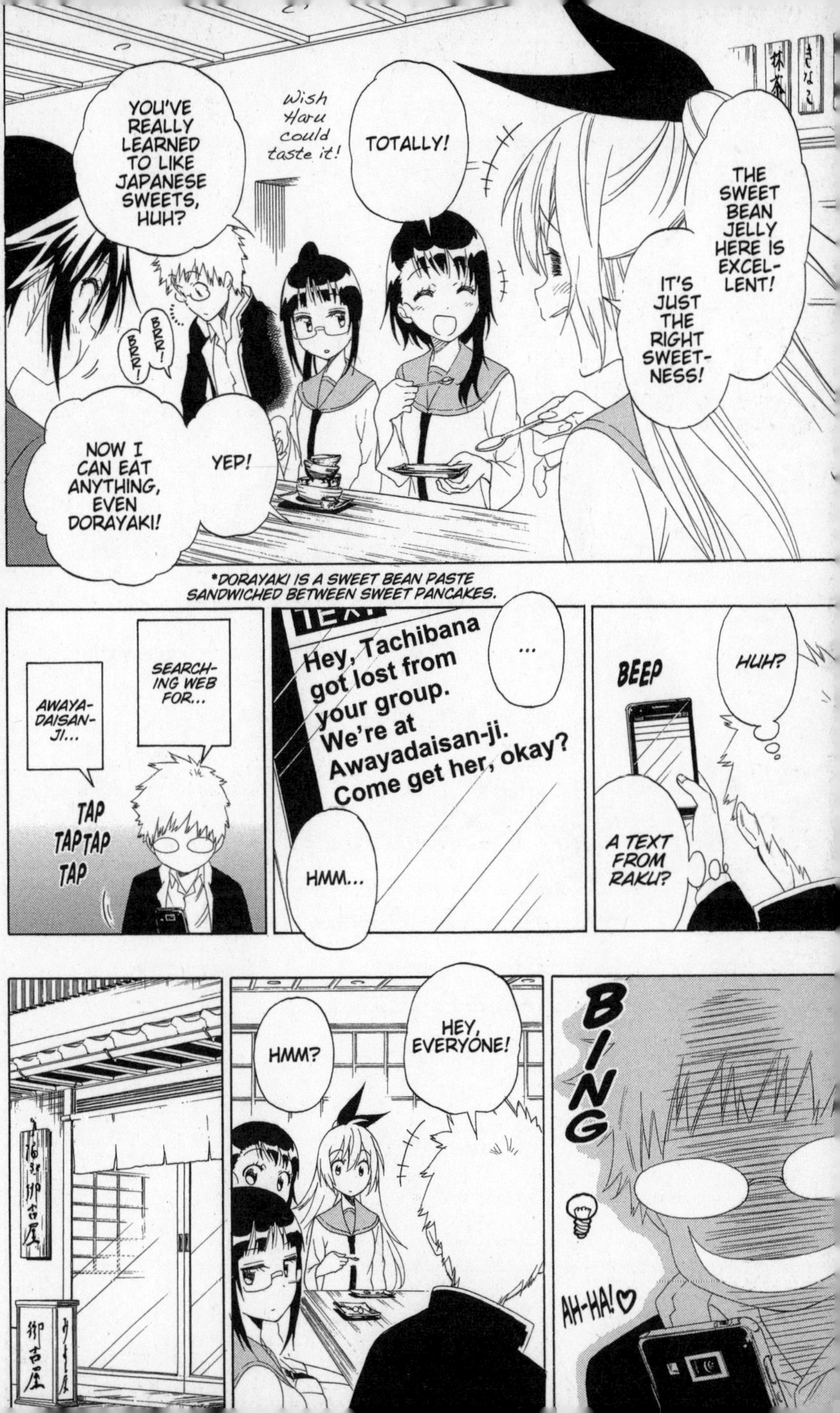
THE SWEET BEAN JELLY HERE IS EXCEL-LENT!
IT'S JUST THE RIGHT SWEET-NESS!
TOTALLY!
Wish Haru could taste it!
YOU'VE REALLY LEARNED TO LIKE JAPANESE SWEETS, HUH?
BRR! BRR!
YEP!
NOW I CAN EAT ANYTHING, EVEN DORAYAKI!
HUH?
BEEP
A TEXT FROM RAKU?
...
Hey, Tachibana got lost from your group. We're at Awayadaisan-ji. Come get her, okay?
HMM...
SEARCH-ING WEB FOR...
AWAYA-DAISAN-JI...
TAP TAP TAP TAP
BING
AH-HA!♡
HEY, EVERYONE!
HMM?

*DORAYAKI IS A SWEET BEAN PASTE SANDWICHED BETWEEN SWEET PANCAKES.

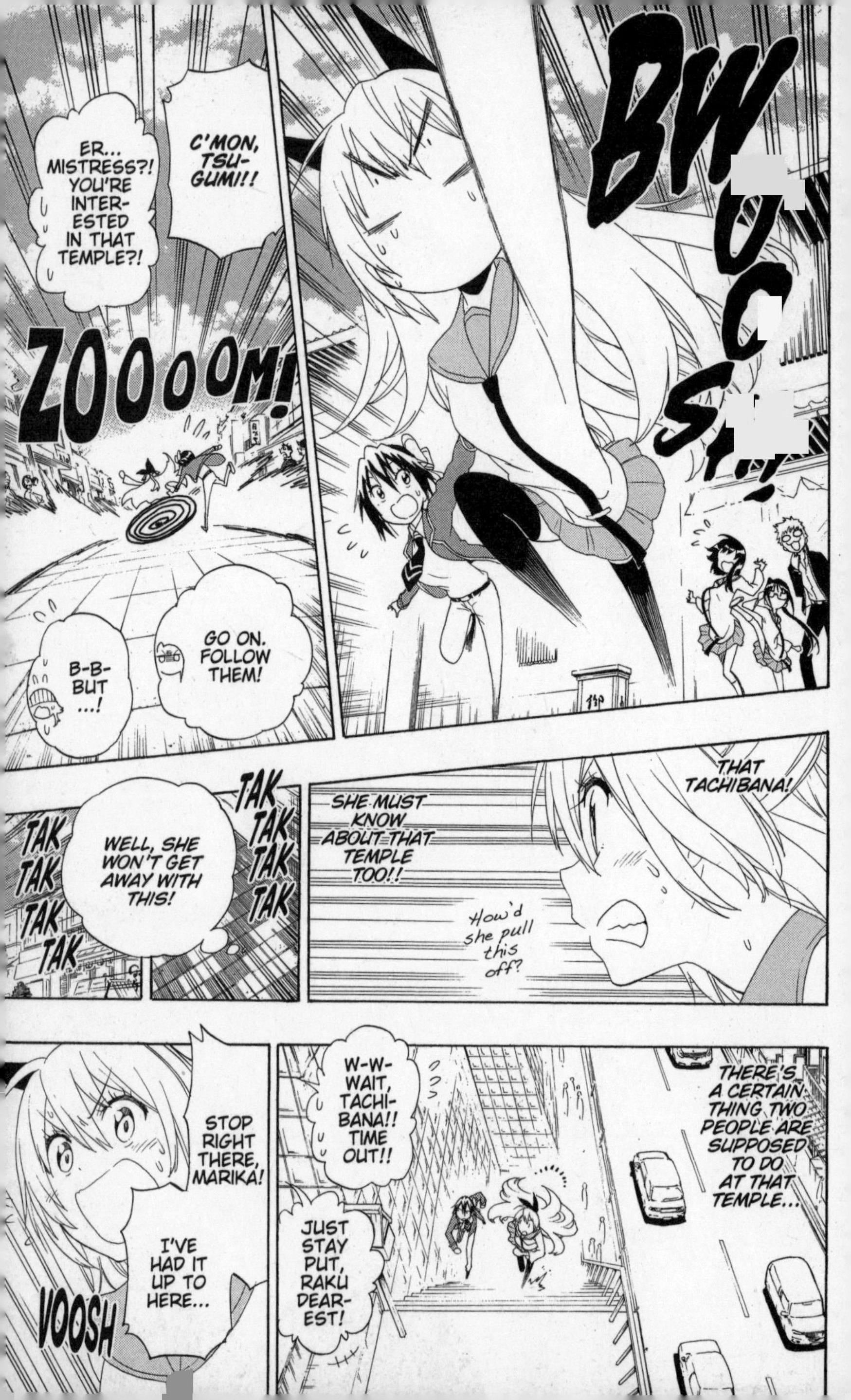
BWOOSH!!
C'MON, TSUGUMI!!
ER... MISTRESS?! YOU'RE INTERESTED IN THAT TEMPLE?!
ZOOOOOM!
GO ON. FOLLOW THEM!
B-B-BUT ...!
THAT TACHIBANA!
SHE MUST KNOW ABOUT THAT TEMPLE TOO!!
How'd she pull this off?
TAK TAK TAK TAK TAK
WELL, SHE WON'T GET AWAY WITH THIS!
TAK TAK TAK TAK
THERE'S A CERTAIN THING TWO PEOPLE ARE SUPPOSED TO DO AT THAT TEMPLE...
W-W-WAIT, TACHIBANA!! TIME OUT!!
JUST STAY PUT, RAKU DEAREST!
STOP RIGHT THERE, MARIKA!
I'VE HAD IT UP TO HERE...
VOOSH

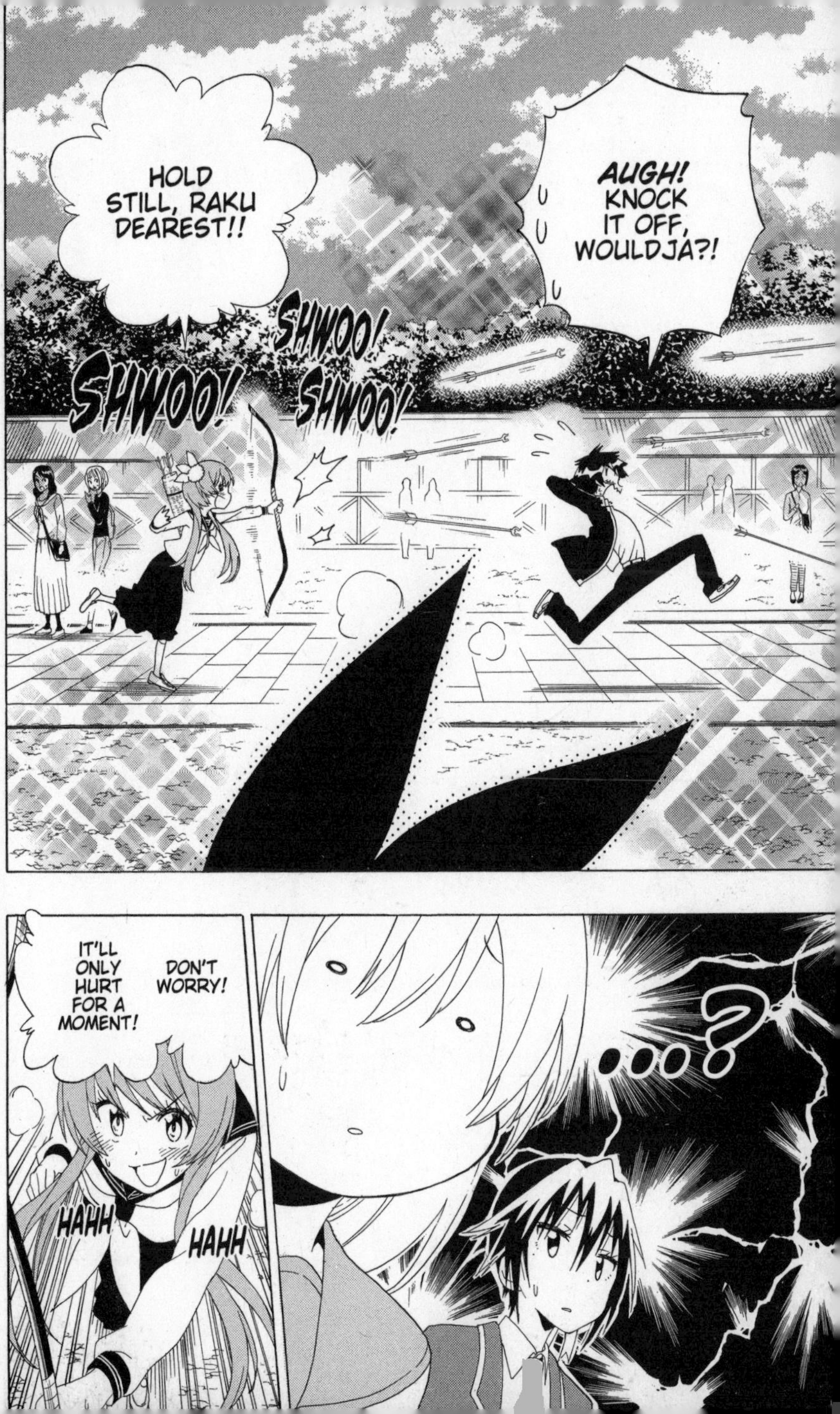
AUGH! KNOCK IT OFF, WOULDJA?!
HOLD STILL, RAKU DEAREST!!
SHWOO!
SHWOO!
SHWOO!
...?
DON'T WORRY!
IT'LL ONLY HURT FOR A MOMENT!
HAHH
HAHH

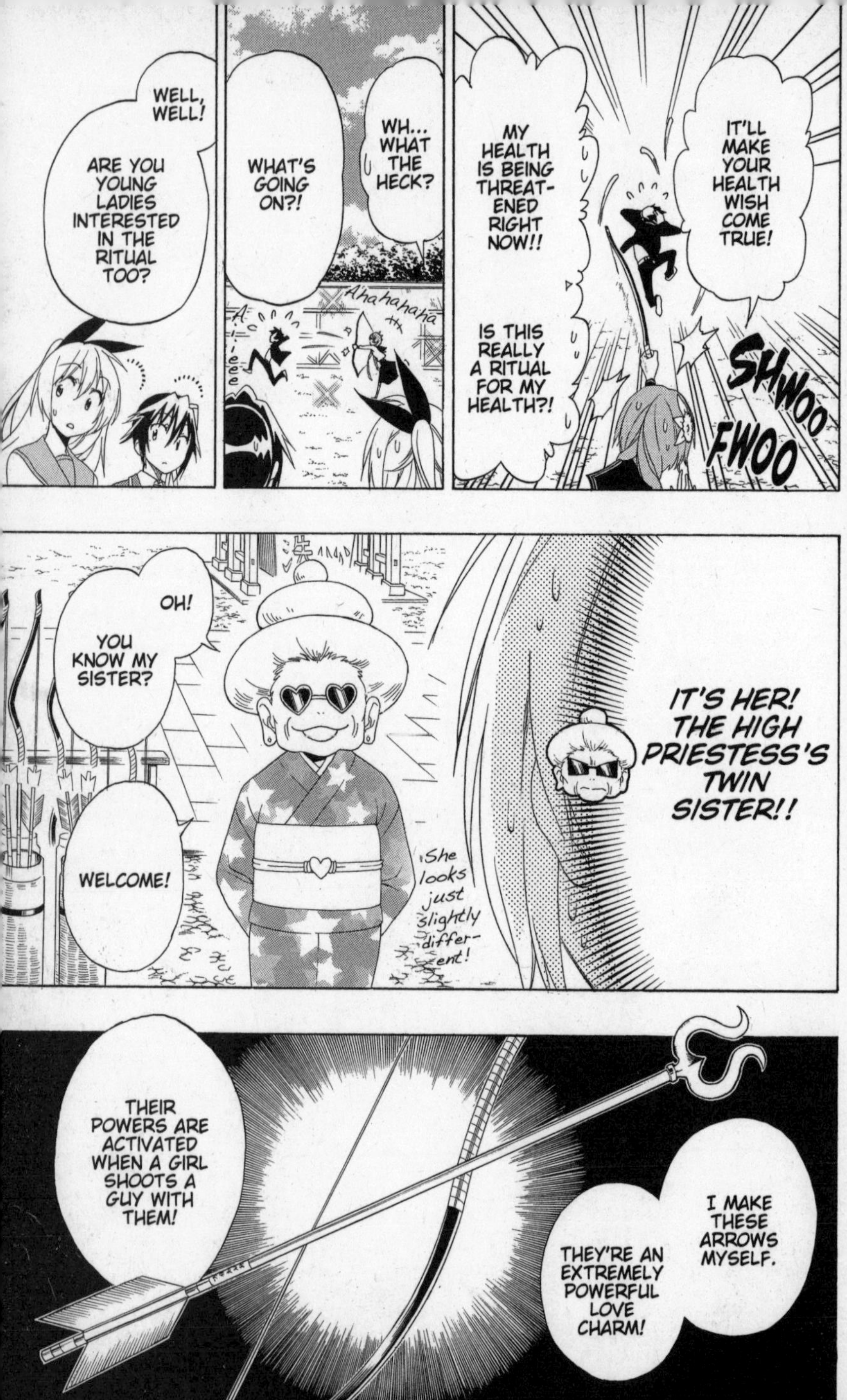
IT'LL MAKE YOUR HEALTH WISH COME TRUE!
SHWOO
FWOO
MY HEALTH IS BEING THREAT-ENED RIGHT NOW!!
IS THIS REALLY A RITUAL FOR MY HEALTH?!
WH... WHAT THE HECK?
WHAT'S GOING ON?!
Ahahahaha
A-ieee
WELL, WELL!
ARE YOU YOUNG LADIES INTERESTED IN THE RITUAL TOO?
IT'S HER! THE HIGH PRIESTESS'S TWIN SISTER!!
She looks just slightly differ-ent!
OH!
YOU KNOW MY SISTER?
WELCOME!
I MAKE THESE ARROWS MYSELF.
THEY'RE AN EXTREMELY POWERFUL LOVE CHARM!
THEIR POWERS ARE ACTIVATED WHEN A GIRL SHOOTS A GUY WITH THEM!

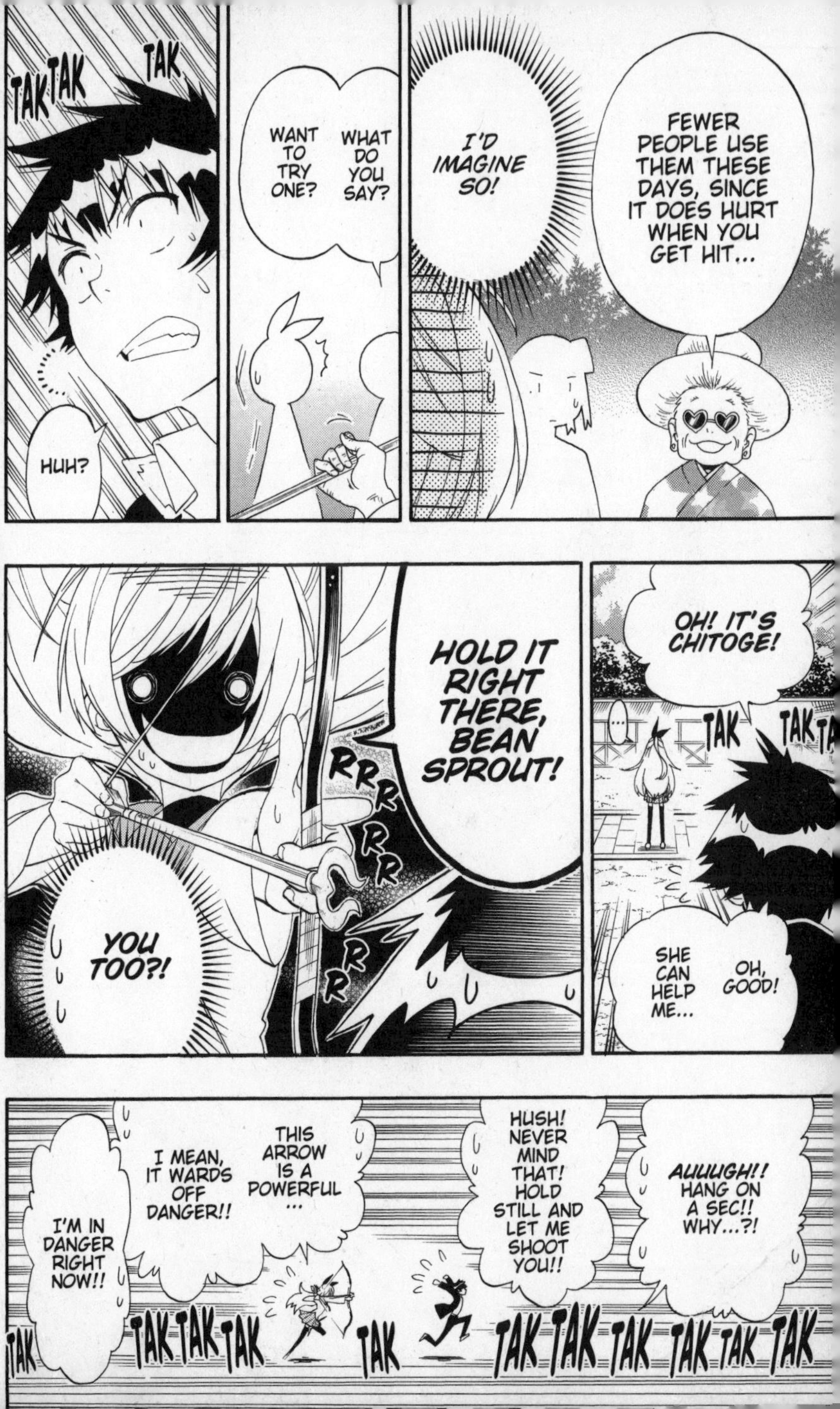
FEWER PEOPLE USE THEM THESE DAYS, SINCE IT DOES HURT WHEN YOU GET HIT...
I'D IMAGINE SO!
WHAT DO YOU SAY?
WANT TO TRY ONE?
TAK
TAK TAK
HUH?
OH! IT'S CHITOGE!
...
TAK TAK TA
OH, GOOD!
SHE CAN HELP ME...
HOLD IT RIGHT THERE, BEAN SPROUT!
RRRRRRRRR
YOU TOO?!
AUUUGH!! HANG ON A SEC!! WHY...?!
HUSH! NEVER MIND THAT! HOLD STILL AND LET ME SHOOT YOU!!
THIS ARROW IS A POWERFUL...
I MEAN, IT WARDS OFF DANGER!!
I'M IN DANGER RIGHT NOW!!
TAK TAK TAK TAK TAK TAK TAK TAK TAK TAK TAK TAK

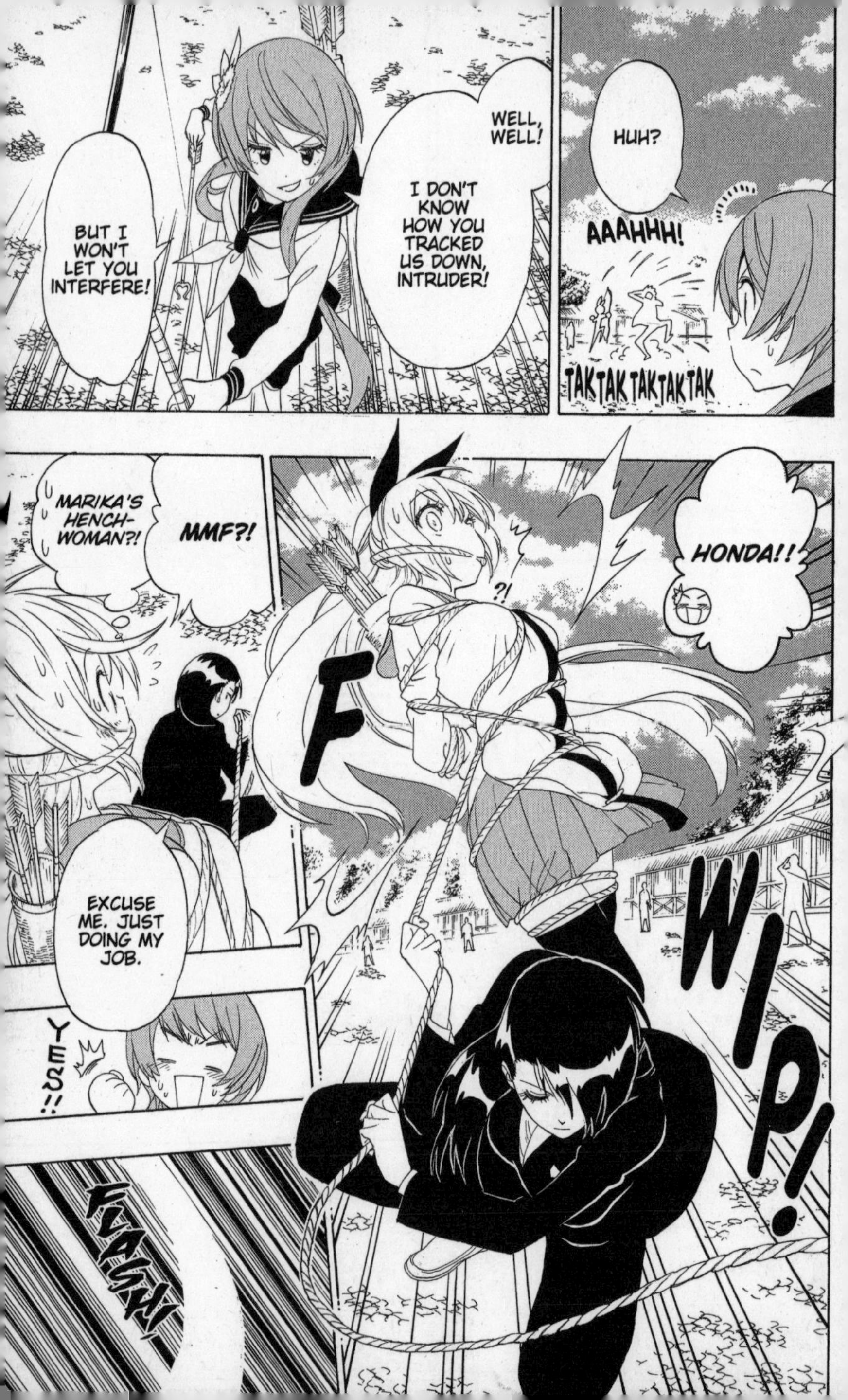
HUH?
AAAHHH!
TAKTAK TAKTAKTAK
WELL, WELL!
I DON'T KNOW HOW YOU TRACKED US DOWN, INTRUDER!
BUT I WON'T LET YOU INTERFERE!
HONDA!!
?!
F
WIP!
MMF?!
MARIKA'S HENCH-WOMAN?!
EXCUSE ME. JUST DOING MY JOB.
YES!!
FLASH!

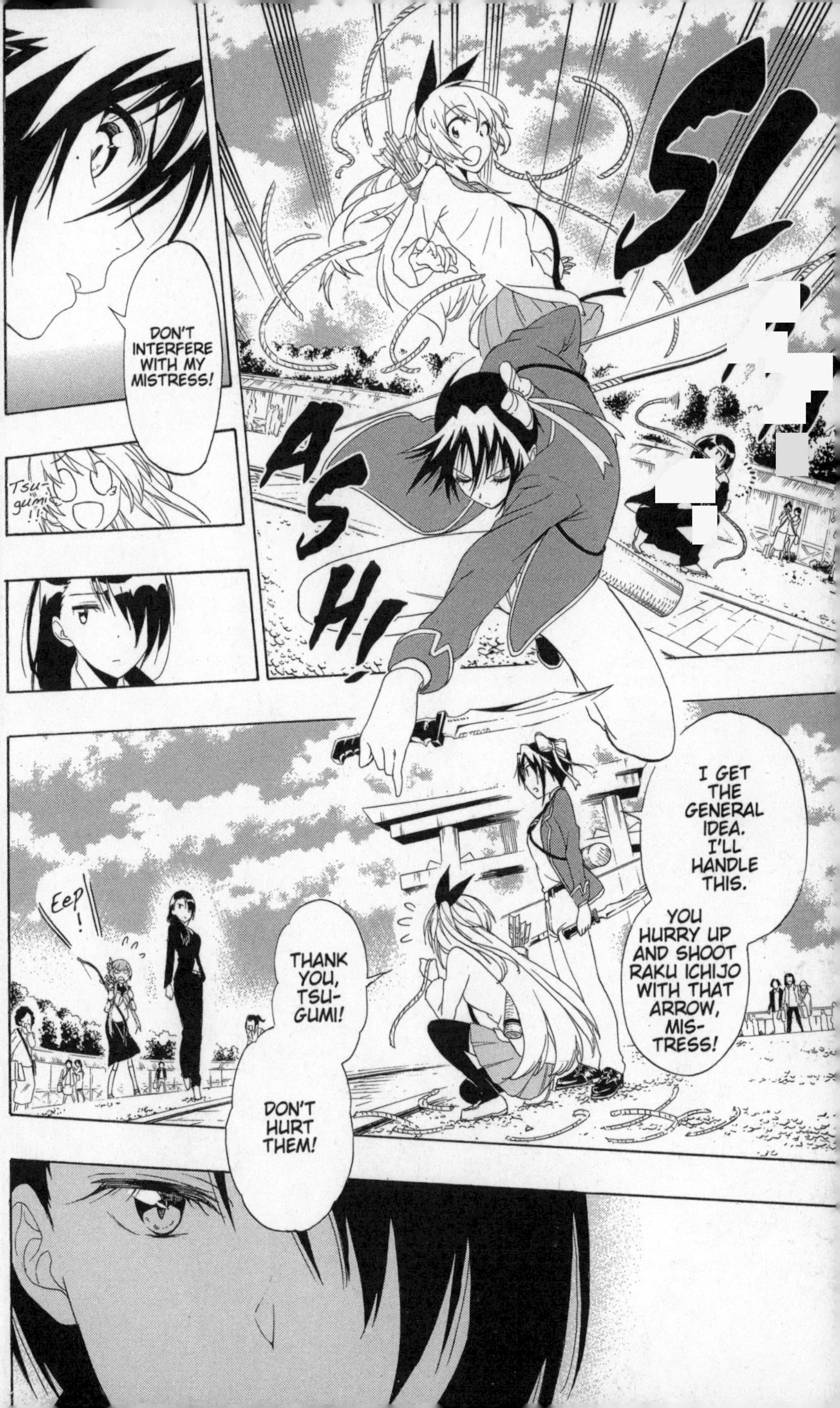

SL
ASH!
DON'T INTERFERE WITH MY MISTRESS!
Tsu-gumi!!
I GET THE GENERAL IDEA. I'LL HANDLE THIS.
YOU HURRY UP AND SHOOT RAKU ICHIJO WITH THAT ARROW, MIS-TRESS!
THANK YOU, TSU-GUMI!
DON'T HURT THEM!
Eep!

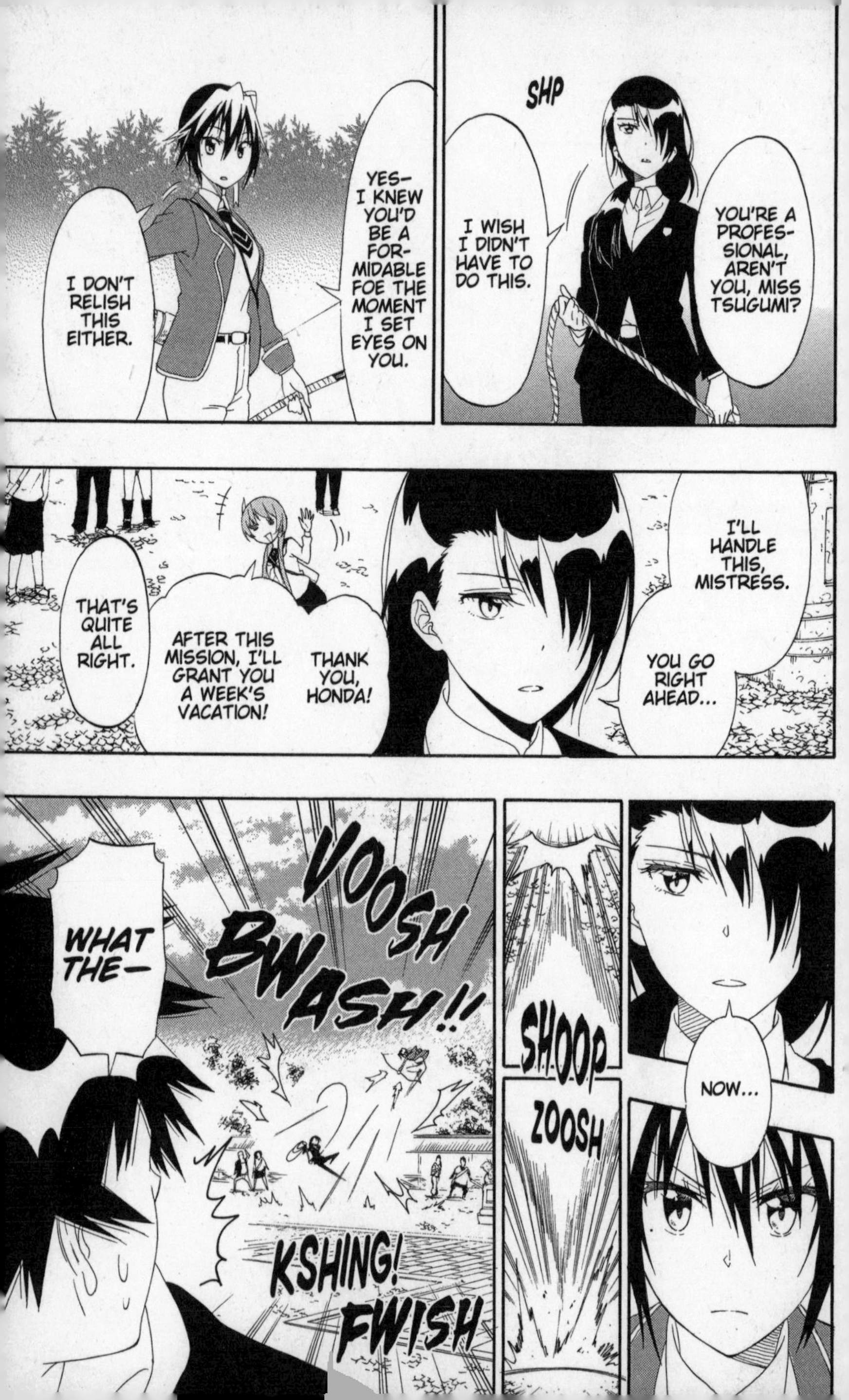
SHP
YOU'RE A PROFES-SIONAL, AREN'T YOU, MISS TSUGUMI?
I WISH I DIDN'T HAVE TO DO THIS.
YES— I KNEW YOU'D BE A FOR-MIDABLE FOE THE MOMENT I SET EYES ON YOU.
I DON'T RELISH THIS EITHER.
I'LL HANDLE THIS, MISTRESS.
YOU GO RIGHT AHEAD...
THANK YOU, HONDA!
AFTER THIS MISSION, I'LL GRANT YOU A WEEK'S VACATION!
THAT'S QUITE ALL RIGHT.
NOW...
SHOOP
ZOOSH
WHAT THE—
VOOSH
BWASH!!
KSHING!
FWISH

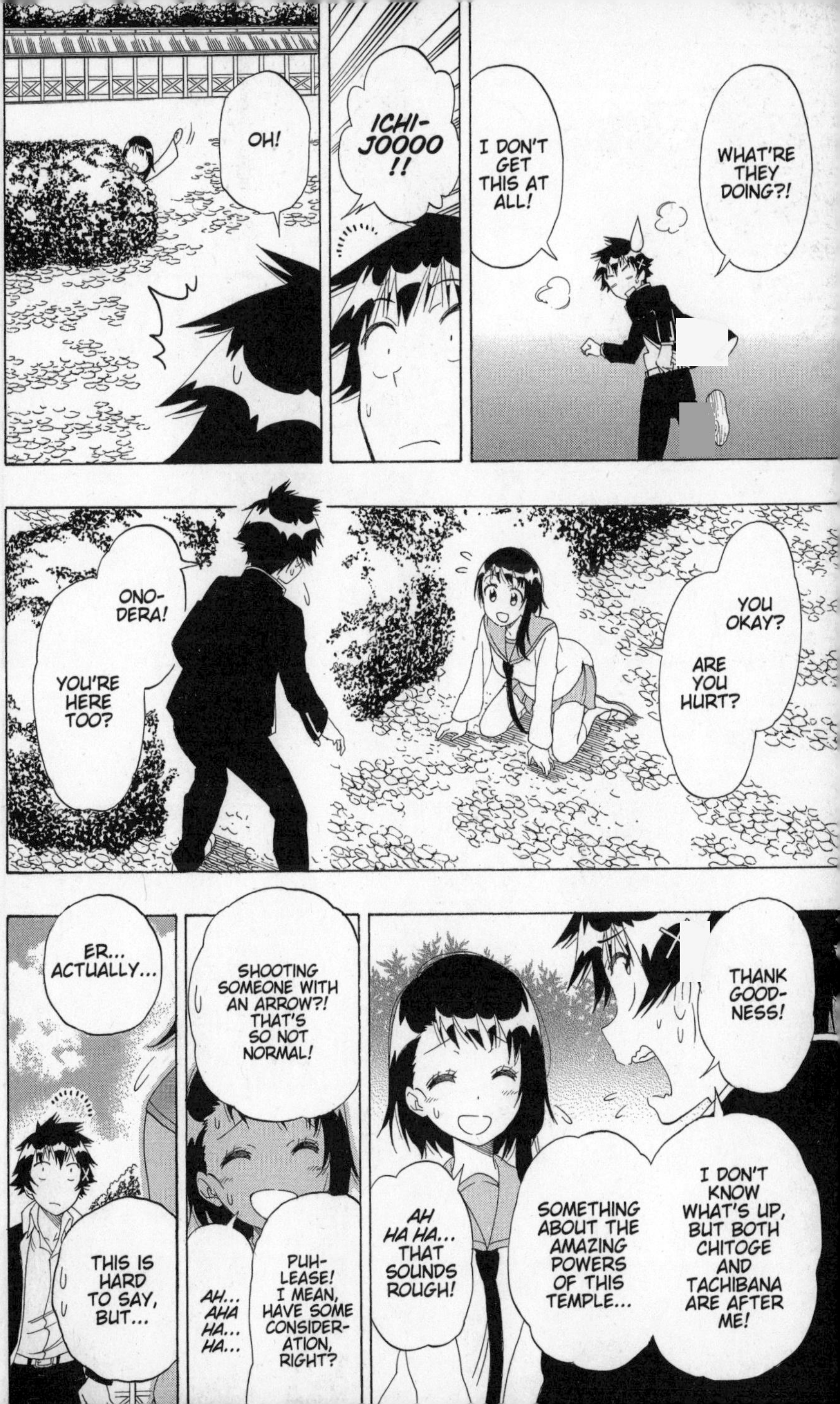
WHAT'RE THEY DOING?!
I DON'T GET THIS AT ALL!
ICHI-JOOOO!!
OH!
YOU OKAY? ARE YOU HURT?
ONO-DERA! YOU'RE HERE TOO?
THANK GOODNESS!
I DON'T KNOW WHAT'S UP, BUT BOTH CHITOGE AND TACHIBANA ARE AFTER ME!
SOMETHING ABOUT THE AMAZING POWERS OF THIS TEMPLE...
AH HA HA... THAT SOUNDS ROUGH!
SHOOTING SOMEONE WITH AN ARROW?! THAT'S SO NOT NORMAL!
PUH-LEASE! I MEAN, HAVE SOME CONSIDERATION, RIGHT?
AH... AHA HA... HA...
ER... ACTUALLY...
THIS IS HARD TO SAY, BUT...

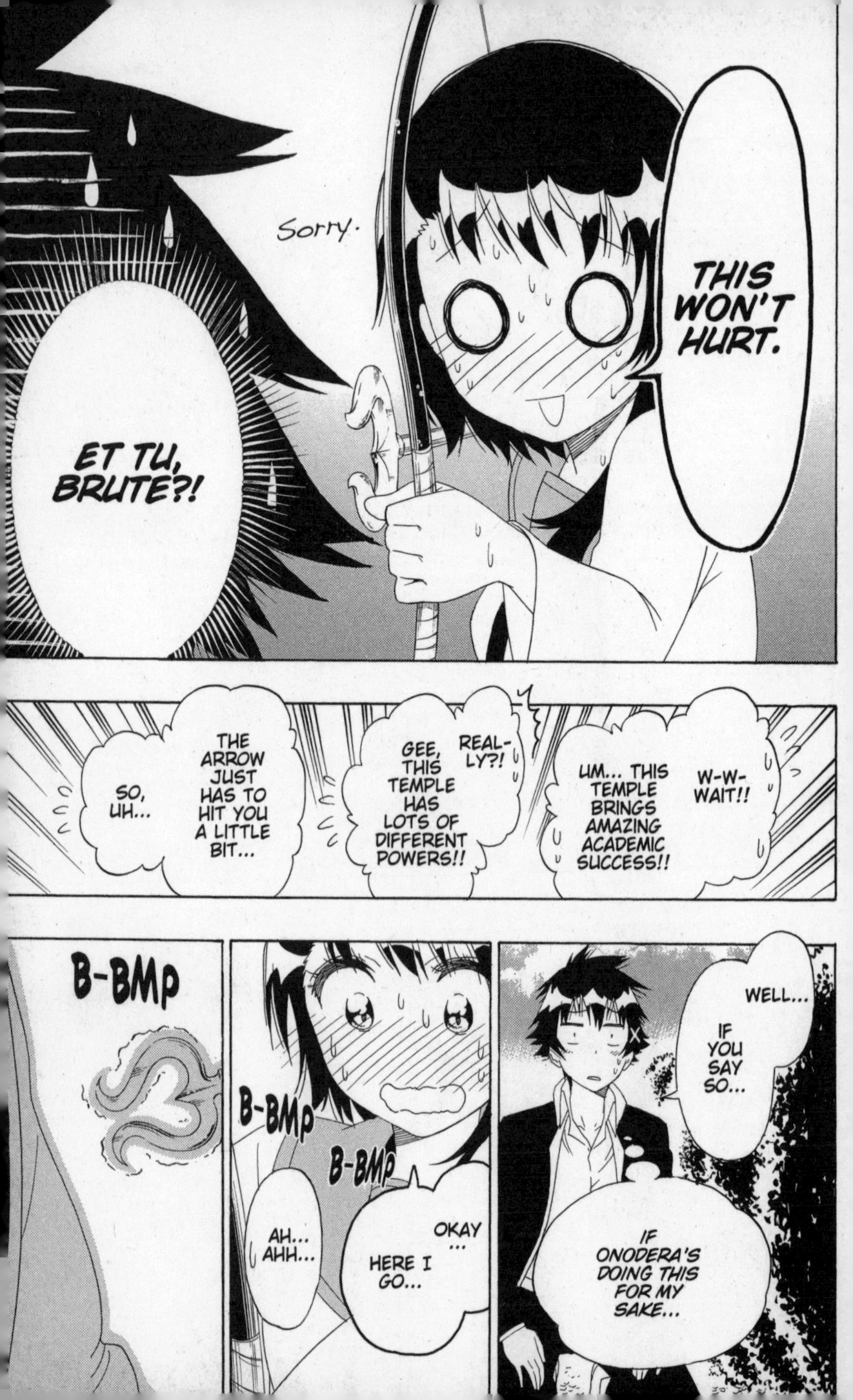
THIS WON'T HURT.
Sorry.
ET TU, BRUTE?!
W-W-WAIT!!
UM... THIS TEMPLE BRINGS AMAZING ACADEMIC SUCCESS!!
REAL-LY?!
GEE, THIS TEMPLE HAS LOTS OF DIFFERENT POWERS!!
THE ARROW JUST HAS TO HIT YOU A LITTLE BIT...
SO, UH...
WELL... IF YOU SAY SO...
IF ONODERA'S DOING THIS FOR MY SAKE...
B-BMP
B-BMP
OKAY... HERE I GO...
AH... AHH...
B-BMP

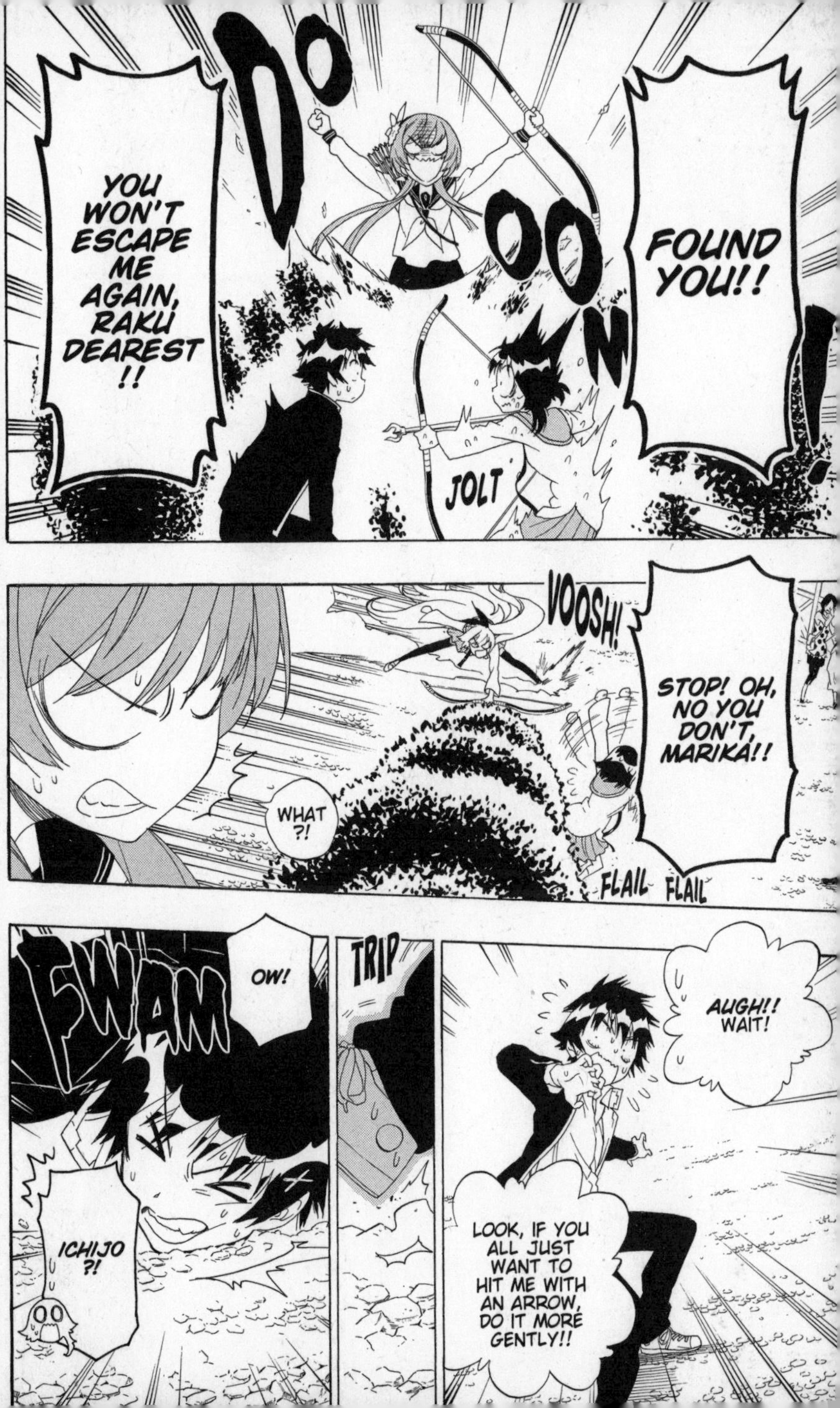
FOUND YOU!!
DOOOON!
YOU WON'T ESCAPE ME AGAIN, RAKU DEAREST!!
JOLT
STOP! OH, NO YOU DON'T, MARIKA!!
VOOSH!
WHAT?!
FLAIL FLAIL
AUGH!! WAIT!
LOOK, IF YOU ALL JUST WANT TO HIT ME WITH AN ARROW, DO IT MORE GENTLY!!
TRIP
OW!
FWAM
ICHIJO?!

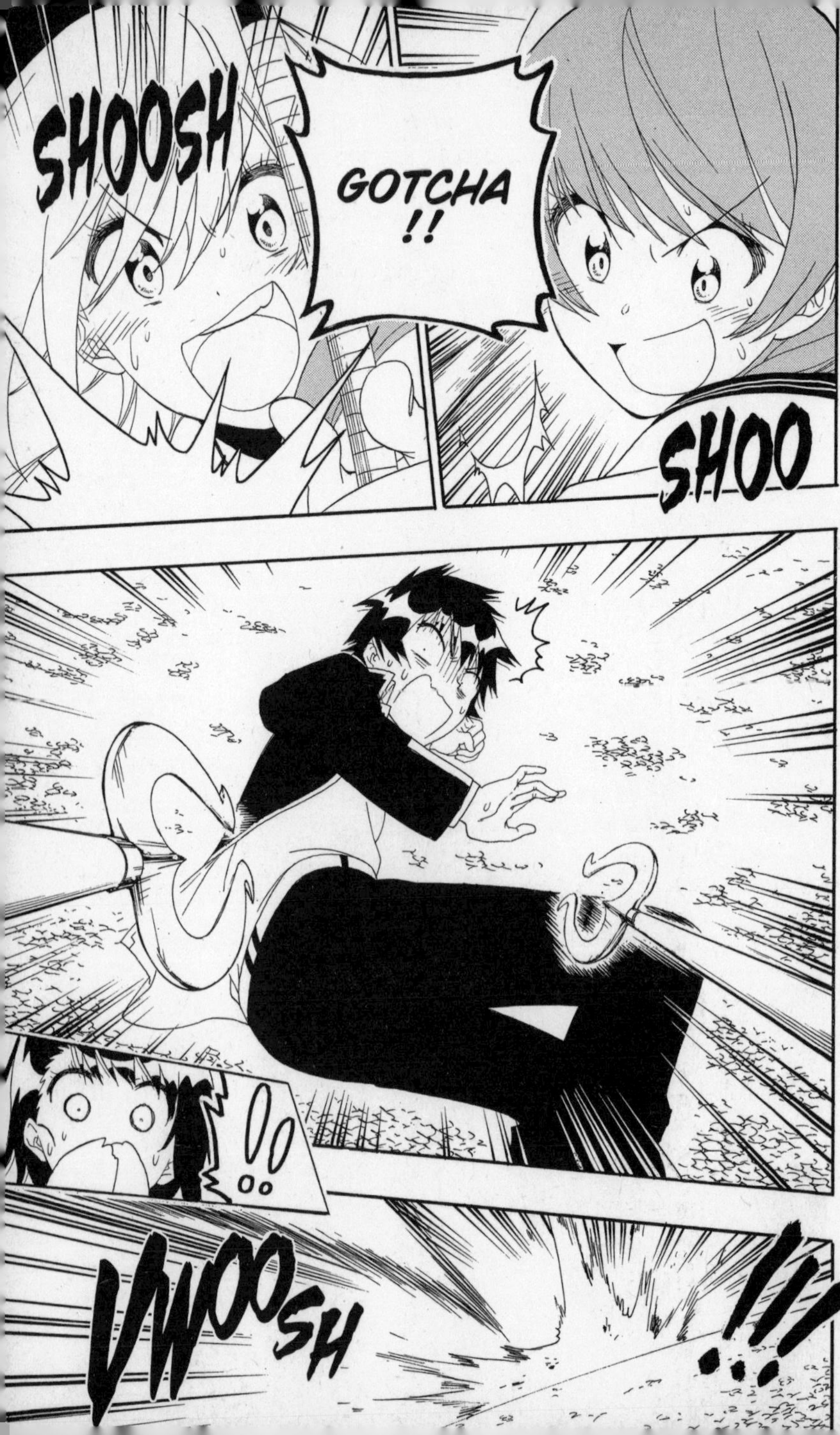
SHOO
GOTCHA !!
SHOOSH
!!
!!!
VWOOSH

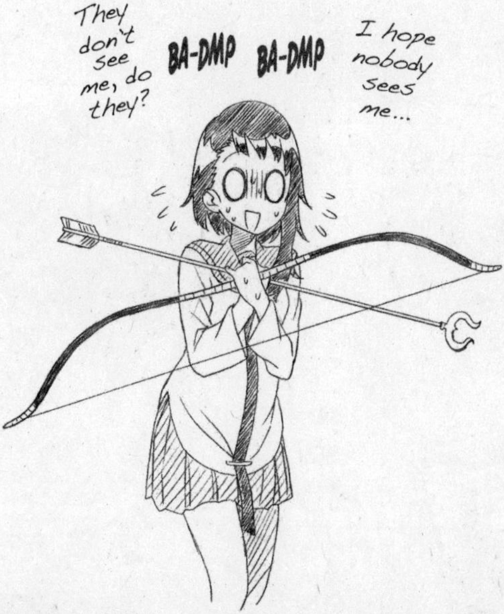
I hope nobody sees me...
BA-DMP
BA-DMP
They don't see me, do they?

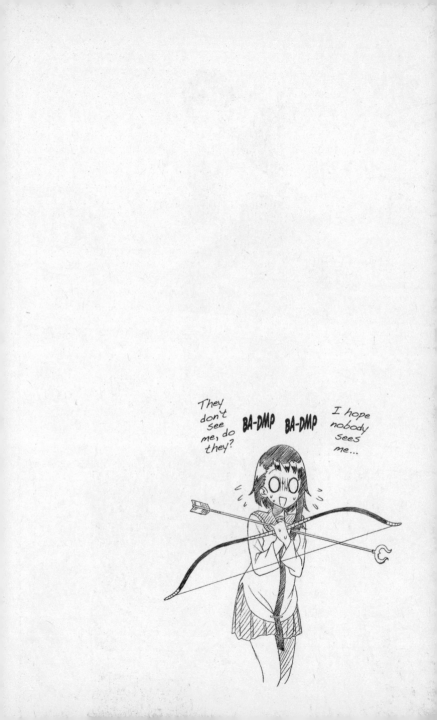

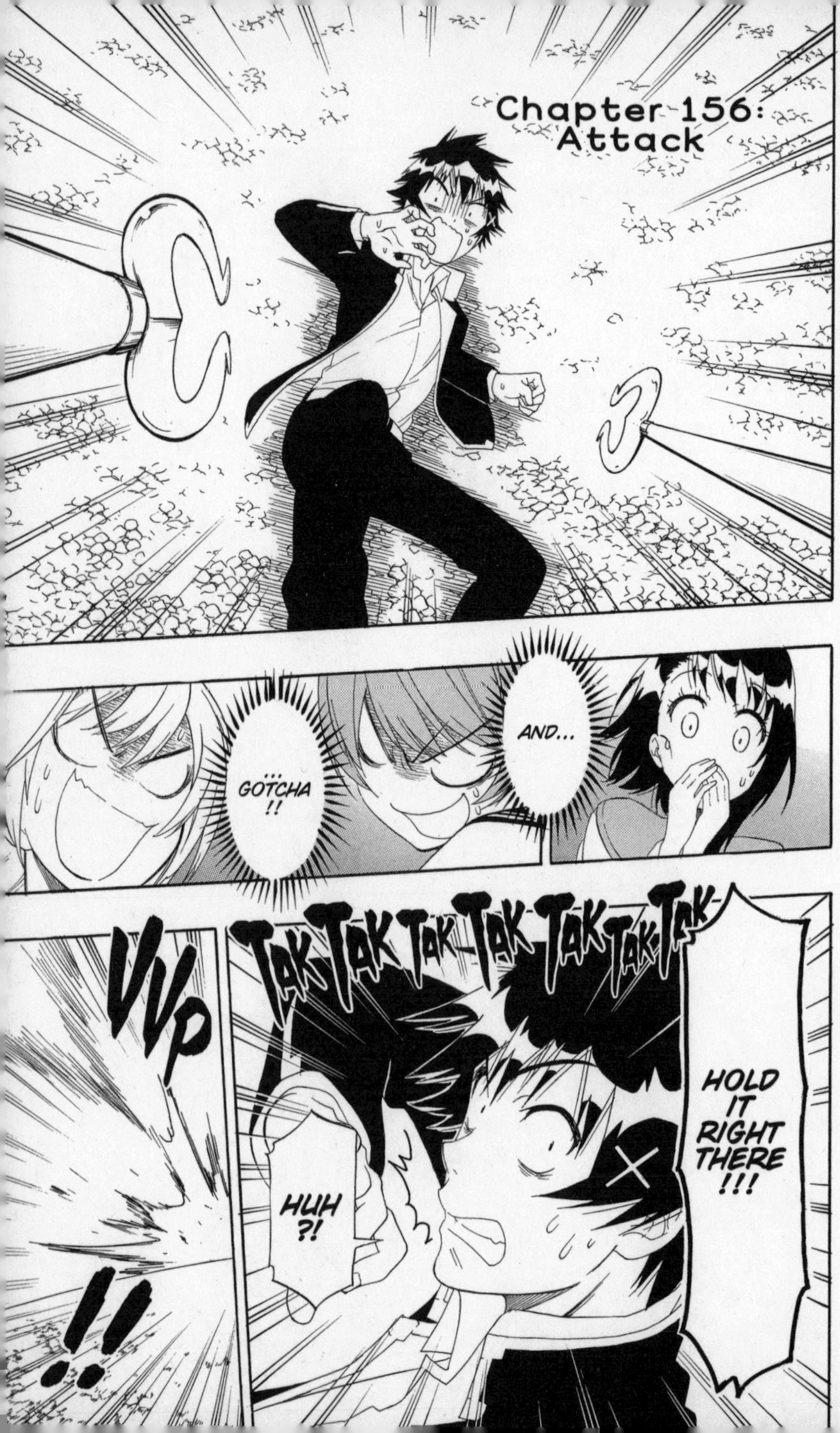
Chapter 156: Attack
AND...
...GOTCHA!!
HOLD IT RIGHT THERE!!!
TAK-TAK TAK-TAK TAK-TAK-TAK
HUH?!
VVP
!!

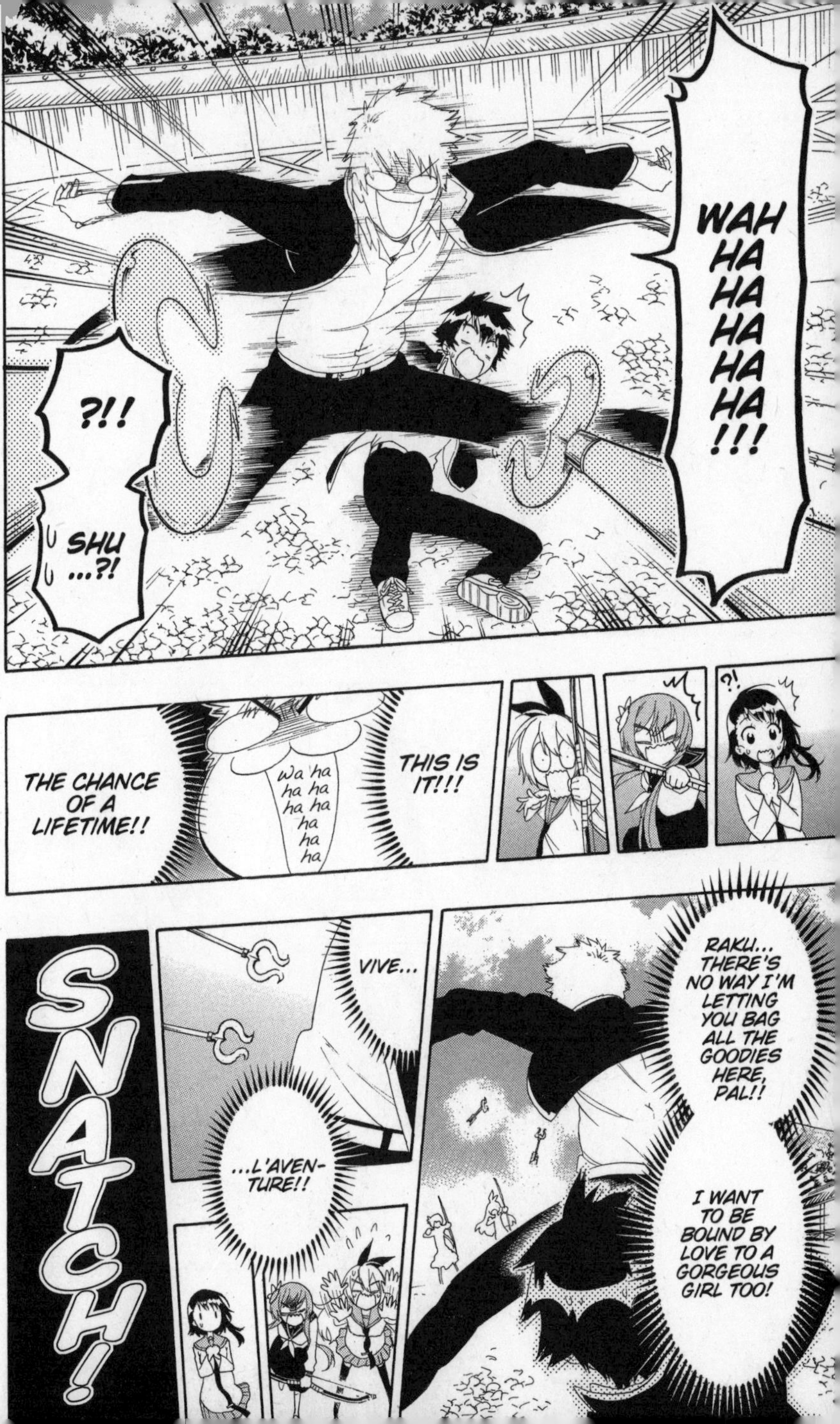
WAH HA HA HA HA HA!!!
?!!
SHU ...?!
?!
THIS IS IT!!!
Wa ha ha ha ha ha ha ha ha ha ha
THE CHANCE OF A LIFETIME!!
RAKU... THERE'S NO WAY I'M LETTING YOU BAG ALL THE GOODIES HERE, PAL!!
I WANT TO BE BOUND BY LOVE TO A GORGEOUS GIRL TOO!
VIVE...
...L'AVEN- TURE!!
SNATCH!

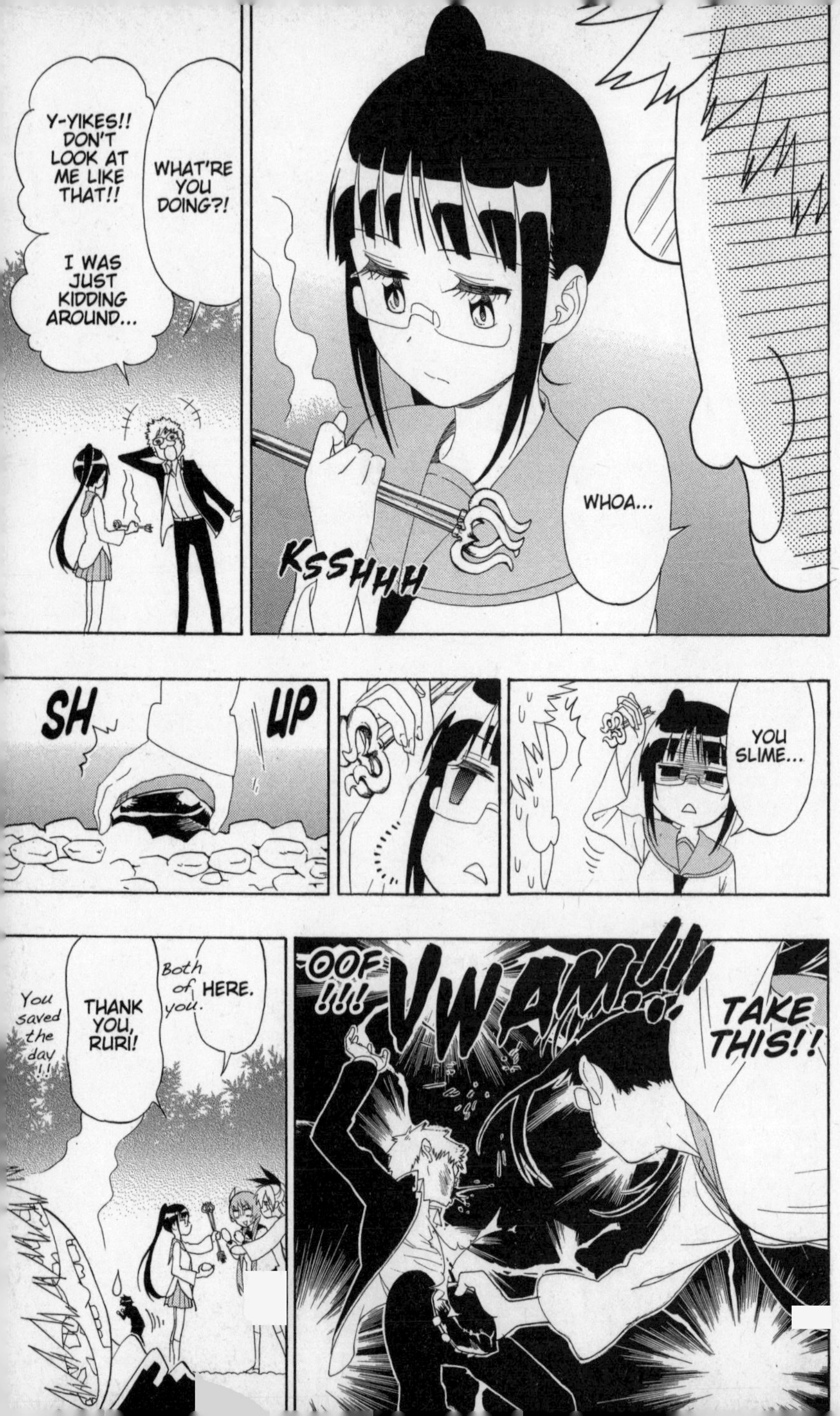
WHOA...
KSSHHH
WHAT'RE YOU DOING?!
Y-YIKES!! DON'T LOOK AT ME LIKE THAT!!
I WAS JUST KIDDING AROUND...
YOU SLIME...
SH
UP
TAKE THIS!!
VWAM!!!
OOF!!!
HERE.
Both of you.
THANK YOU, RURI!
You saved the day!!

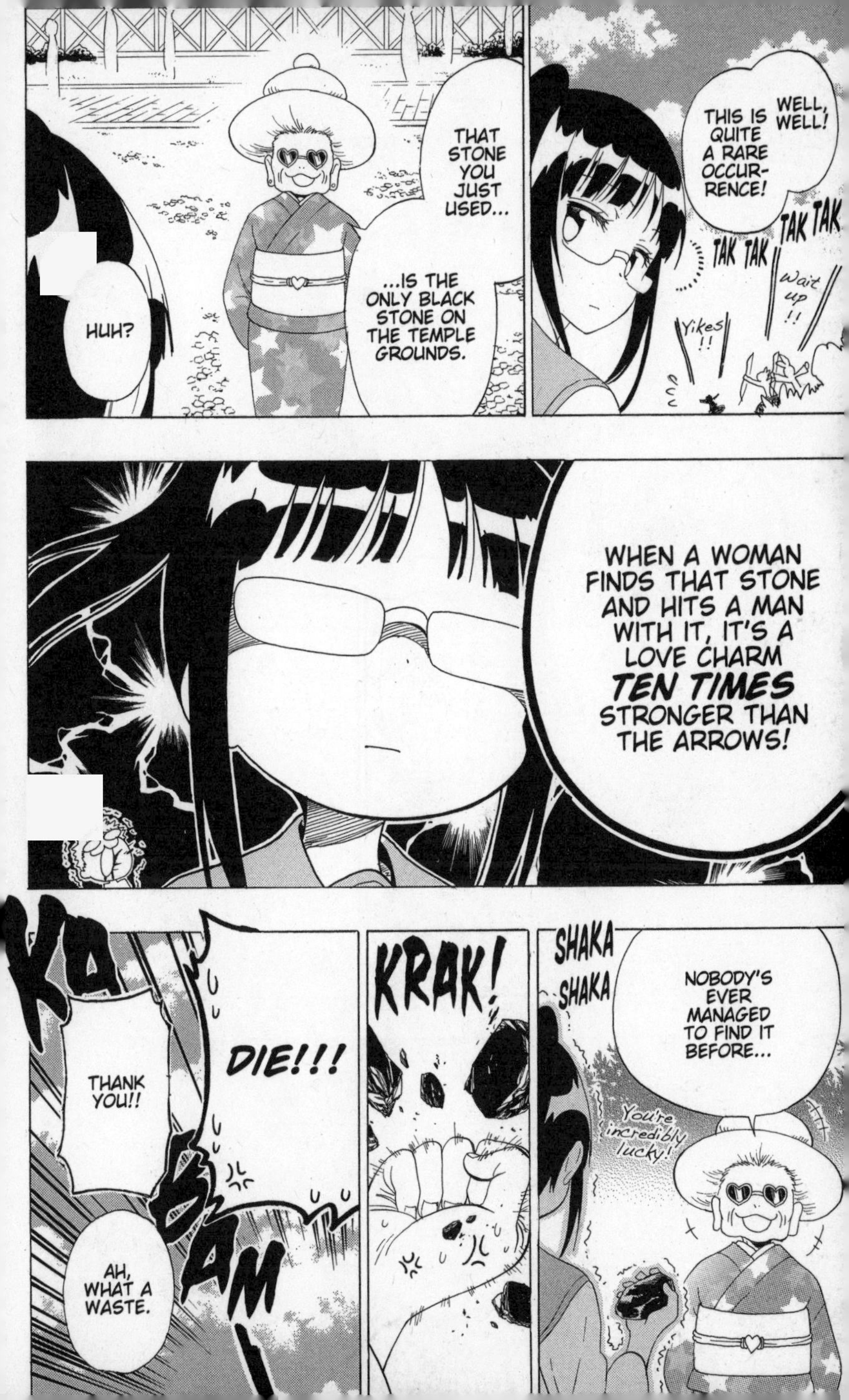
WELL, WELL!
THIS IS QUITE A RARE OCCURRENCE!
TAK TAK
TAK TAK
Wait up!!
Yikes!!
THAT STONE YOU JUST USED...
...IS THE ONLY BLACK STONE ON THE TEMPLE GROUNDS.
HUH?
WHEN A WOMAN FINDS THAT STONE AND HITS A MAN WITH IT, IT'S A LOVE CHARM *TEN TIMES* STRONGER THAN THE ARROWS!
SHAKA SHAKA
NOBODY'S EVER MANAGED TO FIND IT BEFORE...
You're incredibly lucky!
KRAK!
DIE!!!
KA
THANK YOU!!
BAM
AH, WHAT A WASTE.

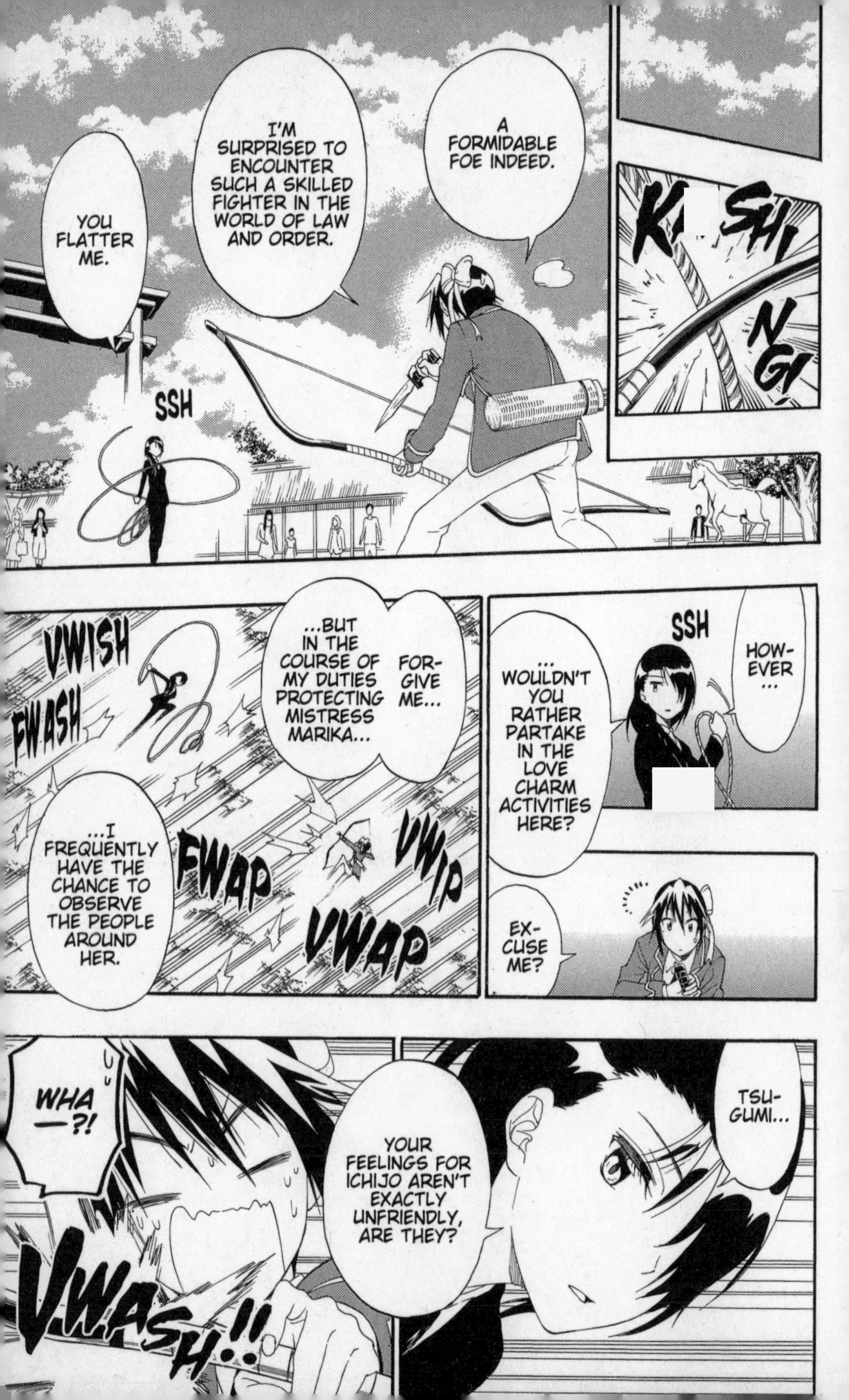
K SHI NG!
A FORMIDABLE FOE INDEED.
I'M SURPRISED TO ENCOUNTER SUCH A SKILLED FIGHTER IN THE WORLD OF LAW AND ORDER.
YOU FLATTER ME.
SSH
HOW-EVER...
SSH
...WOULDN'T YOU RATHER PARTAKE IN THE LOVE CHARM ACTIVITIES HERE?
EX-CUSE ME?
FOR-GIVE ME...
...BUT IN THE COURSE OF MY DUTIES PROTECTING MISTRESS MARIKA...
VWISH
FWASH
VWIP
VWAP
FWAP
...I FREQUENTLY HAVE THE CHANCE TO OBSERVE THE PEOPLE AROUND HER.
TSU-GUMI...
YOUR FEELINGS FOR ICHIJO AREN'T EXACTLY UNFRIENDLY, ARE THEY?
WHA—?!
VWASH!!

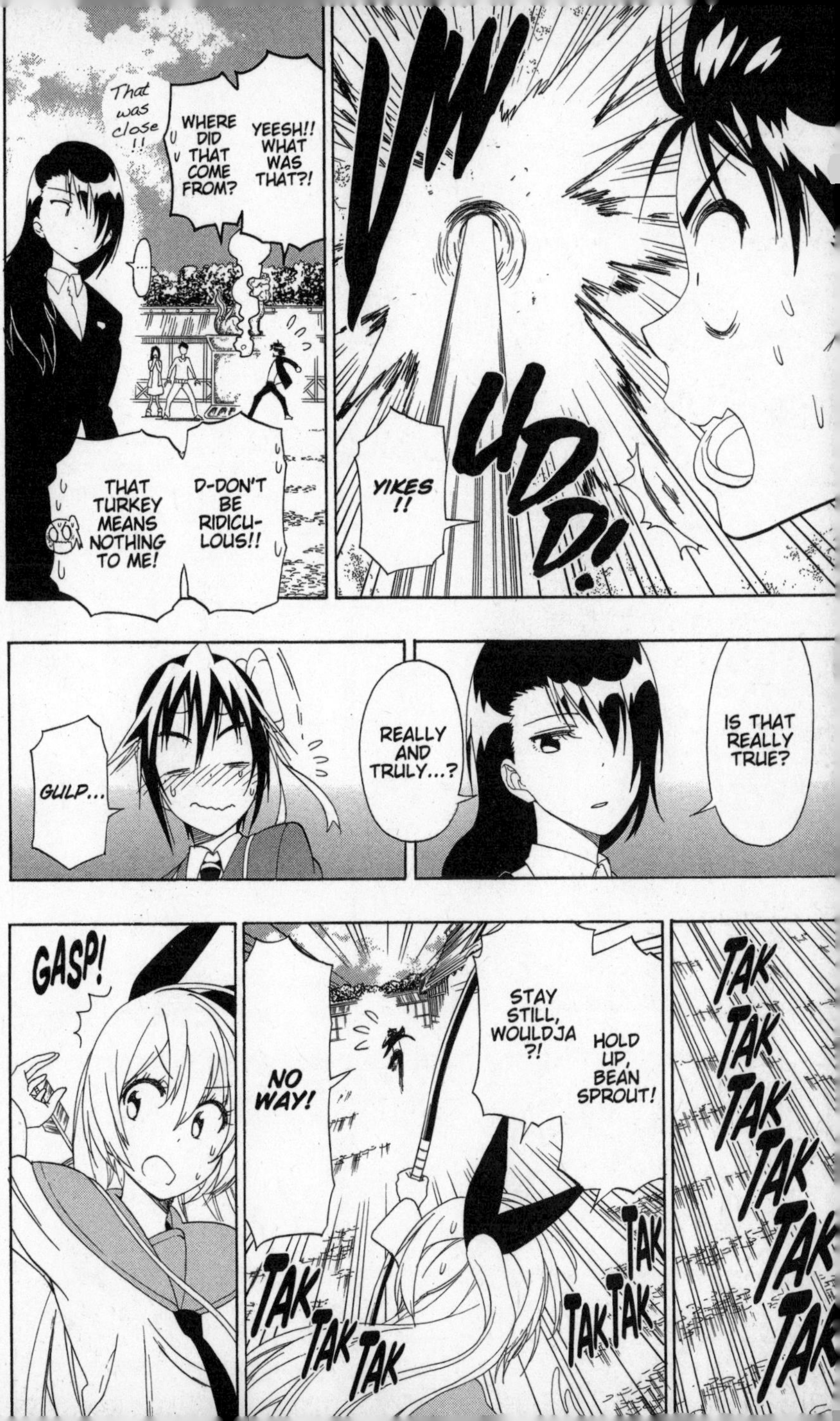
YIKES!!
YEESH!! WHAT WAS THAT?!
WHERE DID THAT COME FROM?
That was close!!
...
D-DON'T BE RIDICULOUS!!
THAT TURKEY MEANS NOTHING TO ME!
IS THAT REALLY TRUE?
REALLY AND TRULY...?
GULP...
TAK TAK TAK TAK TAK TAK TAK
HOLD UP, BEAN SPROUT!
STAY STILL, WOULDJA?!
NO WAY!
TAK TAK TAK TAK
TAK TAK TAK
GASP!

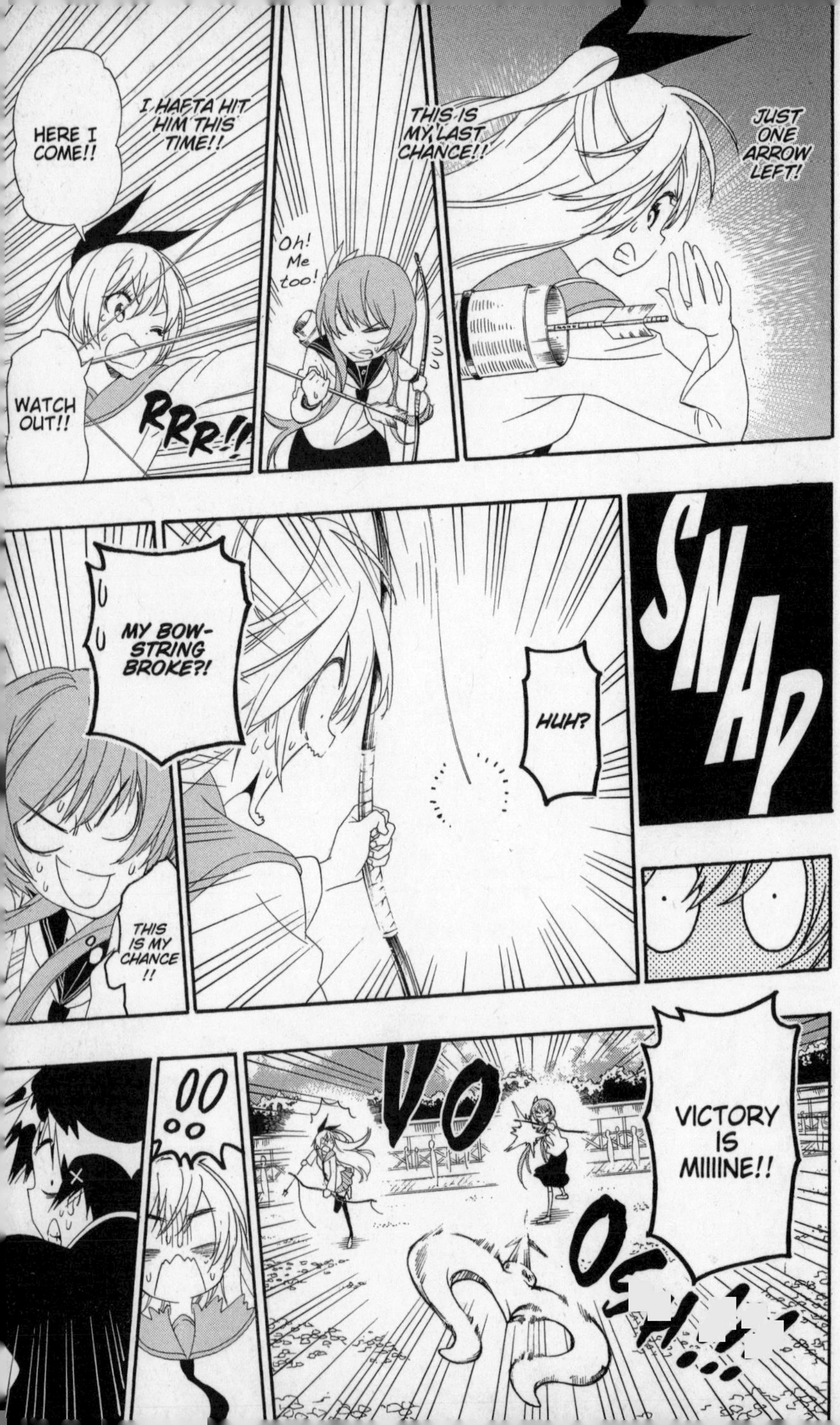
JUST ONE ARROW LEFT!
THIS IS MY LAST CHANCE!!
Oh! Me too!
I HAFTA HIT HIM THIS TIME!!
HERE I COME!!
WATCH OUT!!
RRR!!
SNAP
HUH?
MY BOW-STRING BROKE?!
THIS IS MY CHANCE!!
VICTORY IS MIIIINE!!
VOOOSH!!
OO
OO

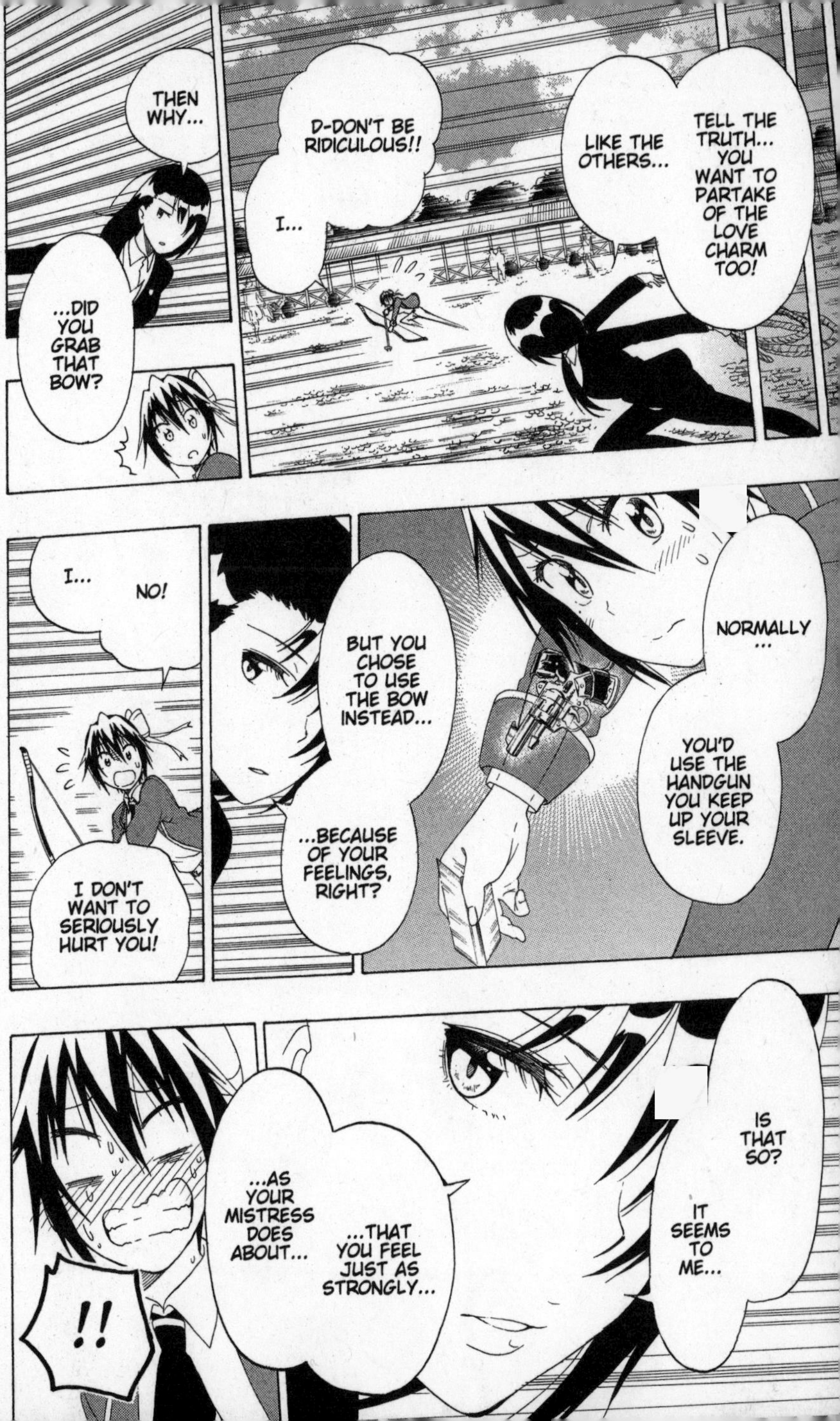
TELL THE TRUTH... YOU WANT TO PARTAKE OF THE LOVE CHARM TOO!
LIKE THE OTHERS...
D-DON'T BE RIDICULOUS!!
I...
THEN WHY...
...DID YOU GRAB THAT BOW?
NORMALLY...
YOU'D USE THE HANDGUN YOU KEEP UP YOUR SLEEVE.
BUT YOU CHOSE TO USE THE BOW INSTEAD...
...BECAUSE OF YOUR FEELINGS, RIGHT?
I... NO!
I DON'T WANT TO SERIOUSLY HURT YOU!
IS THAT SO?
IT SEEMS TO ME...
...THAT YOU FEEL JUST AS STRONGLY...
...AS YOUR MISTRESS DOES ABOUT...
!!

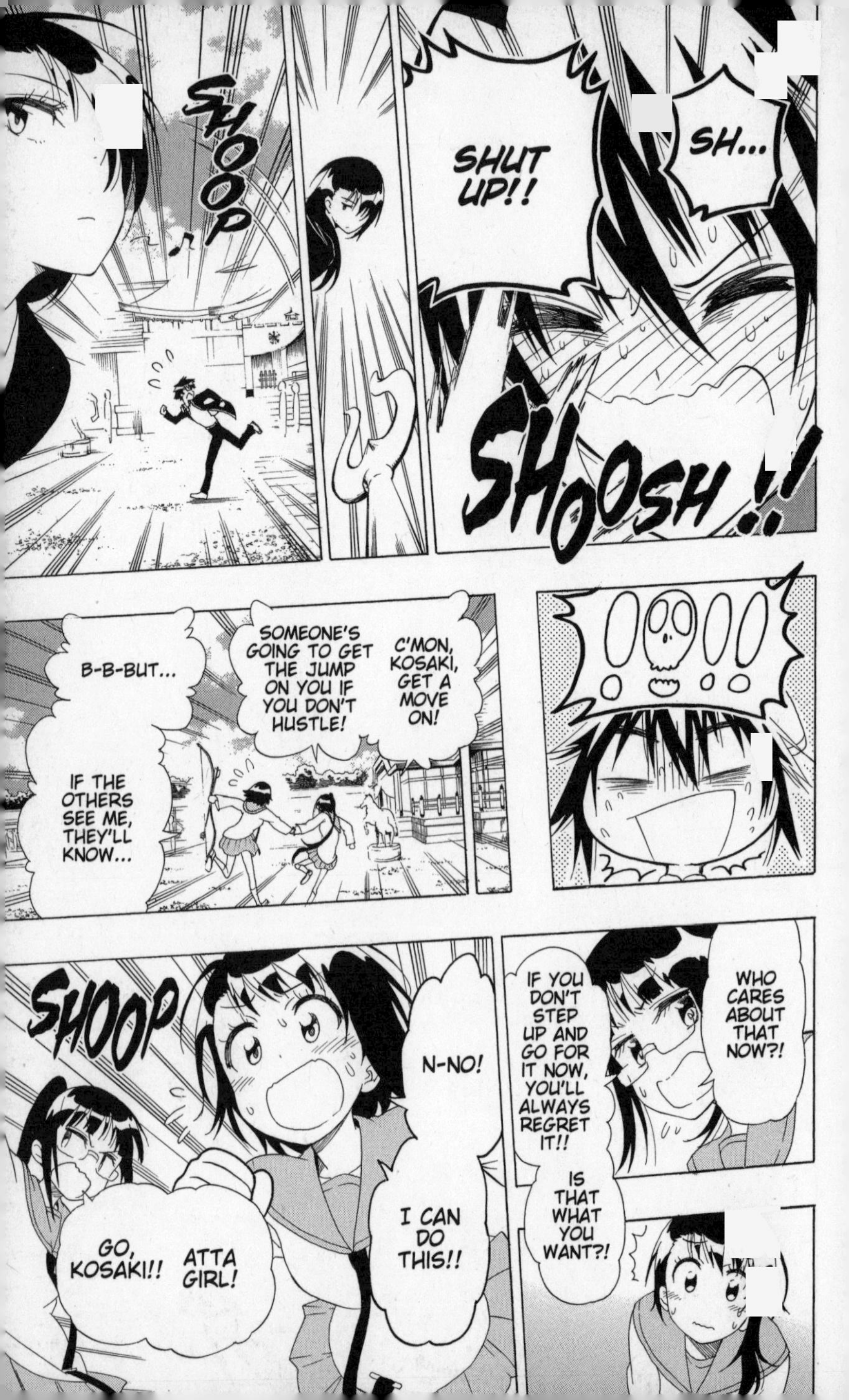
SH...
SHUT UP!!
SHOOSH!!
SHOOP
C'MON, KOSAKI, GET A MOVE ON!
SOMEONE'S GOING TO GET THE JUMP ON YOU IF YOU DON'T HUSTLE!
B-B-BUT...
IF THE OTHERS SEE ME, THEY'LL KNOW...
WHO CARES ABOUT THAT NOW?!
IF YOU DON'T STEP UP AND GO FOR IT NOW, YOU'LL ALWAYS REGRET IT!!
IS THAT WHAT YOU WANT?!
N-NO!
I CAN DO THIS!!
SHOOP
ATTA GIRL!
GO, KOSAKI!!

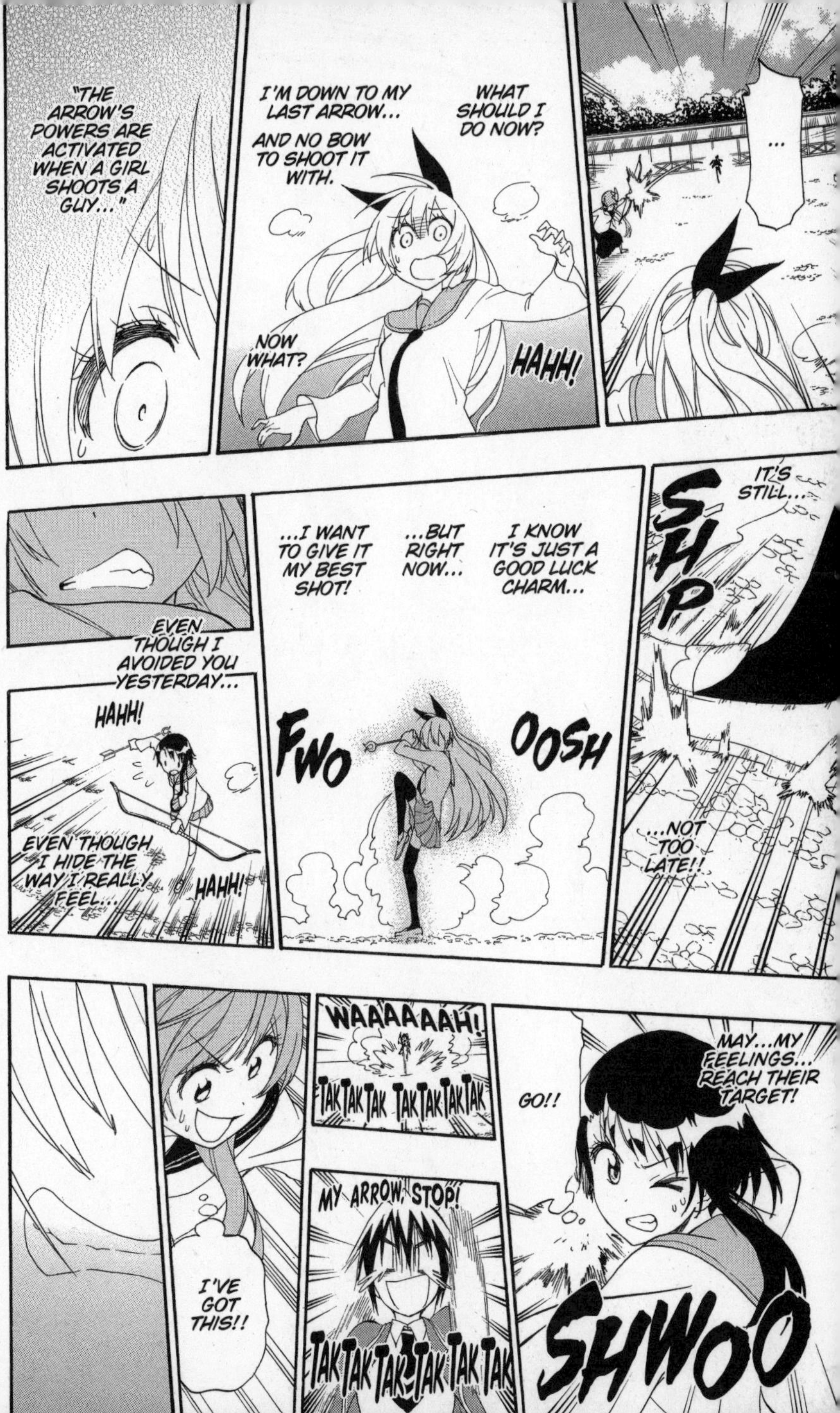
...
WHAT SHOULD I DO NOW?
I'M DOWN TO MY LAST ARROW...
AND NO BOW TO SHOOT IT WITH.
HAHH!
NOW WHAT?
"THE ARROW'S POWERS ARE ACTIVATED WHEN A GIRL SHOOTS A GUY..."
SHP
IT'S STILL...
...NOT TOO LATE!!
I KNOW IT'S JUST A GOOD LUCK CHARM...
...BUT RIGHT NOW...
...I WANT TO GIVE IT MY BEST SHOT!
FWO
OOSH
EVEN THOUGH I AVOIDED YOU YESTERDAY...
HAHH!
EVEN THOUGH I HIDE THE WAY I REALLY FEEL...
HAHH!
MAY...MY FEELINGS... REACH THEIR TARGET!
GO!!
SHWOO
WAAAAAAH!
TAKTAKTAK TAKTAKTAKTAK
MY ARROW, STOP!
TAKTAKTAK TAKTAKTAK
I'VE GOT THIS!!

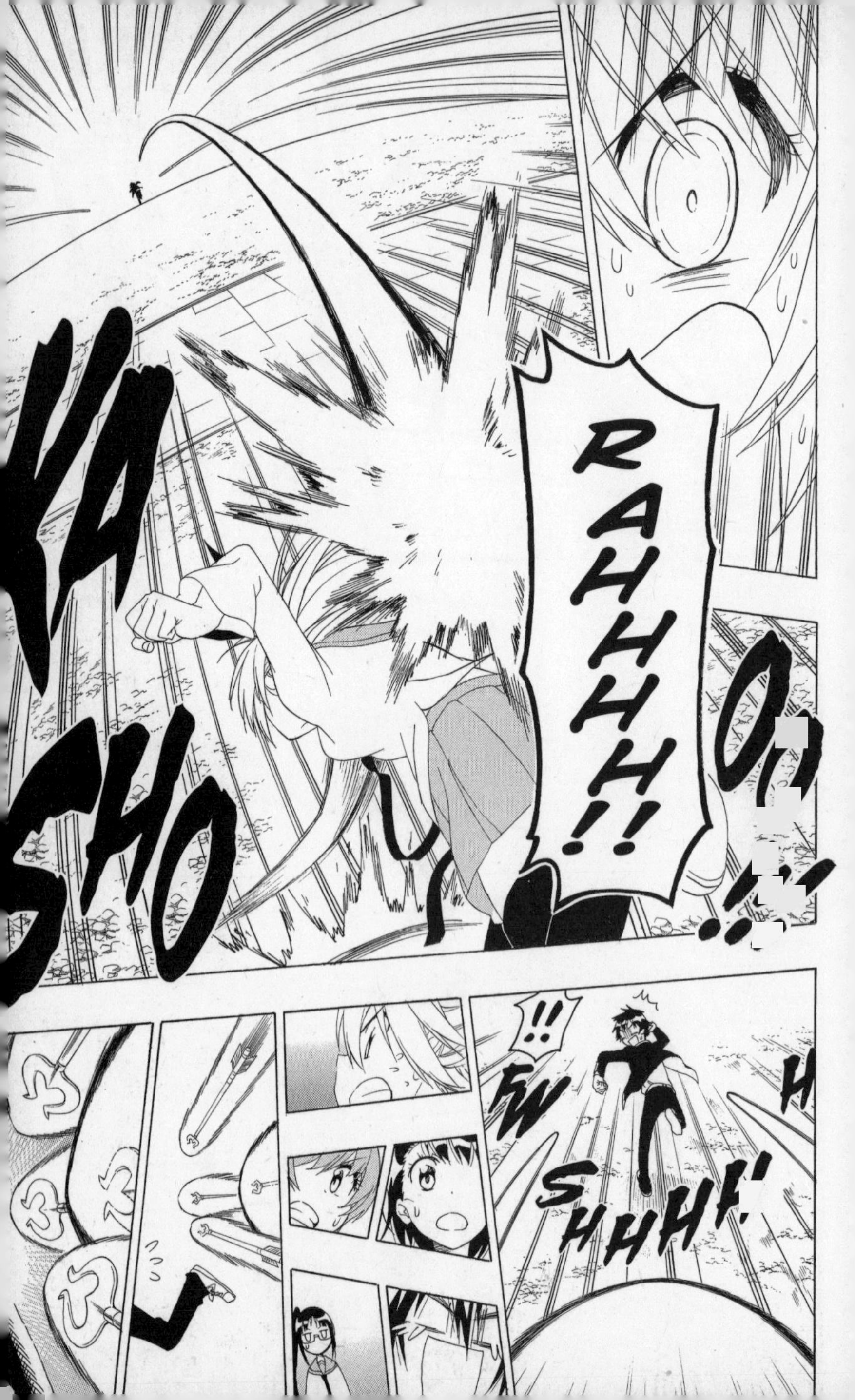
RAHHHH!!
O!!
SHO
!!
H
FW
SHHH!

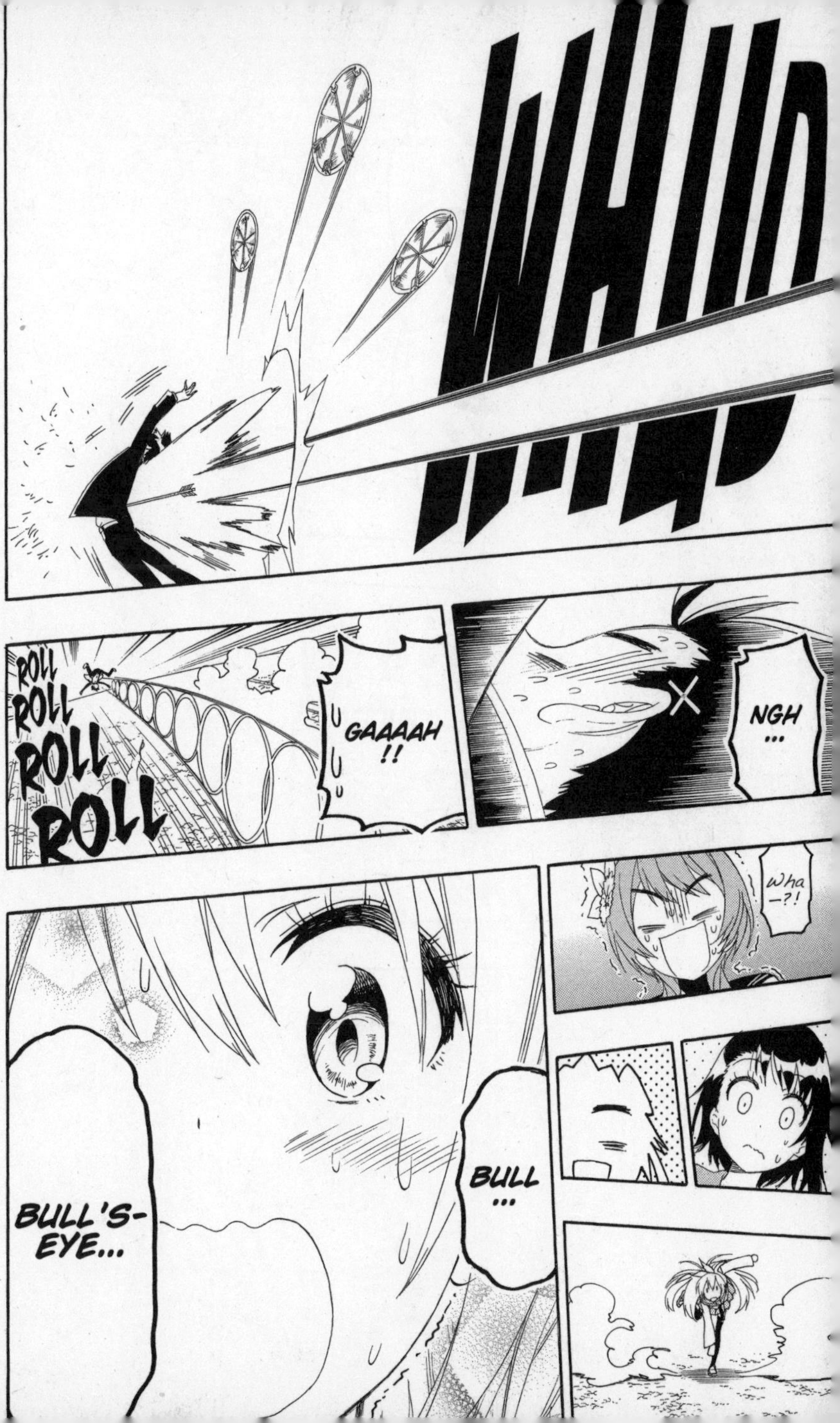
WHUD
NGH ...
GAAAAH !!
ROLL ROLL ROLL ROLL
Wha—?!
BULL ...
BULL'S-EYE...

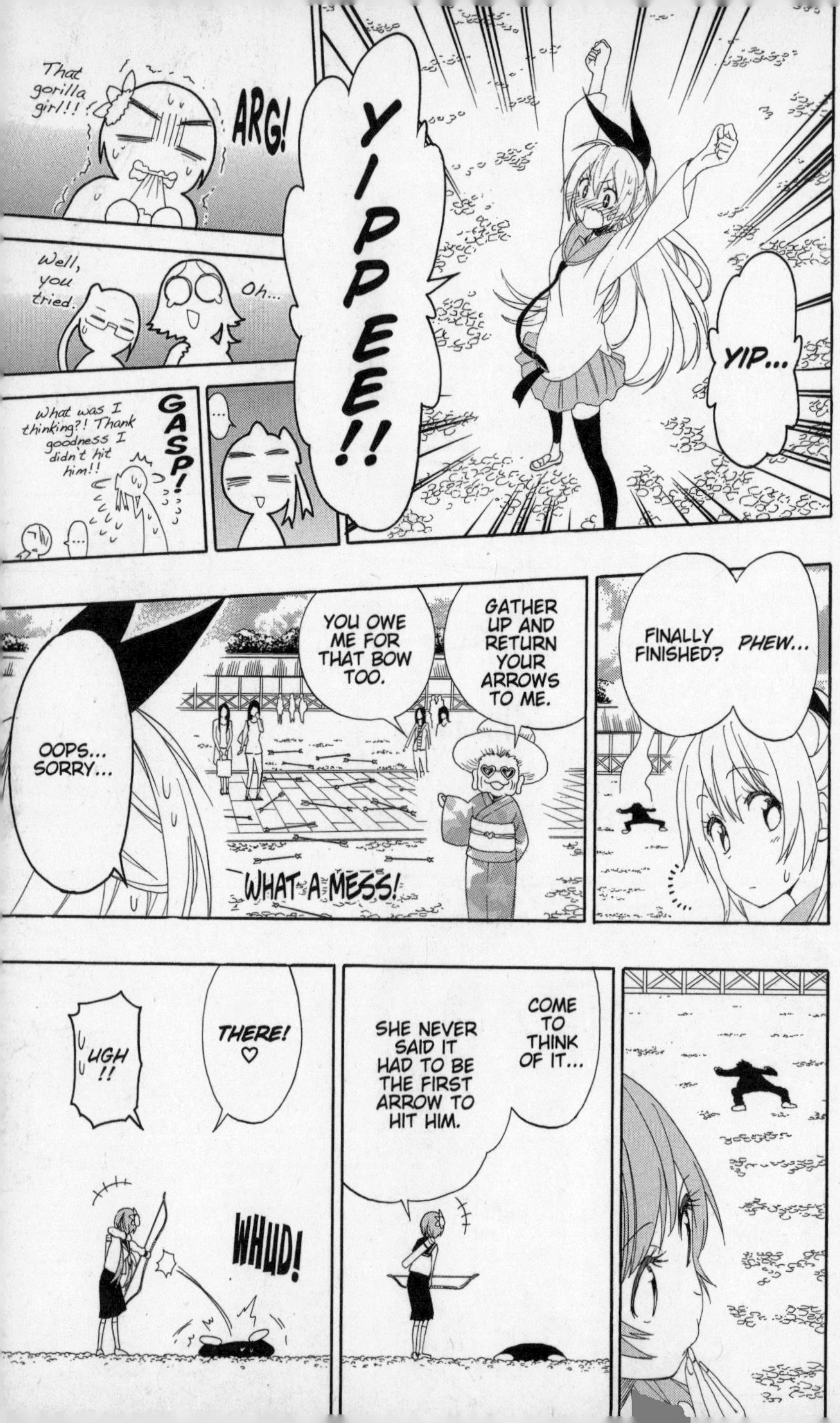
YIP...
YIPPEE!!
That gorilla girl!!!
ARG!
Well, you tried.
Oh...
...
What was I thinking?! Thank goodness I didn't hit him!!
GASP!
...
PHEW...
FINALLY FINISHED?
GATHER UP AND RETURN YOUR ARROWS TO ME.
YOU OWE ME FOR THAT BOW TOO.
WHAT A MESS!
OOPS... SORRY...
COME TO THINK OF IT...
SHE NEVER SAID IT HAD TO BE THE FIRST ARROW TO HIT HIM.
THERE! ♡
UGH!!
WHUD!

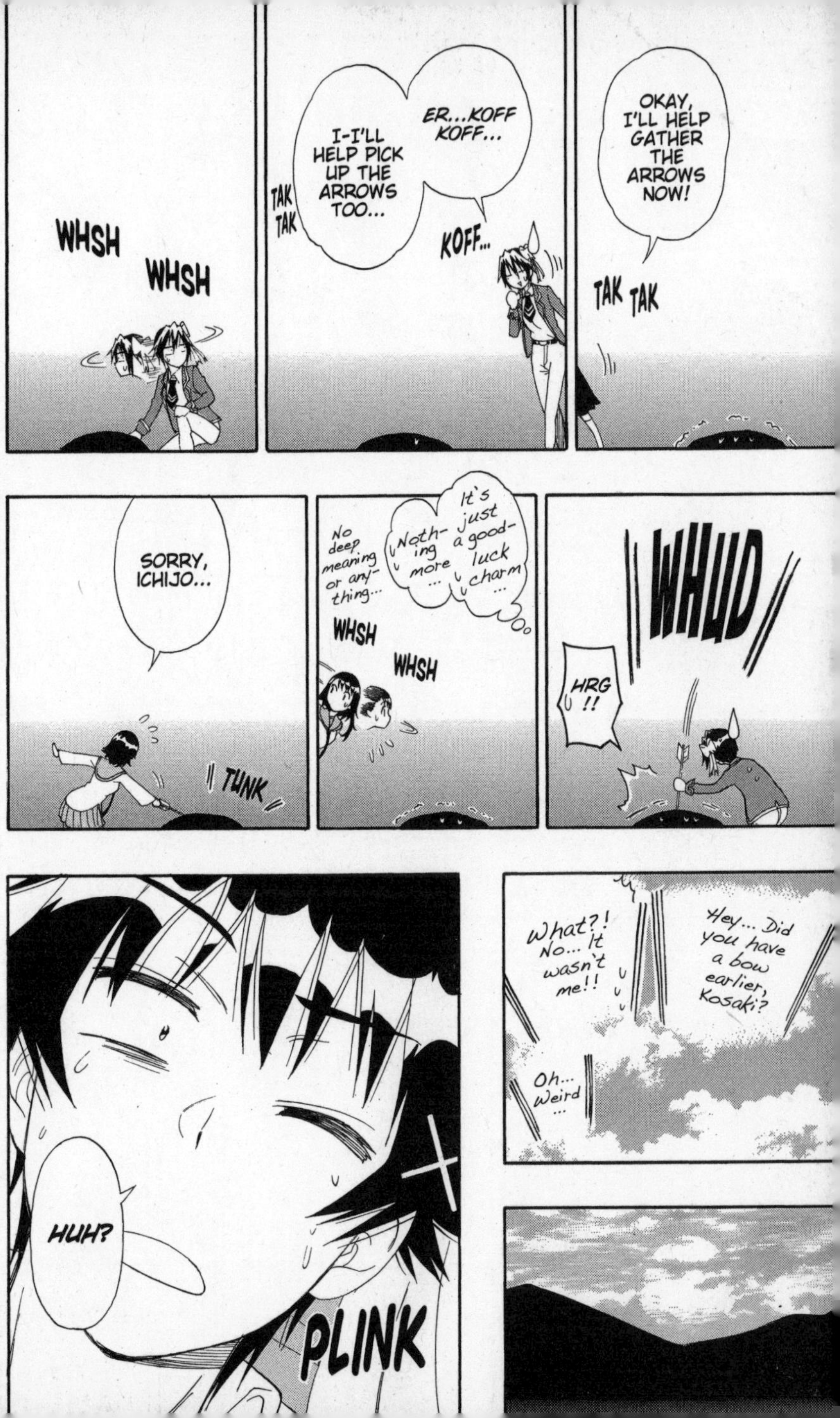
OKAY, I'LL HELP GATHER THE ARROWS NOW!
TAK TAK
ER...KOFF KOFF...
KOFF...
I-I'LL HELP PICK UP THE ARROWS TOO...
TAK TAK
WHSH
WHSH
WHUD
HRG!!
It's just a good-luck charm...
Nothing more...
No deep meaning or anything...
WHSH
WHSH
SORRY, ICHIJO...
TUNK
Hey... Did you have a bow earlier, Kosaki?
What?! No... It wasn't me!!
Oh... Weird...
HUH?
PLINK

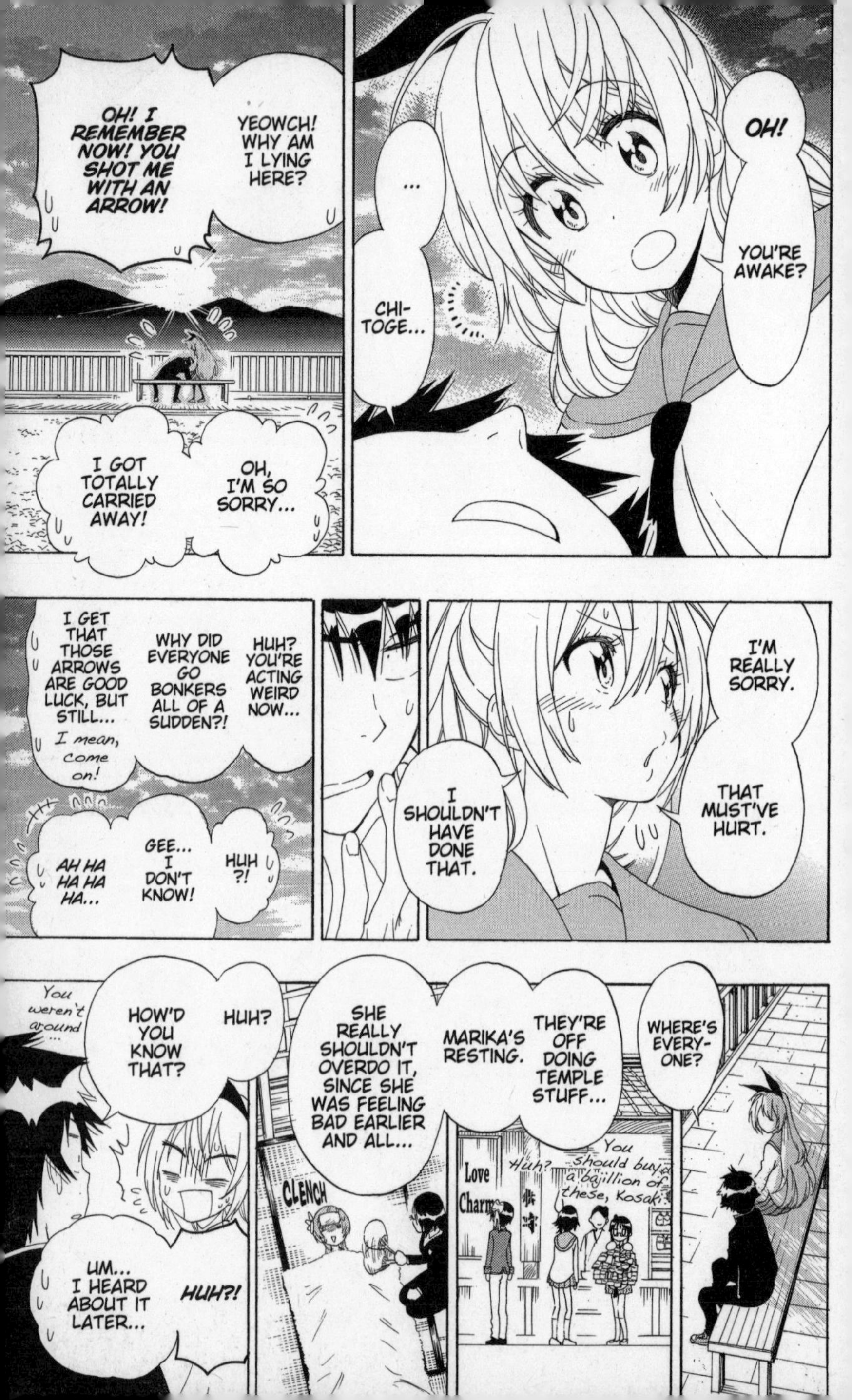

OH!
YOU'RE AWAKE?
...
CHI-TOGE...
YEOWCH! WHY AM I LYING HERE?
OH! I REMEMBER NOW! YOU SHOT ME WITH AN ARROW!
OH, I'M SO SORRY...
I GOT TOTALLY CARRIED AWAY!
I'M REALLY SORRY.
THAT MUST'VE HURT.
I SHOULDN'T HAVE DONE THAT.
HUH? YOU'RE ACTING WEIRD NOW...
WHY DID EVERYONE GO BONKERS ALL OF A SUDDEN?!
I GET THAT THOSE ARROWS ARE GOOD LUCK, BUT STILL...
I mean, come on!
HUH ?!
GEE... I DON'T KNOW!
AH HA HA HA HA...
WHERE'S EVERY-ONE?
THEY'RE OFF DOING TEMPLE STUFF...
MARIKA'S RESTING.
SHE REALLY SHOULDN'T OVERDO IT, SINCE SHE WAS FEELING BAD EARLIER AND ALL...
You should buy a bajillion of these, Kosaki.
Huh?
Love Charm
CLENCH
HUH?
HOW'D YOU KNOW THAT?
You weren't around...
HUH?!
UM... I HEARD ABOUT IT LATER...

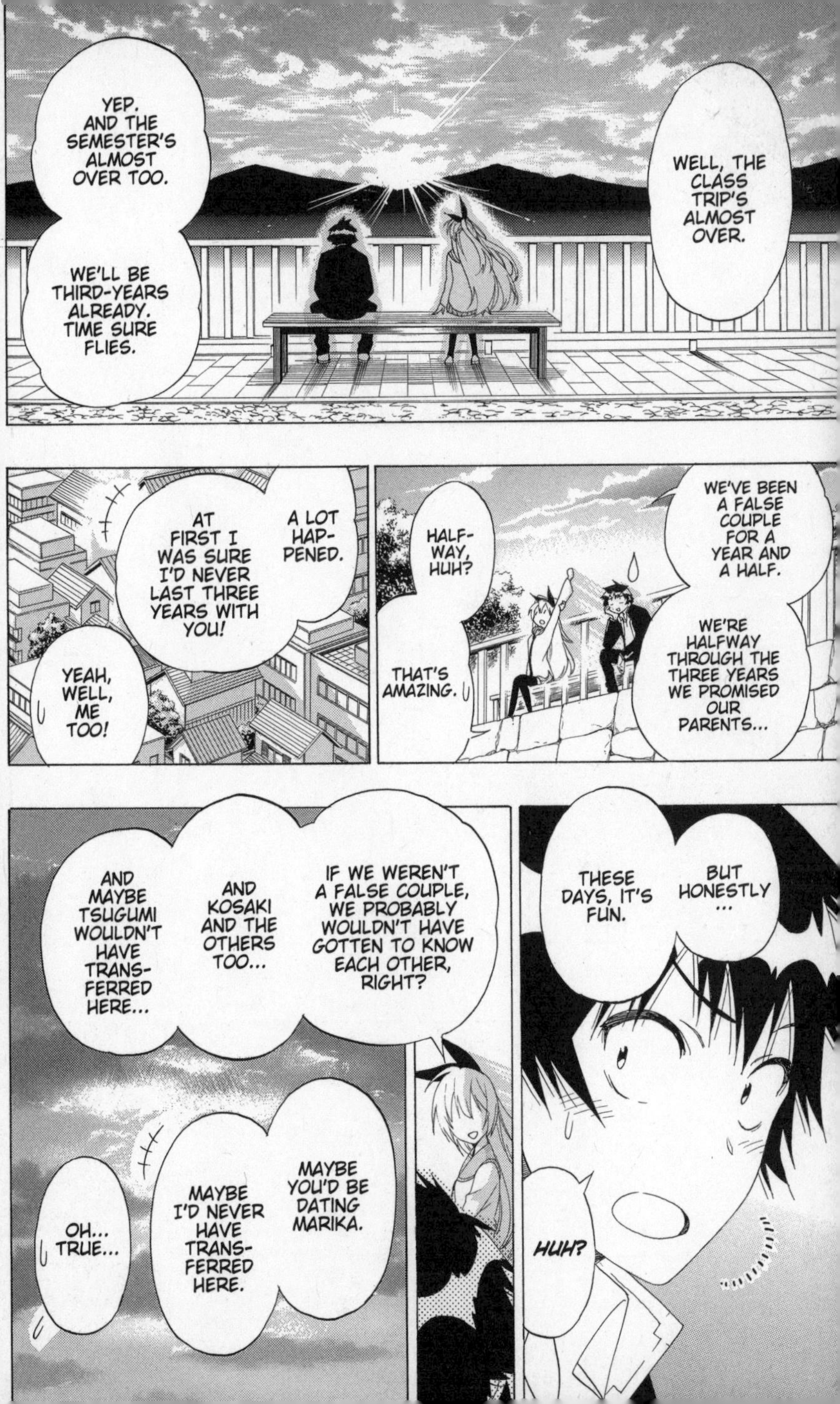
WELL, THE CLASS TRIP'S ALMOST OVER.
YEP. AND THE SEMESTER'S ALMOST OVER TOO.
WE'LL BE THIRD-YEARS ALREADY. TIME SURE FLIES.
WE'VE BEEN A FALSE COUPLE FOR A YEAR AND A HALF.
WE'RE HALFWAY THROUGH THE THREE YEARS WE PROMISED OUR PARENTS...
HALF-WAY, HUH?
THAT'S AMAZING.
A LOT HAP-PENED.
AT FIRST I WAS SURE I'D NEVER LAST THREE YEARS WITH YOU!
YEAH, WELL, ME TOO!
BUT HONESTLY...
THESE DAYS, IT'S FUN.
HUH?
IF WE WEREN'T A FALSE COUPLE, WE PROBABLY WOULDN'T HAVE GOTTEN TO KNOW EACH OTHER, RIGHT?
AND KOSAKI AND THE OTHERS TOO...
AND MAYBE TSUGUMI WOULDN'T HAVE TRANS-FERRED HERE...
MAYBE YOU'D BE DATING MARIKA.
MAYBE I'D NEVER HAVE TRANS-FERRED HERE.
OH... TRUE...

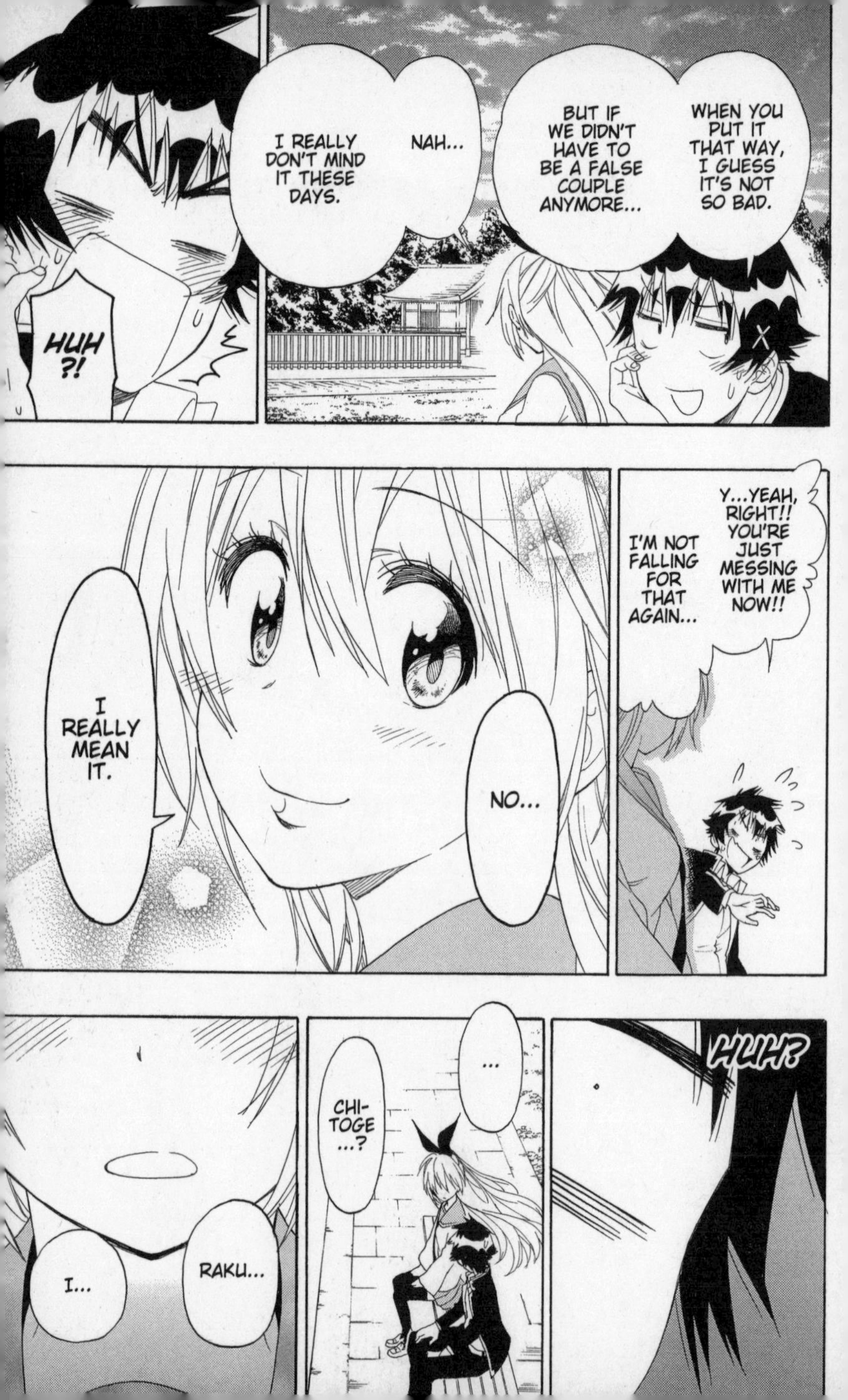
WHEN YOU PUT IT THAT WAY, I GUESS IT'S NOT SO BAD.
BUT IF WE DIDN'T HAVE TO BE A FALSE COUPLE ANYMORE...
NAH...
I REALLY DON'T MIND IT THESE DAYS.
HUH?!
Y...YEAH, RIGHT!! YOU'RE JUST MESSING WITH ME NOW!!
I'M NOT FALLING FOR THAT AGAIN...
NO...
I REALLY MEAN IT.
HUH?
...
CHI-TOGE...?
RAKU...
I...

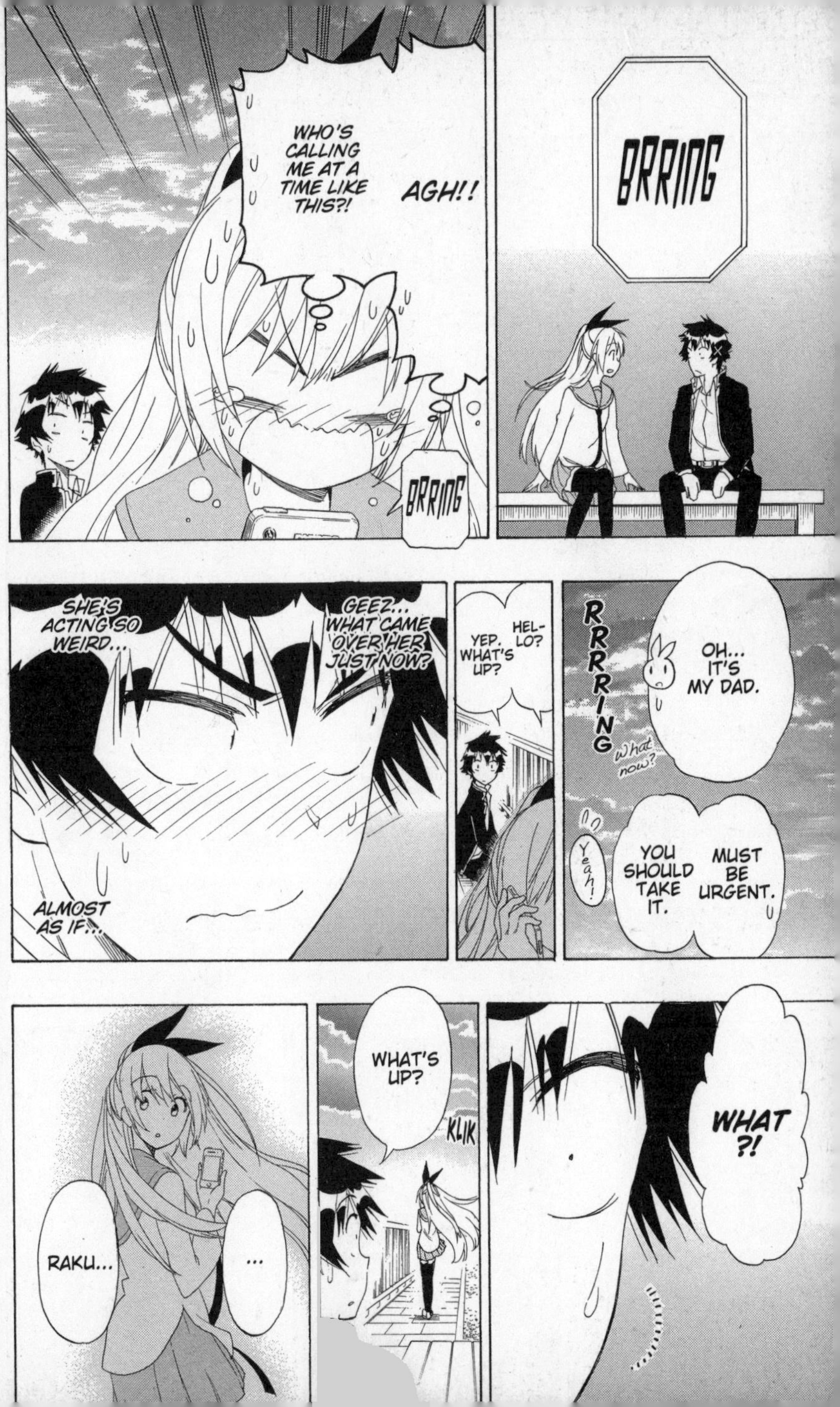
BRRING
AGH!!
WHO'S CALLING ME AT A TIME LIKE THIS?!
BRRING
RRRRING
OH... IT'S MY DAD.
What now?
MUST BE URGENT.
YOU SHOULD TAKE IT.
Yeah!
HEL-LO?
YEP. WHAT'S UP?
GEEZ... WHAT CAME OVER HER JUST NOW?
SHE'S ACTING SO WEIRD...
ALMOST AS IF...
WHAT?!
WHAT'S UP?
KLIK
...
RAKU...

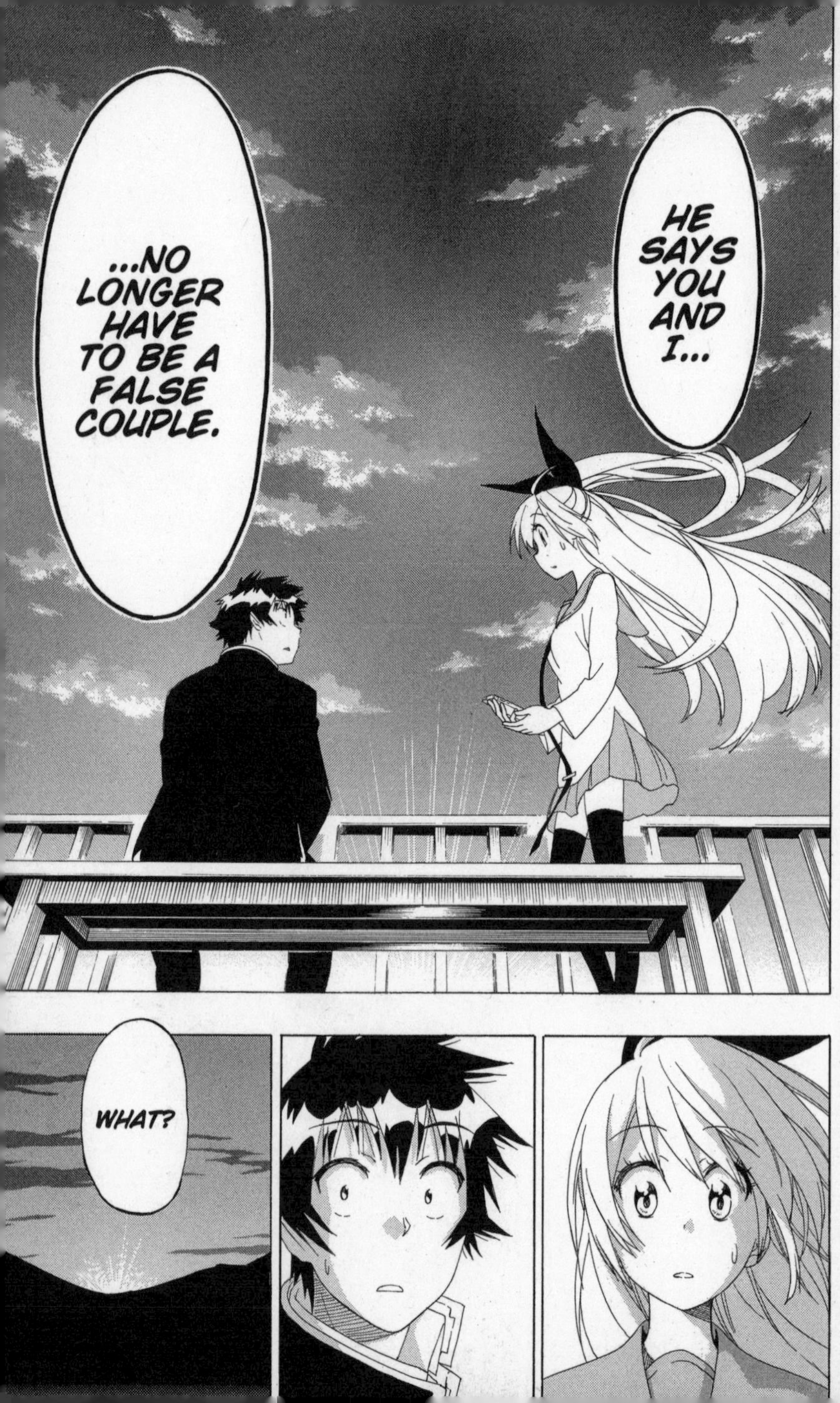
HE SAYS YOU AND I...
...NO LONGER HAVE TO BE A FALSE COUPLE.
WHAT?

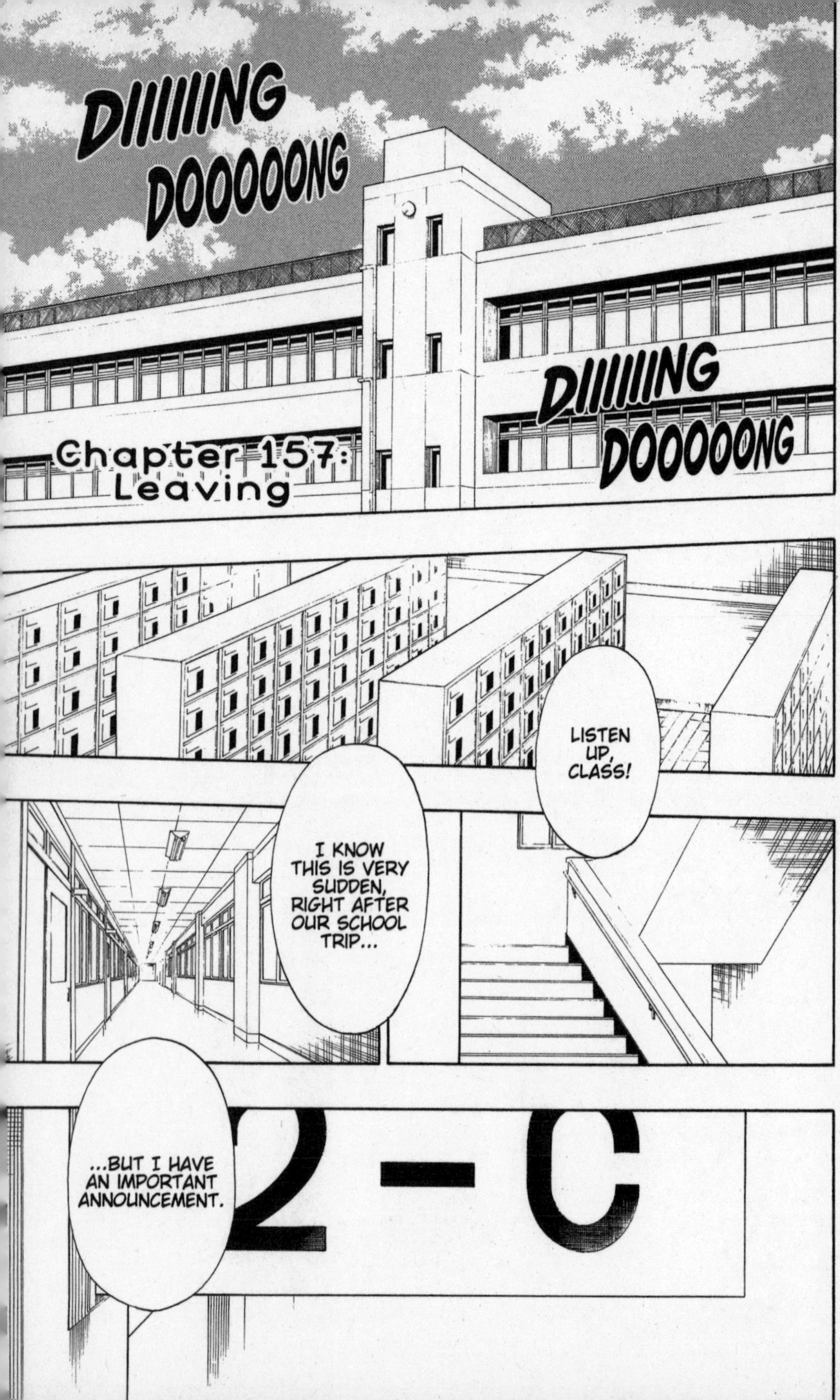
DIIIIING DOOOOONG
DIIIIING DOOOOONG
Chapter 157: Leaving
LISTEN UP, CLASS!
I KNOW THIS IS VERY SUDDEN, RIGHT AFTER OUR SCHOOL TRIP...
...BUT I HAVE AN IMPORTANT ANNOUNCEMENT.
2-C

Chapter 157: Leaving

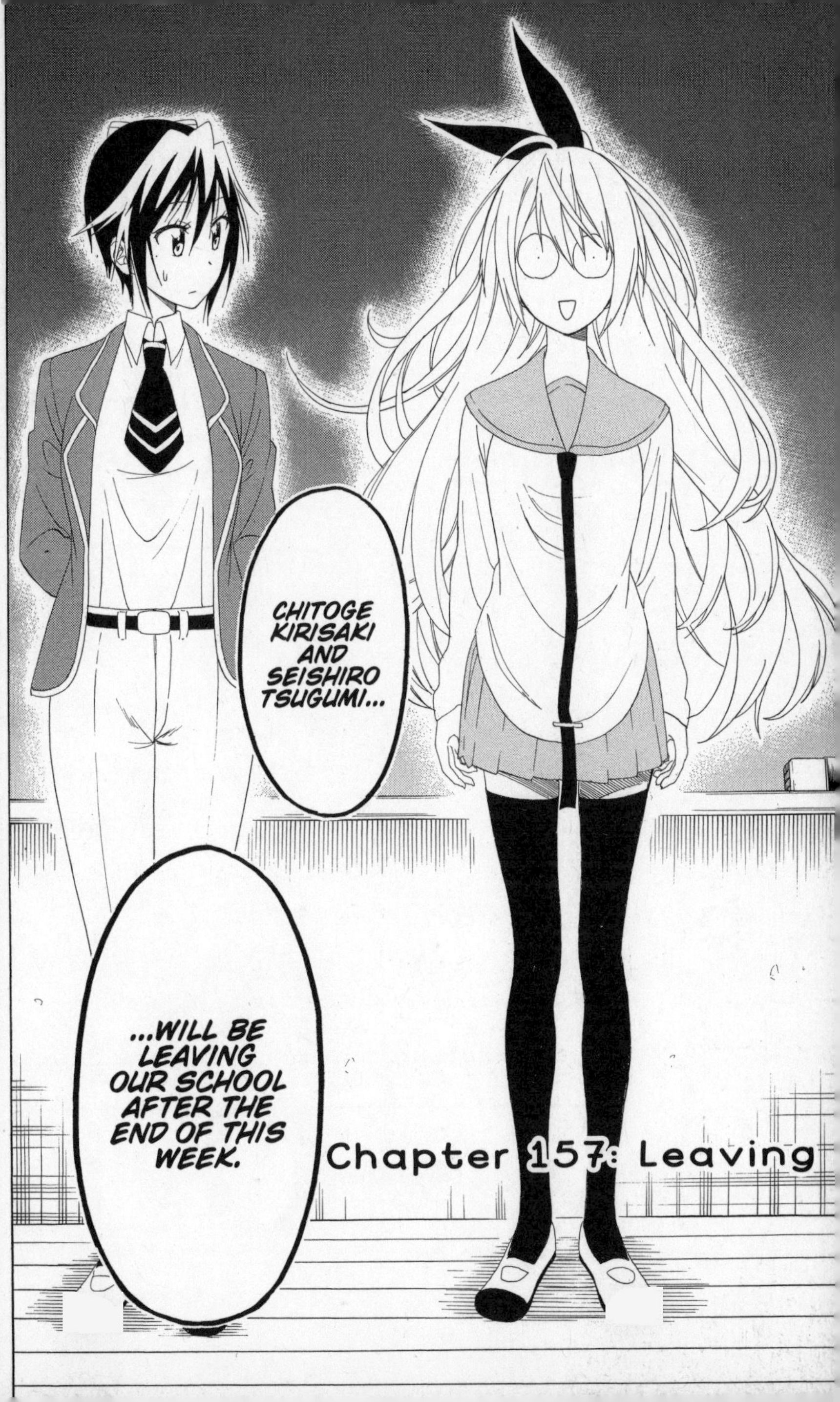
CHITOGE KIRISAKI AND SEISHIRO TSUGUMI...
...WILL BE LEAVING OUR SCHOOL AFTER THE END OF THIS WEEK.

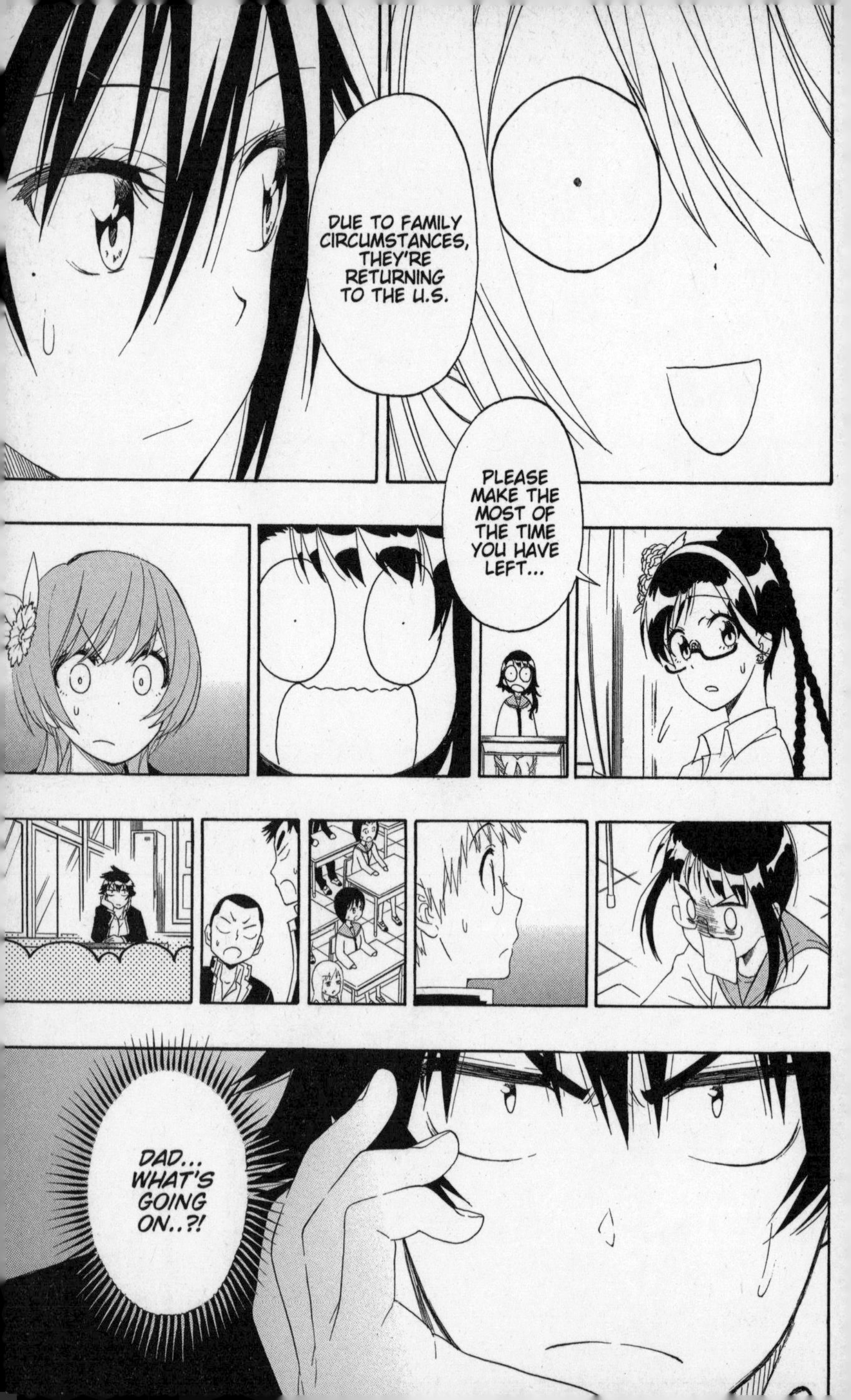
DUE TO FAMILY CIRCUMSTANCES, THEY'RE RETURNING TO THE U.S.
PLEASE MAKE THE MOST OF THE TIME YOU HAVE LEFT...
DAD... WHAT'S GOING ON..?!

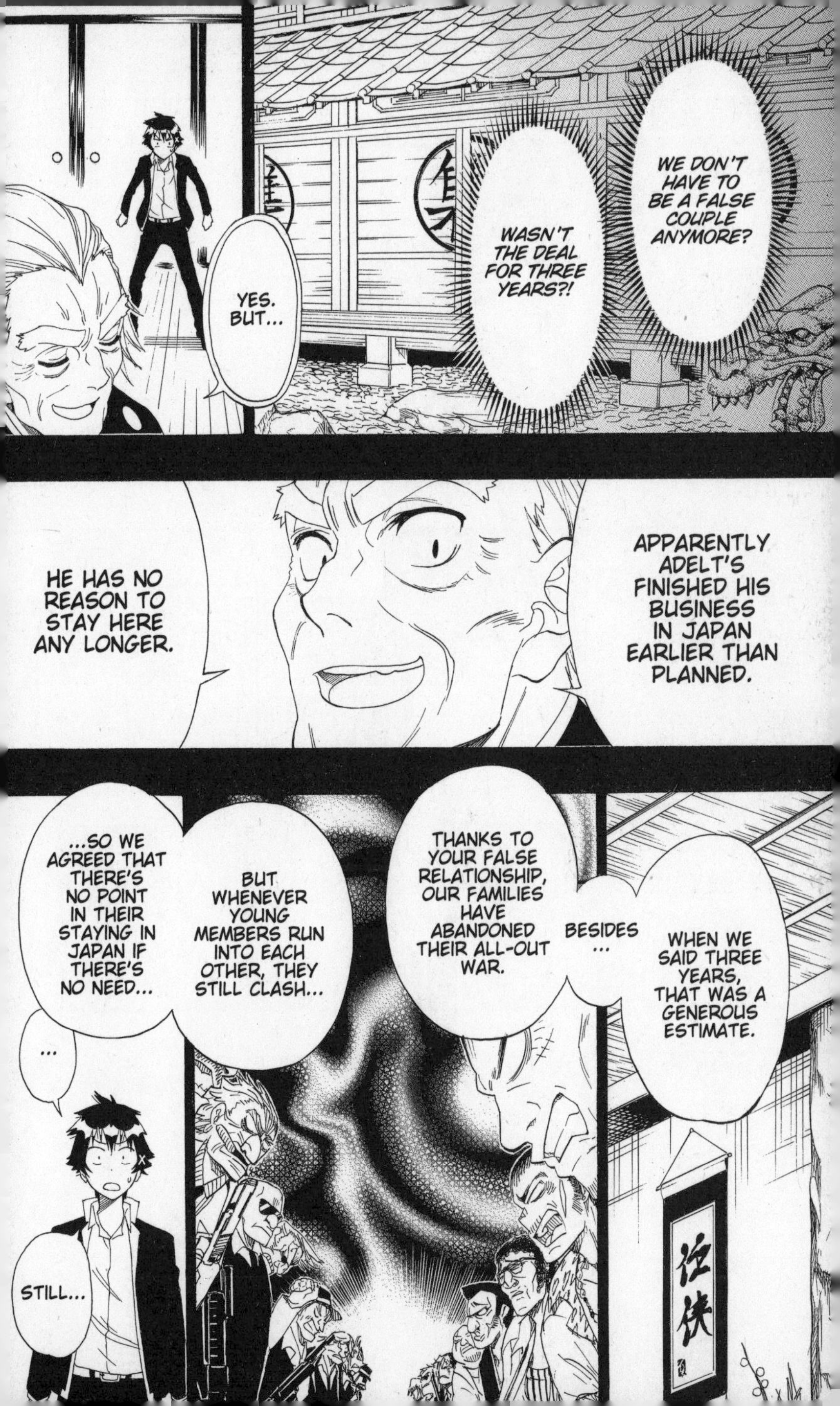
WE DON'T HAVE TO BE A FALSE COUPLE ANYMORE?
WASN'T THE DEAL FOR THREE YEARS?!
YES. BUT...
APPARENTLY ADELT'S FINISHED HIS BUSINESS IN JAPAN EARLIER THAN PLANNED.
HE HAS NO REASON TO STAY HERE ANY LONGER.
WHEN WE SAID THREE YEARS, THAT WAS A GENEROUS ESTIMATE.
BESIDES...
THANKS TO YOUR FALSE RELATIONSHIP, OUR FAMILIES HAVE ABANDONED THEIR ALL-OUT WAR.
BUT WHENEVER YOUNG MEMBERS RUN INTO EACH OTHER, THEY STILL CLASH...
...SO WE AGREED THAT THERE'S NO POINT IN THEIR STAYING IN JAPAN IF THERE'S NO NEED...
...
STILL...

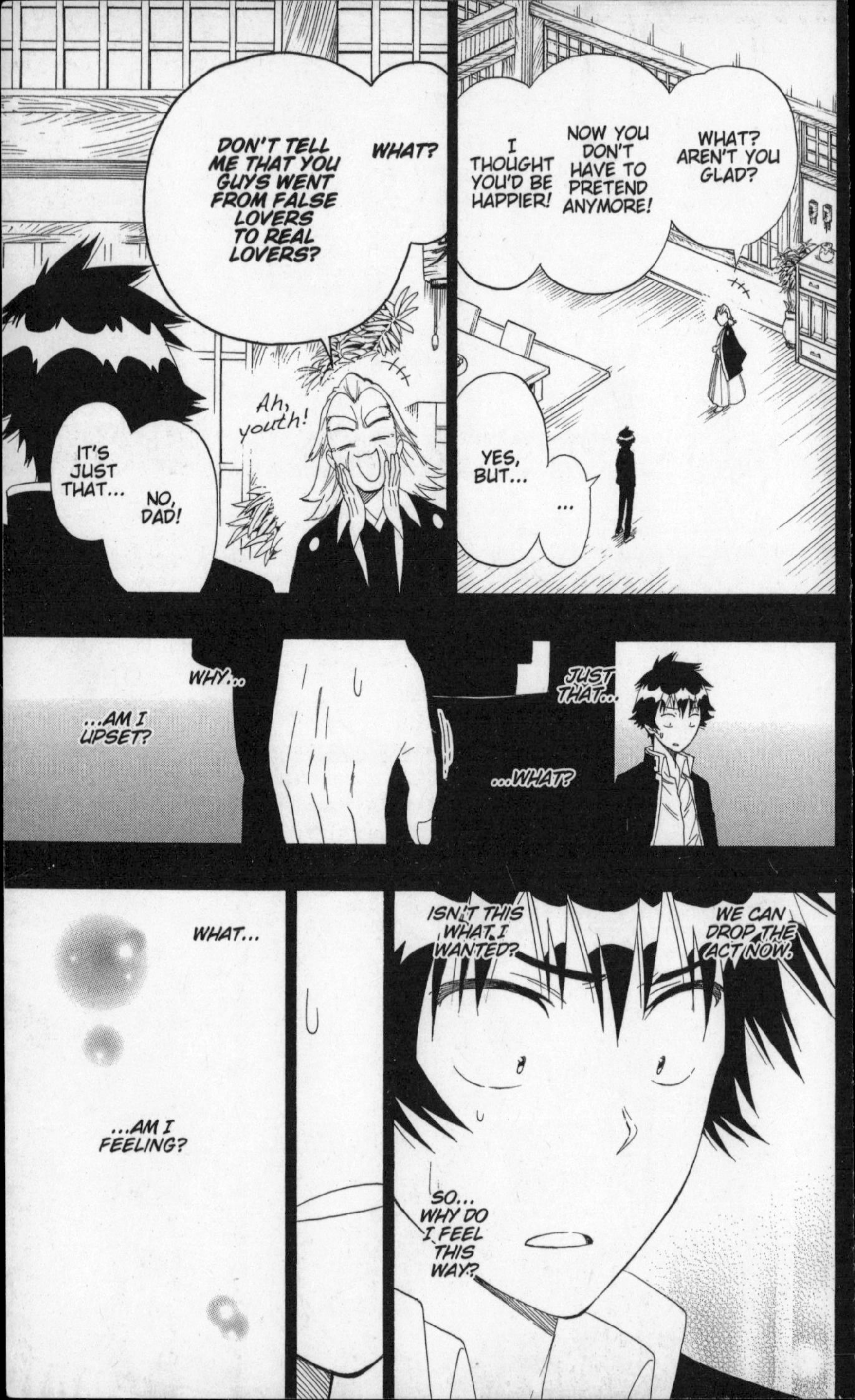
WHAT? AREN'T YOU GLAD?
NOW YOU DON'T HAVE TO PRETEND ANYMORE!
I THOUGHT YOU'D BE HAPPIER!
YES, BUT...
...
WHAT?
DON'T TELL ME THAT YOU GUYS WENT FROM FALSE LOVERS TO REAL LOVERS?
Ah, youth!
NO, DAD!
IT'S JUST THAT...
JUST THAT...
...WHAT?
WHY...
...AM I UPSET?
WE CAN DROP THE ACT NOW.
ISN'T THIS WHAT I WANTED?
SO... WHY DO I FEEL THIS WAY?
WHAT...
...AM I FEELING?

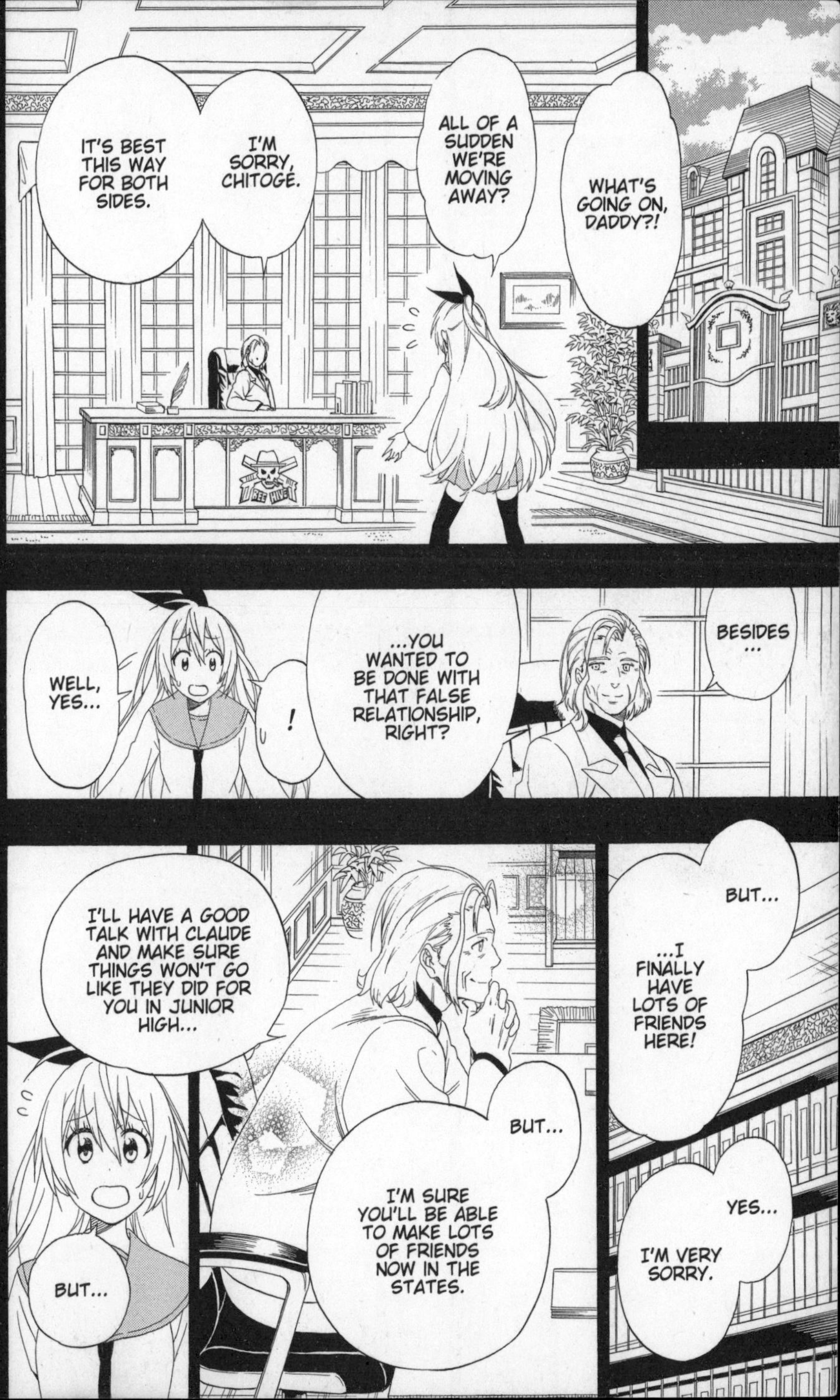
WHAT'S GOING ON, DADDY?!
ALL OF A SUDDEN WE'RE MOVING AWAY?
I'M SORRY, CHITOGE.
IT'S BEST THIS WAY FOR BOTH SIDES.
BESIDES...
...YOU WANTED TO BE DONE WITH THAT FALSE RELATIONSHIP, RIGHT?
!
WELL, YES...
BUT...
...I FINALLY HAVE LOTS OF FRIENDS HERE!
YES...
I'M VERY SORRY.
I'LL HAVE A GOOD TALK WITH CLAUDE AND MAKE SURE THINGS WON'T GO LIKE THEY DID FOR YOU IN JUNIOR HIGH...
BUT...
I'M SURE YOU'LL BE ABLE TO MAKE LOTS OF FRIENDS NOW IN THE STATES.
BUT...

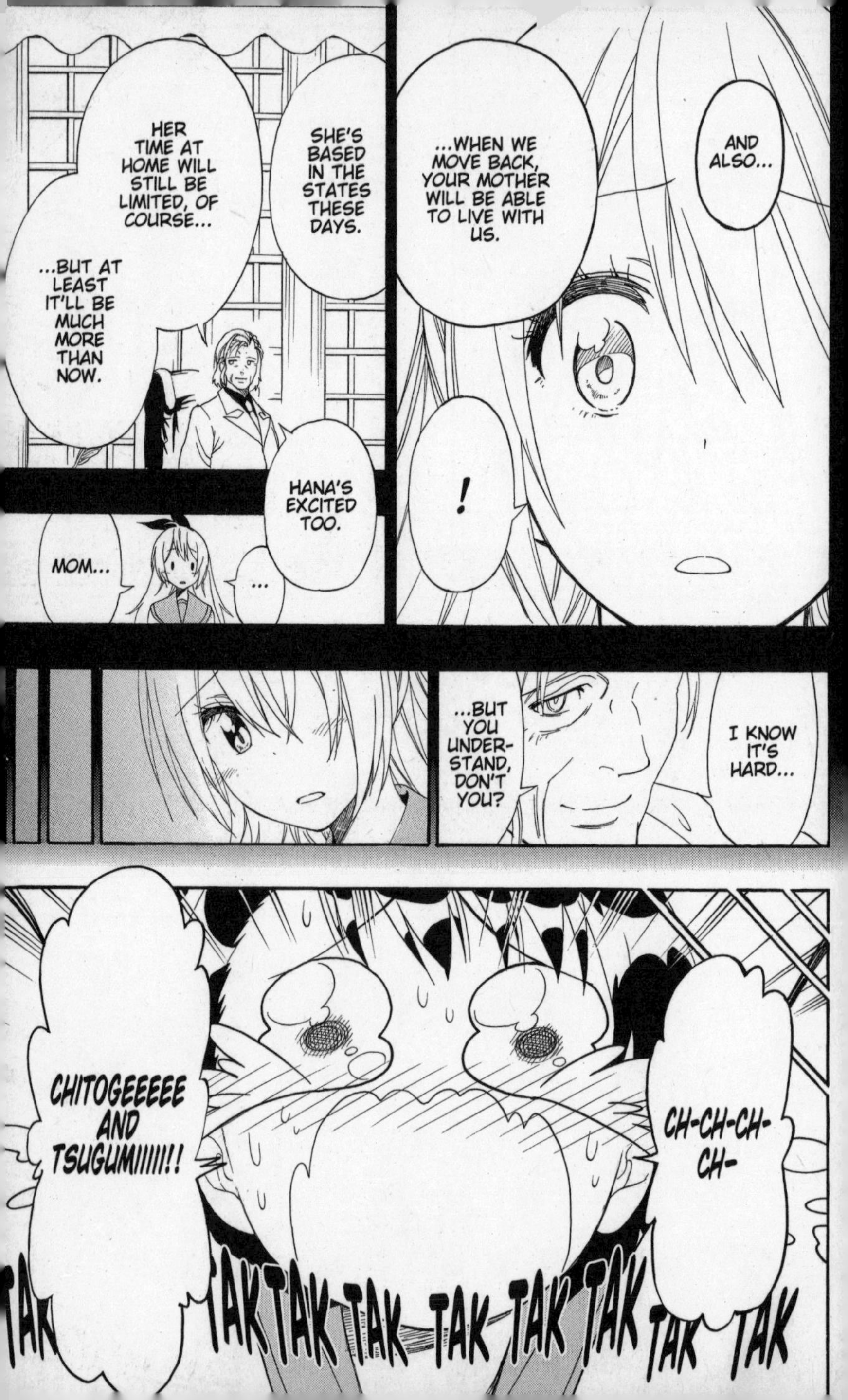
AND ALSO...
...WHEN WE MOVE BACK, YOUR MOTHER WILL BE ABLE TO LIVE WITH US.
!
SHE'S BASED IN THE STATES THESE DAYS.
HER TIME AT HOME WILL STILL BE LIMITED, OF COURSE...
...BUT AT LEAST IT'LL BE MUCH MORE THAN NOW.
HANA'S EXCITED TOO.
...
MOM...
I KNOW IT'S HARD...
...BUT YOU UNDER-STAND, DON'T YOU?
CH-CH-CH-CH-
CHITOGEEEEE AND TSUGUMIIIIII!!
TAK TAK TAK TAK TAK TAK TAK TAK TAK

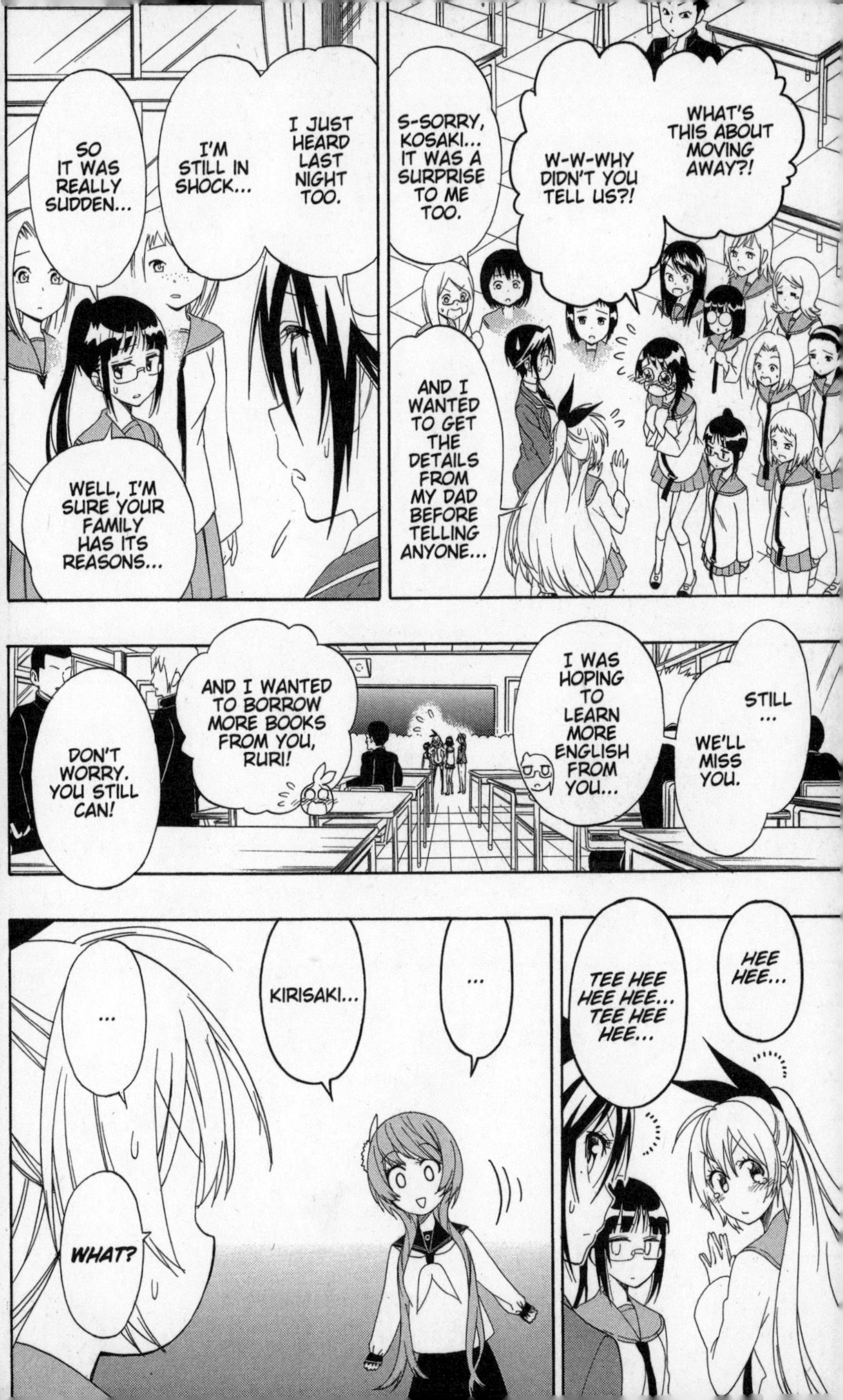
WHAT'S THIS ABOUT MOVING AWAY?!
W-W-WHY DIDN'T YOU TELL US?!
S-SORRY, KOSAKI... IT WAS A SURPRISE TO ME TOO.
AND I WANTED TO GET THE DETAILS FROM MY DAD BEFORE TELLING ANYONE...
I JUST HEARD LAST NIGHT TOO.
I'M STILL IN SHOCK...
SO IT WAS REALLY SUDDEN...
WELL, I'M SURE YOUR FAMILY HAS ITS REASONS...
STILL... WE'LL MISS YOU.
I WAS HOPING TO LEARN MORE ENGLISH FROM YOU...
AND I WANTED TO BORROW MORE BOOKS FROM YOU, RURI!
DON'T WORRY. YOU STILL CAN!
HEE HEE...
TEE HEE HEE HEE... TEE HEE HEE...
...
KIRISAKI...
...
WHAT?

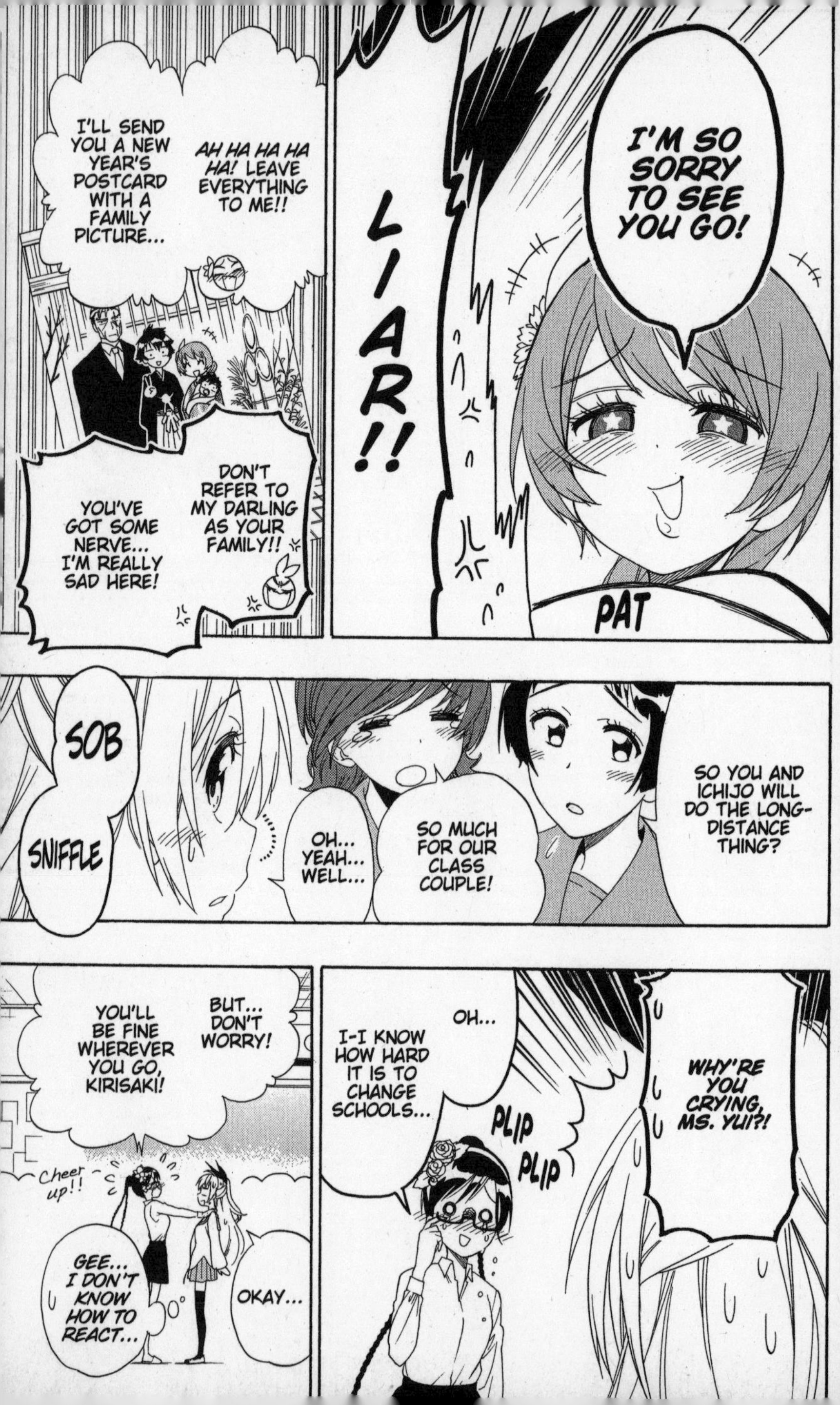
I'M SO SORRY TO SEE YOU GO!
LIAR!!
PAT
AH HA HA HA HA! LEAVE EVERYTHING TO ME!!
I'LL SEND YOU A NEW YEAR'S POSTCARD WITH A FAMILY PICTURE...
DON'T REFER TO MY DARLING AS YOUR FAMILY!!
YOU'VE GOT SOME NERVE... I'M REALLY SAD HERE!
SO YOU AND ICHIJO WILL DO THE LONG-DISTANCE THING?
SO MUCH FOR OUR CLASS COUPLE!
OH... YEAH... WELL...
SOB
SNIFFLE
WHY'RE YOU CRYING, MS. YUI?!
OH...
I-I KNOW HOW HARD IT IS TO CHANGE SCHOOLS...
PLIP
PLIP
BUT... DON'T WORRY!
YOU'LL BE FINE WHEREVER YOU GO, KIRISAKI!
Cheer up!!
OKAY...
GEE... I DON'T KNOW HOW TO REACT...

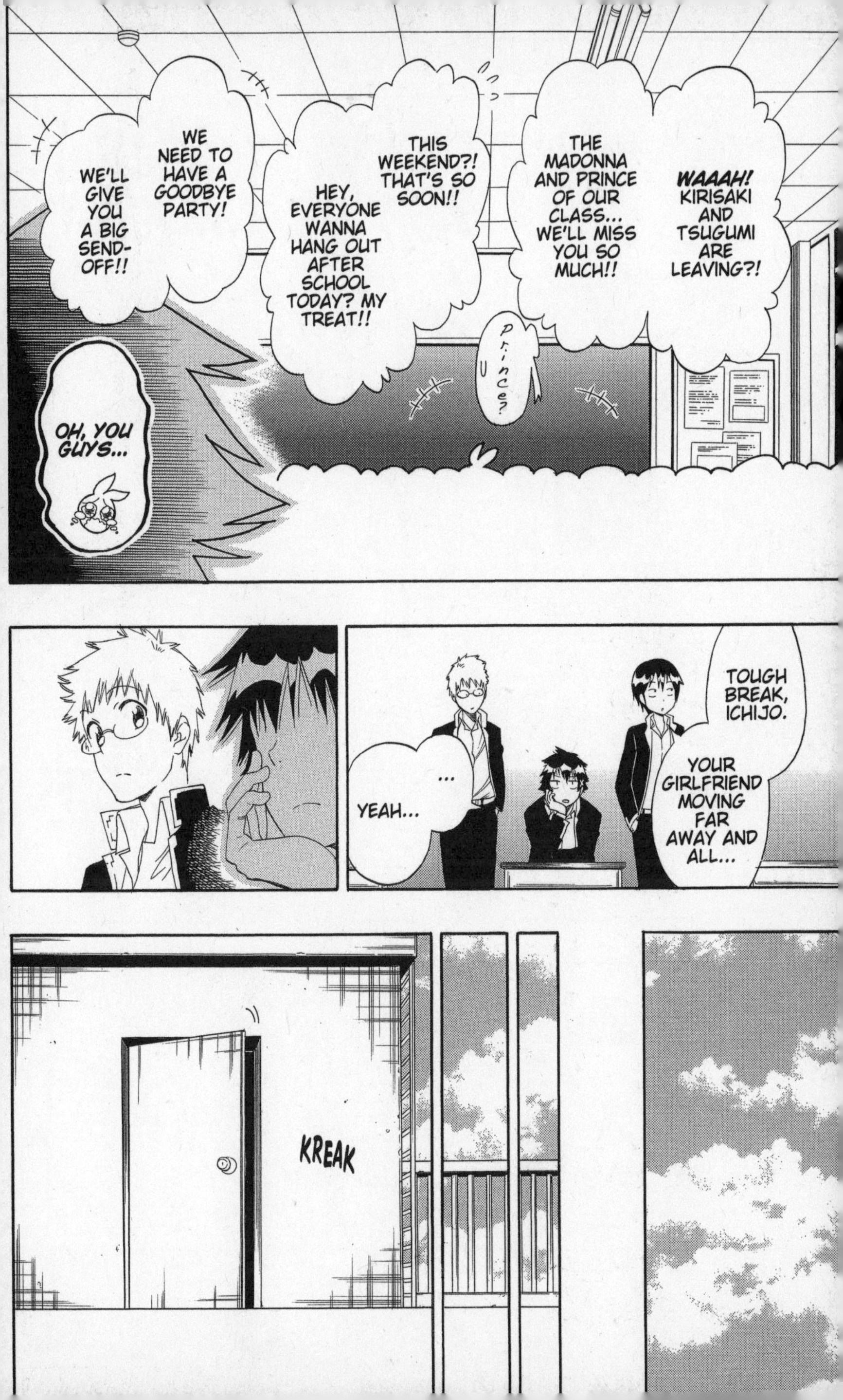
WAAAH! KIRISAKI AND TSUGUMI ARE LEAVING?!
THE MADONNA AND PRINCE OF OUR CLASS... WE'LL MISS YOU SO MUCH!!
Prince?
THIS WEEKEND?! THAT'S SO SOON!!
HEY, EVERYONE WANNA HANG OUT AFTER SCHOOL TODAY? MY TREAT!!
WE NEED TO HAVE A GOODBYE PARTY!
WE'LL GIVE YOU A BIG SEND-OFF!!
OH, YOU GUYS...
TOUGH BREAK, ICHIJO.
YOUR GIRLFRIEND MOVING FAR AWAY AND ALL...
...
YEAH...
KREAK

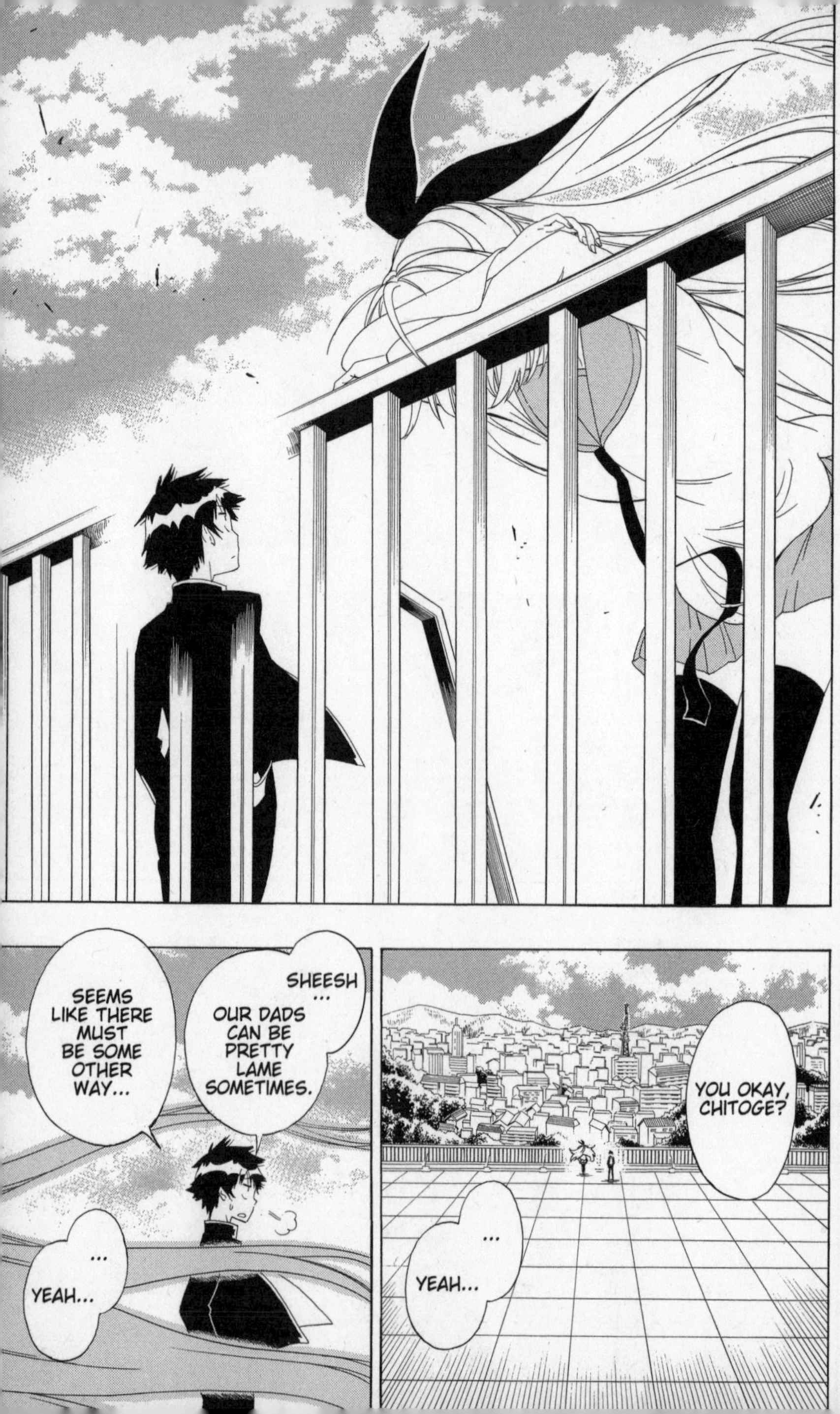

YOU OKAY, CHITOGE?
... YEAH...
SHEESH... OUR DADS CAN BE PRETTY LAME SOMETIMES.
SEEMS LIKE THERE MUST BE SOME OTHER WAY...
... YEAH...

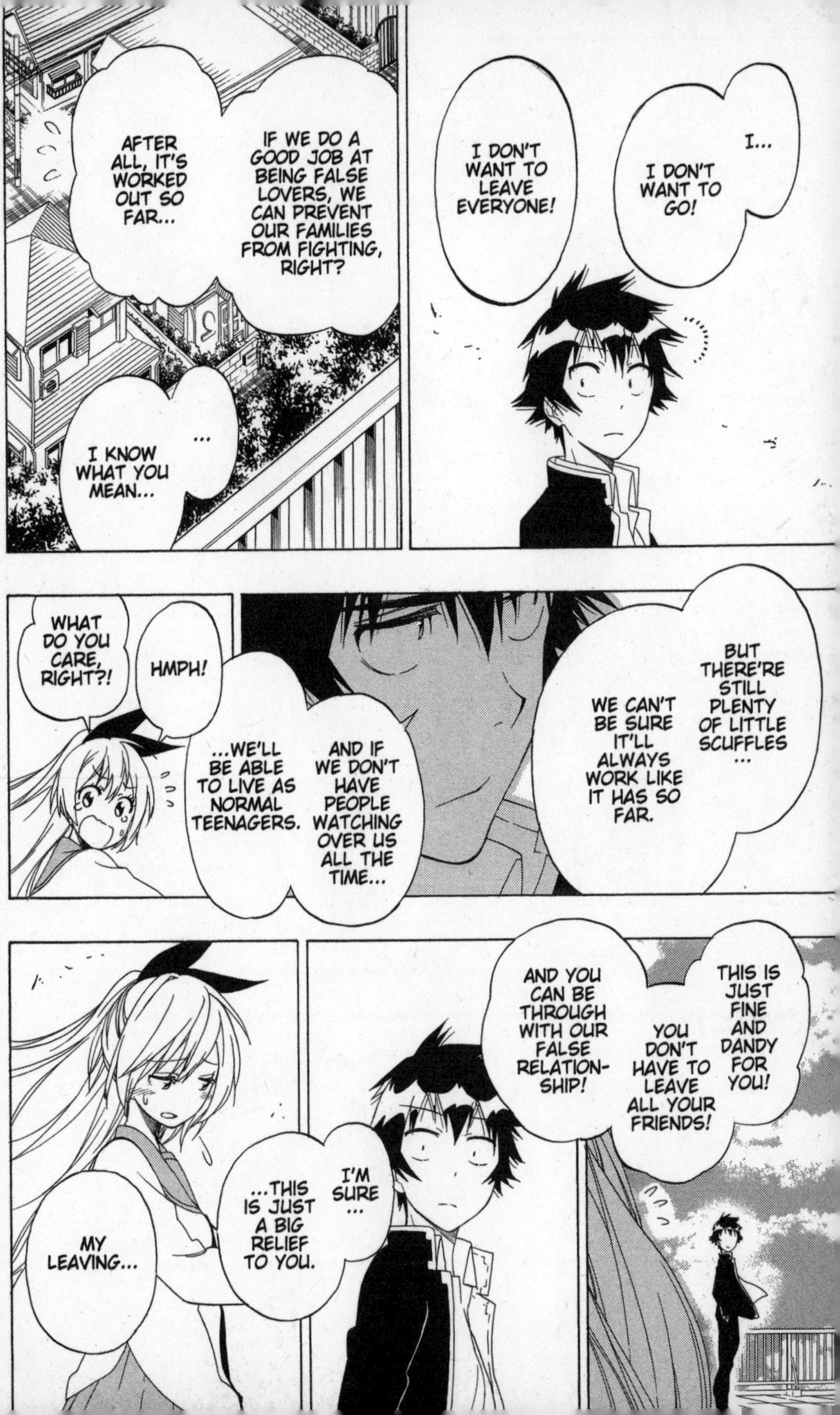
I...
I DON'T WANT TO GO!
I DON'T WANT TO LEAVE EVERYONE!
IF WE DO A GOOD JOB AT BEING FALSE LOVERS, WE CAN PREVENT OUR FAMILIES FROM FIGHTING, RIGHT?
AFTER ALL, IT'S WORKED OUT SO FAR...
...
I KNOW WHAT YOU MEAN...
BUT THERE'RE STILL PLENTY OF LITTLE SCUFFLES...
WE CAN'T BE SURE IT'LL ALWAYS WORK LIKE IT HAS SO FAR.
AND IF WE DON'T HAVE PEOPLE WATCHING OVER US ALL THE TIME...
...WE'LL BE ABLE TO LIVE AS NORMAL TEENAGERS.
HMPH!
WHAT DO YOU CARE, RIGHT?!
THIS IS JUST FINE AND DANDY FOR YOU!
YOU DON'T HAVE TO LEAVE ALL YOUR FRIENDS!
AND YOU CAN BE THROUGH WITH OUR FALSE RELATION-SHIP!
I'M SURE...
...THIS IS JUST A BIG RELIEF TO YOU.
MY LEAVING...

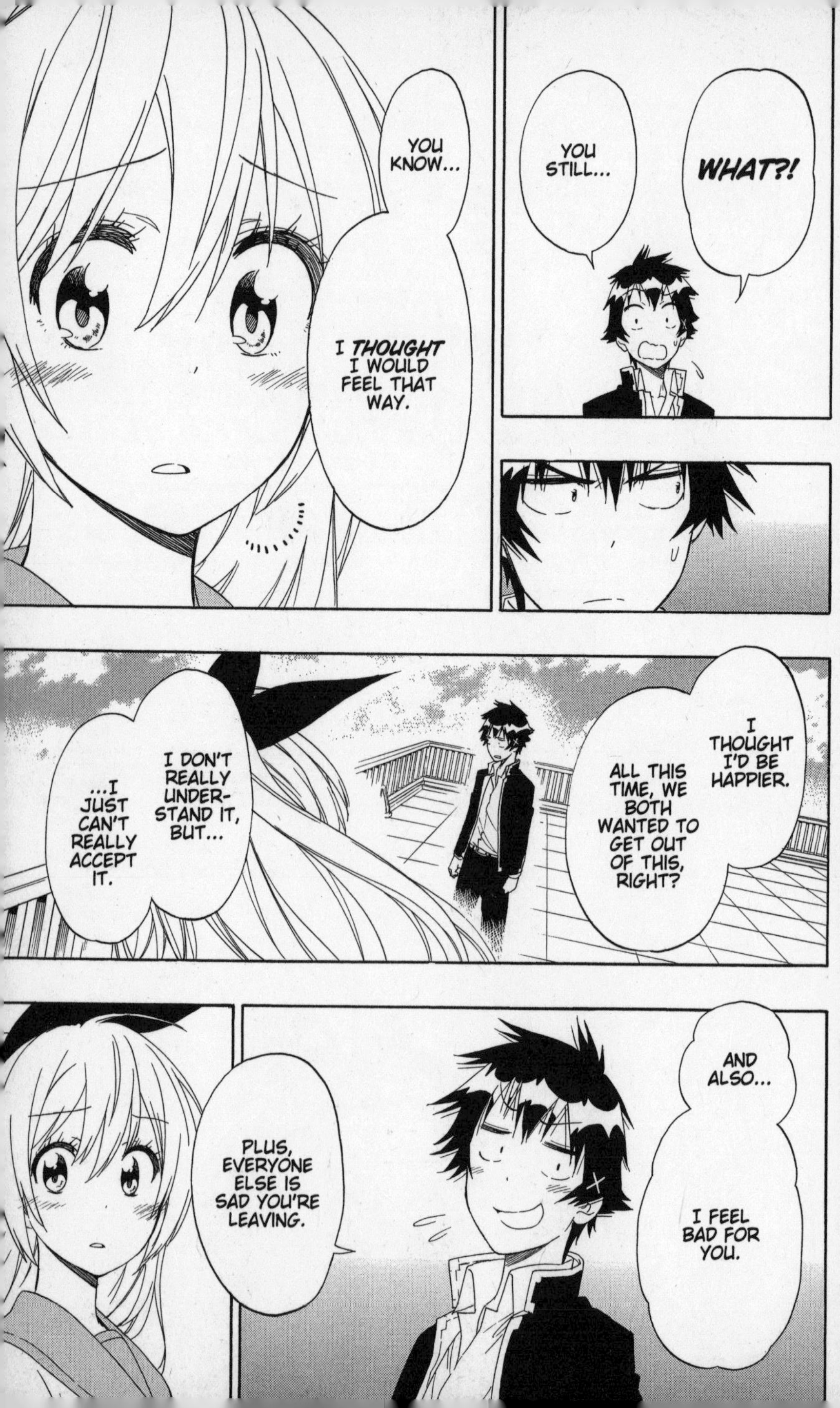
WHAT?!
YOU STILL...
YOU KNOW...
I *THOUGHT* I WOULD FEEL THAT WAY.
I THOUGHT I'D BE HAPPIER.
ALL THIS TIME, WE BOTH WANTED TO GET OUT OF THIS, RIGHT?
I DON'T REALLY UNDERSTAND IT, BUT...
...I JUST CAN'T REALLY ACCEPT IT.
AND ALSO...
I FEEL BAD FOR YOU.
PLUS, EVERYONE ELSE IS SAD YOU'RE LEAVING.

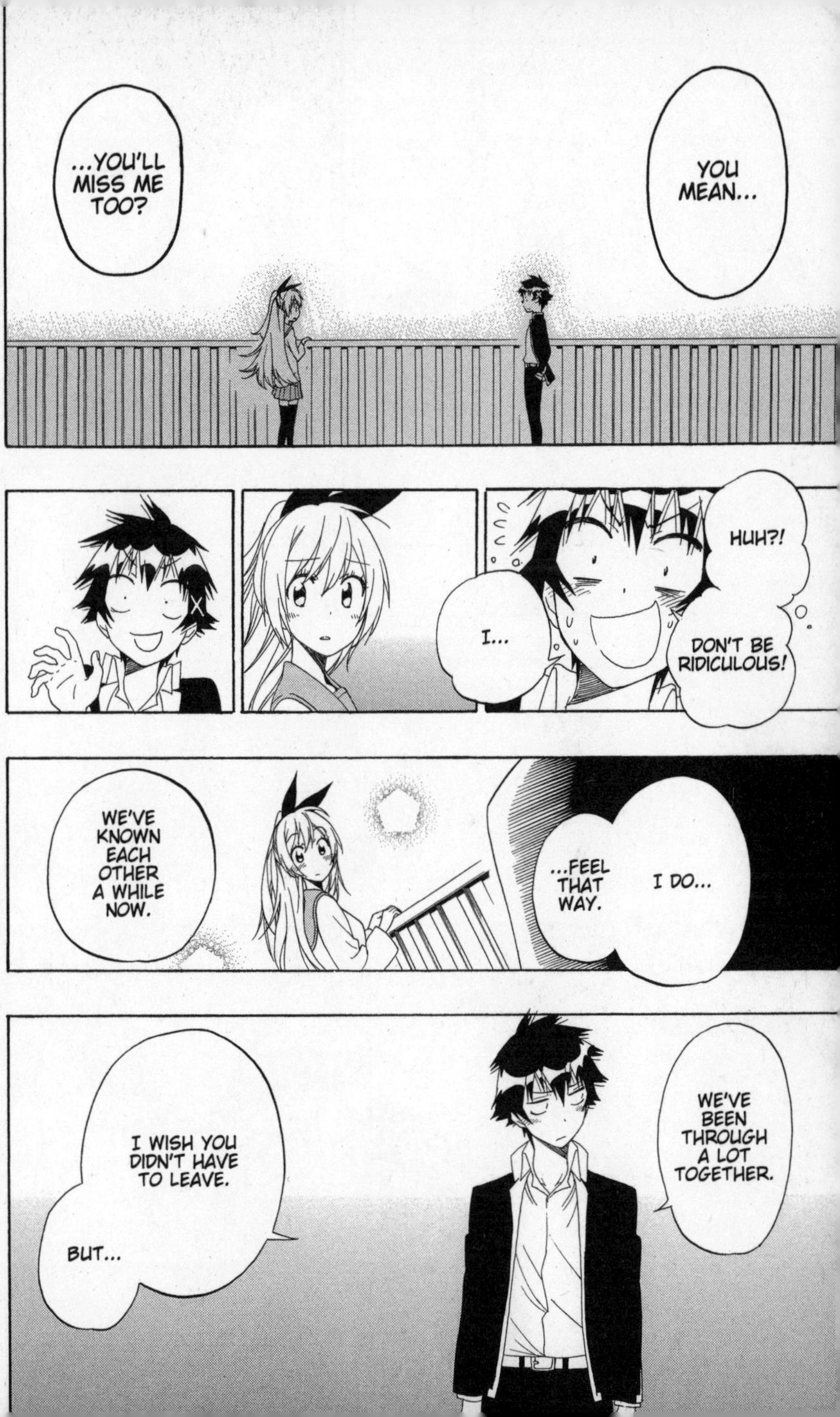
YOU MEAN...
...YOU'LL MISS ME TOO?
HUH?!
DON'T BE RIDICULOUS!
I...
I DO...
...FEEL THAT WAY.
WE'VE KNOWN EACH OTHER A WHILE NOW.
WE'VE BEEN THROUGH A LOT TOGETHER.
I WISH YOU DIDN'T HAVE TO LEAVE.
BUT...

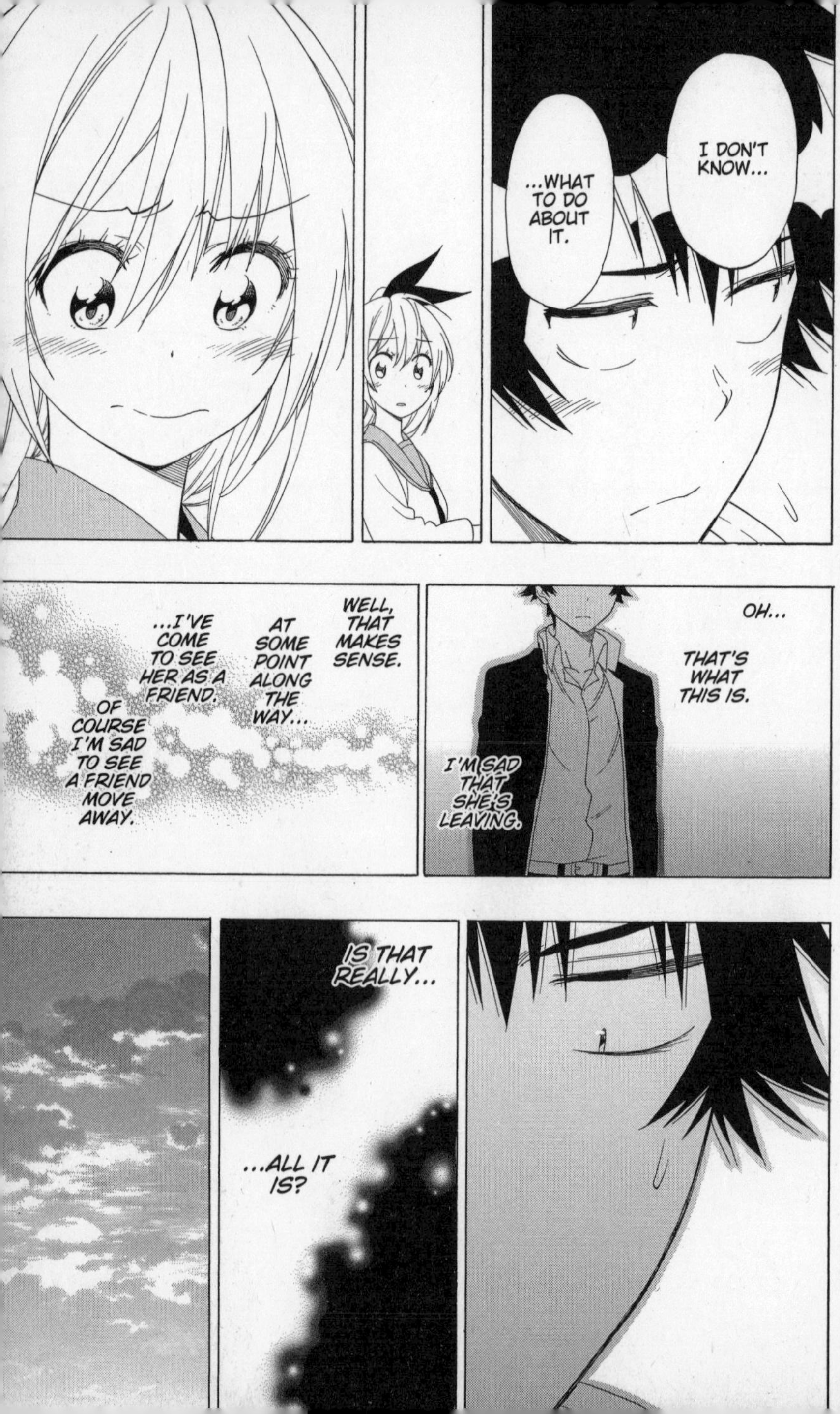
I DON'T KNOW...
...WHAT TO DO ABOUT IT.
OH...
THAT'S WHAT THIS IS.
I'M SAD THAT SHE'S LEAVING.
WELL, THAT MAKES SENSE.
AT SOME POINT ALONG THE WAY...
...I'VE COME TO SEE HER AS A FRIEND.
OF COURSE I'M SAD TO SEE A FRIEND MOVE AWAY.
IS THAT REALLY...
...ALL IT IS?

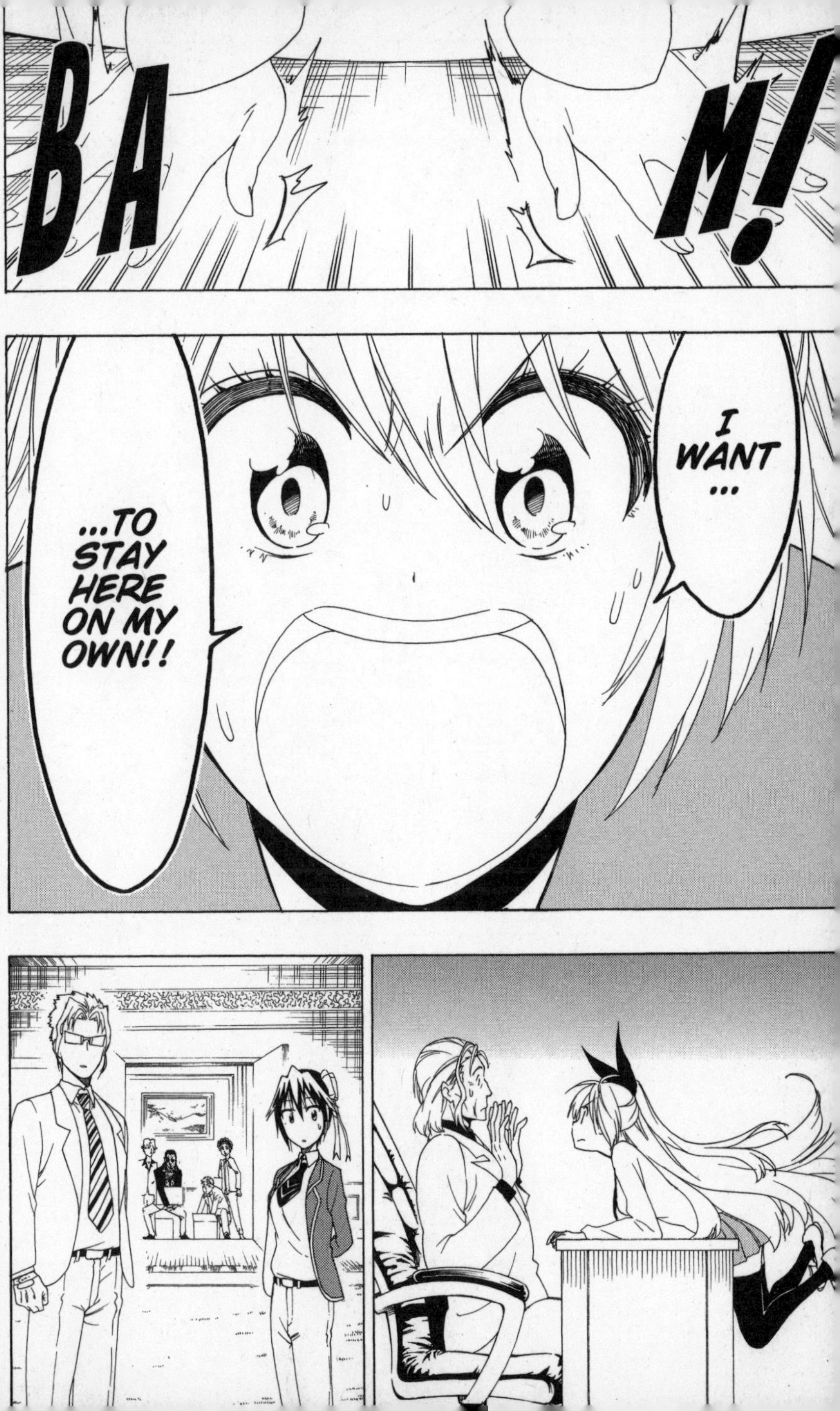
BAM!
I WANT...
...TO STAY HERE ON MY OWN!!

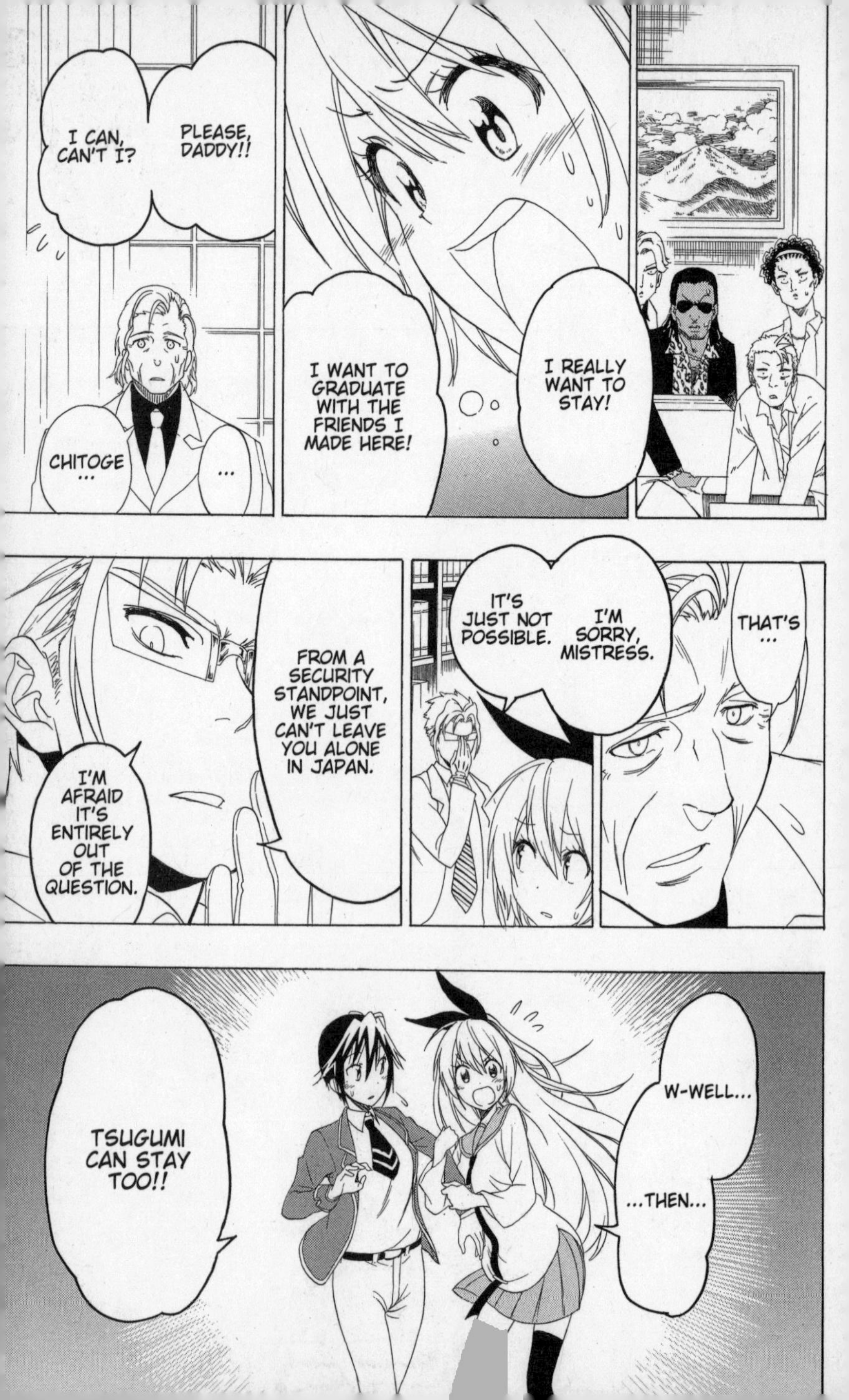
I REALLY WANT TO STAY!
I WANT TO GRADUATE WITH THE FRIENDS I MADE HERE!
PLEASE, DADDY!!
I CAN, CAN'T I?
...
CHITOGE...
THAT'S...
I'M SORRY, MISTRESS.
IT'S JUST NOT POSSIBLE.
FROM A SECURITY STANDPOINT, WE JUST CAN'T LEAVE YOU ALONE IN JAPAN.
I'M AFRAID IT'S ENTIRELY OUT OF THE QUESTION.
W-WELL...
...THEN...
TSUGUMI CAN STAY TOO!!

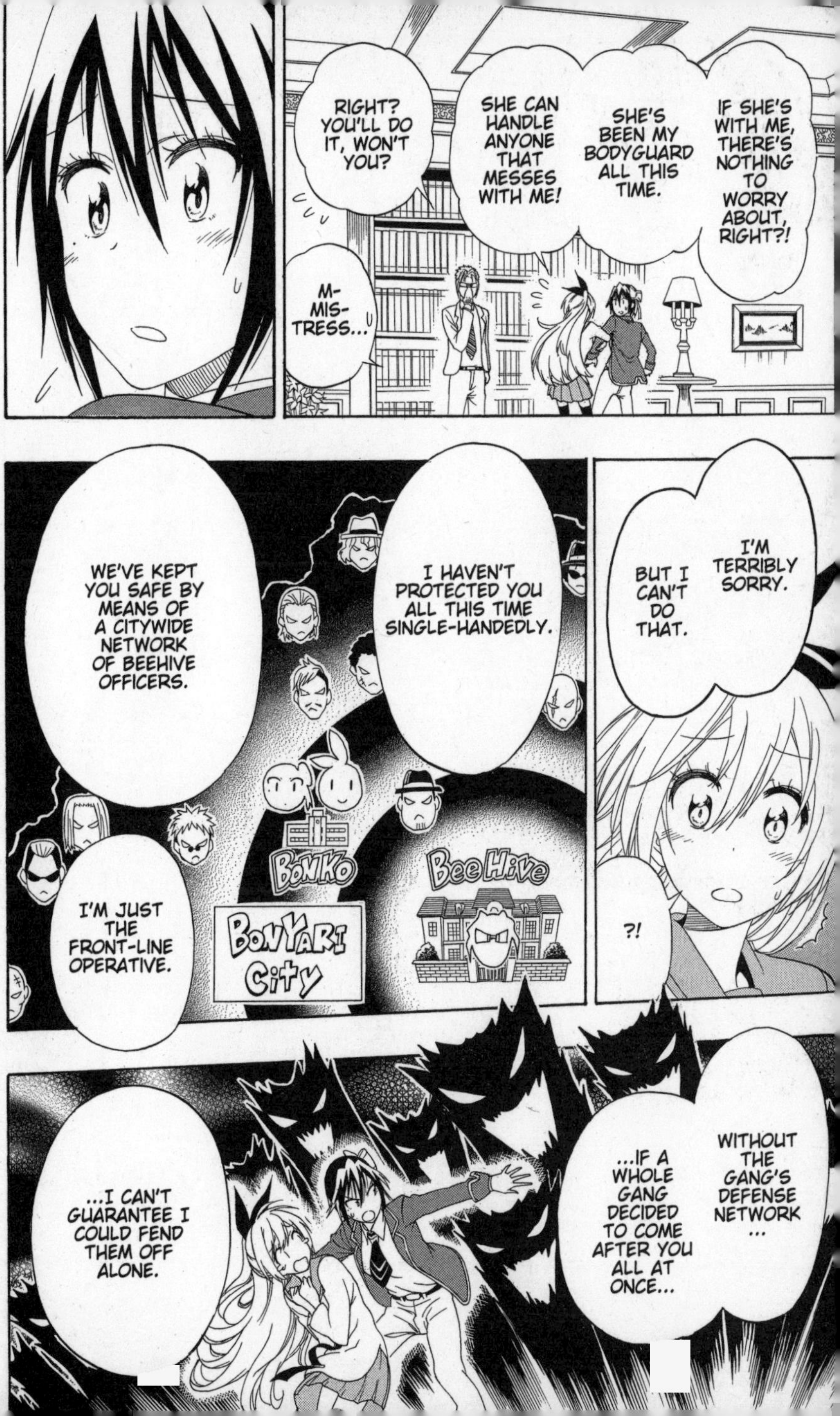
IF SHE'S WITH ME, THERE'S NOTHING TO WORRY ABOUT, RIGHT?!
SHE'S BEEN MY BODYGUARD ALL THIS TIME.
SHE CAN HANDLE ANYONE THAT MESSES WITH ME!
RIGHT? YOU'LL DO IT, WON'T YOU?
M-MIS-TRESS...
I'M TERRIBLY SORRY.
BUT I CAN'T DO THAT.
?!
I HAVEN'T PROTECTED YOU ALL THIS TIME SINGLE-HANDEDLY.
WE'VE KEPT YOU SAFE BY MEANS OF A CITYWIDE NETWORK OF BEEHIVE OFFICERS.
BeeHive
BONKO
I'M JUST THE FRONT-LINE OPERATIVE.
BONYARI City
WITHOUT THE GANG'S DEFENSE NETWORK...
...IF A WHOLE GANG DECIDED TO COME AFTER YOU ALL AT ONCE...
...I CAN'T GUARANTEE I COULD FEND THEM OFF ALONE.

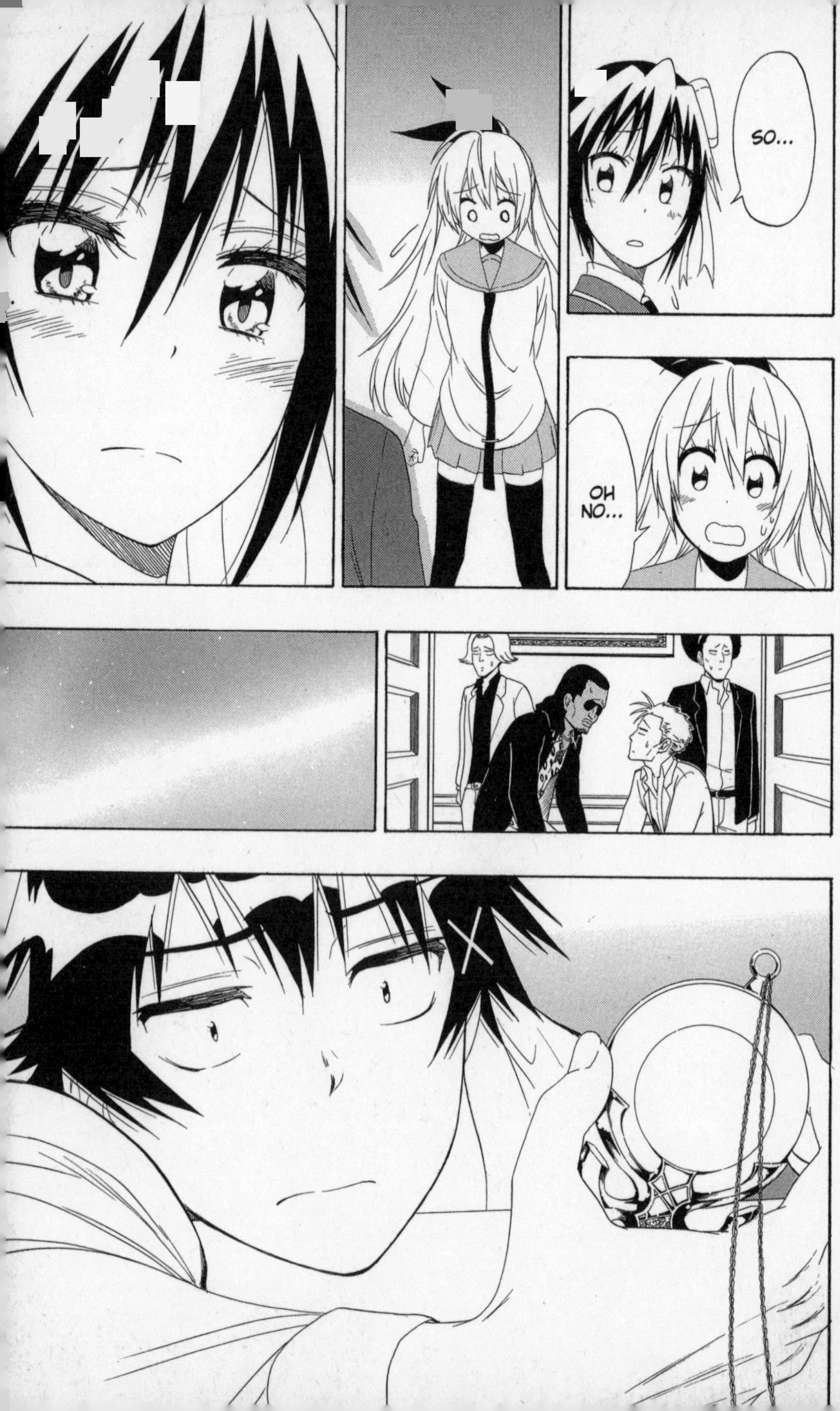
SO...
OH NO...

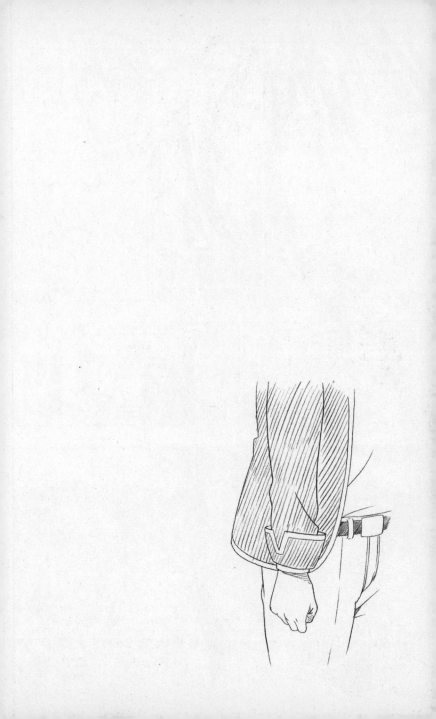

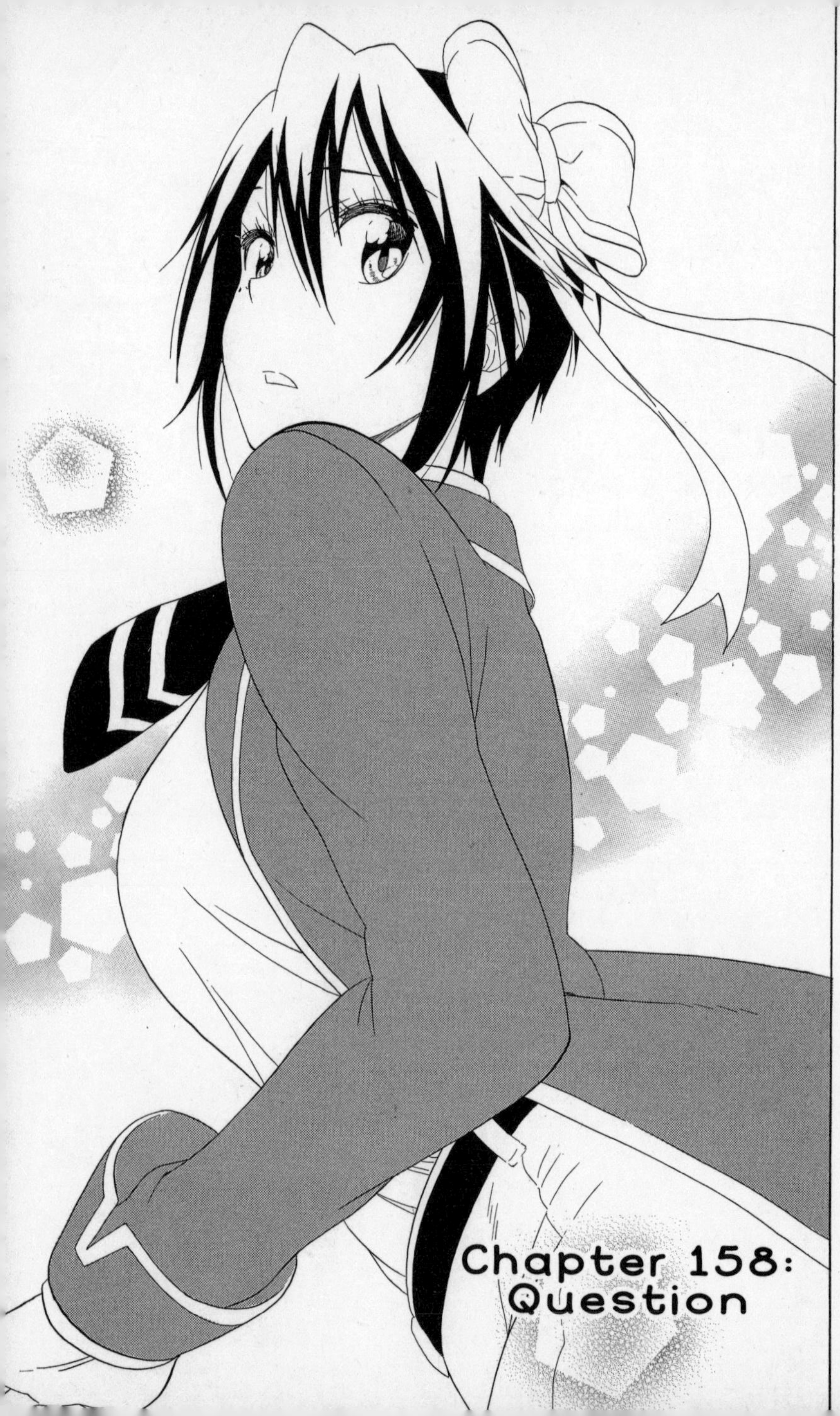
Chapter 158:
Question

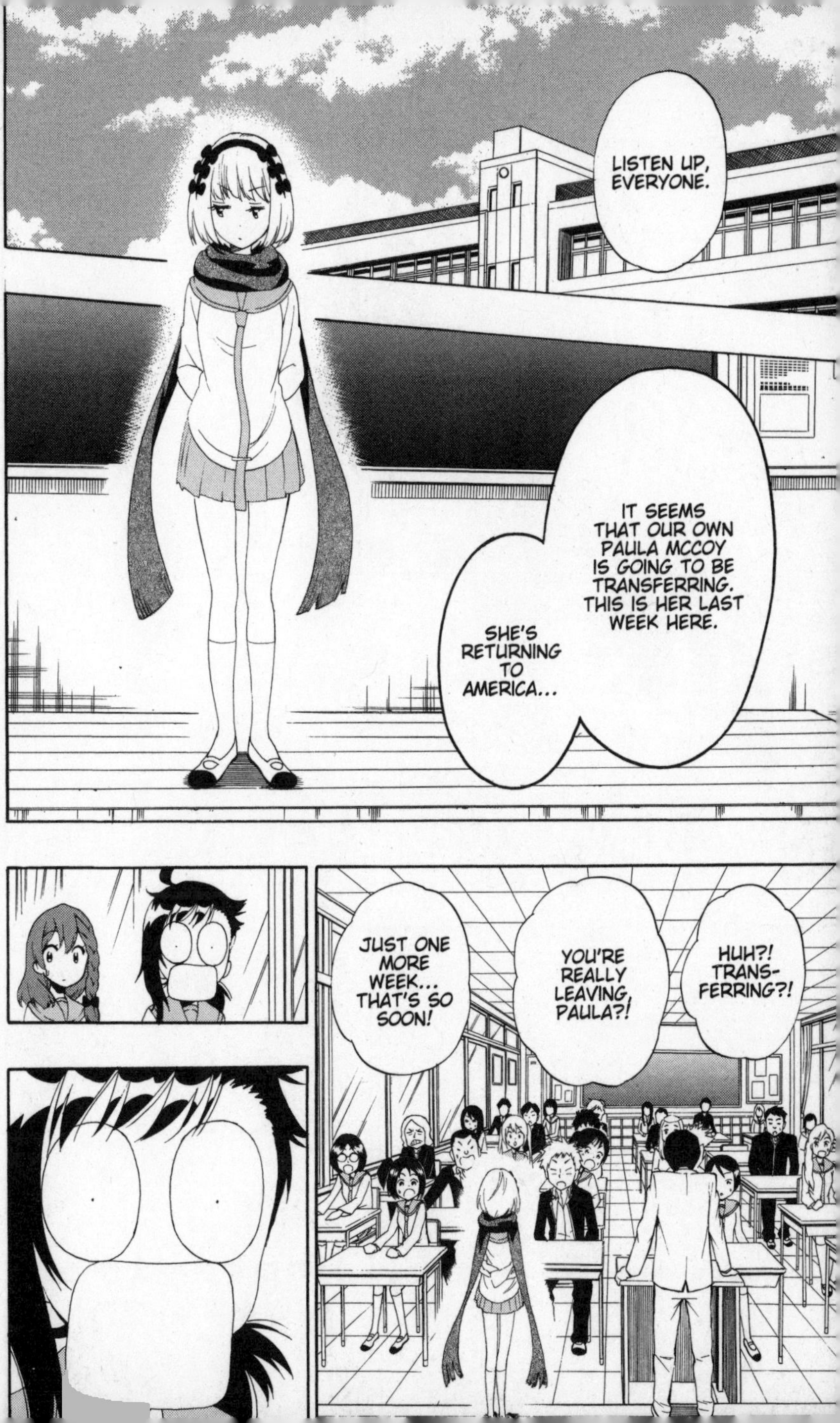
LISTEN UP, EVERYONE.
IT SEEMS THAT OUR OWN PAULA MCCOY IS GOING TO BE TRANSFERRING. THIS IS HER LAST WEEK HERE.
SHE'S RETURNING TO AMERICA...
HUH?! TRANS-FERRING?!
YOU'RE REALLY LEAVING, PAULA?!
JUST ONE MORE WEEK... THAT'S SO SOON!

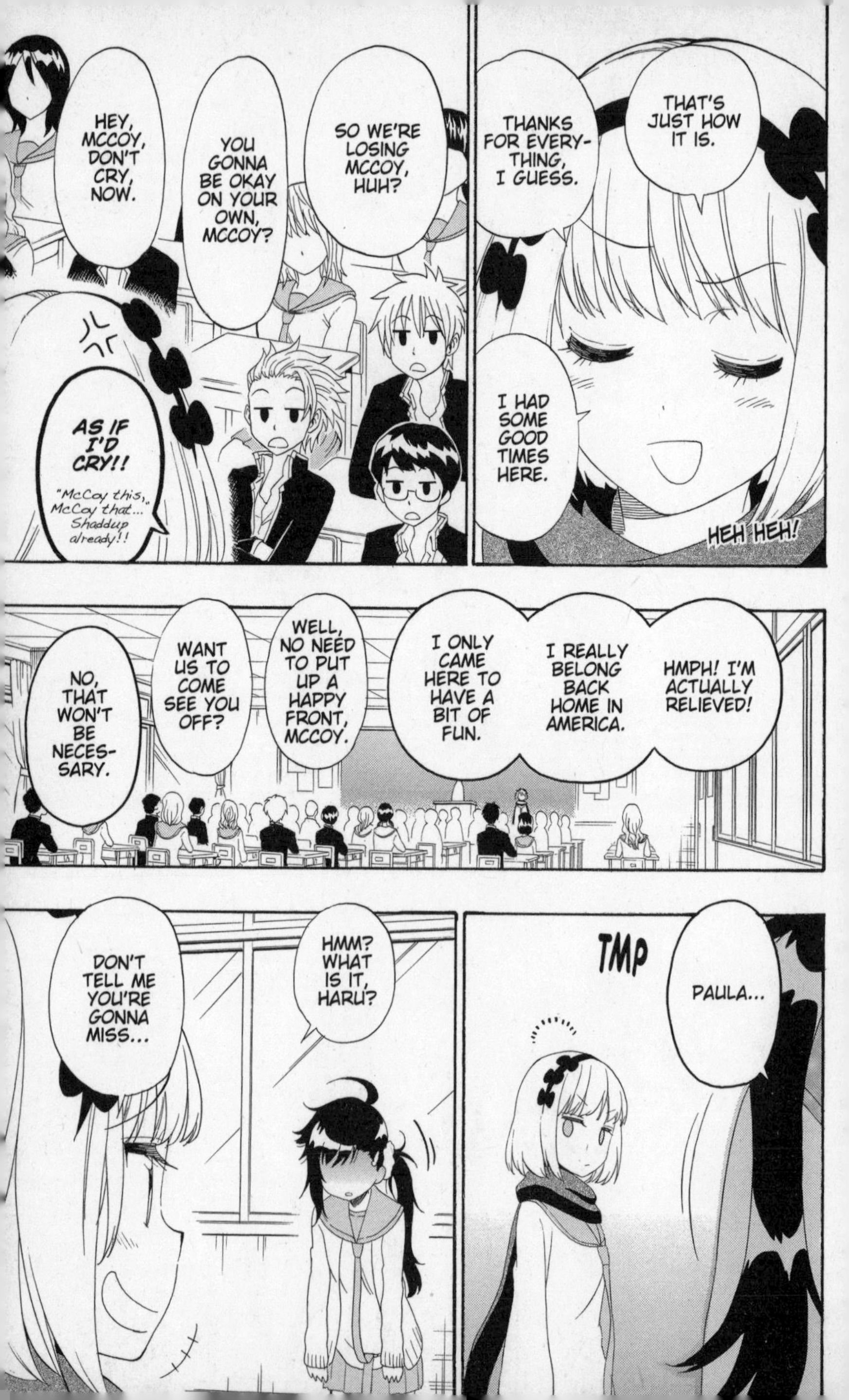
THAT'S JUST HOW IT IS.
THANKS FOR EVERYTHING, I GUESS.
I HAD SOME GOOD TIMES HERE.
HEH HEH!
SO WE'RE LOSING MCCOY, HUH?
YOU GONNA BE OKAY ON YOUR OWN, MCCOY?
HEY, MCCOY, DON'T CRY, NOW.
AS IF I'D CRY!!
"McCoy this, McCoy that..." Shaddup already!!
HMPH! I'M ACTUALLY RELIEVED!
I REALLY BELONG BACK HOME IN AMERICA.
I ONLY CAME HERE TO HAVE A BIT OF FUN.
WELL, NO NEED TO PUT UP A HAPPY FRONT, MCCOY.
WANT US TO COME SEE YOU OFF?
NO, THAT WON'T BE NECESSARY.
PAULA...
TMP
HMM? WHAT IS IT, HARU?
DON'T TELL ME YOU'RE GONNA MISS...

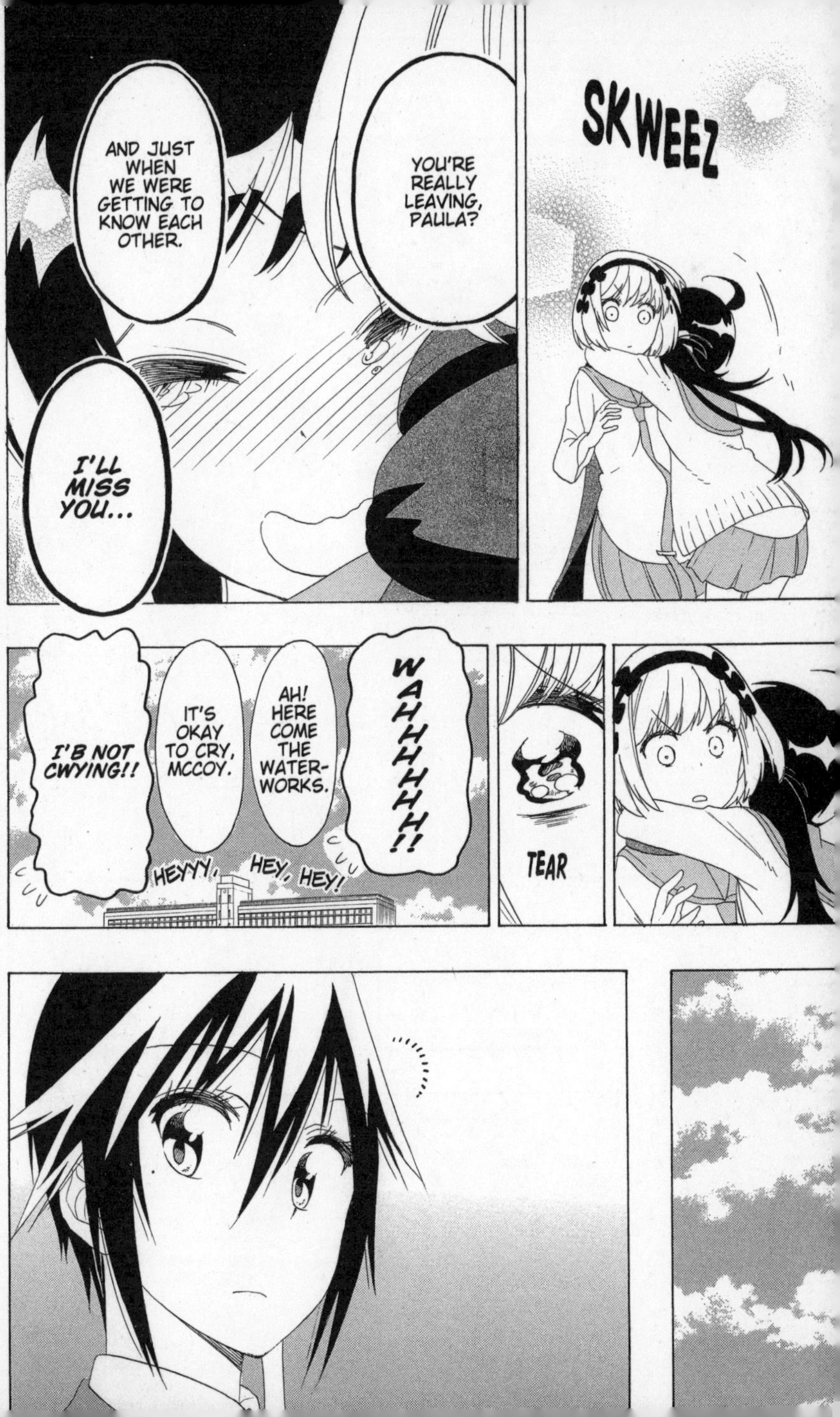
SKWEEZ
YOU'RE REALLY LEAVING, PAULA?
AND JUST WHEN WE WERE GETTING TO KNOW EACH OTHER.
I'LL MISS YOU...
TEAR
WAHHHHHHH!!
AH! HERE COME THE WATER-WORKS.
IT'S OKAY TO CRY, MCCOY.
I'B NOT CWYING!!
HEY, HEY!
HEYYY,

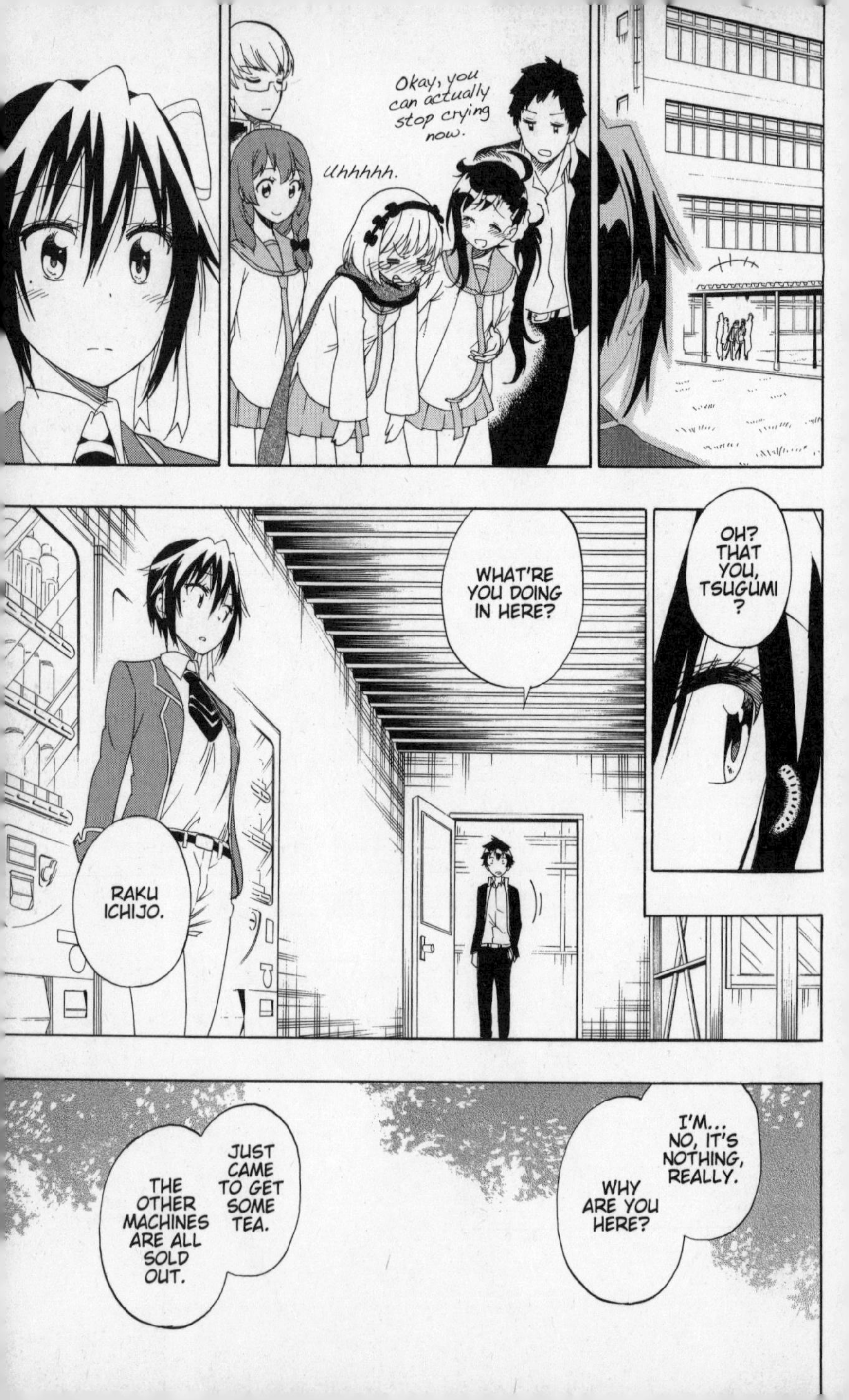
Okay, you can actually stop crying now.
Uhhhhh.
OH? THAT YOU, TSUGUMI?
WHAT'RE YOU DOING IN HERE?
RAKU ICHIJO.
I'M... NO, IT'S NOTHING, REALLY.
WHY ARE YOU HERE?
JUST CAME TO GET SOME TEA.
THE OTHER MACHINES ARE ALL SOLD OUT.

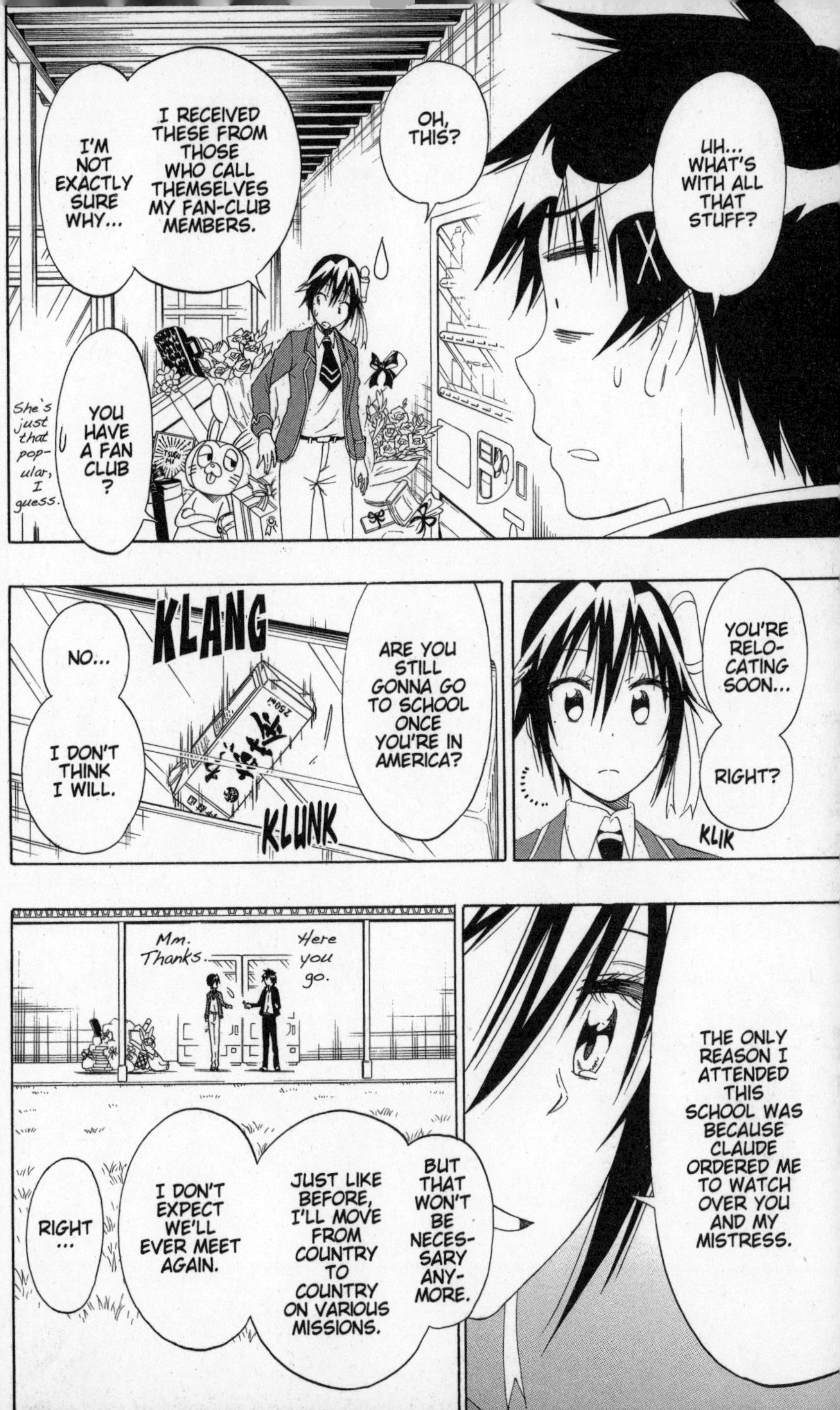
UH... WHAT'S WITH ALL THAT STUFF?
OH, THIS?
I RECEIVED THESE FROM THOSE WHO CALL THEMSELVES MY FAN-CLUB MEMBERS.
I'M NOT EXACTLY SURE WHY...
YOU HAVE A FAN CLUB?
She's just that popular, I guess.
YOU'RE RELOCATING SOON...
RIGHT?
KLIK
...
ARE YOU STILL GONNA GO TO SCHOOL ONCE YOU'RE IN AMERICA?
KLANG
KLUNK
NO...
I DON'T THINK I WILL.
THE ONLY REASON I ATTENDED THIS SCHOOL WAS BECAUSE CLAUDE ORDERED ME TO WATCH OVER YOU AND MY MISTRESS.
Here you go.
Mm. Thanks.
BUT THAT WON'T BE NECESSARY ANYMORE.
JUST LIKE BEFORE, I'LL MOVE FROM COUNTRY TO COUNTRY ON VARIOUS MISSIONS.
I DON'T EXPECT WE'LL EVER MEET AGAIN.
RIGHT...

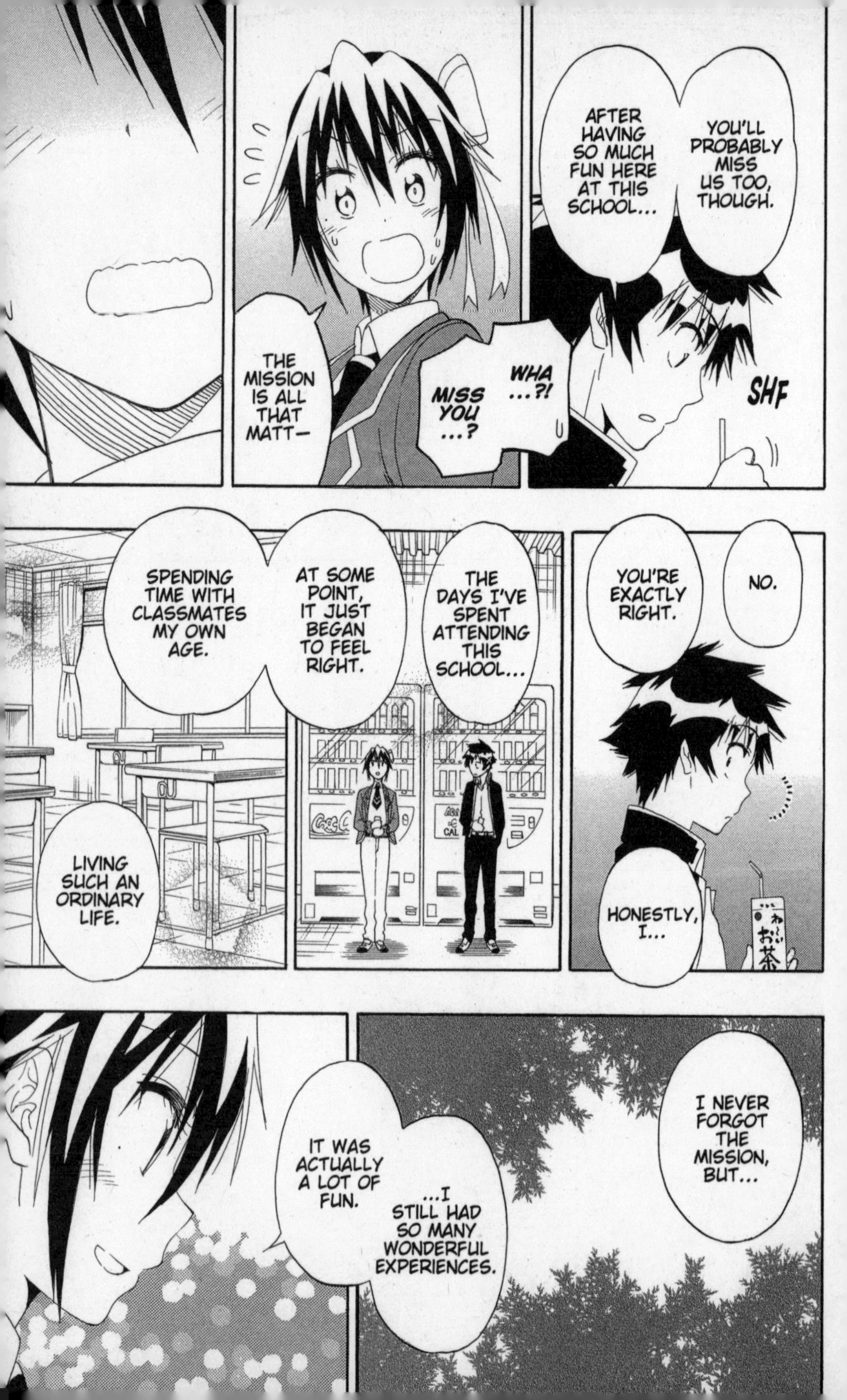
YOU'LL PROBABLY MISS US TOO, THOUGH.
AFTER HAVING SO MUCH FUN HERE AT THIS SCHOOL...
SHF
WHA ...?!
MISS YOU ...?
THE MISSION IS ALL THAT MATT—
NO.
YOU'RE EXACTLY RIGHT.
HONESTLY, I...
THE DAYS I'VE SPENT ATTENDING THIS SCHOOL...
AT SOME POINT, IT JUST BEGAN TO FEEL RIGHT.
SPENDING TIME WITH CLASSMATES MY OWN AGE.
LIVING SUCH AN ORDINARY LIFE.
I NEVER FORGOT THE MISSION, BUT...
...I STILL HAD SO MANY WONDERFUL EXPERIENCES.
IT WAS ACTUALLY A LOT OF FUN.

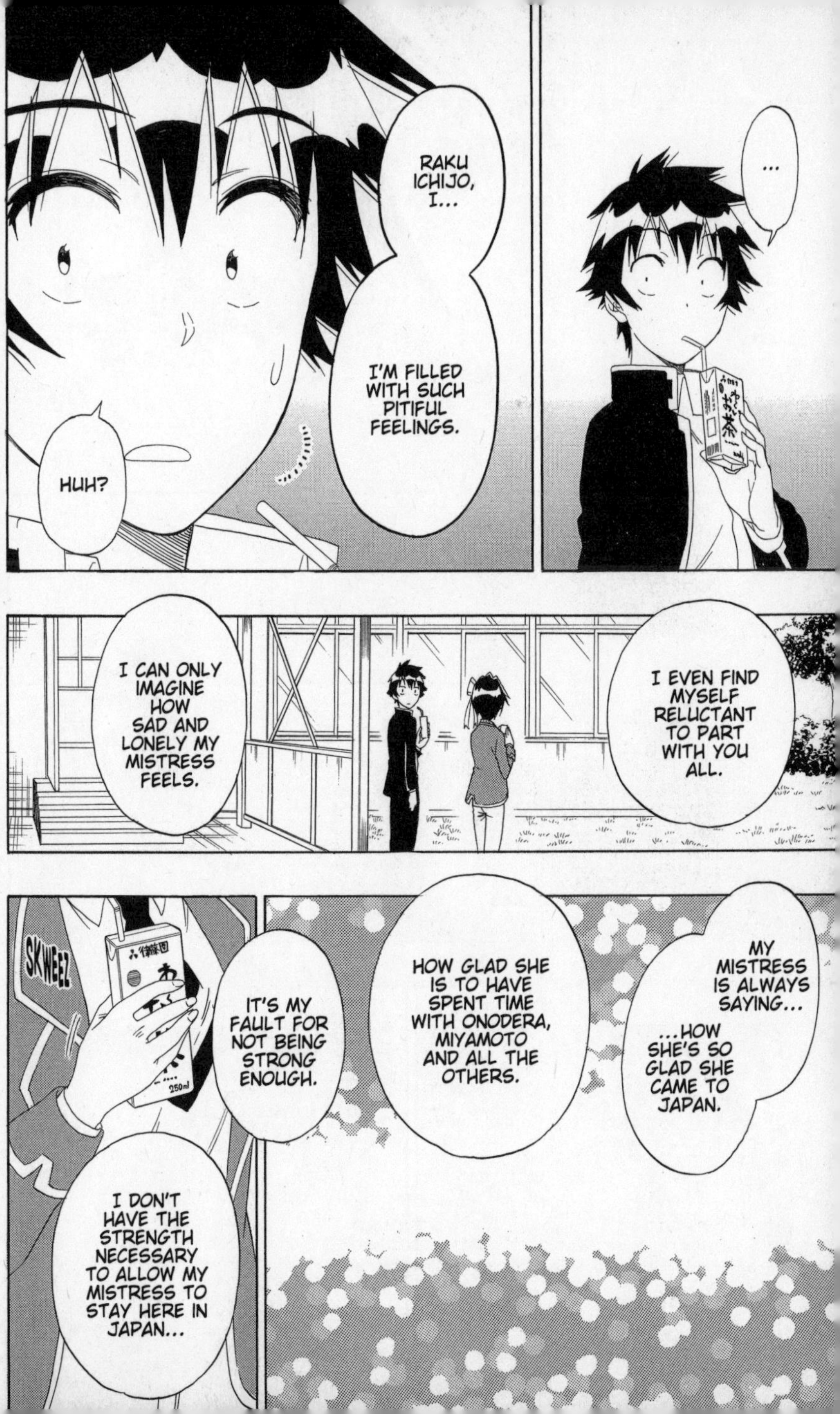
...
RAKU ICHIJO, I...
I'M FILLED WITH SUCH PITIFUL FEELINGS.
HUH?
I EVEN FIND MYSELF RELUCTANT TO PART WITH YOU ALL.
I CAN ONLY IMAGINE HOW SAD AND LONELY MY MISTRESS FEELS.
MY MISTRESS IS ALWAYS SAYING...
...HOW SHE'S SO GLAD SHE CAME TO JAPAN.
HOW GLAD SHE IS TO HAVE SPENT TIME WITH ONODERA, MIYAMOTO AND ALL THE OTHERS.
SKWEEZ
IT'S MY FAULT FOR NOT BEING STRONG ENOUGH.
I DON'T HAVE THE STRENGTH NECESSARY TO ALLOW MY MISTRESS TO STAY HERE IN JAPAN...

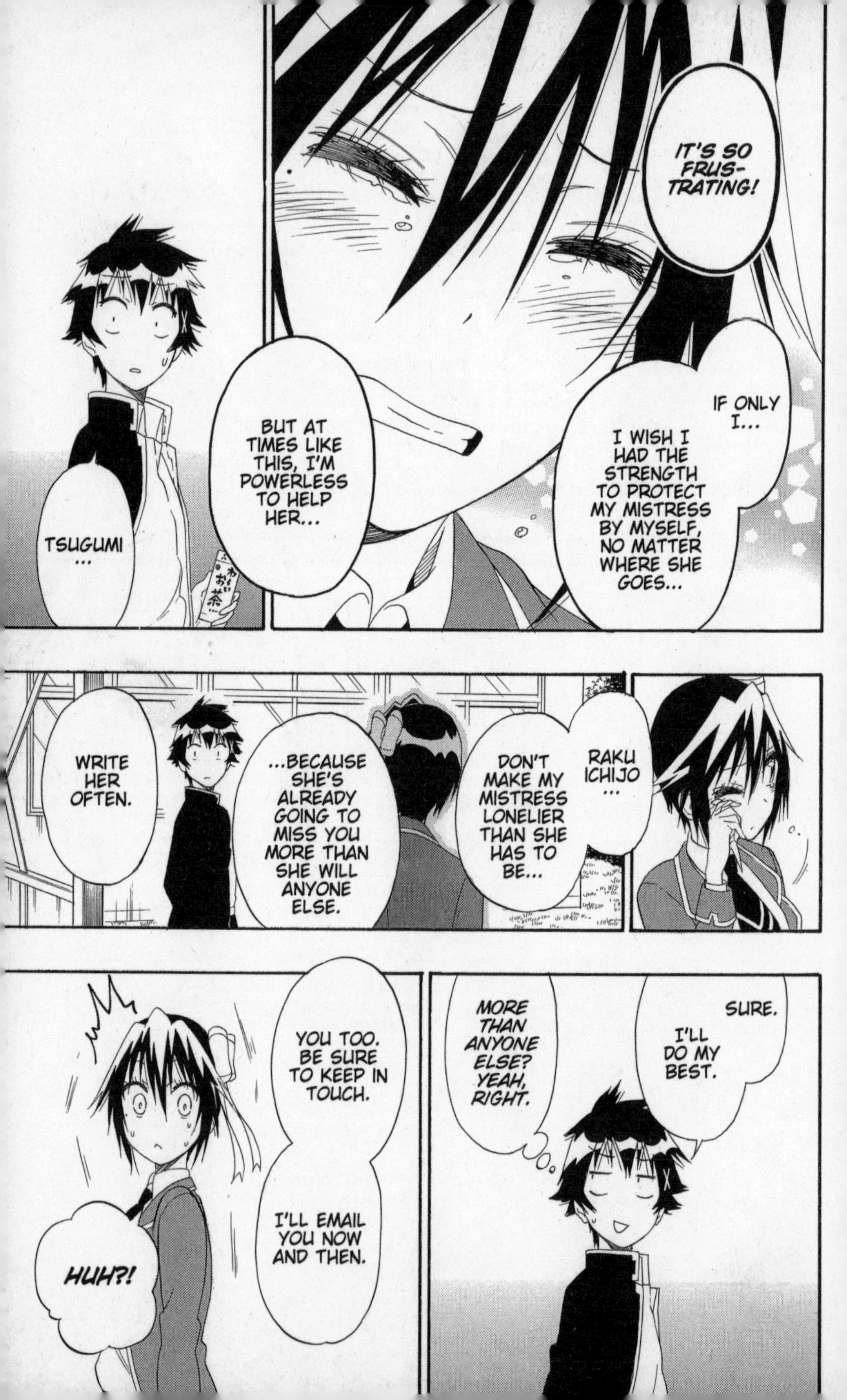
IT'S SO FRUS-TRATING!
IF ONLY I...
I WISH I HAD THE STRENGTH TO PROTECT MY MISTRESS BY MYSELF, NO MATTER WHERE SHE GOES...
BUT AT TIMES LIKE THIS, I'M POWERLESS TO HELP HER...
TSUGUMI...
RAKU ICHIJO...
DON'T MAKE MY MISTRESS LONELIER THAN SHE HAS TO BE...
...BECAUSE SHE'S ALREADY GOING TO MISS YOU MORE THAN SHE WILL ANYONE ELSE.
WRITE HER OFTEN.
SURE.
I'LL DO MY BEST.
MORE THAN ANYONE ELSE? YEAH, RIGHT.
YOU TOO. BE SURE TO KEEP IN TOUCH.
I'LL EMAIL YOU NOW AND THEN.
HUH?!

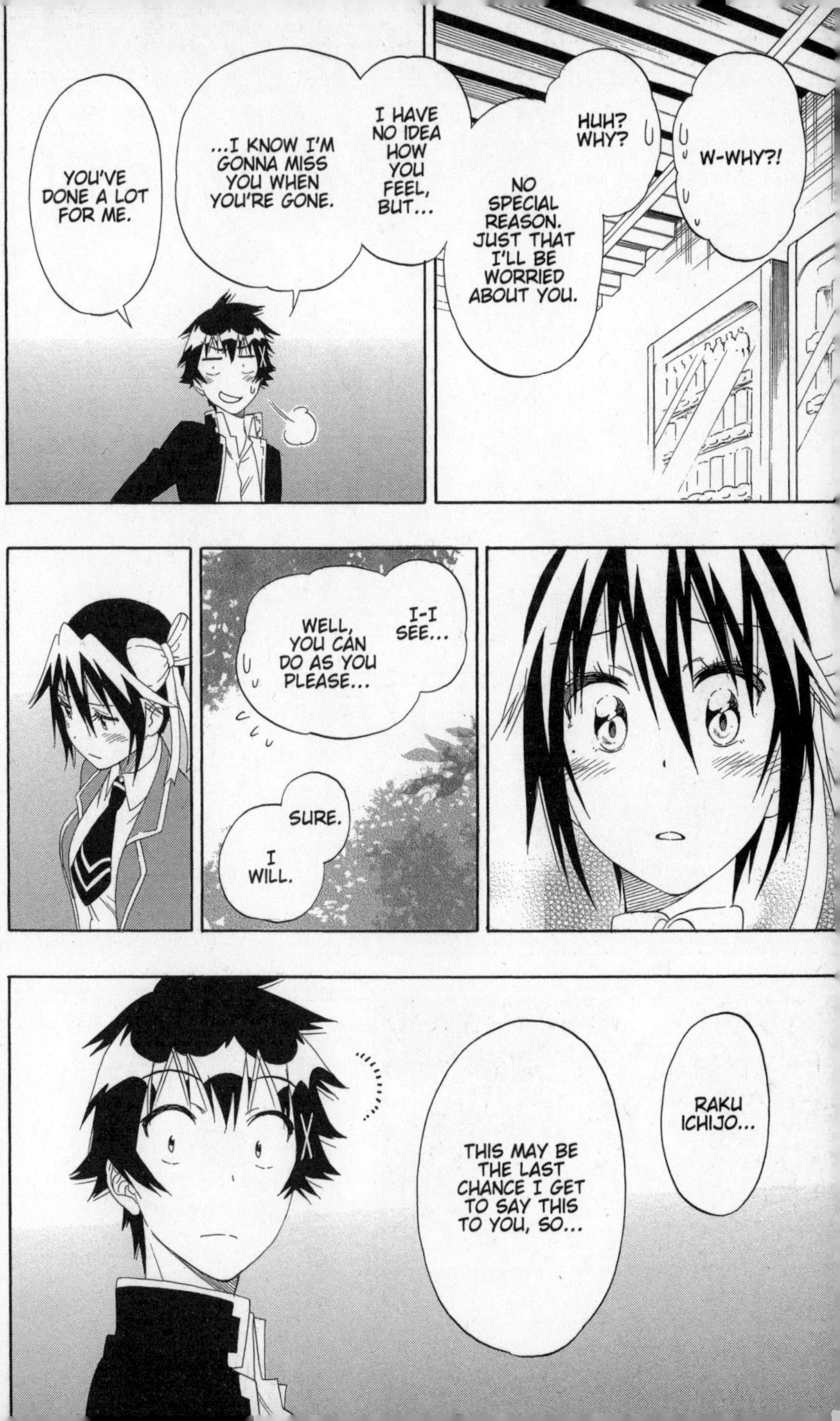
W-WHY?!
HUH? WHY?
NO SPECIAL REASON. JUST THAT I'LL BE WORRIED ABOUT YOU.
I HAVE NO IDEA HOW YOU FEEL, BUT...
...I KNOW I'M GONNA MISS YOU WHEN YOU'RE GONE.
YOU'VE DONE A LOT FOR ME.
I-I SEE...
WELL, YOU CAN DO AS YOU PLEASE...
SURE.
I WILL.
RAKU ICHIJO...
THIS MAY BE THE LAST CHANCE I GET TO SAY THIS TO YOU, SO...

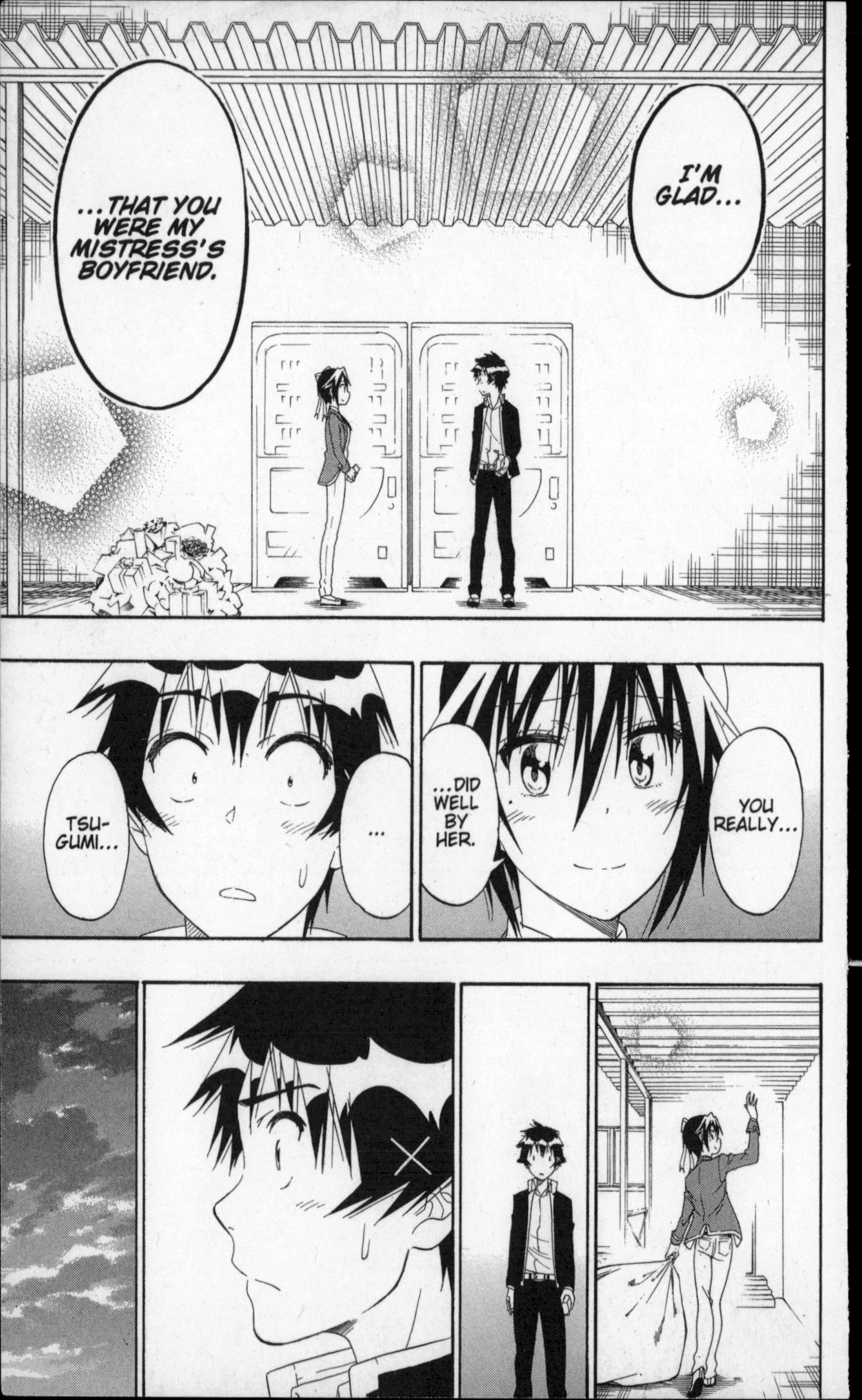
I'M GLAD...
...THAT YOU WERE MY MISTRESS'S BOYFRIEND.
YOU REALLY...
...DID WELL BY HER.
...
TSU-GUMI...

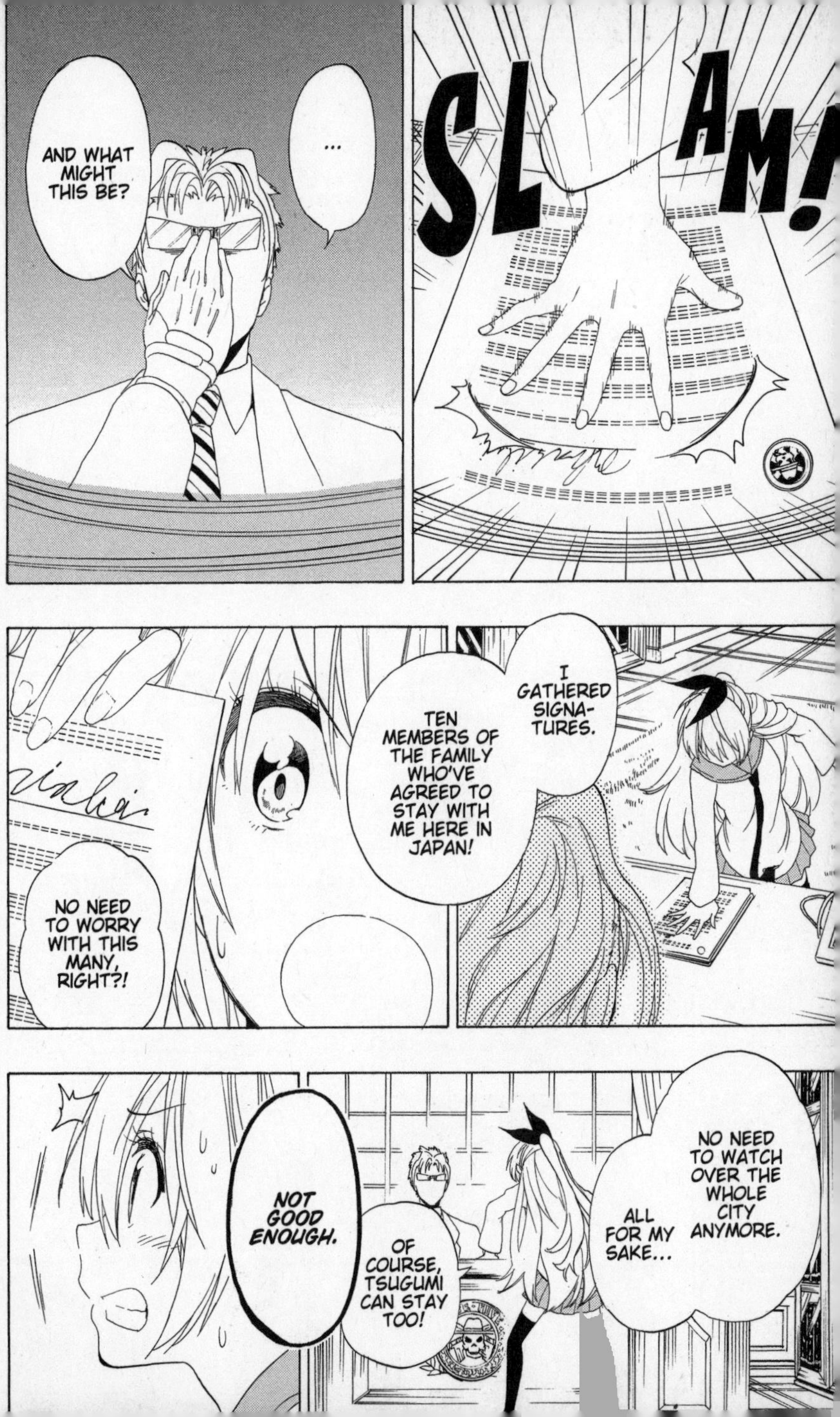
SLAM!
...
AND WHAT MIGHT THIS BE?
I GATHERED SIGNATURES.
TEN MEMBERS OF THE FAMILY WHO'VE AGREED TO STAY WITH ME HERE IN JAPAN!
NO NEED TO WORRY WITH THIS MANY, RIGHT?!
NO NEED TO WATCH OVER THE WHOLE CITY ANYMORE.
ALL FOR MY SAKE...
OF COURSE, TSUGUMI CAN STAY TOO!
NOT GOOD ENOUGH.

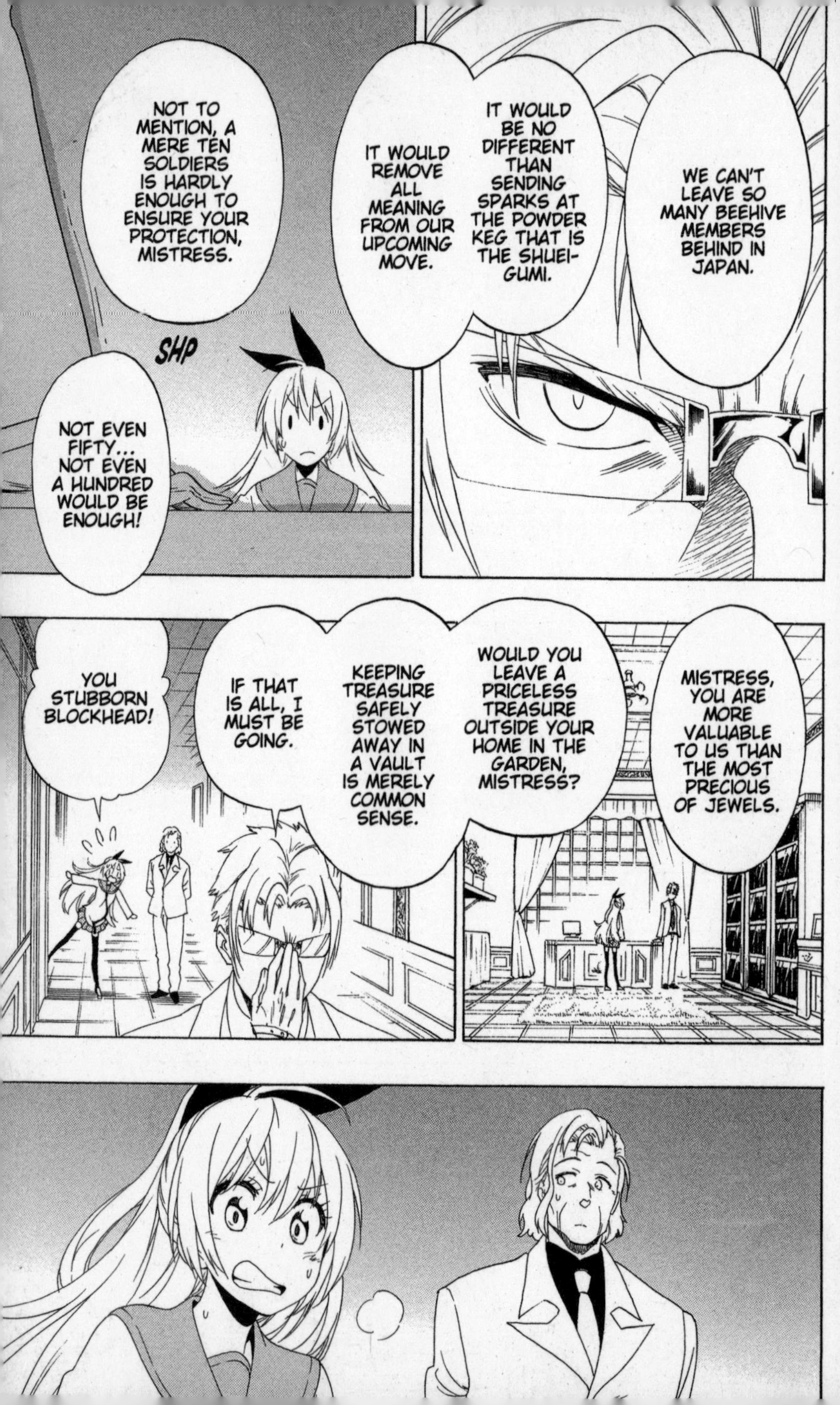
WE CAN'T LEAVE SO MANY BEEHIVE MEMBERS BEHIND IN JAPAN.
IT WOULD BE NO DIFFERENT THAN SENDING SPARKS AT THE POWDER KEG THAT IS THE SHUEI-GUMI.
IT WOULD REMOVE ALL MEANING FROM OUR UPCOMING MOVE.
NOT TO MENTION, A MERE TEN SOLDIERS IS HARDLY ENOUGH TO ENSURE YOUR PROTECTION, MISTRESS.
SHP
NOT EVEN FIFTY... NOT EVEN A HUNDRED WOULD BE ENOUGH!
MISTRESS, YOU ARE MORE VALUABLE TO US THAN THE MOST PRECIOUS OF JEWELS.
WOULD YOU LEAVE A PRICELESS TREASURE OUTSIDE YOUR HOME IN THE GARDEN, MISTRESS?
KEEPING TREASURE SAFELY STOWED AWAY IN A VAULT IS MERELY COMMON SENSE.
IF THAT IS ALL, I MUST BE GOING.
YOU STUBBORN BLOCKHEAD!

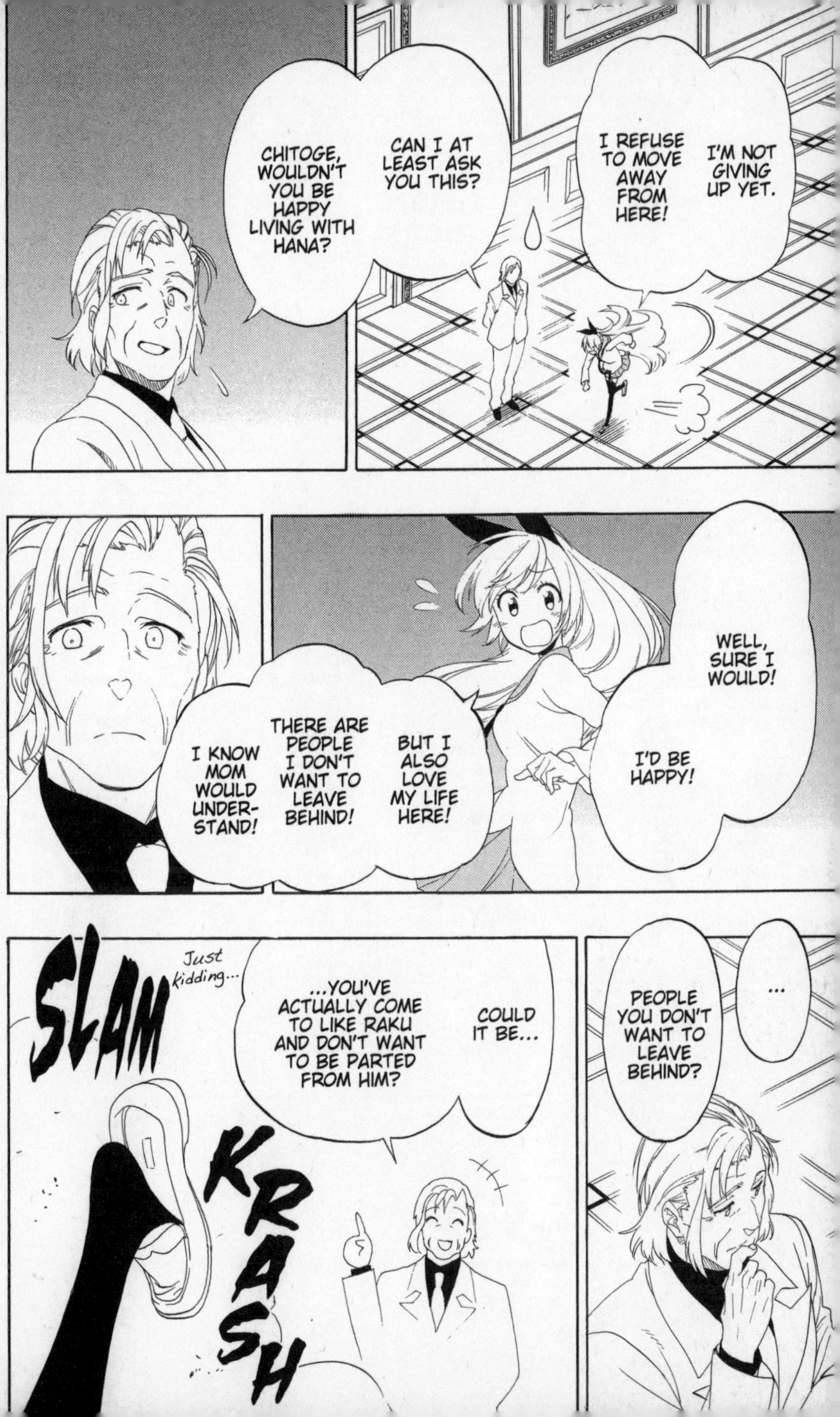
I'M NOT GIVING UP YET.
I REFUSE TO MOVE AWAY FROM HERE!
CAN I AT LEAST ASK YOU THIS?
CHITOGE, WOULDN'T YOU BE HAPPY LIVING WITH HANA?
WELL, SURE I WOULD!
I'D BE HAPPY!
BUT I ALSO LOVE MY LIFE HERE!
THERE ARE PEOPLE I DON'T WANT TO LEAVE BEHIND!
I KNOW MOM WOULD UNDER-STAND!
...
PEOPLE YOU DON'T WANT TO LEAVE BEHIND?
COULD IT BE...
...YOU'VE ACTUALLY COME TO LIKE RAKU AND DON'T WANT TO BE PARTED FROM HIM?
Just kidding...
SLAM
KRASH

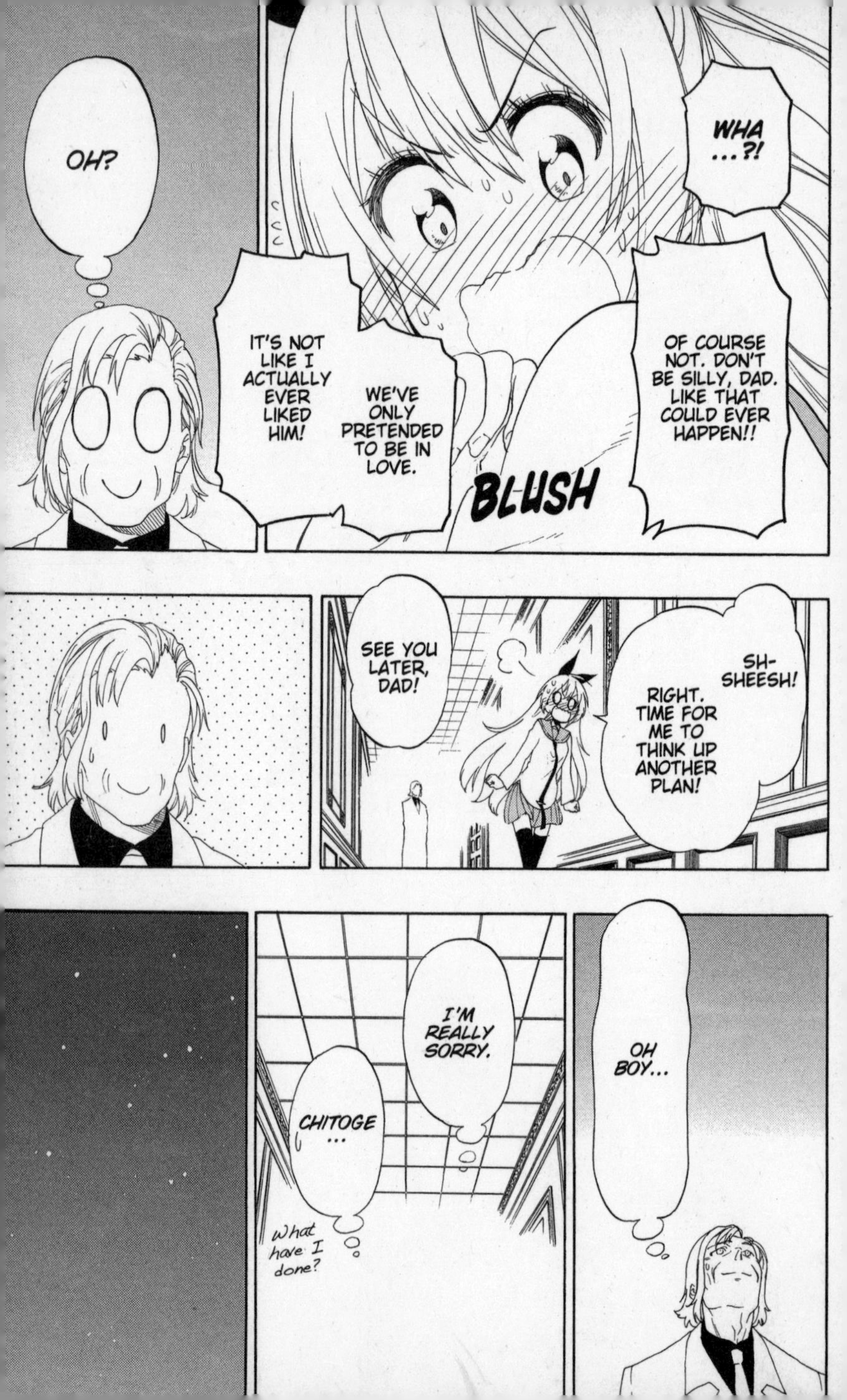
WHA...?!
OF COURSE NOT. DON'T BE SILLY, DAD. LIKE THAT COULD EVER HAPPEN!!
BLUSH
WE'VE ONLY PRETENDED TO BE IN LOVE.
IT'S NOT LIKE I ACTUALLY EVER LIKED HIM!
OH?
SH-SHEESH!
RIGHT. TIME FOR ME TO THINK UP ANOTHER PLAN!
SEE YOU LATER, DAD!
OH BOY...
I'M REALLY SORRY.
CHITOGE...
What have I done?

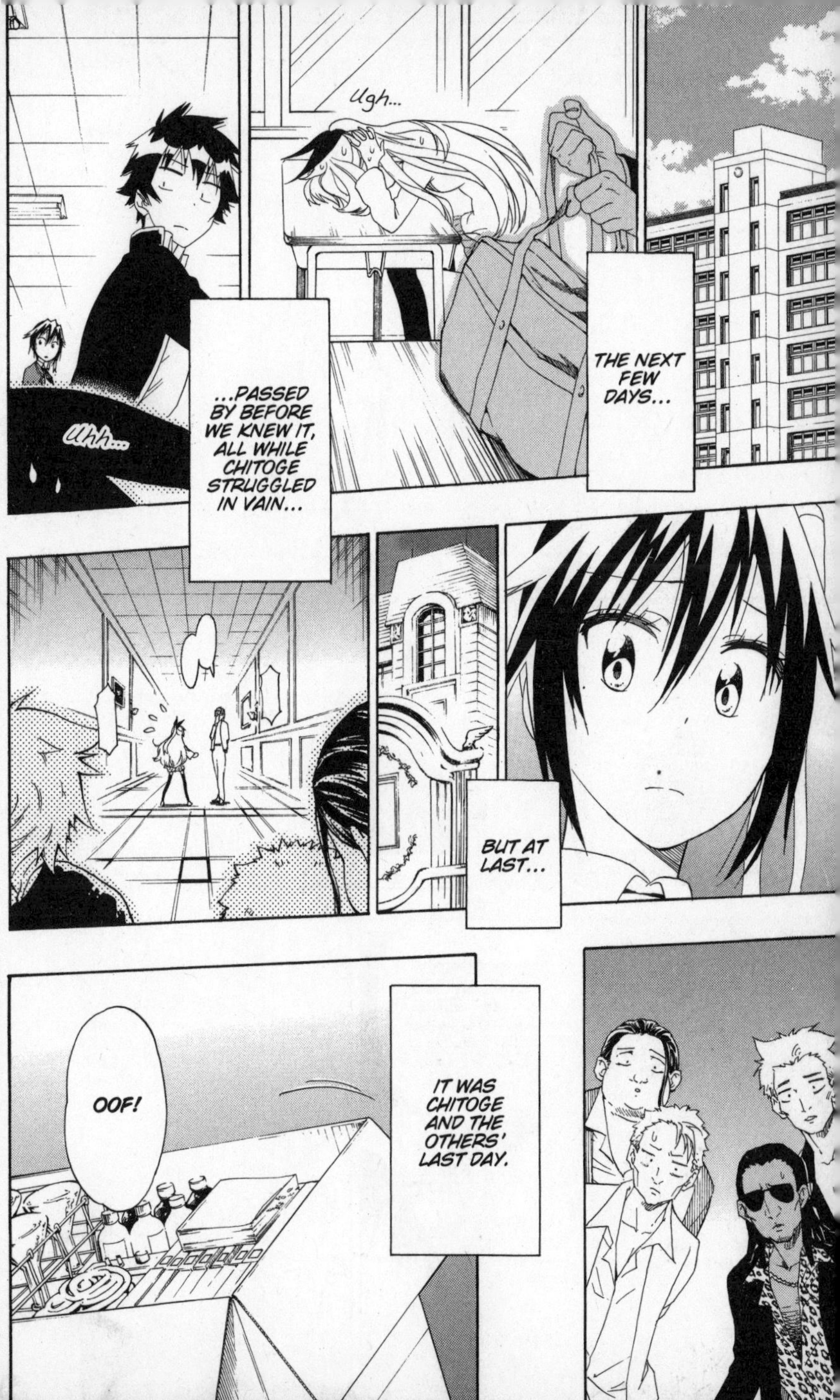
THE NEXT FEW DAYS...
Ugh...
...PASSED BY BEFORE WE KNEW IT, ALL WHILE CHITOGE STRUGGLED IN VAIN...
Uhh...
BUT AT LAST...
IT WAS CHITOGE AND THE OTHERS' LAST DAY.
OOF!

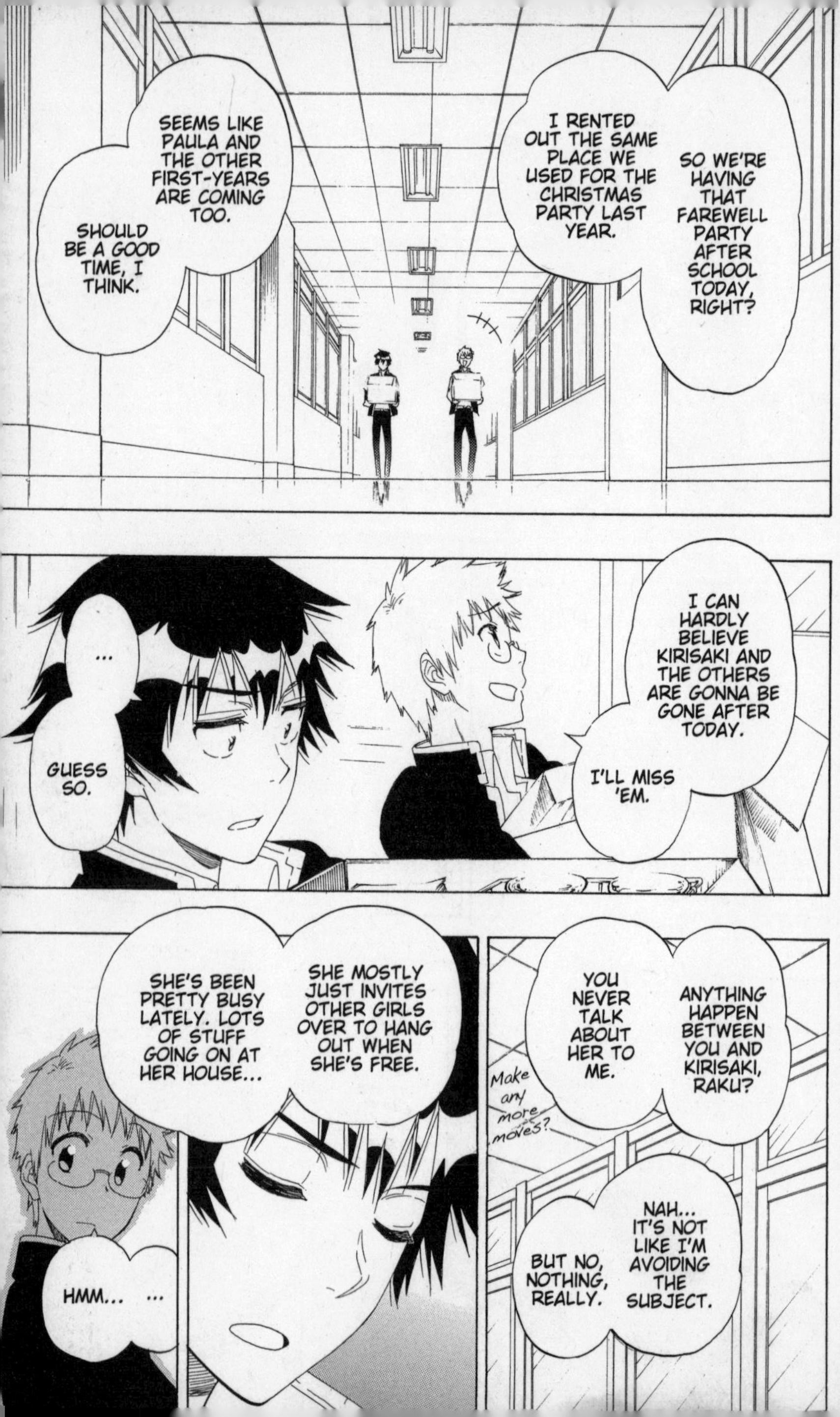
SO WE'RE HAVING THAT FAREWELL PARTY AFTER SCHOOL TODAY, RIGHT?
I RENTED OUT THE SAME PLACE WE USED FOR THE CHRISTMAS PARTY LAST YEAR.
SEEMS LIKE PAULA AND THE OTHER FIRST-YEARS ARE COMING TOO.
SHOULD BE A GOOD TIME, I THINK.
I CAN HARDLY BELIEVE KIRISAKI AND THE OTHERS ARE GONNA BE GONE AFTER TODAY.
I'LL MISS 'EM.
...
GUESS SO.
ANYTHING HAPPEN BETWEEN YOU AND KIRISAKI, RAKU?
YOU NEVER TALK ABOUT HER TO ME.
Make any more moves?
NAH... IT'S NOT LIKE I'M AVOIDING THE SUBJECT.
BUT NO, NOTHING, REALLY.
SHE MOSTLY JUST INVITES OTHER GIRLS OVER TO HANG OUT WHEN SHE'S FREE.
SHE'S BEEN PRETTY BUSY LATELY. LOTS OF STUFF GOING ON AT HER HOUSE...
HMM... ...

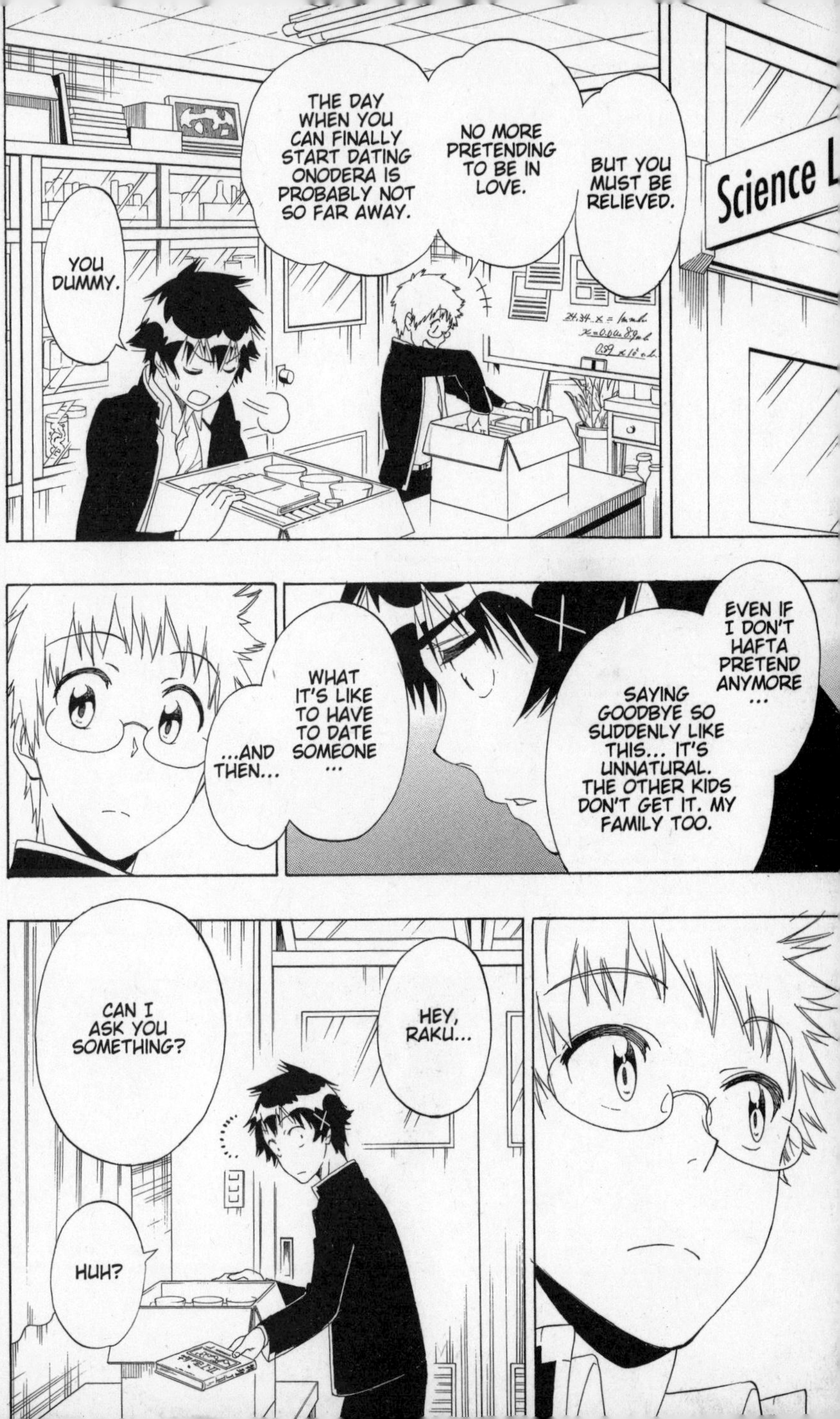
Science L
BUT YOU MUST BE RELIEVED.
NO MORE PRETENDING TO BE IN LOVE.
THE DAY WHEN YOU CAN FINALLY START DATING ONODERA IS PROBABLY NOT SO FAR AWAY.
YOU DUMMY.
EVEN IF I DON'T HAFTA PRETEND ANYMORE...
SAYING GOODBYE SO SUDDENLY LIKE THIS... IT'S UNNATURAL. THE OTHER KIDS DON'T GET IT. MY FAMILY TOO.
WHAT IT'S LIKE TO HAVE TO DATE SOMEONE...
...AND THEN...
HEY, RAKU...
CAN I ASK YOU SOMETHING?
HUH?

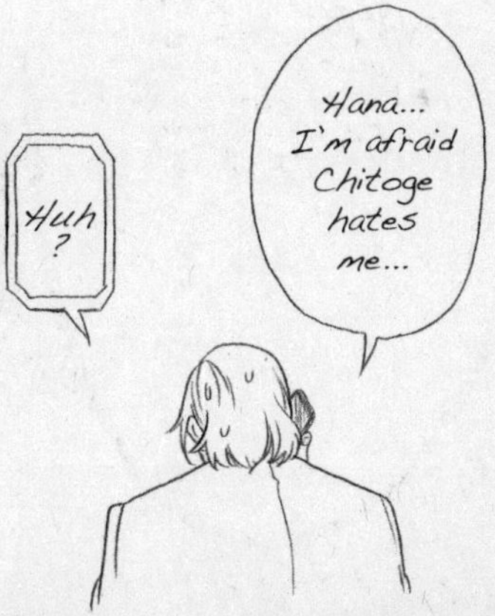
Hana... I'm afraid Chitoge hates me...
Huh?

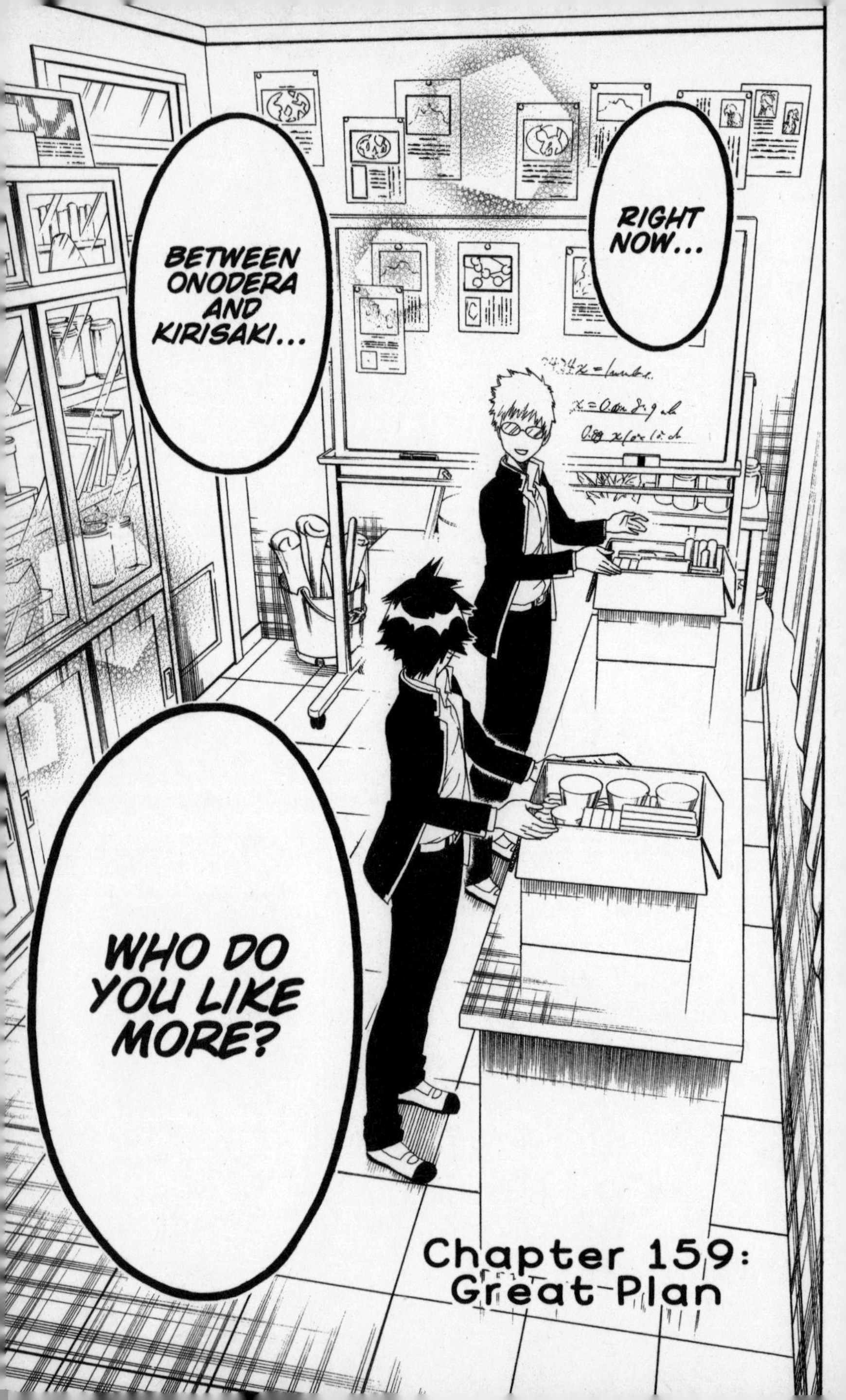
RIGHT NOW...
BETWEEN ONODERA AND KIRISAKI...
WHO DO YOU LIKE MORE?
Chapter 159: Great Plan

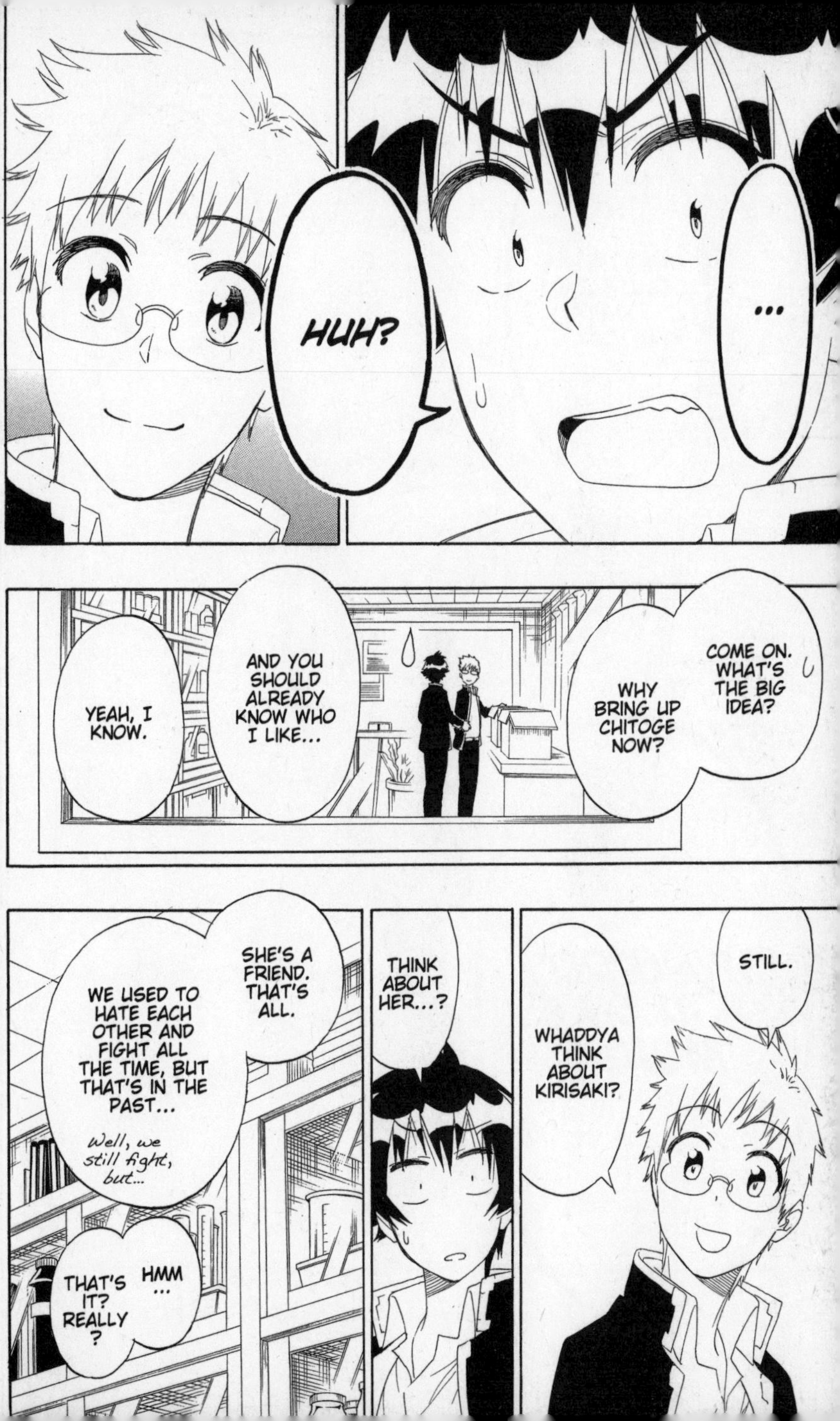
...
HUH?
COME ON. WHAT'S THE BIG IDEA?
WHY BRING UP CHITOGE NOW?
AND YOU SHOULD ALREADY KNOW WHO I LIKE...
YEAH, I KNOW.
STILL.
WHADDYA THINK ABOUT KIRISAKI?
THINK ABOUT HER...?
SHE'S A FRIEND. THAT'S ALL.
WE USED TO HATE EACH OTHER AND FIGHT ALL THE TIME, BUT THAT'S IN THE PAST...
Well, we still fight, but...
HMM...
THAT'S IT? REALLY?

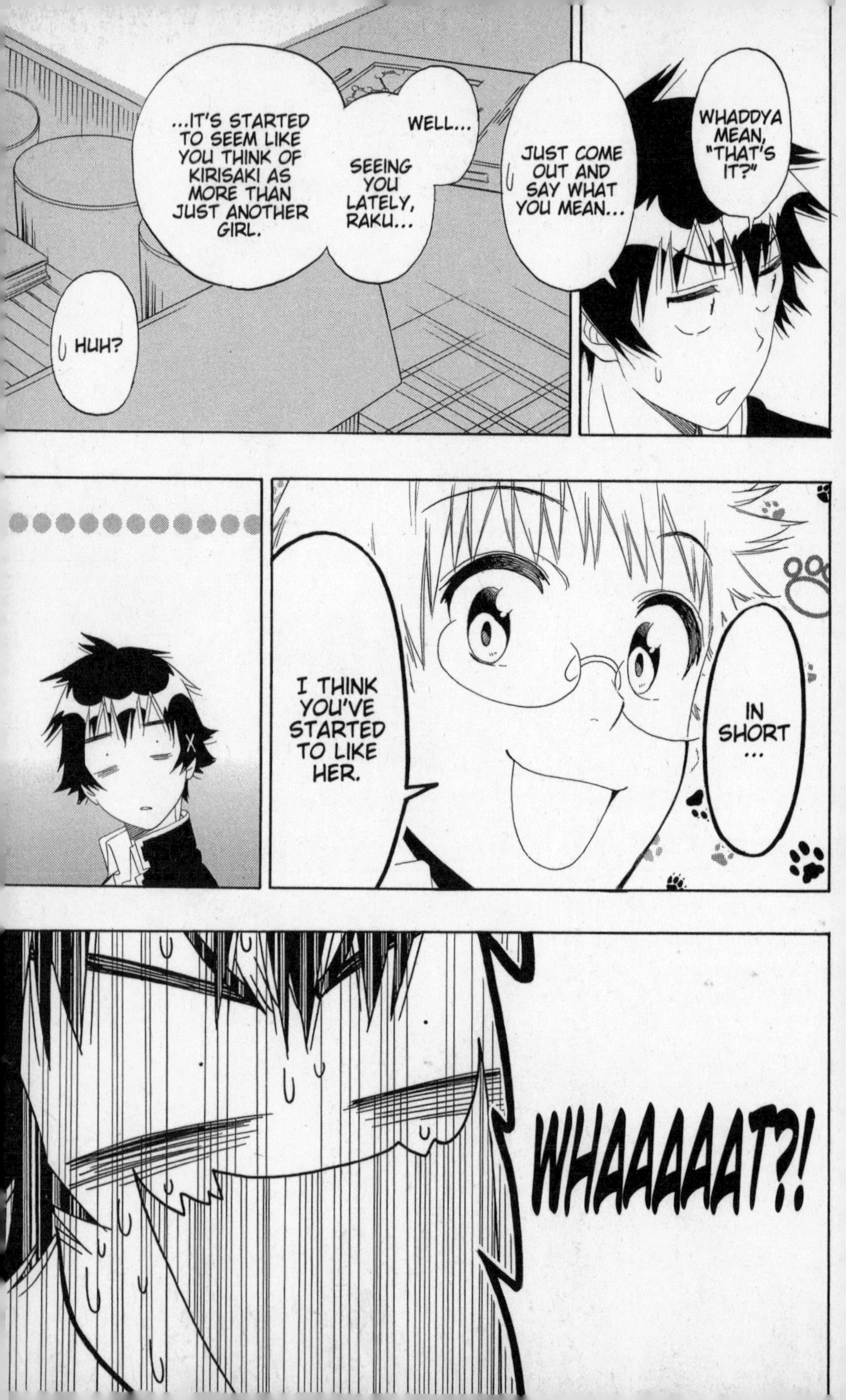
WHADDYA MEAN, "THAT'S IT?"
JUST COME OUT AND SAY WHAT YOU MEAN...
WELL...
SEEING YOU LATELY, RAKU...
...IT'S STARTED TO SEEM LIKE YOU THINK OF KIRISAKI AS MORE THAN JUST ANOTHER GIRL.
HUH?
IN SHORT...
I THINK YOU'VE STARTED TO LIKE HER.
WHAAAAAT?!

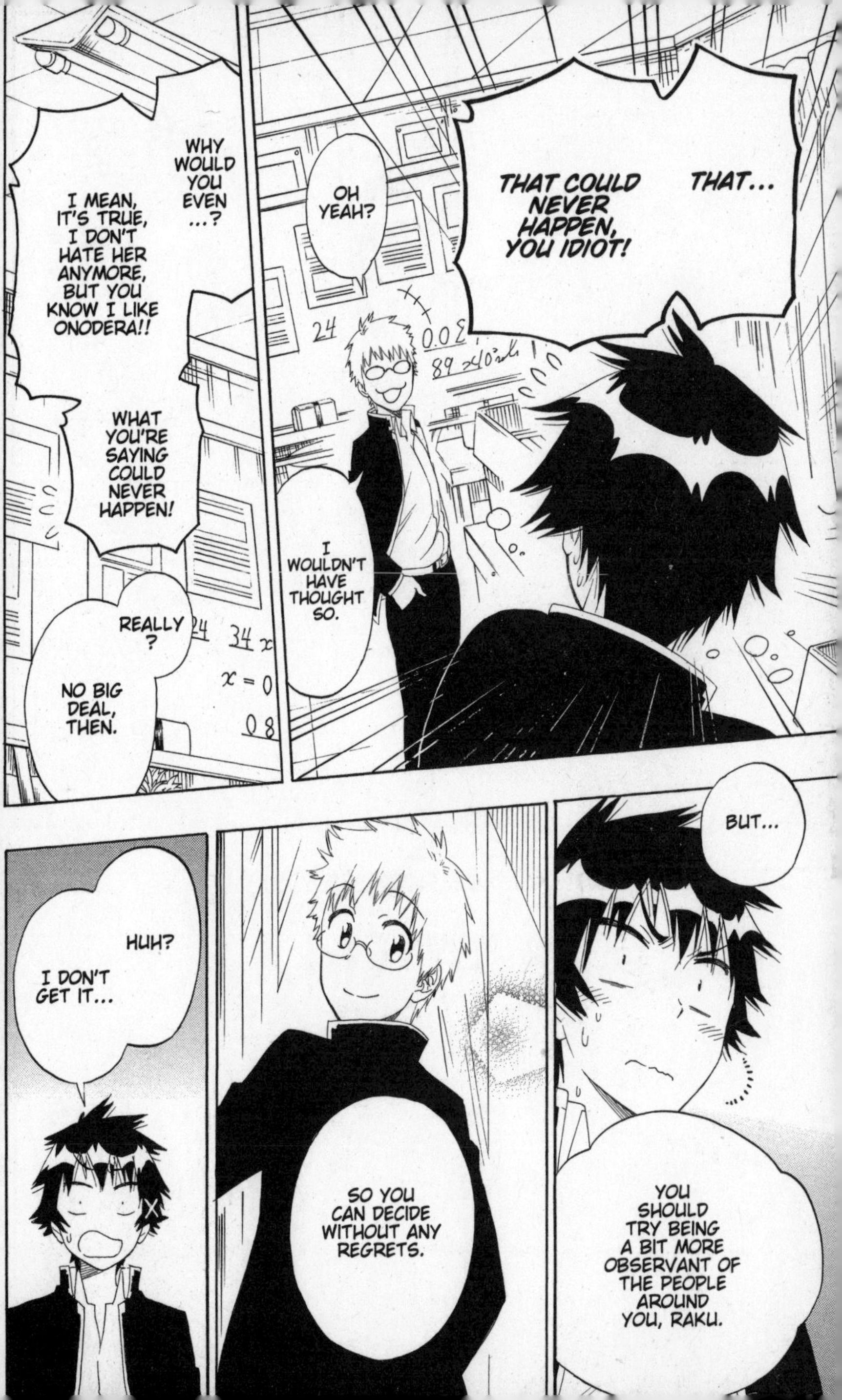
THAT...
THAT COULD NEVER HAPPEN, YOU IDIOT!
OH YEAH?
I WOULDN'T HAVE THOUGHT SO.
WHY WOULD YOU EVEN ...?
I MEAN, IT'S TRUE, I DON'T HATE HER ANYMORE, BUT YOU KNOW I LIKE ONODERA!!
WHAT YOU'RE SAYING COULD NEVER HAPPEN!
REALLY?
NO BIG DEAL, THEN.
BUT...
YOU SHOULD TRY BEING A BIT MORE OBSERVANT OF THE PEOPLE AROUND YOU, RAKU.
SO YOU CAN DECIDE WITHOUT ANY REGRETS.
HUH?
I DON'T GET IT...

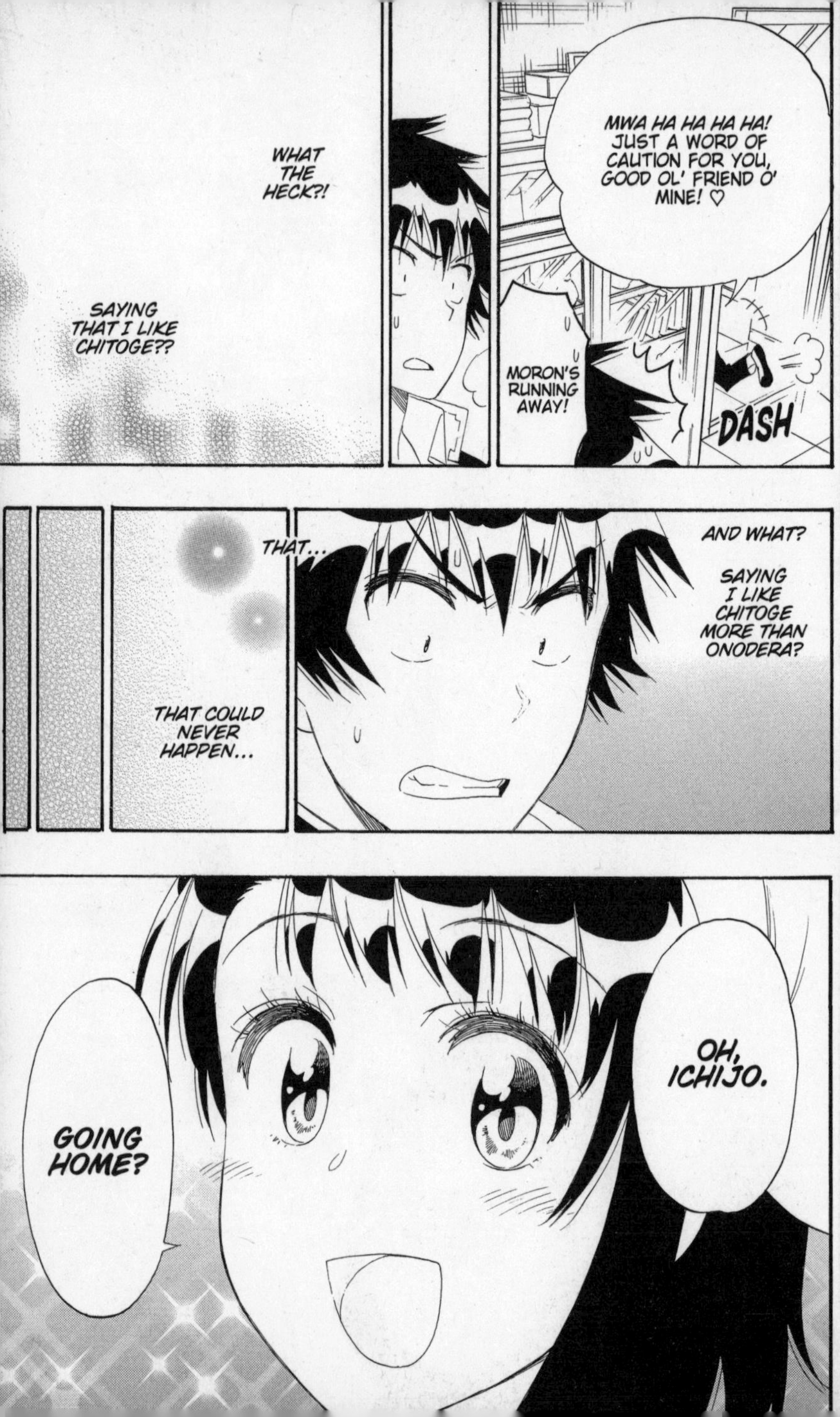
MWA HA HA HA HA! JUST A WORD OF CAUTION FOR YOU, GOOD OL' FRIEND O' MINE! ♡
MORON'S RUNNING AWAY!
DASH
WHAT THE HECK?!
SAYING THAT I LIKE CHITOGE??
AND WHAT?
SAYING I LIKE CHITOGE MORE THAN ONODERA?
THAT...
THAT COULD NEVER HAPPEN...
OH, ICHIJO.
GOING HOME?

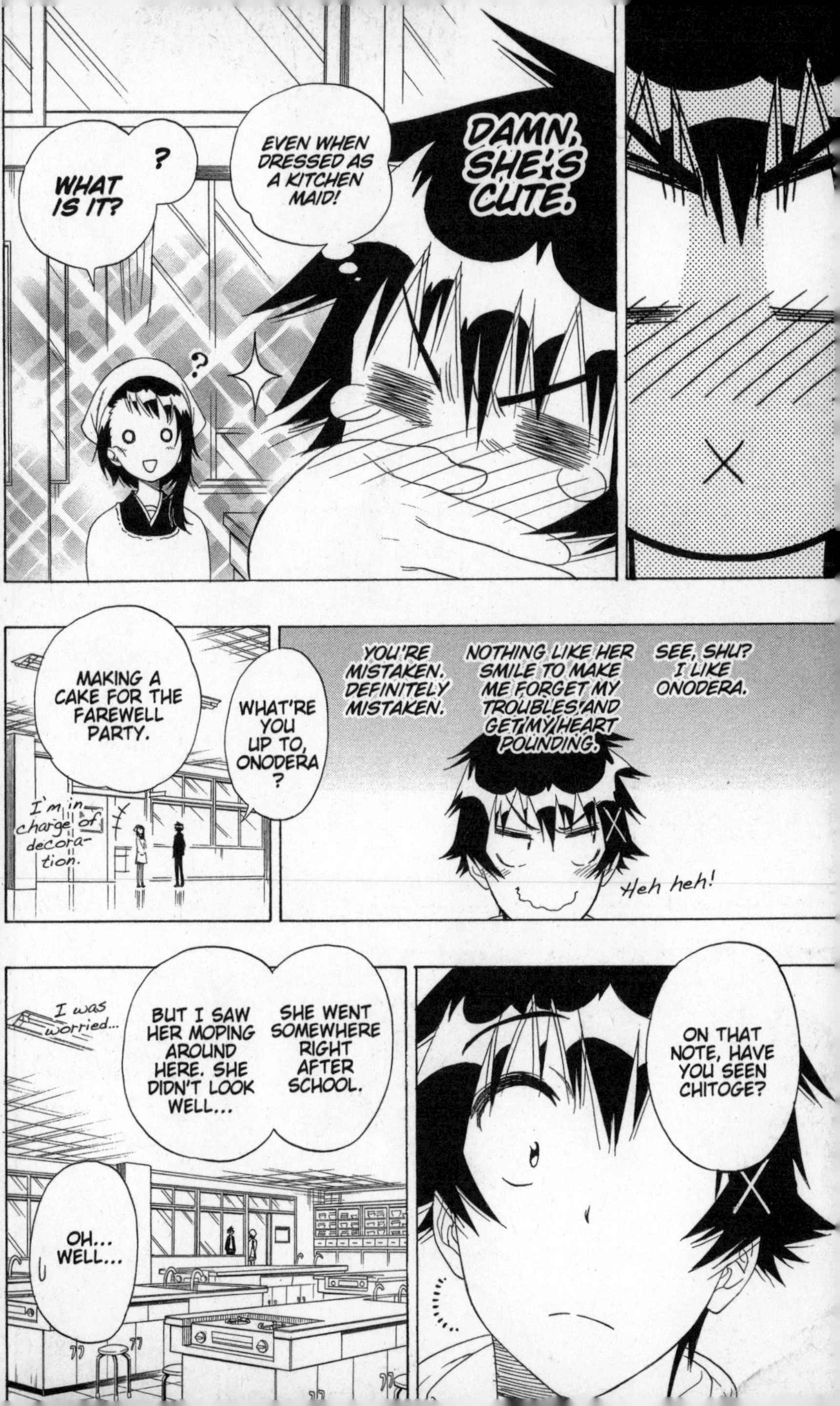
DAMN, SHE'S CUTE.
EVEN WHEN DRESSED AS A KITCHEN MAID!
?
WHAT IS IT?
?
SEE, SHU? I LIKE ONODERA.
NOTHING LIKE HER SMILE TO MAKE ME FORGET MY TROUBLES AND GET MY HEART POUNDING.
YOU'RE MISTAKEN. DEFINITELY MISTAKEN.
Heh heh!
WHAT'RE YOU UP TO, ONODERA?
MAKING A CAKE FOR THE FAREWELL PARTY.
I'm in charge of decoration.
ON THAT NOTE, HAVE YOU SEEN CHITOGE?
SHE WENT SOMEWHERE RIGHT AFTER SCHOOL.
BUT I SAW HER MOPING AROUND HERE. SHE DIDN'T LOOK WELL...
I was worried...
OH... WELL...

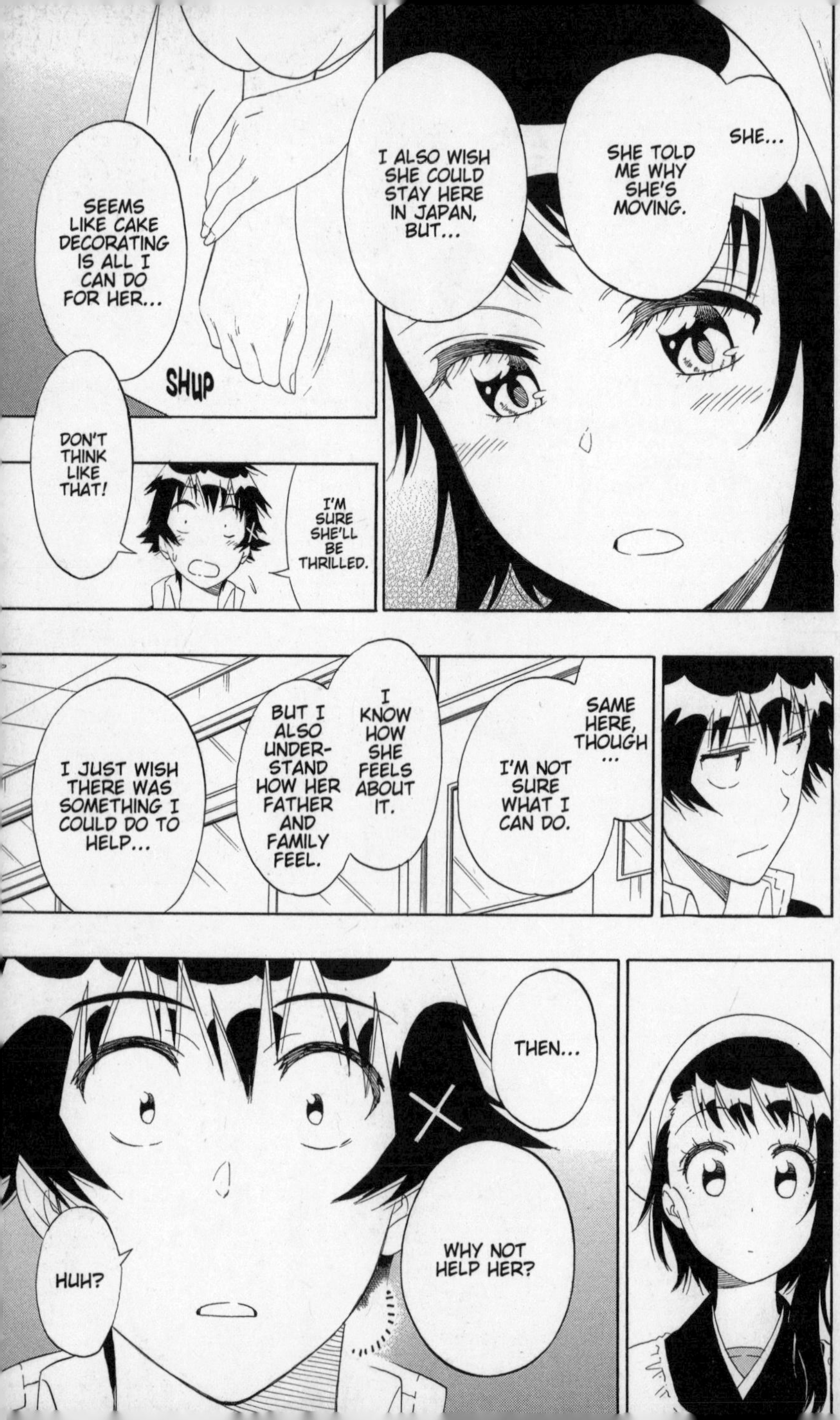

SHE...
SHE TOLD ME WHY SHE'S MOVING.
I ALSO WISH SHE COULD STAY HERE IN JAPAN, BUT...
SEEMS LIKE CAKE DECORATING IS ALL I CAN DO FOR HER...
SHUP
DON'T THINK LIKE THAT!
I'M SURE SHE'LL BE THRILLED.
SAME HERE, THOUGH...
I'M NOT SURE WHAT I CAN DO.
I KNOW HOW SHE FEELS ABOUT IT.
BUT I ALSO UNDERSTAND HOW HER FATHER AND FAMILY FEEL.
I JUST WISH THERE WAS SOMETHING I COULD DO TO HELP...
THEN...
WHY NOT HELP HER?
HUH?

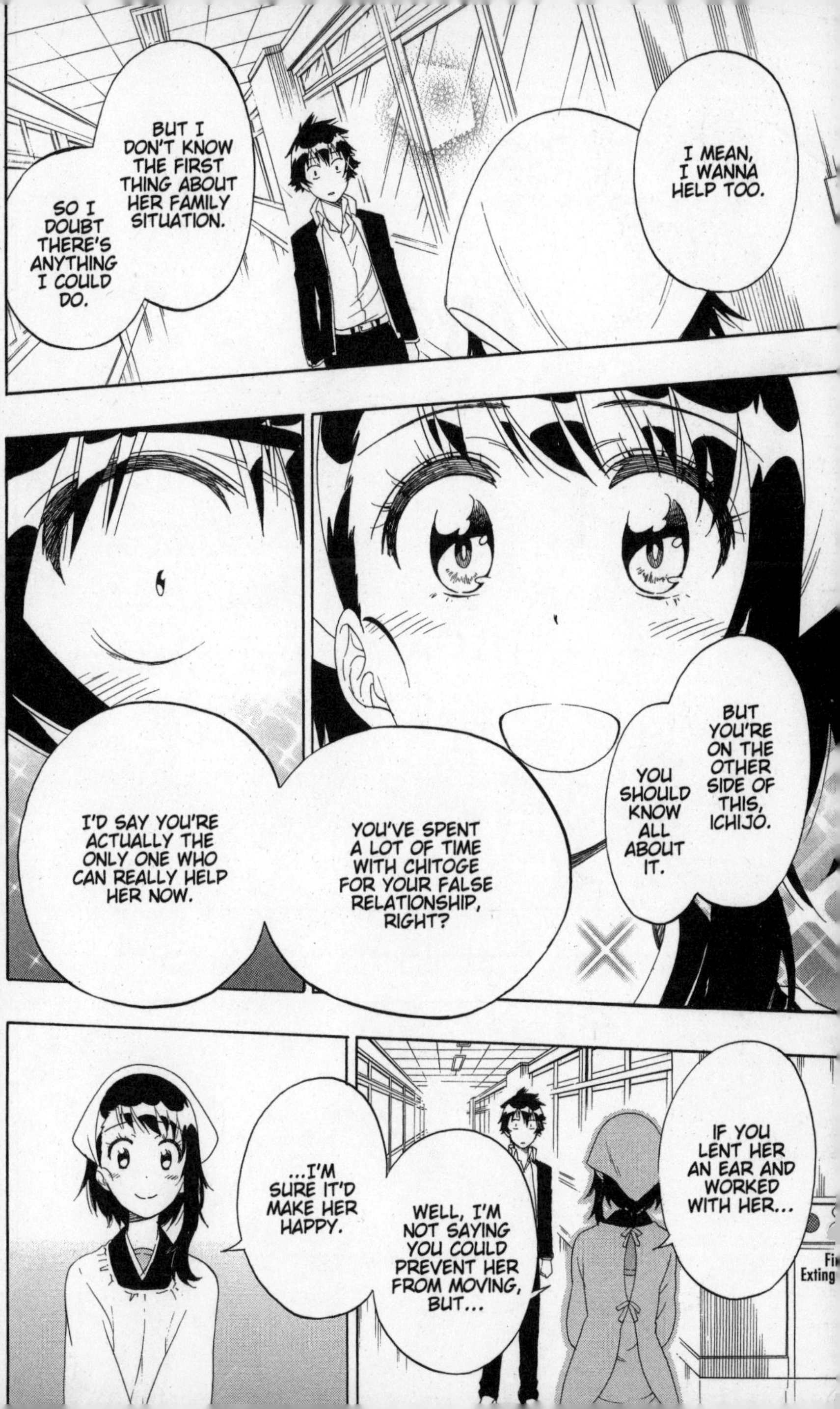
I MEAN, I WANNA HELP TOO.
BUT I DON'T KNOW THE FIRST THING ABOUT HER FAMILY SITUATION.
SO I DOUBT THERE'S ANYTHING I COULD DO.
BUT YOU'RE ON THE OTHER SIDE OF THIS, ICHIJO.
YOU SHOULD KNOW ALL ABOUT IT.
YOU'VE SPENT A LOT OF TIME WITH CHITOGE FOR YOUR FALSE RELATIONSHIP, RIGHT?
I'D SAY YOU'RE ACTUALLY THE ONLY ONE WHO CAN REALLY HELP HER NOW.
IF YOU LENT HER AN EAR AND WORKED WITH HER...
WELL, I'M NOT SAYING YOU COULD PREVENT HER FROM MOVING, BUT...
...I'M SURE IT'D MAKE HER HAPPY.

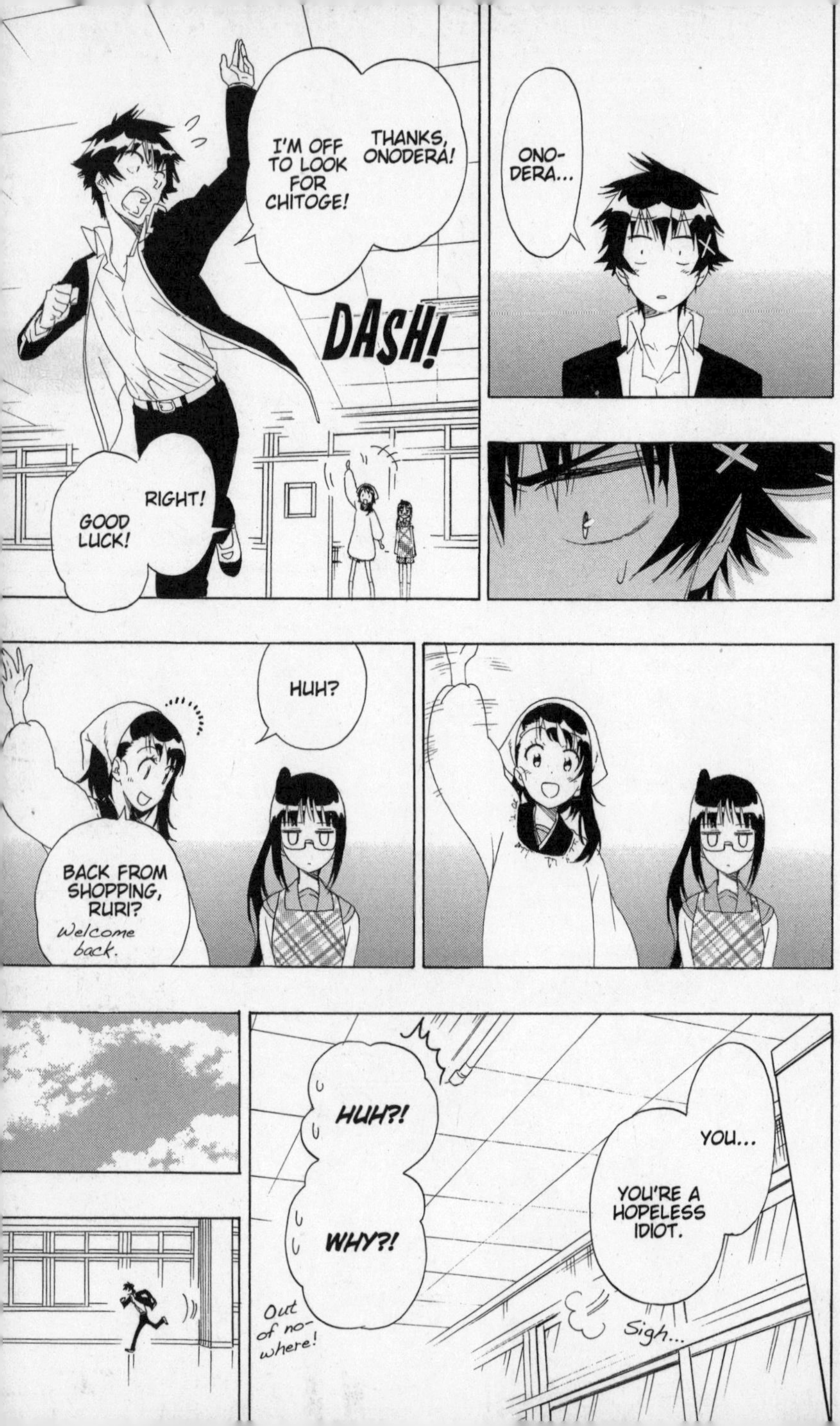
ONO-DERA...
THANKS, ONODERA!
I'M OFF TO LOOK FOR CHITOGE!
DASH!
RIGHT!
GOOD LUCK!
HUH?
BACK FROM SHOPPING, RURI?
Welcome back.
YOU...
YOU'RE A HOPELESS IDIOT.
Sigh...
HUH?!
WHY?!
Out of no-where!

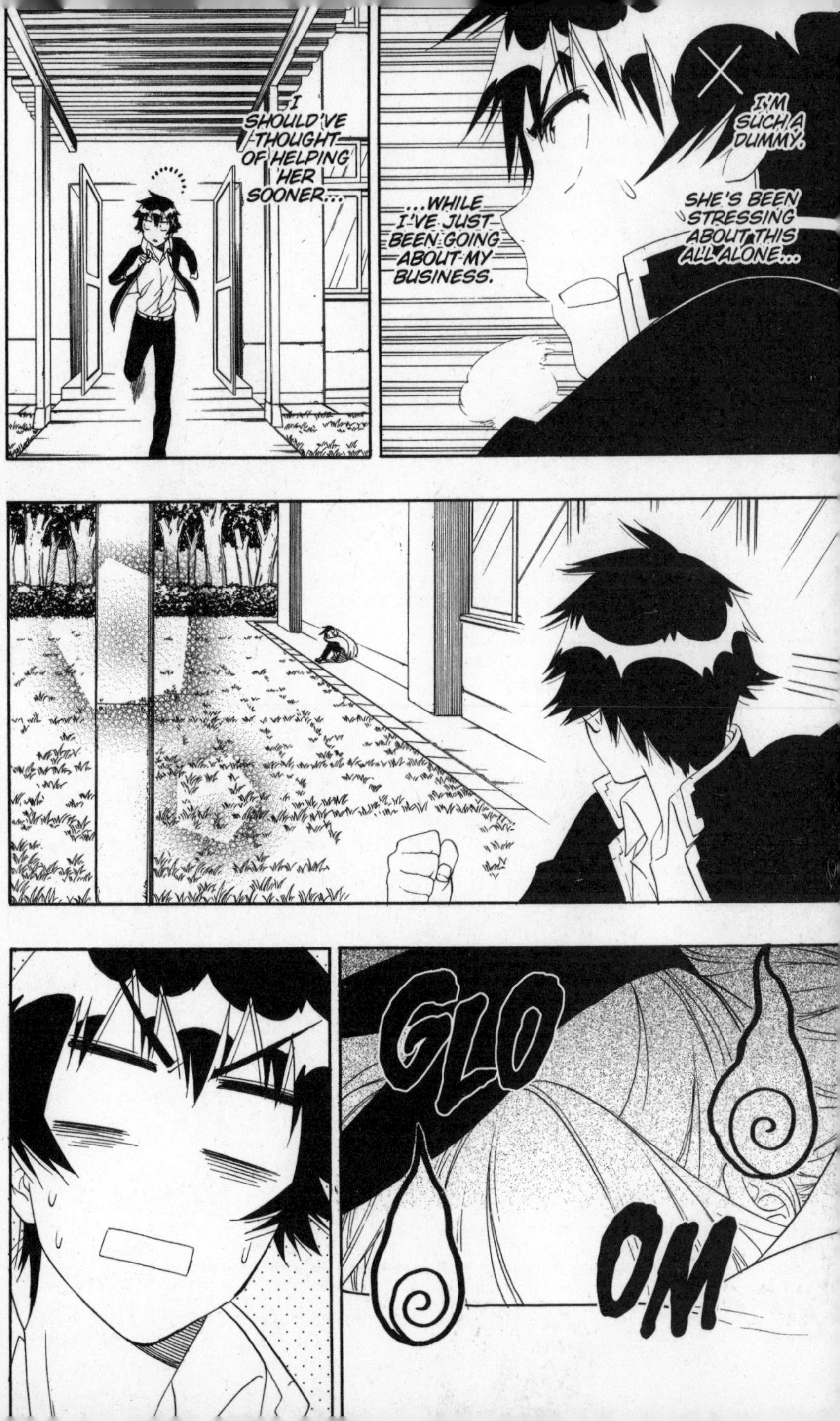
I'M SUCH A DUMMY.
SHE'S BEEN STRESSING ABOUT THIS ALL ALONE...
...WHILE I'VE JUST BEEN GOING ABOUT MY BUSINESS.
I SHOULD'VE THOUGHT OF HELPING HER SOONER...
GLO
OM

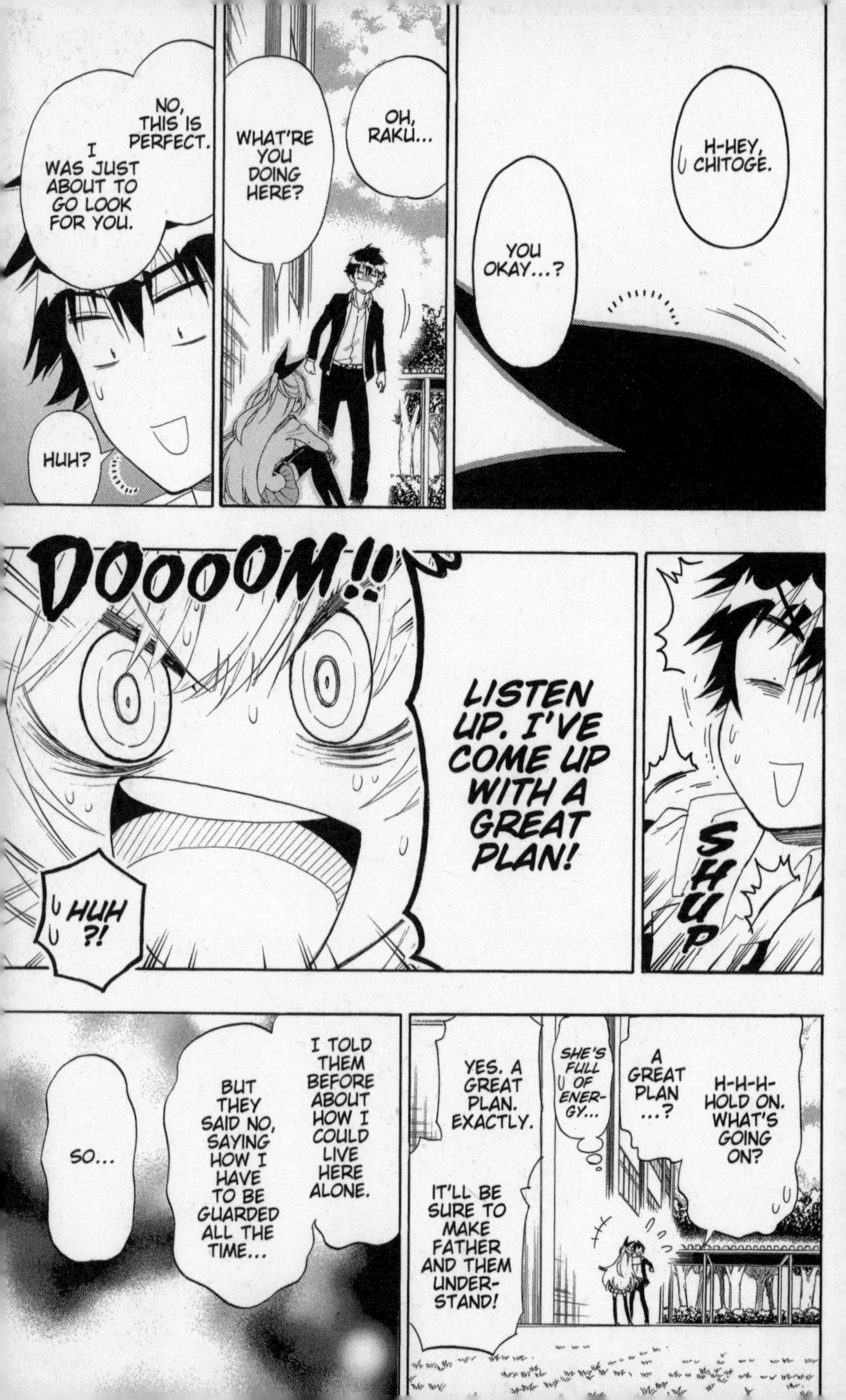
H-HEY, CHITOGE.
YOU OKAY...?
OH, RAKU...
WHAT'RE YOU DOING HERE?
NO, THIS IS PERFECT.
I WAS JUST ABOUT TO GO LOOK FOR YOU.
HUH?
SHUP
DOOOOM!!
LISTEN UP. I'VE COME UP WITH A GREAT PLAN!
HUH ?!
H-H-H-HOLD ON. WHAT'S GOING ON?
A GREAT PLAN ...?
SHE'S FULL OF ENERGY...
YES. A GREAT PLAN. EXACTLY.
IT'LL BE SURE TO MAKE FATHER AND THEM UNDERSTAND!
I TOLD THEM BEFORE ABOUT HOW I COULD LIVE HERE ALONE.
BUT THEY SAID NO, SAYING HOW I HAVE TO BE GUARDED ALL THE TIME...
SO...

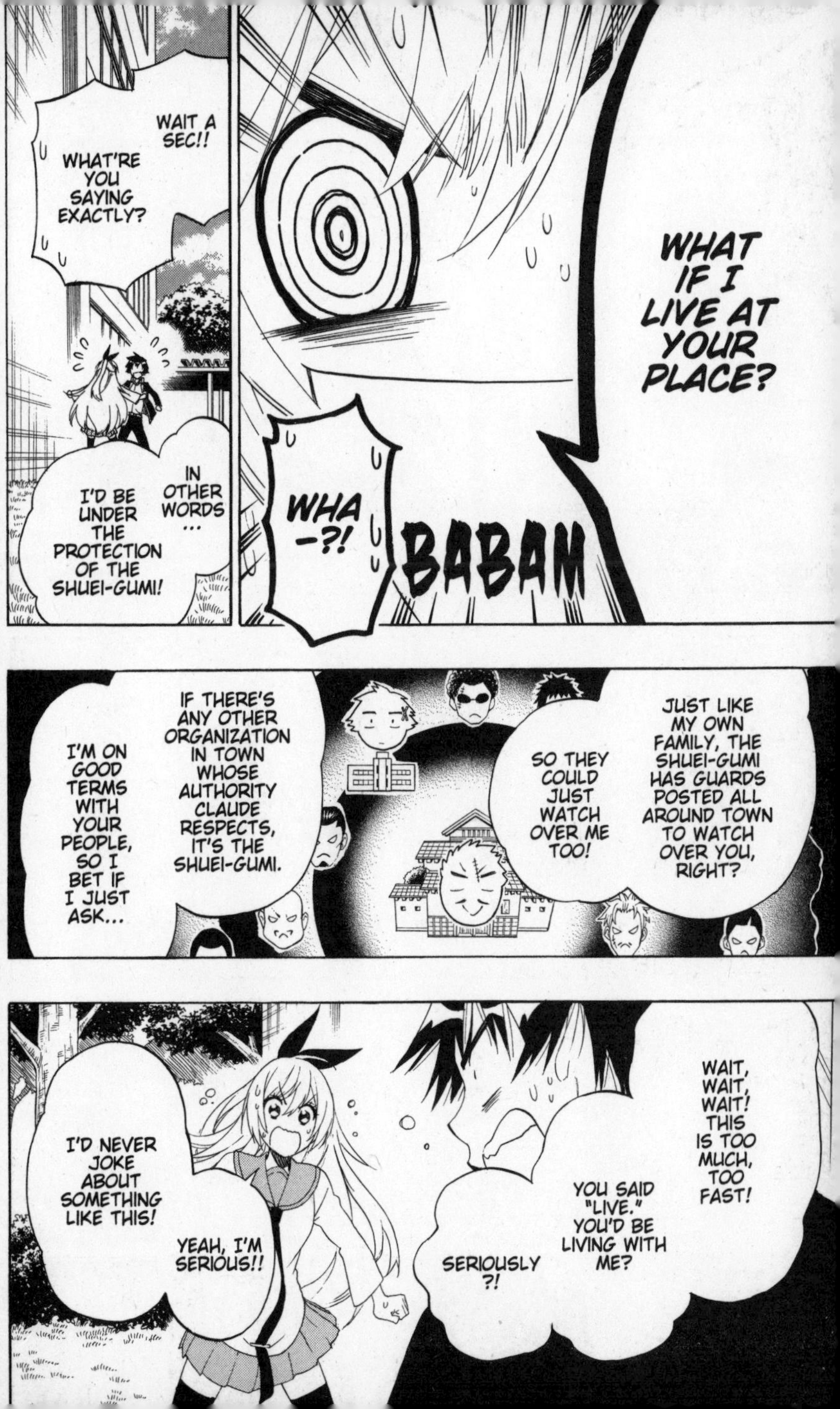
WHAT IF I LIVE AT YOUR PLACE?
WHA-?!
BABAM
WAIT A SEC!!
WHAT'RE YOU SAYING EXACTLY?
IN OTHER WORDS...
I'D BE UNDER THE PROTECTION OF THE SHUEI-GUMI!
JUST LIKE MY OWN FAMILY, THE SHUEI-GUMI HAS GUARDS POSTED ALL AROUND TOWN TO WATCH OVER YOU, RIGHT?
SO THEY COULD JUST WATCH OVER ME TOO!
IF THERE'S ANY OTHER ORGANIZATION IN TOWN WHOSE AUTHORITY CLAUDE RESPECTS, IT'S THE SHUEI-GUMI.
I'M ON GOOD TERMS WITH YOUR PEOPLE, SO I BET IF I JUST ASK...
WAIT, WAIT, WAIT! THIS IS TOO MUCH, TOO FAST!
YOU SAID "LIVE." YOU'D BE LIVING WITH ME?
SERIOUSLY?!
YEAH, I'M SERIOUS!!
I'D NEVER JOKE ABOUT SOMETHING LIKE THIS!

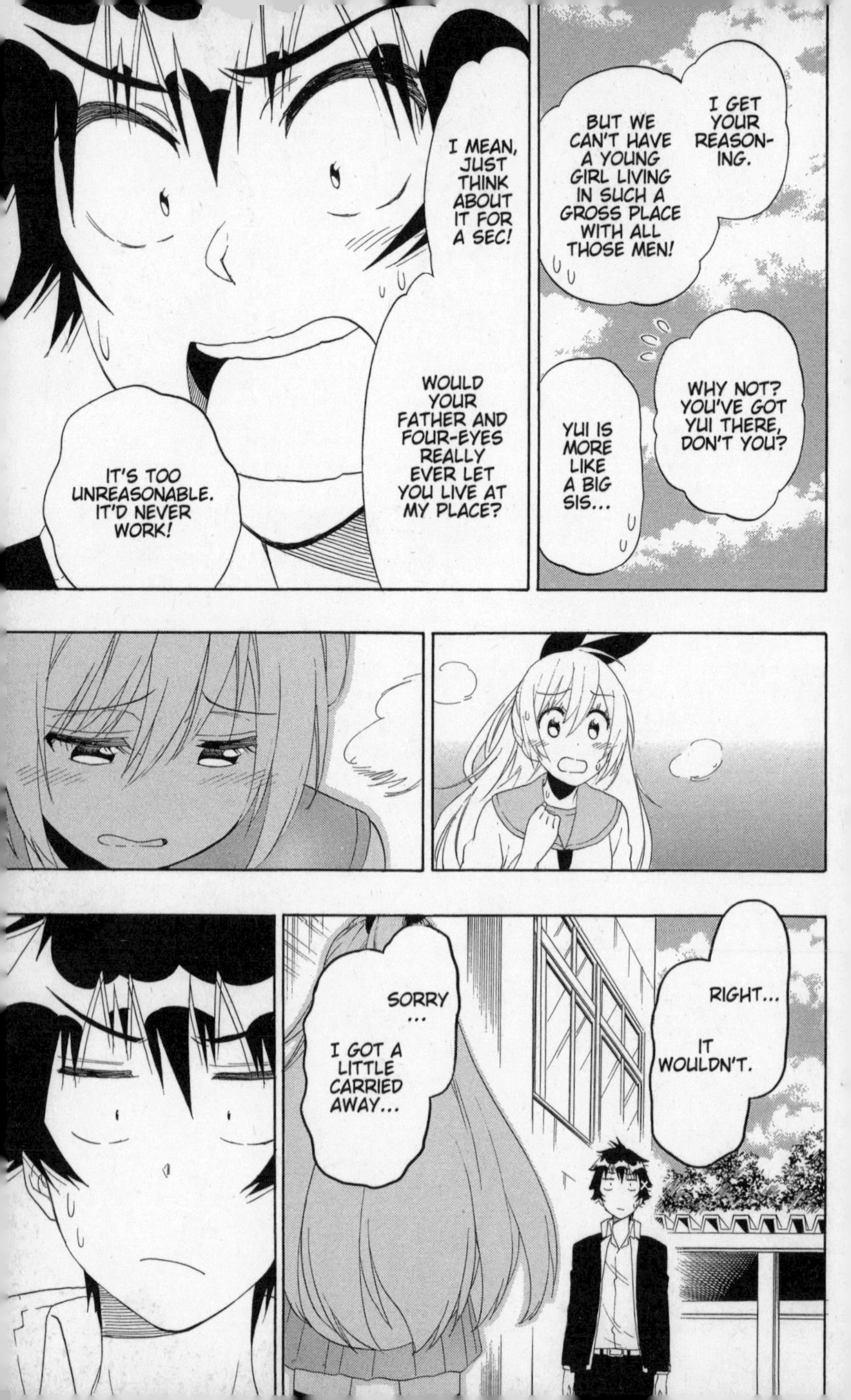
I GET YOUR REASONING.
BUT WE CAN'T HAVE A YOUNG GIRL LIVING IN SUCH A GROSS PLACE WITH ALL THOSE MEN!
WHY NOT? YOU'VE GOT YUI THERE, DON'T YOU?
YUI IS MORE LIKE A BIG SIS...
I MEAN, JUST THINK ABOUT IT FOR A SEC!
WOULD YOUR FATHER AND FOUR-EYES REALLY EVER LET YOU LIVE AT MY PLACE?
IT'S TOO UNREASONABLE. IT'D NEVER WORK!
RIGHT...
IT WOULDN'T.
SORRY...
I GOT A LITTLE CARRIED AWAY...

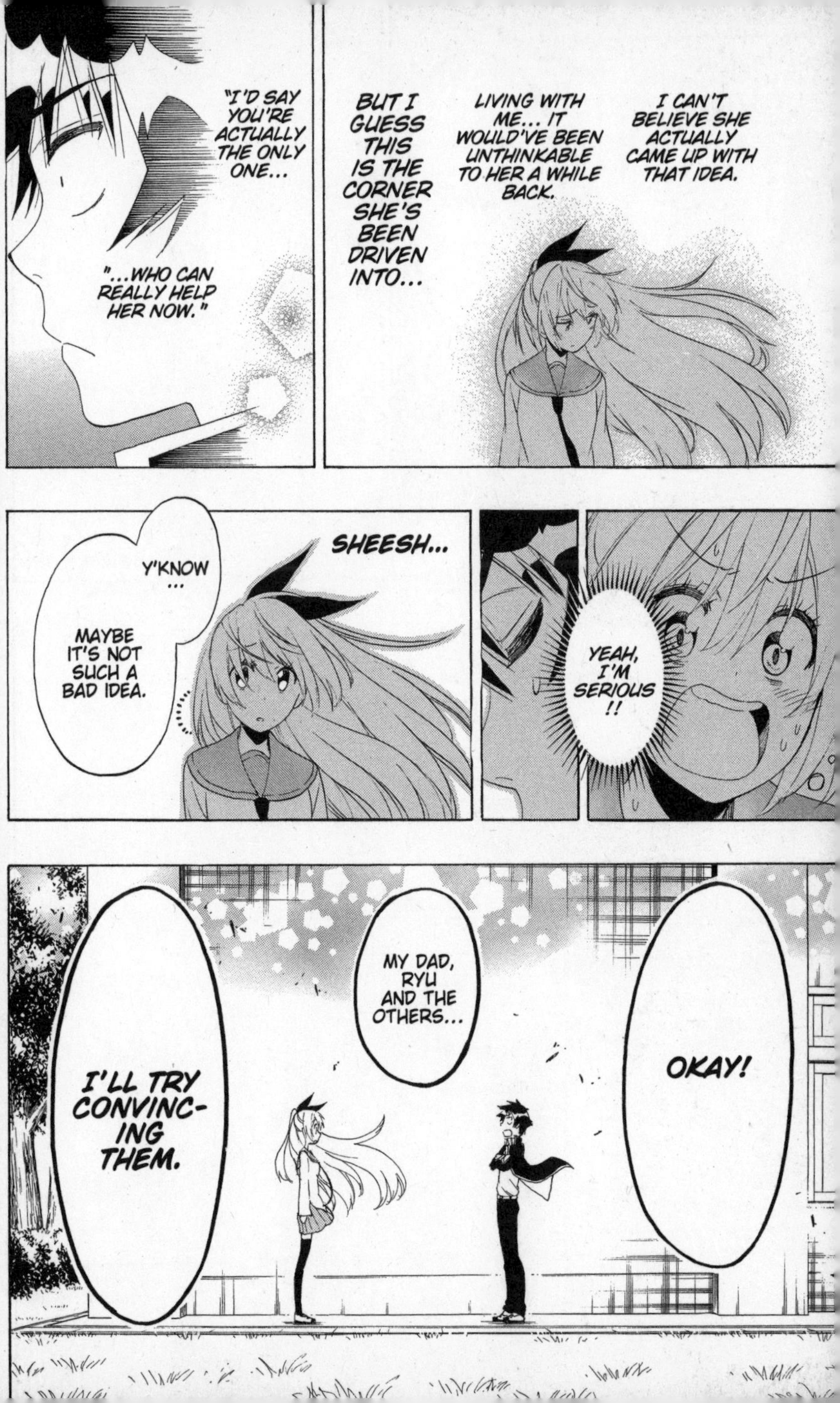
I CAN'T BELIEVE SHE ACTUALLY CAME UP WITH THAT IDEA.
LIVING WITH ME... IT WOULD'VE BEEN UNTHINKABLE TO HER A WHILE BACK.
BUT I GUESS THIS IS THE CORNER SHE'S BEEN DRIVEN INTO...
"I'D SAY YOU'RE ACTUALLY THE ONLY ONE...
"...WHO CAN REALLY HELP HER NOW."
YEAH, I'M SERIOUS!!
SHEESH...
Y'KNOW... MAYBE IT'S NOT SUCH A BAD IDEA.
OKAY!
MY DAD, RYU AND THE OTHERS...
I'LL TRY CONVINCING THEM.

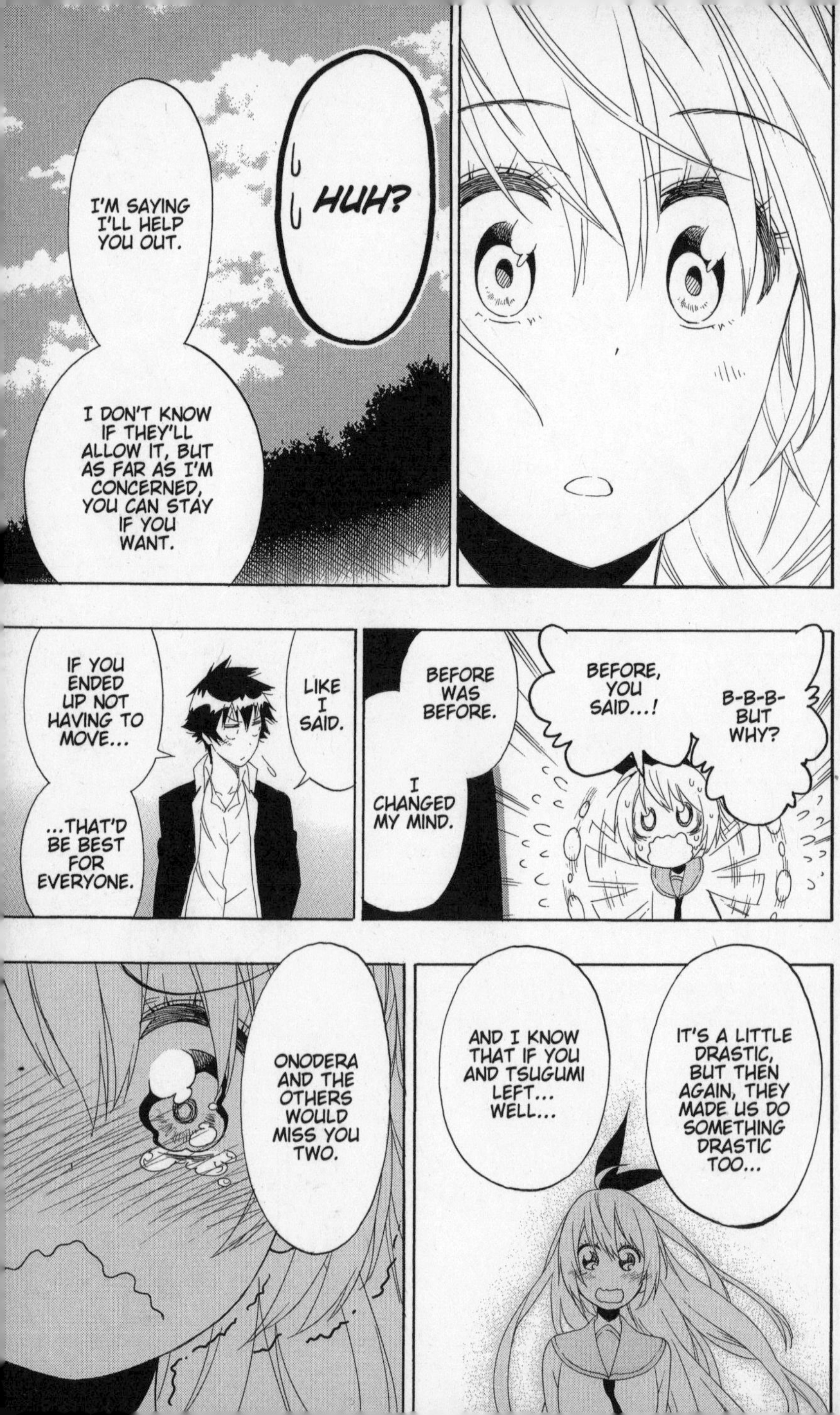
HUH?
I'M SAYING I'LL HELP YOU OUT.
I DON'T KNOW IF THEY'LL ALLOW IT, BUT AS FAR AS I'M CONCERNED, YOU CAN STAY IF YOU WANT.
B-B-B-BUT WHY?
BEFORE, YOU SAID...!
BEFORE WAS BEFORE.
I CHANGED MY MIND.
LIKE I SAID.
IF YOU ENDED UP NOT HAVING TO MOVE...
...THAT'D BE BEST FOR EVERYONE.
IT'S A LITTLE DRASTIC, BUT THEN AGAIN, THEY MADE US DO SOMETHING DRASTIC TOO...
AND I KNOW THAT IF YOU AND TSUGUMI LEFT... WELL...
ONODERA AND THE OTHERS WOULD MISS YOU TWO.

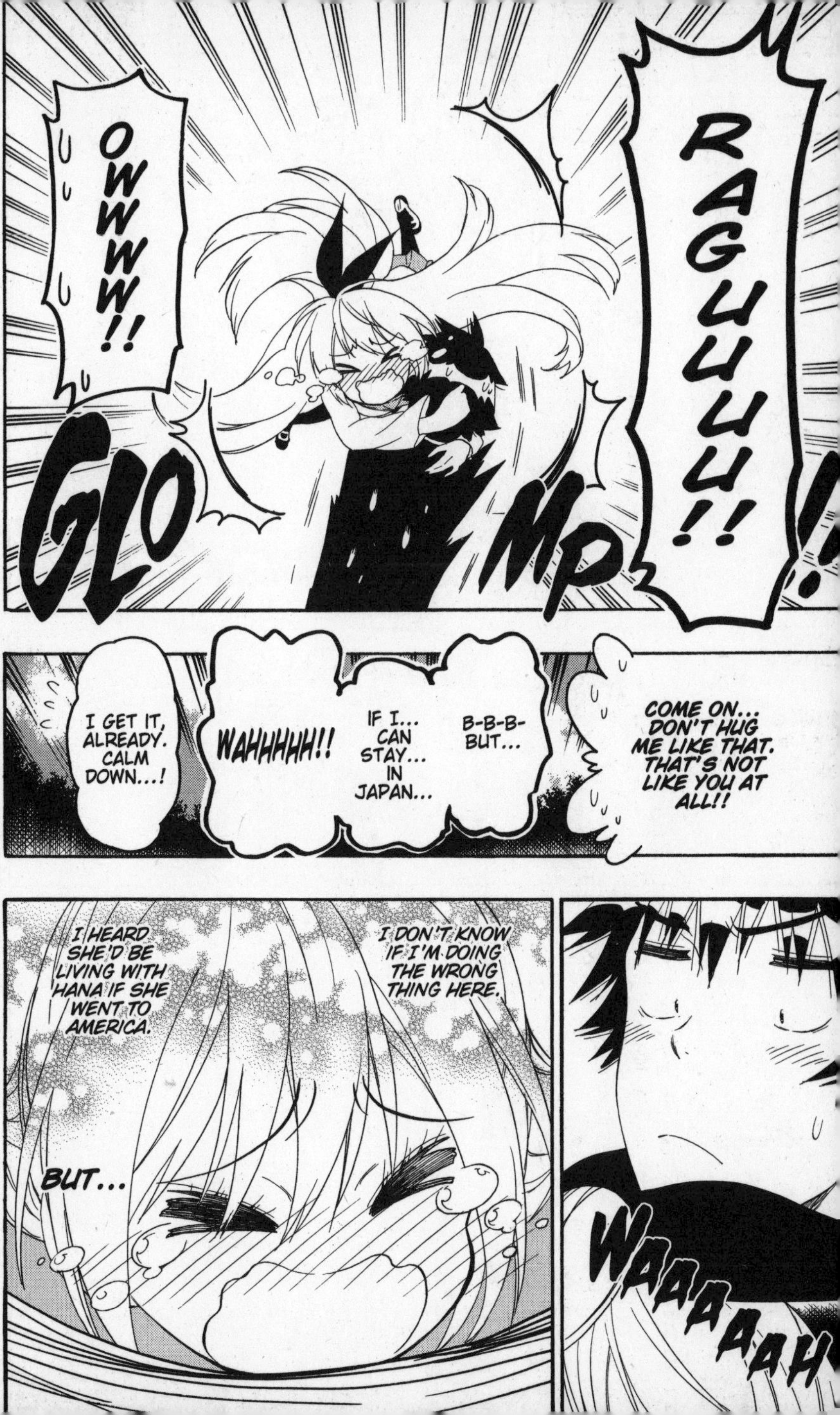
RAGUUUUU!!
OWWWWW!!
GLOMP
COME ON... DON'T HUG ME LIKE THAT. THAT'S NOT LIKE YOU AT ALL!!
B-B-B-BUT...
IF I... CAN STAY... IN JAPAN...
WAHHHHH!!
I GET IT, ALREADY. CALM DOWN...!
WAAAAAAH
I DON'T KNOW IF I'M DOING THE WRONG THING HERE.
I HEARD SHE'D BE LIVING WITH HANA IF SHE WENT TO AMERICA.
BUT...

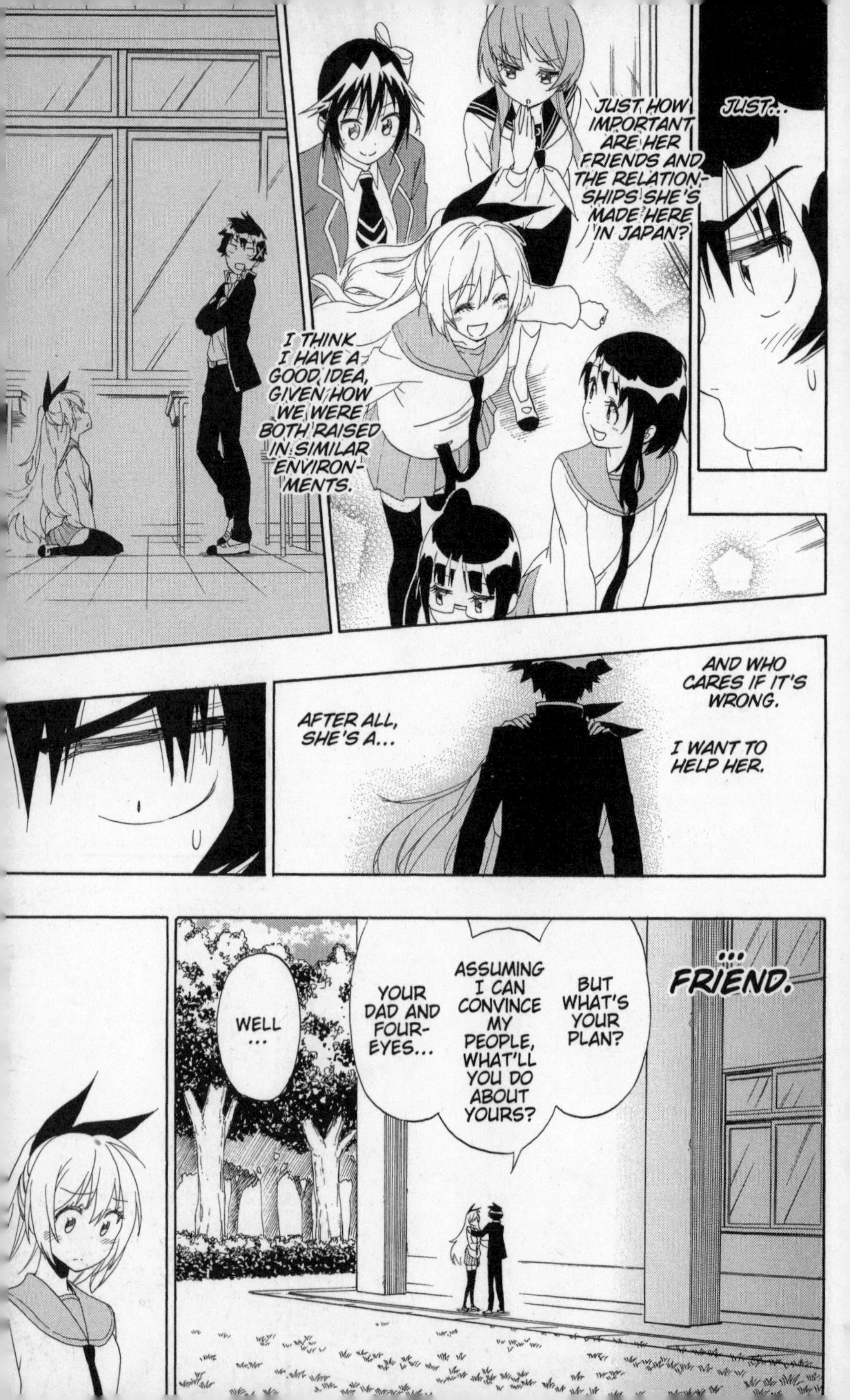
JUST...
JUST HOW IMPORTANT ARE HER FRIENDS AND THE RELATIONSHIPS SHE'S MADE HERE IN JAPAN?
I THINK I HAVE A GOOD IDEA, GIVEN HOW WE WERE BOTH RAISED IN SIMILAR ENVIRONMENTS.
AND WHO CARES IF IT'S WRONG.
I WANT TO HELP HER.
AFTER ALL, SHE'S A...
...FRIEND.
BUT WHAT'S YOUR PLAN?
ASSUMING I CAN CONVINCE MY PEOPLE, WHAT'LL YOU DO ABOUT YOURS?
YOUR DAD AND FOUR-EYES...
WELL...

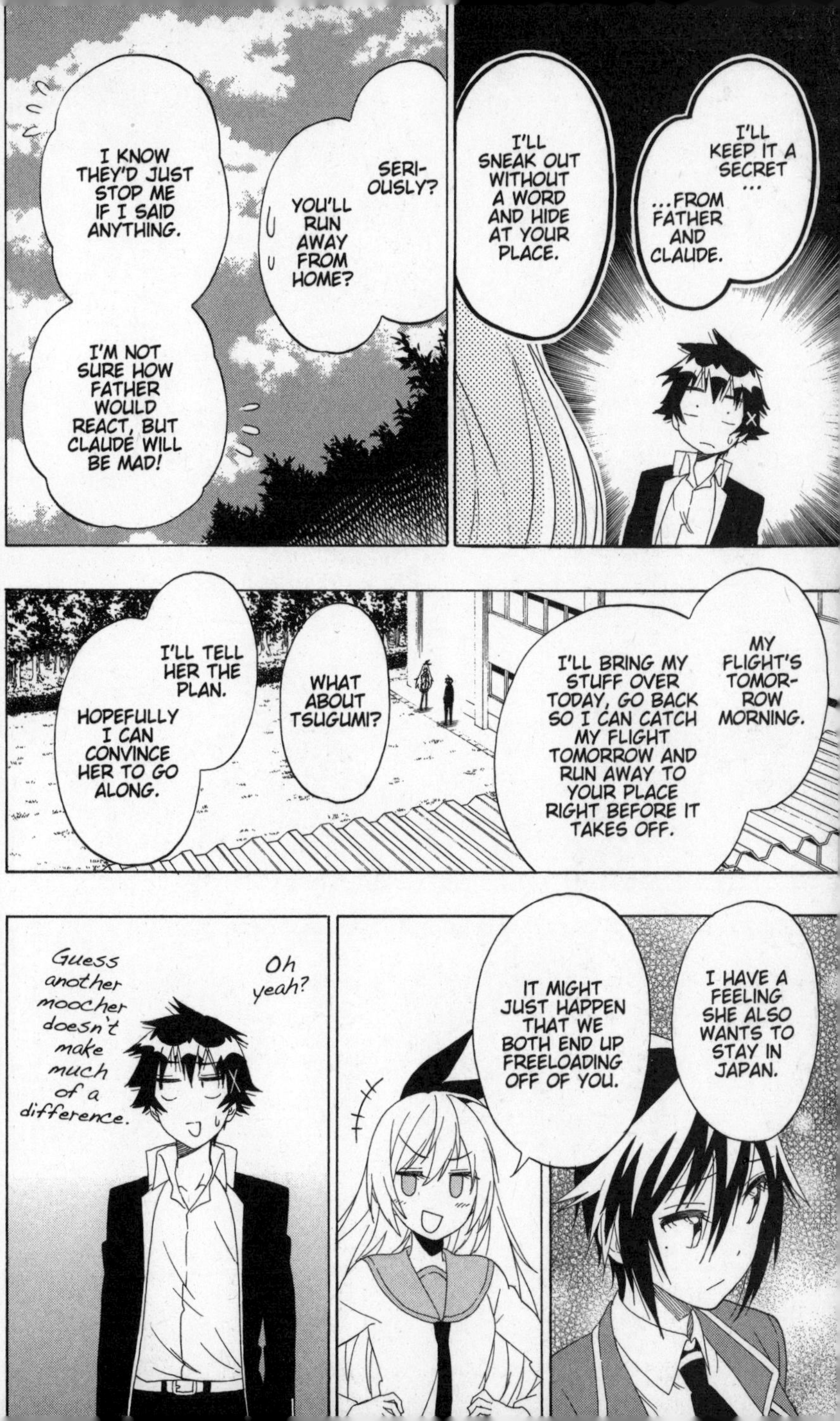
I'LL KEEP IT A SECRET ...
...FROM FATHER AND CLAUDE.
I'LL SNEAK OUT WITHOUT A WORD AND HIDE AT YOUR PLACE.
SERI-OUSLY?
YOU'LL RUN AWAY FROM HOME?
I KNOW THEY'D JUST STOP ME IF I SAID ANYTHING.
I'M NOT SURE HOW FATHER WOULD REACT, BUT CLAUDE WILL BE MAD!
MY FLIGHT'S TOMORROW MORNING.
I'LL BRING MY STUFF OVER TODAY, GO BACK SO I CAN CATCH MY FLIGHT TOMORROW AND RUN AWAY TO YOUR PLACE RIGHT BEFORE IT TAKES OFF.
WHAT ABOUT TSUGUMI?
I'LL TELL HER THE PLAN.
HOPEFULLY I CAN CONVINCE HER TO GO ALONG.
I HAVE A FEELING SHE ALSO WANTS TO STAY IN JAPAN.
IT MIGHT JUST HAPPEN THAT WE BOTH END UP FREELOADING OFF OF YOU.
Oh yeah?
Guess another moocher doesn't make much of a difference.

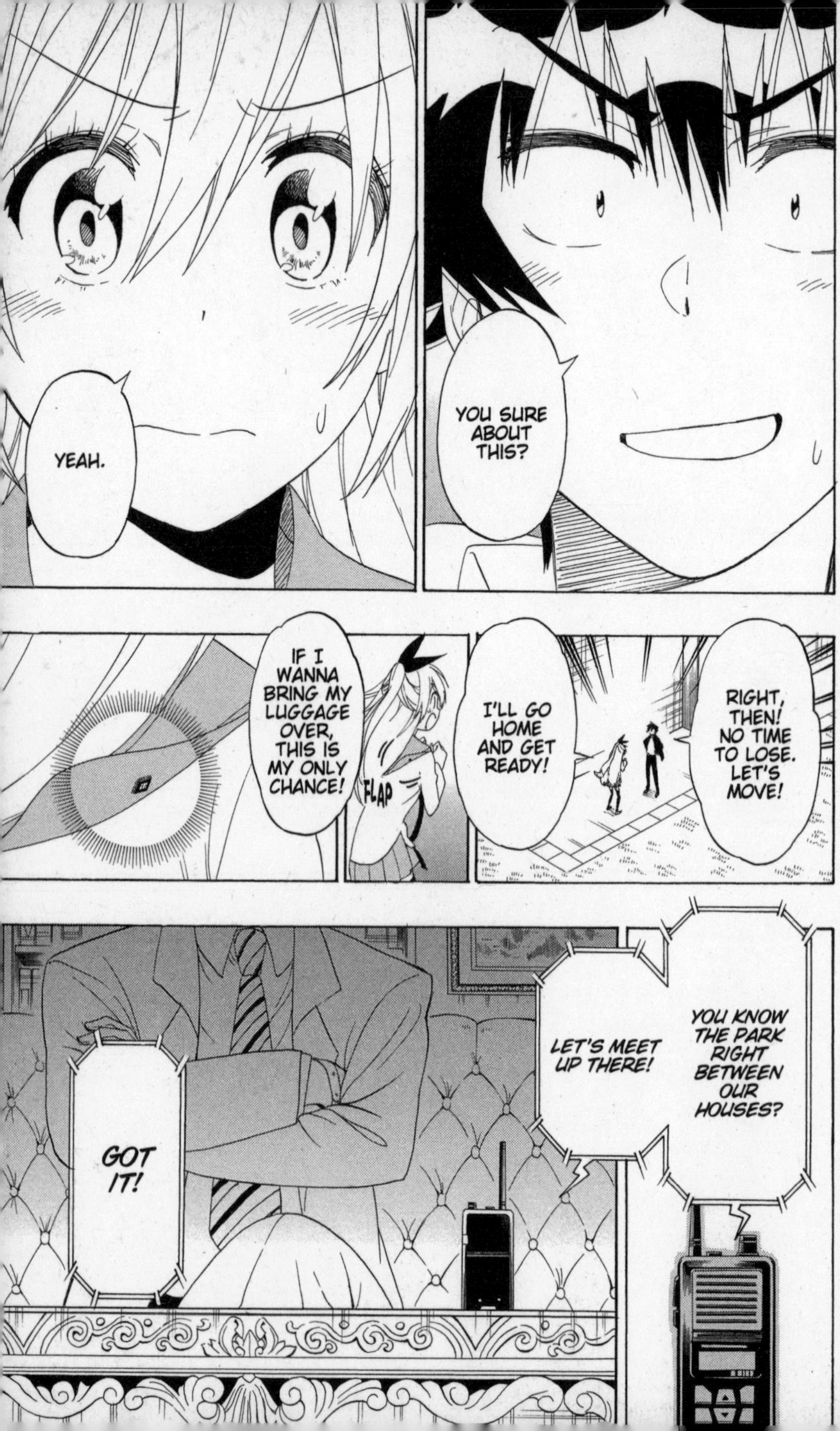
YOU SURE ABOUT THIS?
YEAH.
RIGHT, THEN! NO TIME TO LOSE. LET'S MOVE!
I'LL GO HOME AND GET READY!
IF I WANNA BRING MY LUGGAGE OVER, THIS IS MY ONLY CHANCE!
FLAP
YOU KNOW THE PARK RIGHT BETWEEN OUR HOUSES?
LET'S MEET UP THERE!
GOT IT!

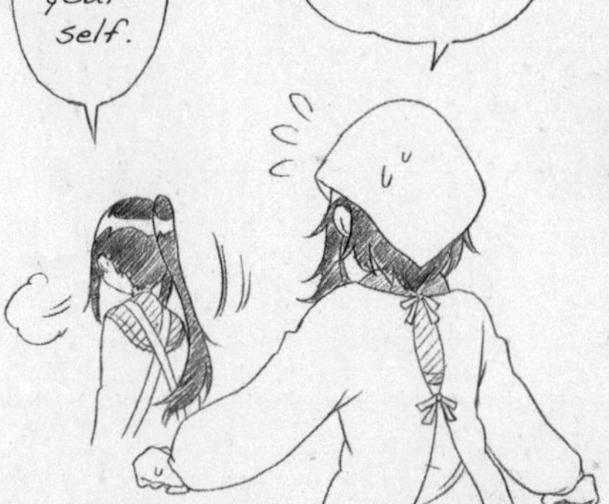
What do you mean, a hopeless idiot?
Figure it out your-self.

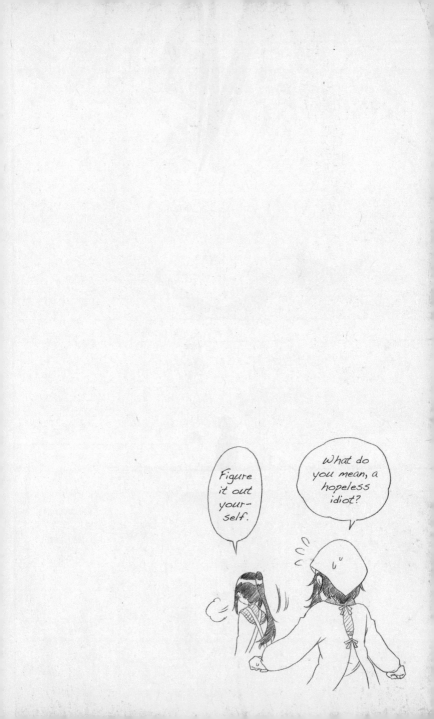

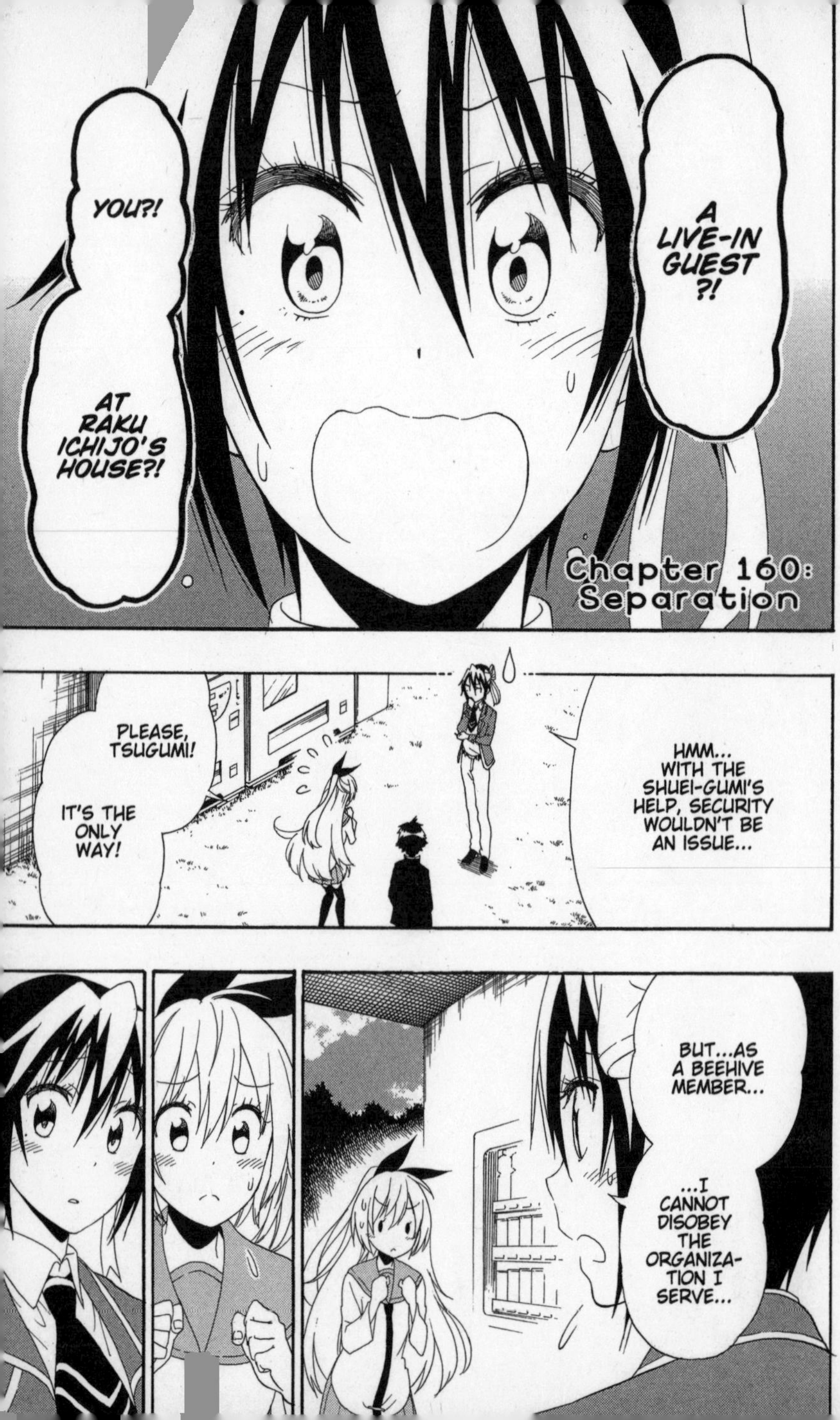
A LIVE-IN GUEST ?!
YOU?!
AT RAKU ICHIJO'S HOUSE?!
Chapter 160: Separation
HMM... WITH THE SHUEI-GUMI'S HELP, SECURITY WOULDN'T BE AN ISSUE...
PLEASE, TSUGUMI!
IT'S THE ONLY WAY!
BUT...AS A BEEHIVE MEMBER...
...I CANNOT DISOBEY THE ORGANIZATION I SERVE...

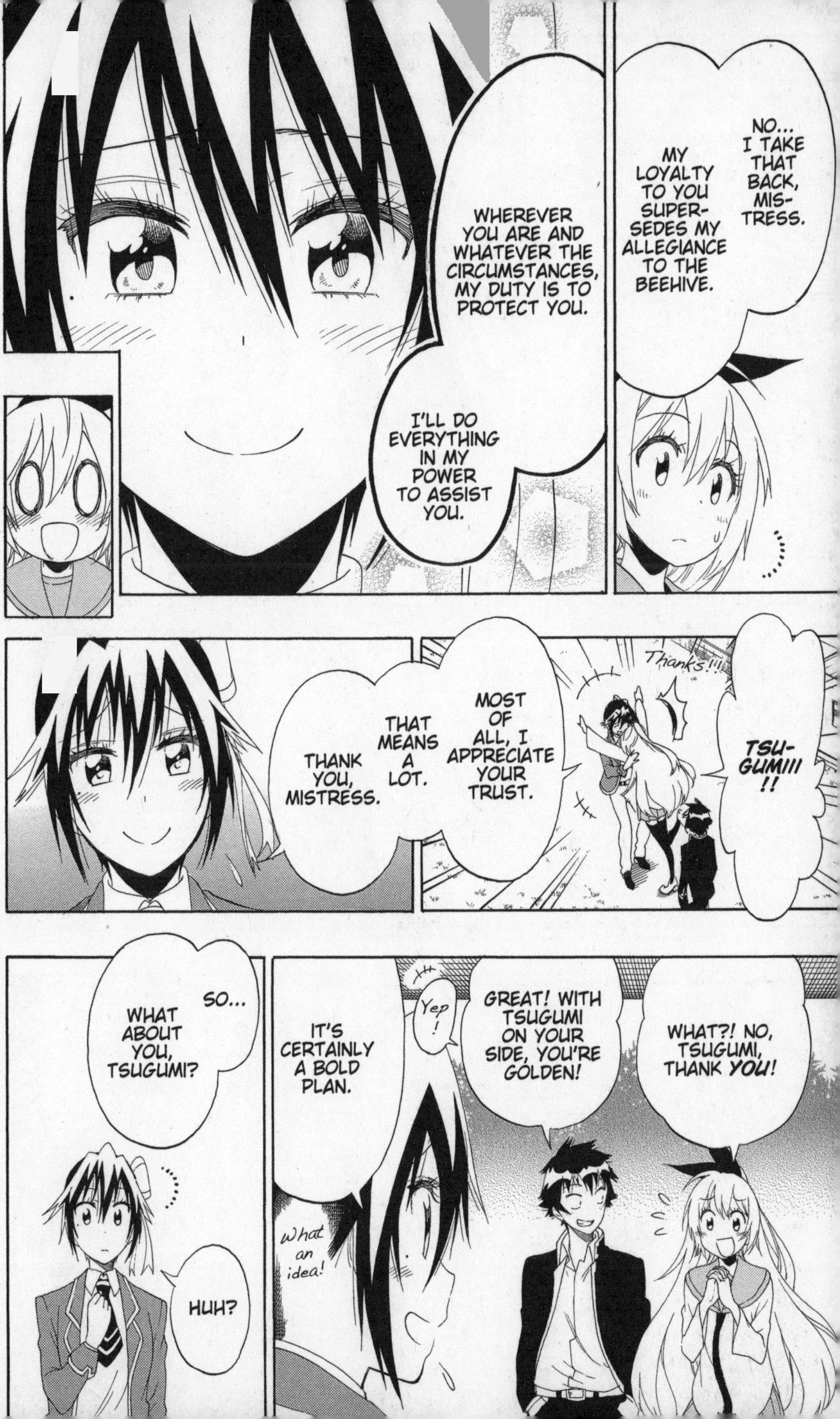
NO... I TAKE THAT BACK, MISTRESS.
MY LOYALTY TO YOU SUPERSEDES MY ALLEGIANCE TO THE BEEHIVE.
WHEREVER YOU ARE AND WHATEVER THE CIRCUMSTANCES, MY DUTY IS TO PROTECT YOU.
I'LL DO EVERYTHING IN MY POWER TO ASSIST YOU.
......
Thanks!!!
TSUGUMIII!!
MOST OF ALL, I APPRECIATE YOUR TRUST.
THAT MEANS A LOT.
THANK YOU, MISTRESS.
WHAT?! NO, TSUGUMI, THANK YOU!
GREAT! WITH TSUGUMI ON YOUR SIDE, YOU'RE GOLDEN!
Yep!
IT'S CERTAINLY A BOLD PLAN.
What an idea!
SO...
WHAT ABOUT YOU, TSUGUMI?
HUH?

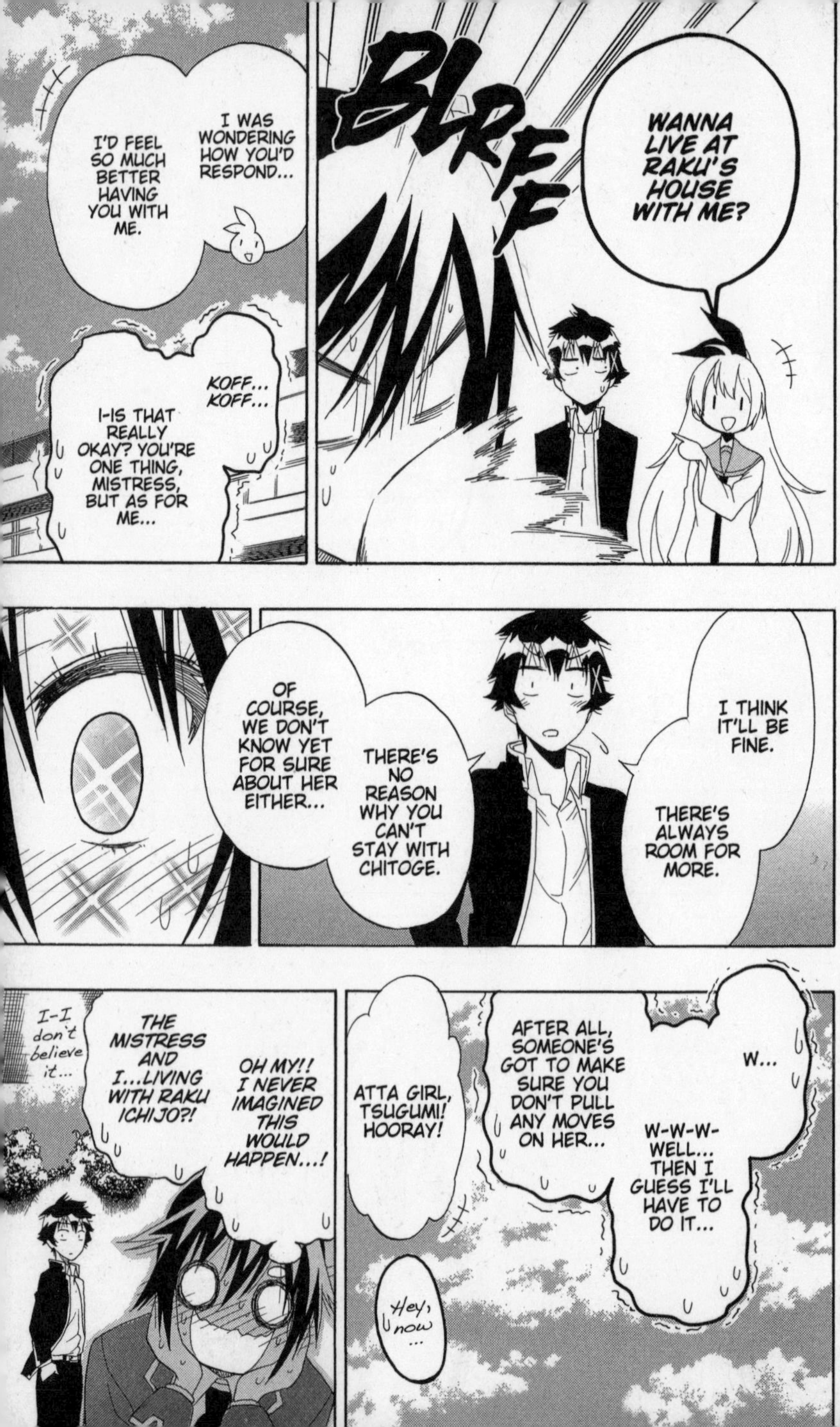
WANNA LIVE AT RAKU'S HOUSE WITH ME?
BLRFF
I WAS WONDERING HOW YOU'D RESPOND...
I'D FEEL SO MUCH BETTER HAVING YOU WITH ME.
KOFF... KOFF...
I-IS THAT REALLY OKAY? YOU'RE ONE THING, MISTRESS, BUT AS FOR ME...
I THINK IT'LL BE FINE.
THERE'S ALWAYS ROOM FOR MORE.
THERE'S NO REASON WHY YOU CAN'T STAY WITH CHITOGE.
OF COURSE, WE DON'T KNOW YET FOR SURE ABOUT HER EITHER...
W...
W-W-W-WELL... THEN I GUESS I'LL HAVE TO DO IT...
AFTER ALL, SOMEONE'S GOT TO MAKE SURE YOU DON'T PULL ANY MOVES ON HER...
ATTA GIRL, TSUGUMI! HOORAY!
Hey, now...
OH MY!! I NEVER IMAGINED THIS WOULD HAPPEN...!
THE MISTRESS AND I...LIVING WITH RAKU ICHIJO?!
I-I don't believe it...

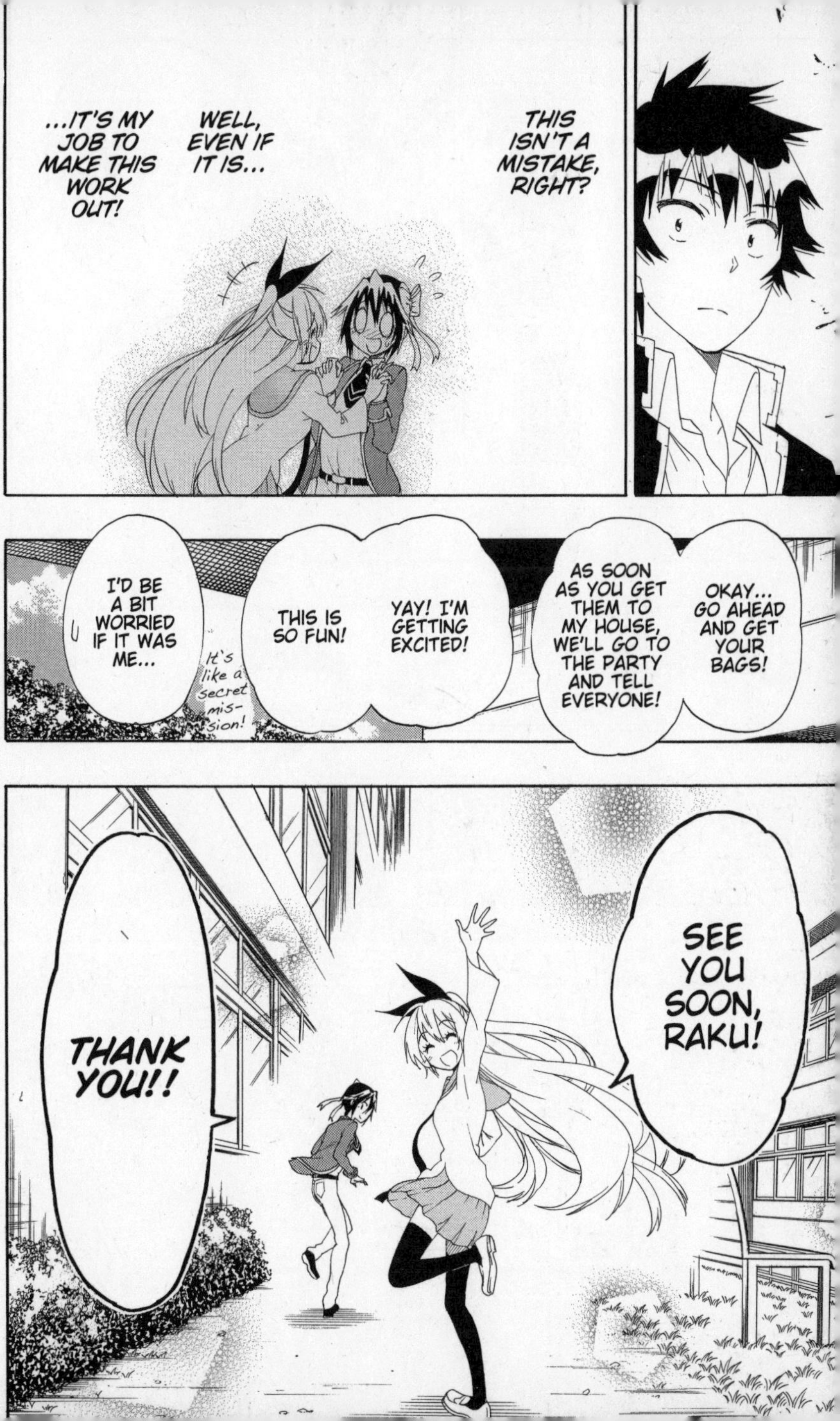
THIS ISN'T A MISTAKE, RIGHT?
WELL, EVEN IF IT IS...
...IT'S MY JOB TO MAKE THIS WORK OUT!
OKAY... GO AHEAD AND GET YOUR BAGS!
AS SOON AS YOU GET THEM TO MY HOUSE, WE'LL GO TO THE PARTY AND TELL EVERYONE!
YAY! I'M GETTING EXCITED!
THIS IS SO FUN!
It's like a secret mission!
I'D BE A BIT WORRIED IF IT WAS ME...
SEE YOU SOON, RAKU!
THANK YOU!!

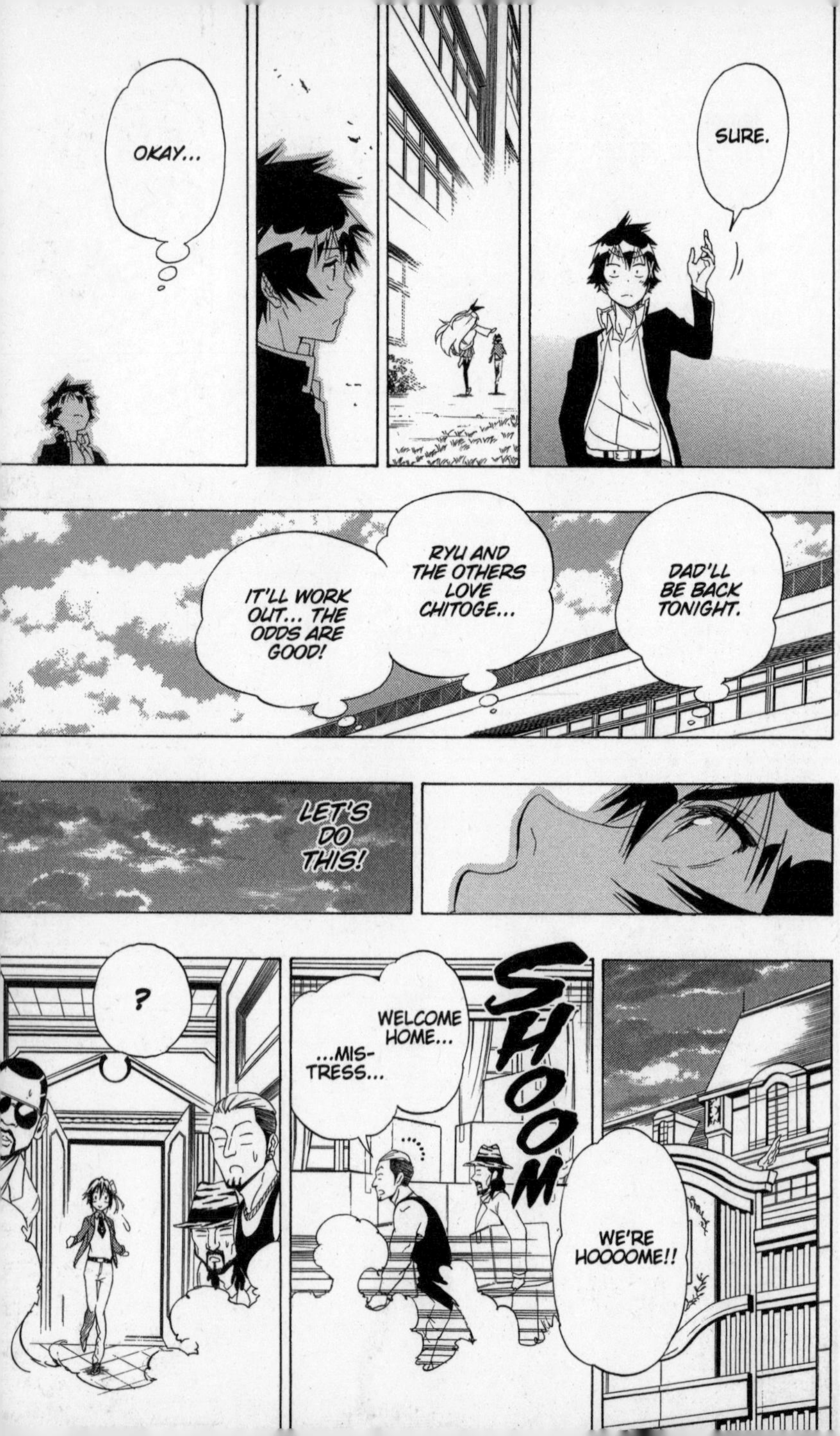
SURE.
OKAY...
DAD'LL BE BACK TONIGHT.
RYU AND THE OTHERS LOVE CHITOGE...
IT'LL WORK OUT... THE ODDS ARE GOOD!
LET'S DO THIS!
WE'RE HOOOOME!!
SHOOM
WELCOME HOME...
...MIS-TRESS...
?

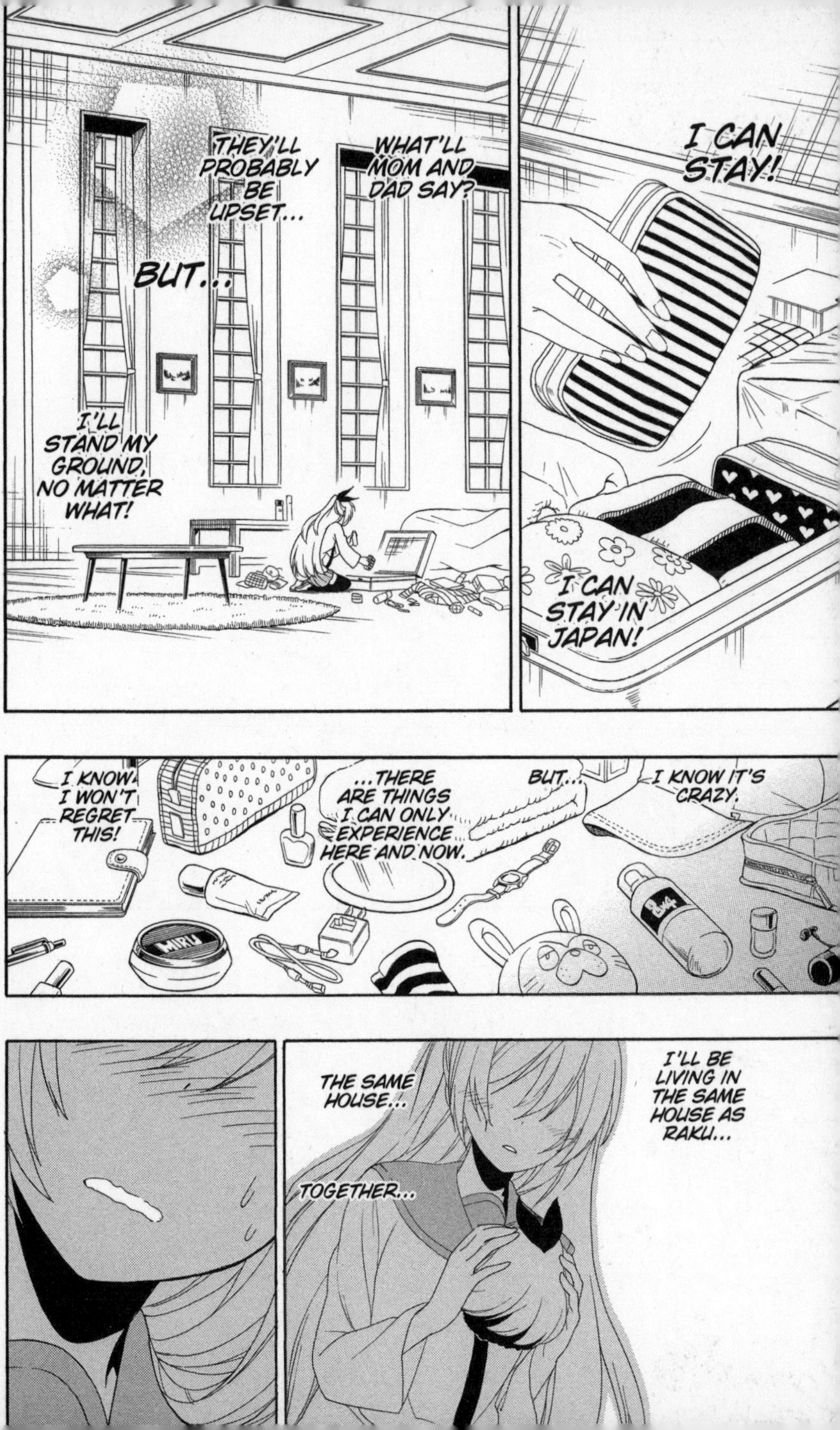
I CAN STAY!
I CAN STAY IN JAPAN!
WHAT'LL MOM AND DAD SAY?
THEY'LL PROBABLY BE UPSET...
BUT...
I'LL STAND MY GROUND, NO MATTER WHAT!
I KNOW IT'S CRAZY.
BUT...
...THERE ARE THINGS I CAN ONLY EXPERIENCE HERE AND NOW.
I KNOW I WON'T REGRET THIS!
MIRU
I'LL BE LIVING IN THE SAME HOUSE AS RAKU...
THE SAME HOUSE...
TOGETHER...

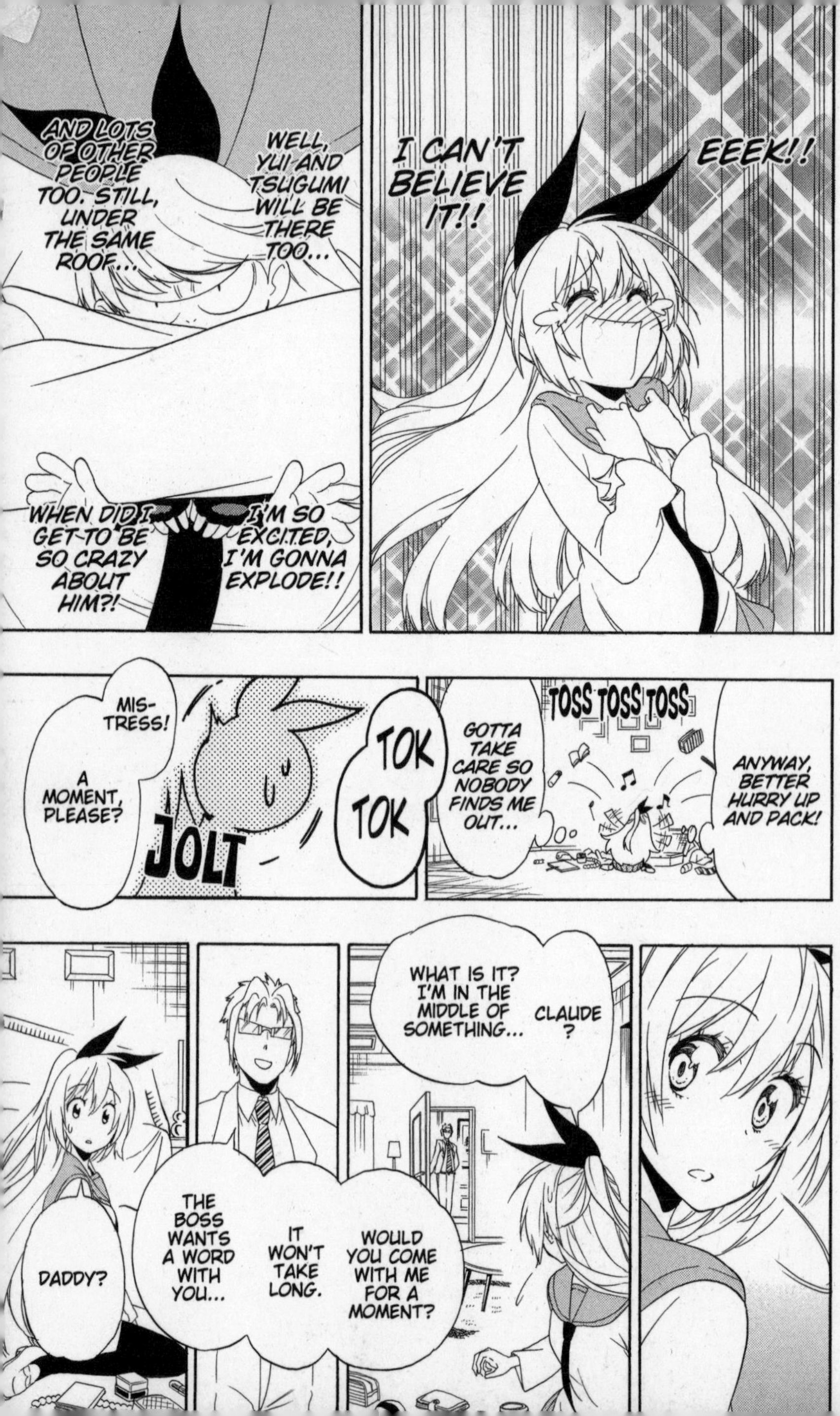
EEEK!!
I CAN'T BELIEVE IT!!
WELL, YUI AND TSUGUMI WILL BE THERE TOO...
AND LOTS OF OTHER PEOPLE TOO. STILL, UNDER THE SAME ROOF...
I'M SO EXCITED, I'M GONNA EXPLODE!!
WHEN DID I GET TO BE SO CRAZY ABOUT HIM?!
ANYWAY, BETTER HURRY UP AND PACK!
TOSS TOSS TOSS
GOTTA TAKE CARE SO NOBODY FINDS ME OUT...
TOK TOK
JOLT
MIS-TRESS!
A MOMENT, PLEASE?
CLAUDE?
WHAT IS IT? I'M IN THE MIDDLE OF SOMETHING...
WOULD YOU COME WITH ME FOR A MOMENT?
IT WON'T TAKE LONG.
THE BOSS WANTS A WORD WITH YOU...
DADDY?

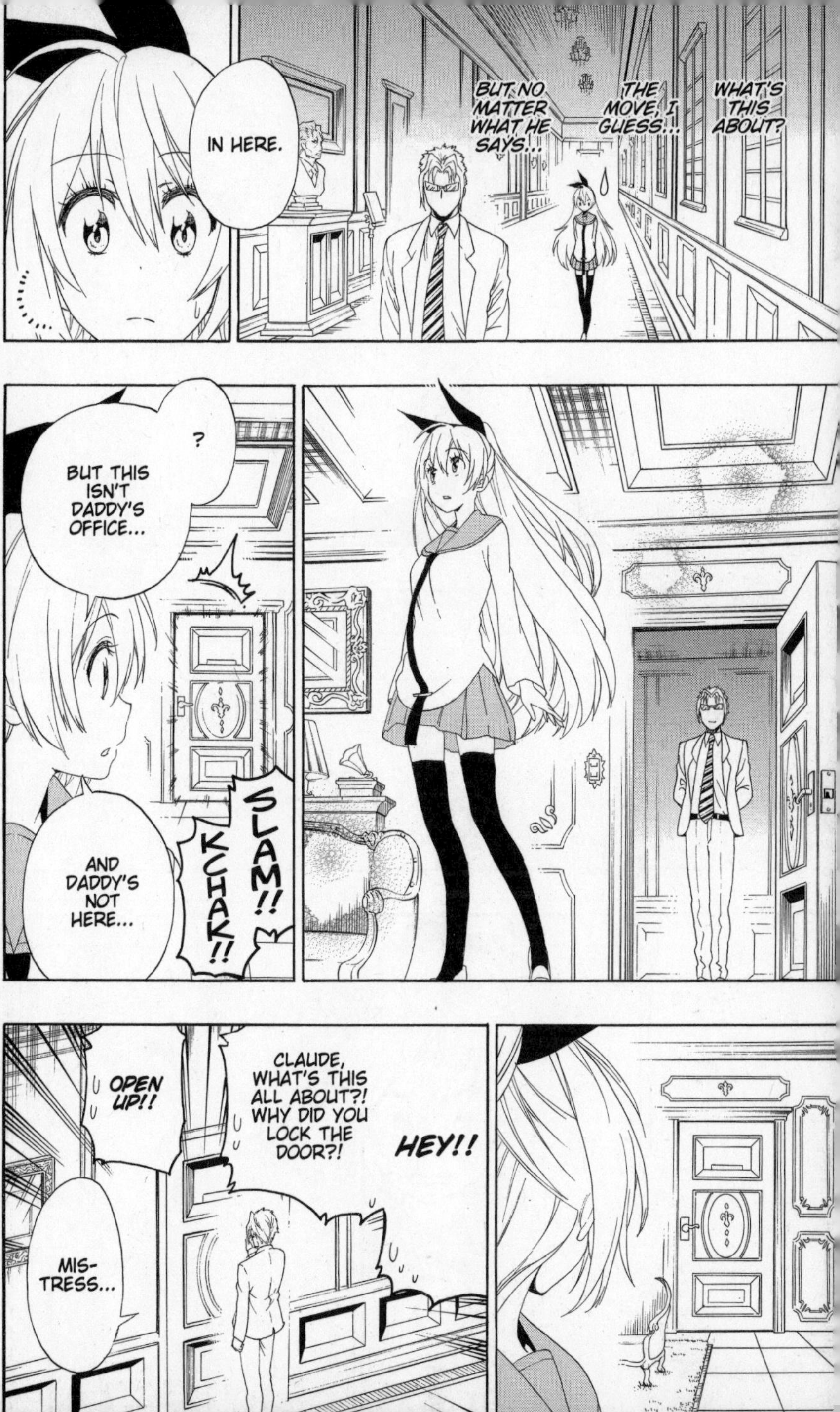
WHAT'S THIS ABOUT?
THE MOVE, I GUESS...
BUT NO MATTER WHAT HE SAYS...
IN HERE.
?
BUT THIS ISN'T DADDY'S OFFICE...
AND DADDY'S NOT HERE...
SLAM!!
KCHAK!!
HEY!!
CLAUDE, WHAT'S THIS ALL ABOUT?! WHY DID YOU LOCK THE DOOR?!
OPEN UP!!
MIS-TRESS...

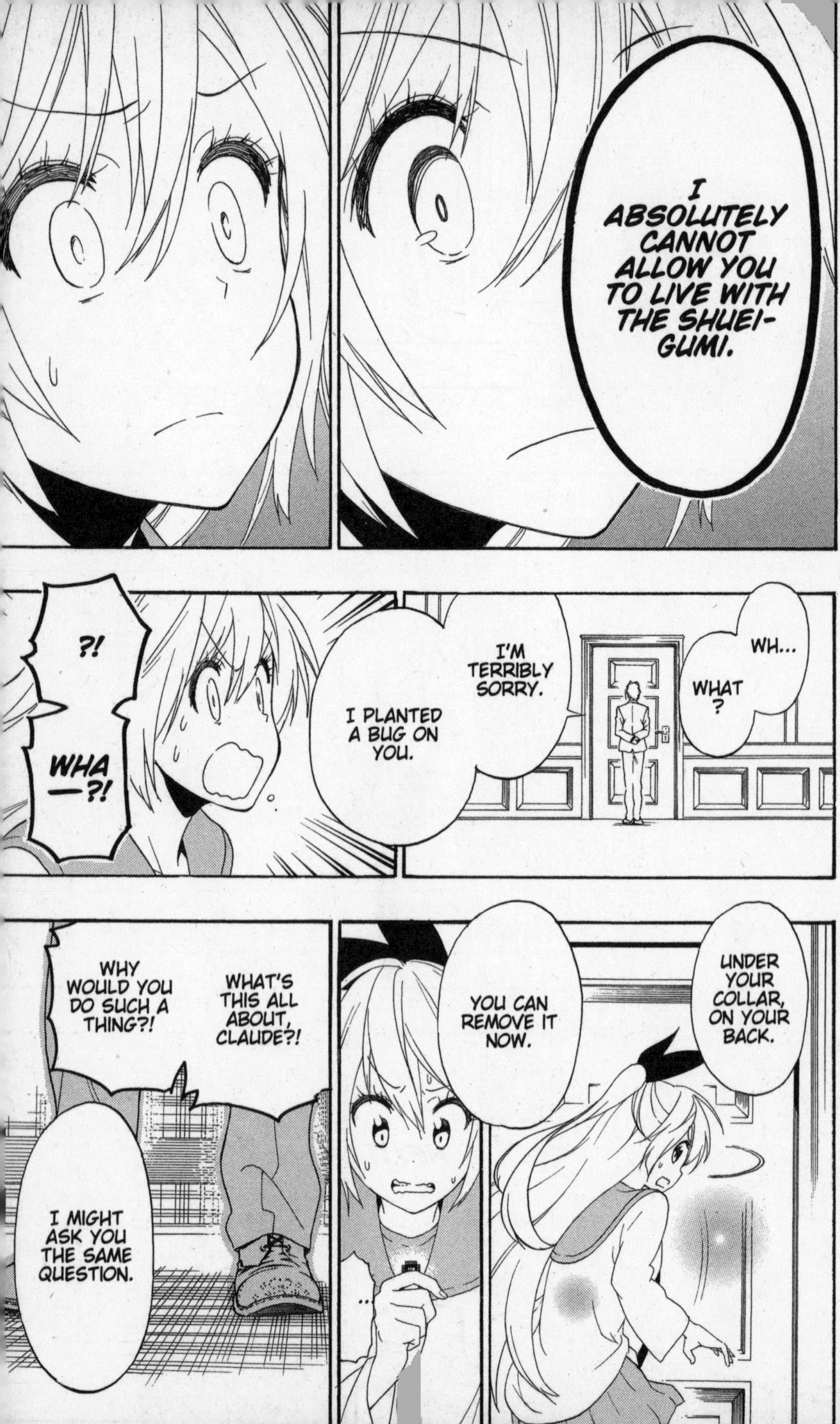
I ABSOLUTELY CANNOT ALLOW YOU TO LIVE WITH THE SHUEI-GUMI.
WH... WHAT?
I'M TERRIBLY SORRY.
I PLANTED A BUG ON YOU.
?! WHA—?!
UNDER YOUR COLLAR, ON YOUR BACK.
YOU CAN REMOVE IT NOW.
...
WHAT'S THIS ALL ABOUT, CLAUDE?!
WHY WOULD YOU DO SUCH A THING?!
I MIGHT ASK YOU THE SAME QUESTION.

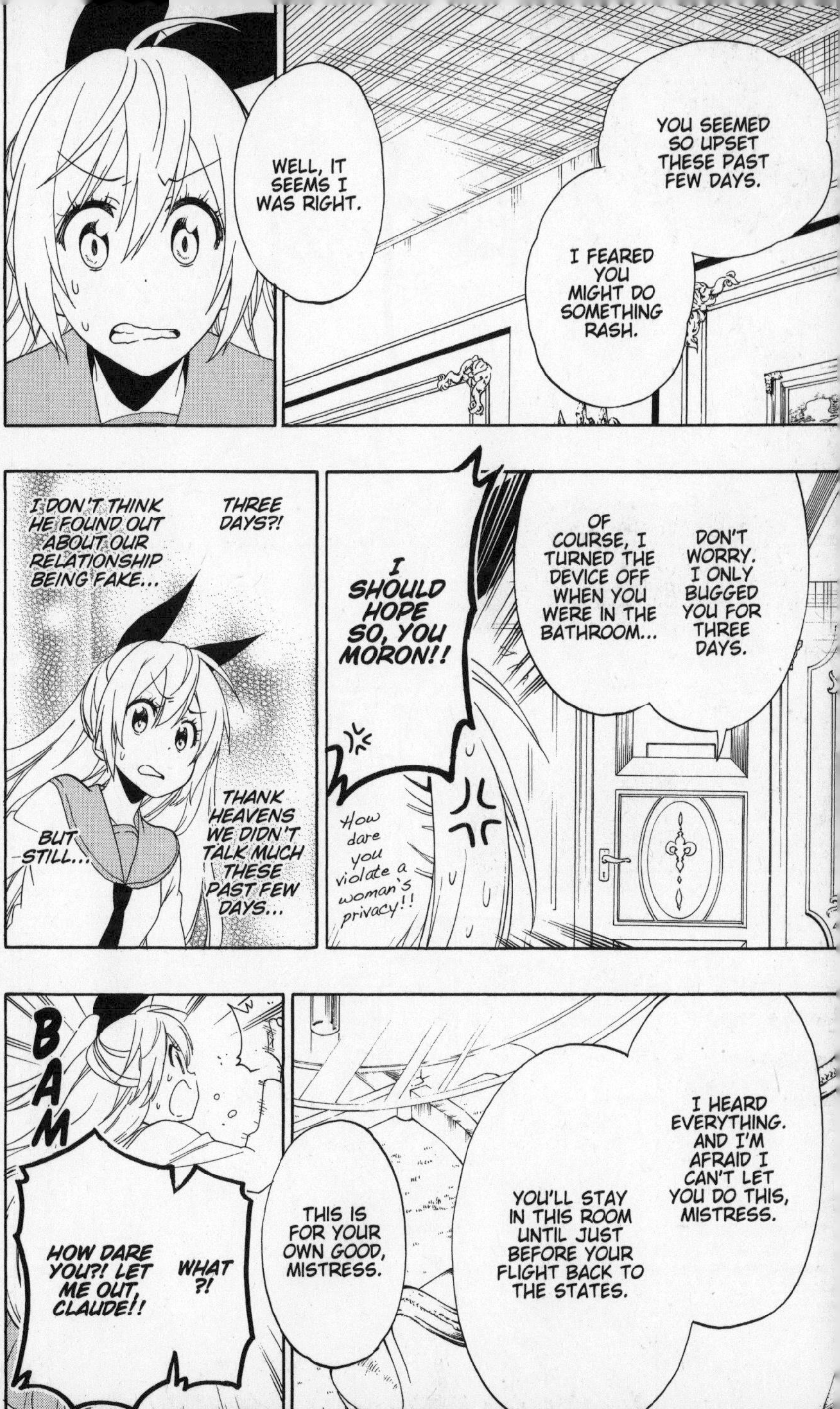
YOU SEEMED SO UPSET THESE PAST FEW DAYS.
I FEARED YOU MIGHT DO SOMETHING RASH.
WELL, IT SEEMS I WAS RIGHT.
DON'T WORRY. I ONLY BUGGED YOU FOR THREE DAYS.
OF COURSE, I TURNED THE DEVICE OFF WHEN YOU WERE IN THE BATHROOM...
I SHOULD HOPE SO, YOU MORON!!
How dare you violate a woman's privacy!!
THREE DAYS?!
I DON'T THINK HE FOUND OUT ABOUT OUR RELATIONSHIP BEING FAKE...
THANK HEAVENS WE DIDN'T TALK MUCH THESE PAST FEW DAYS...
BUT STILL...
I HEARD EVERYTHING. AND I'M AFRAID I CAN'T LET YOU DO THIS, MISTRESS.
YOU'LL STAY IN THIS ROOM UNTIL JUST BEFORE YOUR FLIGHT BACK TO THE STATES.
THIS IS FOR YOUR OWN GOOD, MISTRESS.
BAM
WHAT?!
HOW DARE YOU?! LET ME OUT, CLAUDE!!

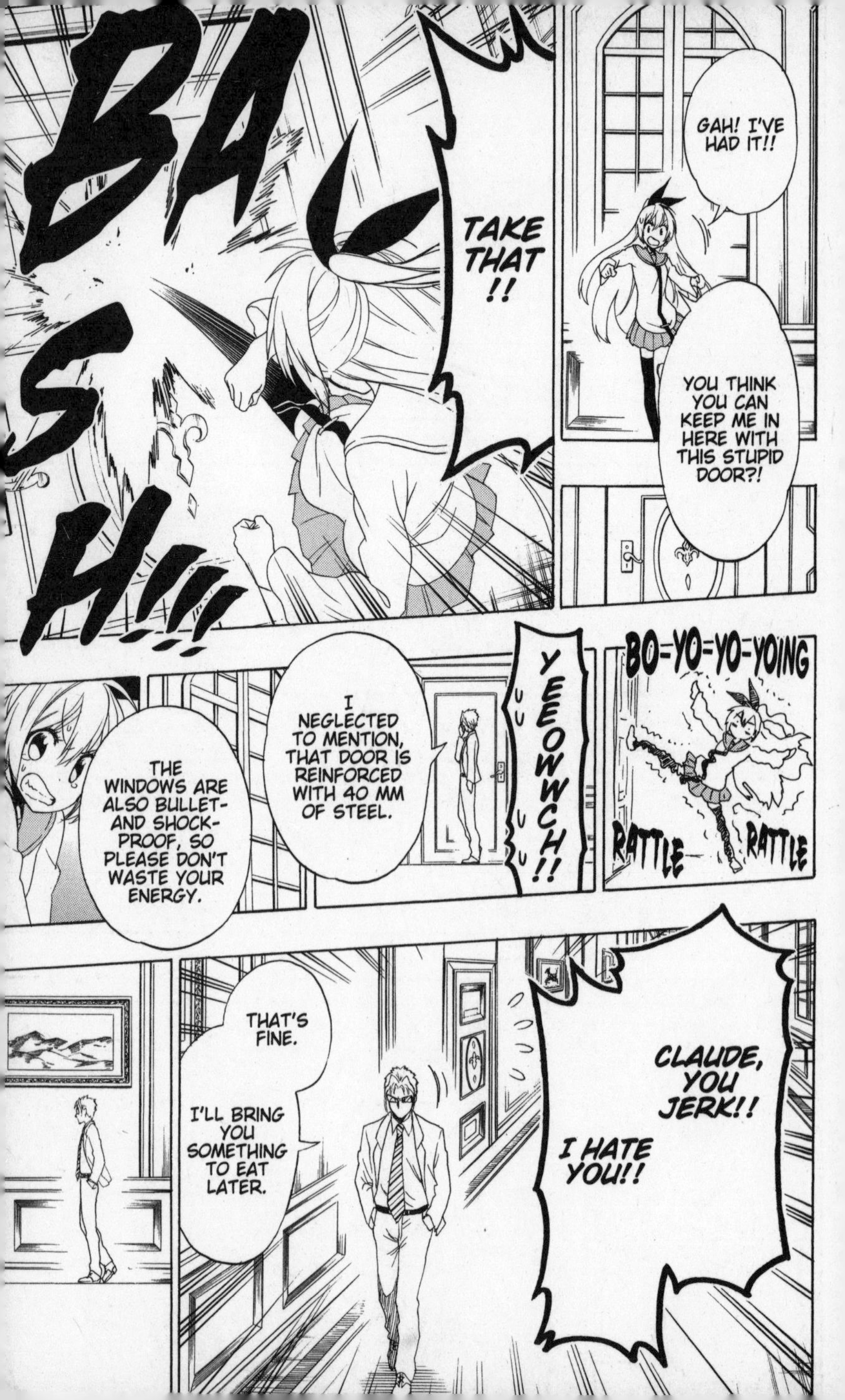
GAH! I'VE HAD IT!!
YOU THINK YOU CAN KEEP ME IN HERE WITH THIS STUPID DOOR?!
TAKE THAT!!
BASH!!
BO-YO=YO-YOING
RATTLE RATTLE
YEEOWWCH!!
I NEGLECTED TO MENTION, THAT DOOR IS REINFORCED WITH 40 MM OF STEEL.
THE WINDOWS ARE ALSO BULLET- AND SHOCK-PROOF, SO PLEASE DON'T WASTE YOUR ENERGY.
CLAUDE, YOU JERK!!
I HATE YOU!!
THAT'S FINE.
I'LL BRING YOU SOMETHING TO EAT LATER.

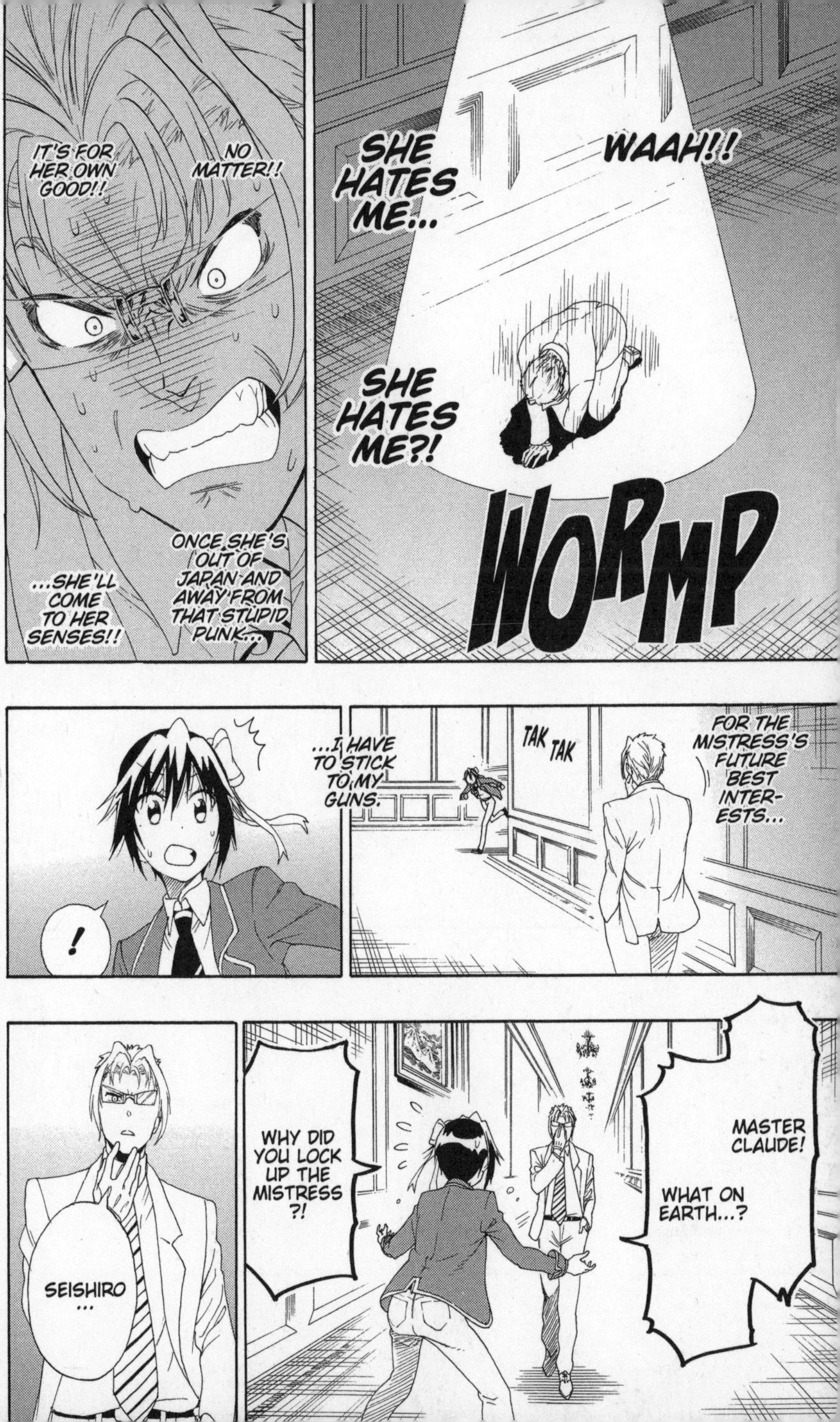
WAAH!!
SHE HATES ME...
SHE HATES ME?!
WORMP
NO MATTER!!
IT'S FOR HER OWN GOOD!!
ONCE SHE'S OUT OF JAPAN AND AWAY FROM THAT STUPID PUNK...
...SHE'LL COME TO HER SENSES!!
FOR THE MISTRESS'S FUTURE BEST INTER-ESTS...
TAK TAK
...I HAVE TO STICK TO MY GUNS.
!
MASTER CLAUDE!
WHAT ON EARTH...?
WHY DID YOU LOCK UP THE MISTRESS?!
SEISHIRO...

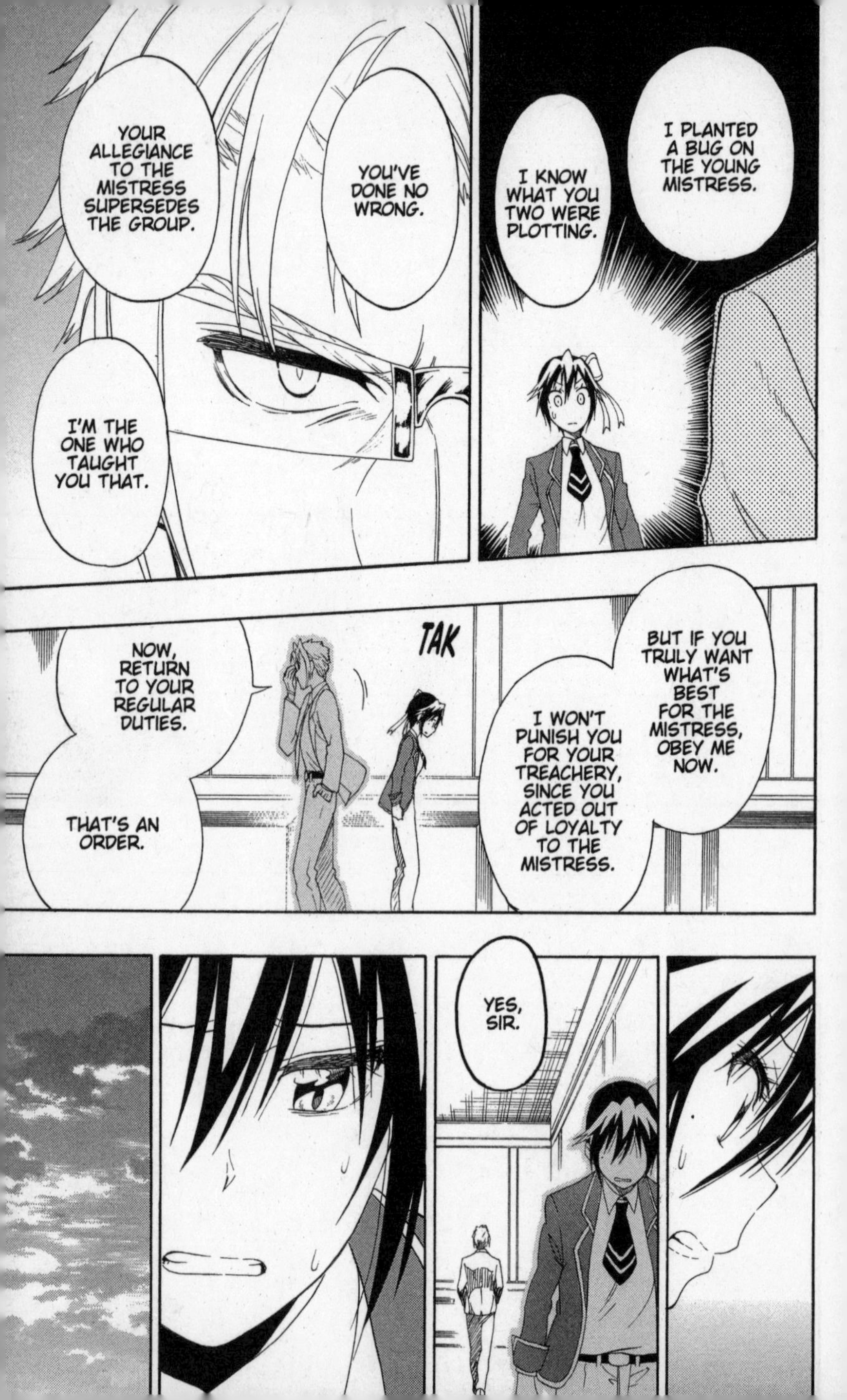
I PLANTED A BUG ON THE YOUNG MISTRESS.
I KNOW WHAT YOU TWO WERE PLOTTING.
YOU'VE DONE NO WRONG.
YOUR ALLEGIANCE TO THE MISTRESS SUPERSEDES THE GROUP.
I'M THE ONE WHO TAUGHT YOU THAT.
BUT IF YOU TRULY WANT WHAT'S BEST FOR THE MISTRESS, OBEY ME NOW.
I WON'T PUNISH YOU FOR YOUR TREACHERY, SINCE YOU ACTED OUT OF LOYALTY TO THE MISTRESS.
TAK
NOW, RETURN TO YOUR REGULAR DUTIES.
THAT'S AN ORDER.
YES, SIR.

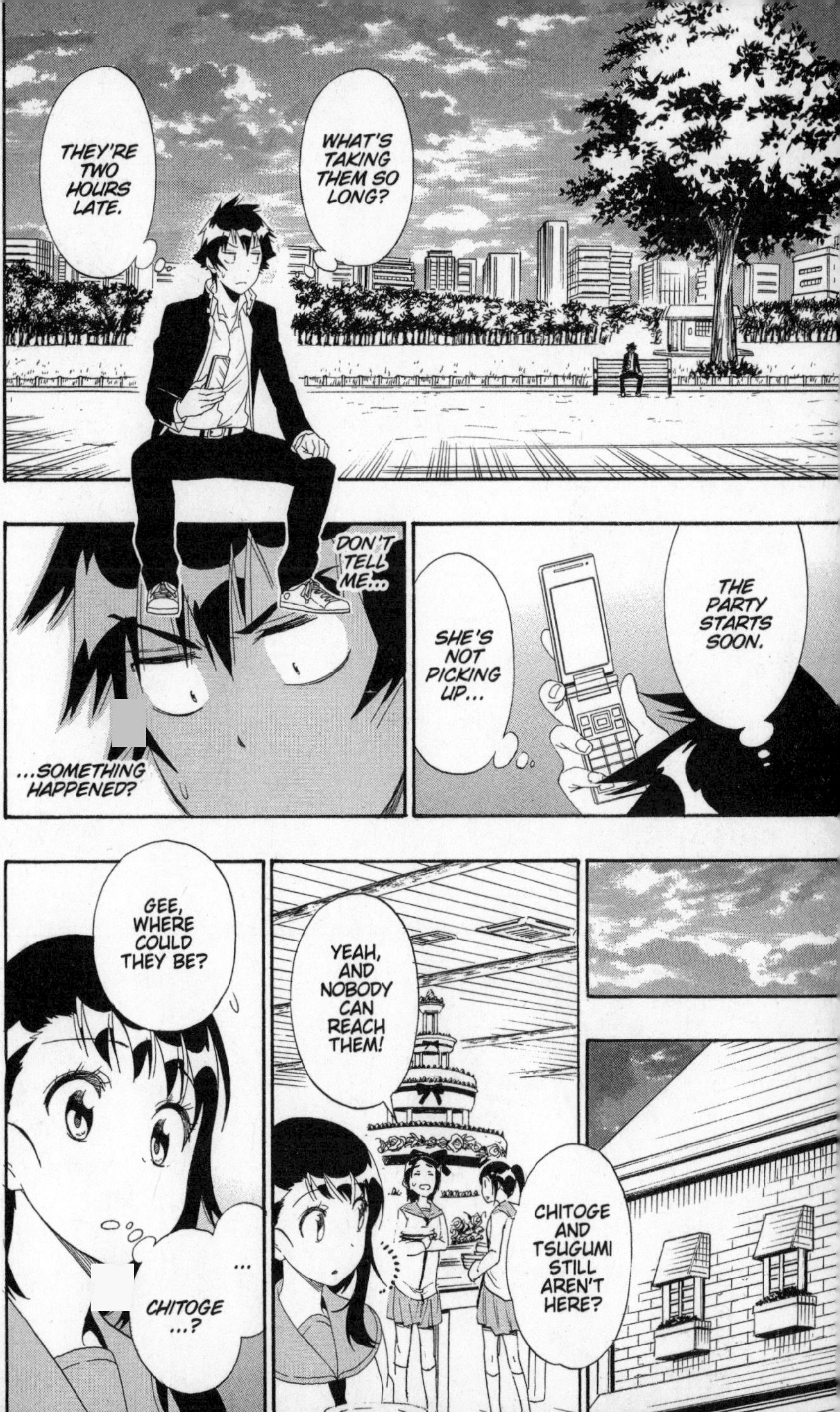
WHAT'S TAKING THEM SO LONG?
THEY'RE TWO HOURS LATE.
THE PARTY STARTS SOON.
SHE'S NOT PICKING UP...
DON'T TELL ME...
...SOMETHING HAPPENED?
CHITOGE AND TSUGUMI STILL AREN'T HERE?
YEAH, AND NOBODY CAN REACH THEM!
GEE, WHERE COULD THEY BE?
...
CHITOGE ...?

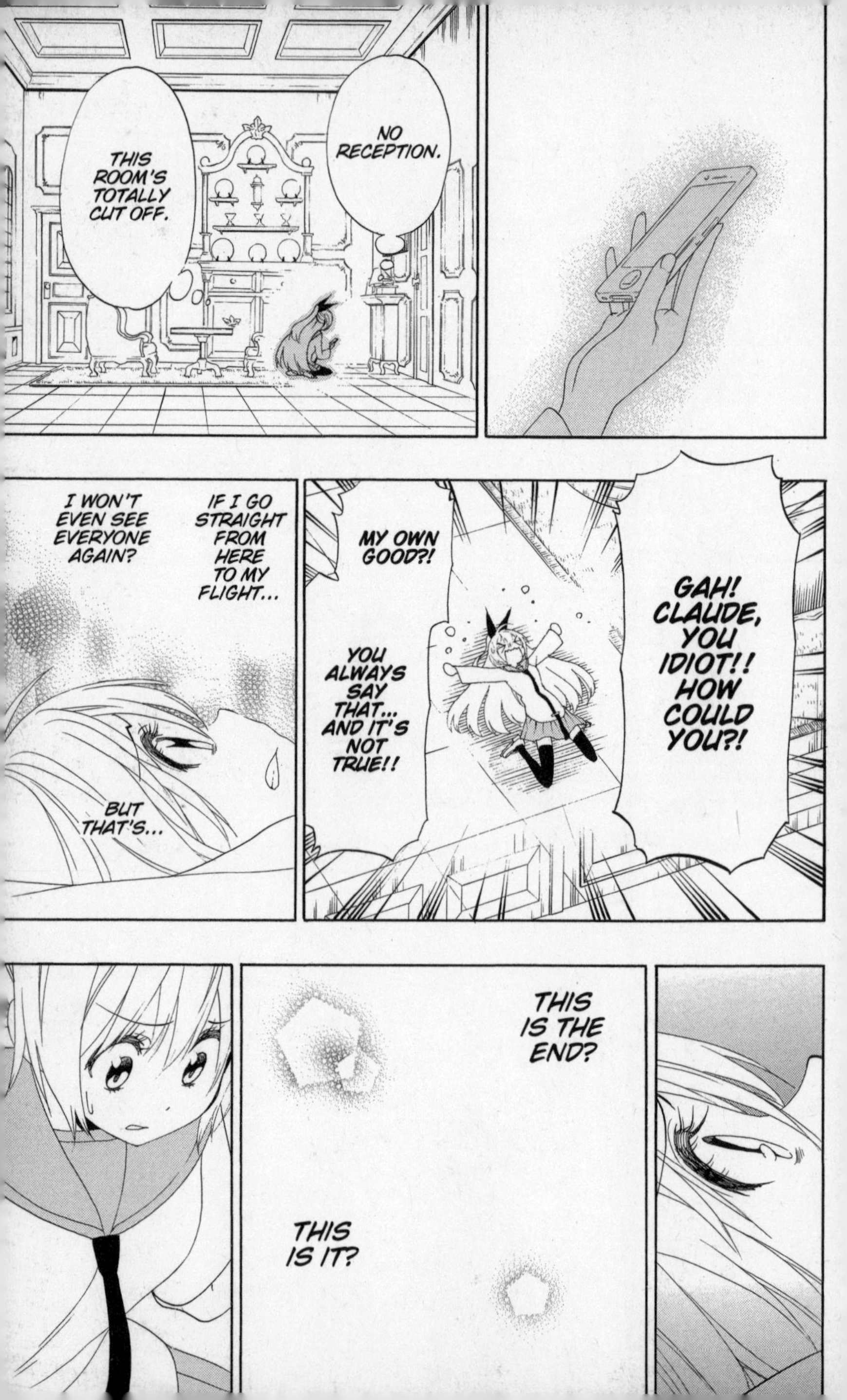
NO RECEPTION.
THIS ROOM'S TOTALLY CUT OFF.
GAH! CLAUDE, YOU IDIOT!! HOW COULD YOU?!
MY OWN GOOD?!
YOU ALWAYS SAY THAT... AND IT'S NOT TRUE!!
IF I GO STRAIGHT FROM HERE TO MY FLIGHT...
I WON'T EVEN SEE EVERYONE AGAIN?
BUT THAT'S...
THIS IS THE END?
THIS IS IT?

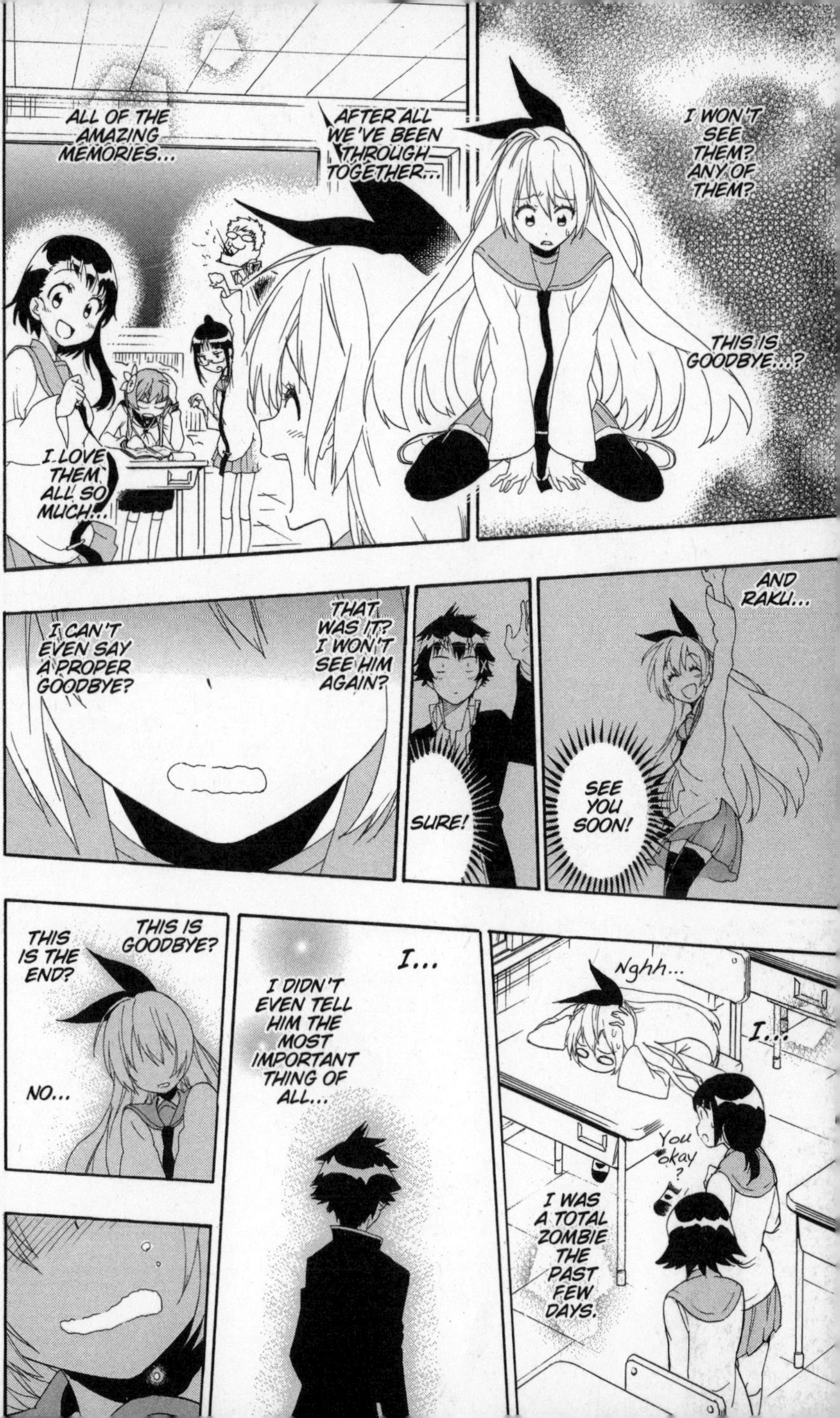
I WON'T SEE THEM? ANY OF THEM?
THIS IS GOODBYE...?
AFTER ALL WE'VE BEEN THROUGH TOGETHER...
ALL OF THE AMAZING MEMORIES...
I LOVE THEM ALL SO MUCH!...
AND RAKU...
SEE YOU SOON!
SURE!
THAT WAS IT? I WON'T SEE HIM AGAIN?
I CAN'T EVEN SAY A PROPER GOODBYE?
Nghh...
I...
You okay?
I WAS A TOTAL ZOMBIE THE PAST FEW DAYS.
I...
I DIDN'T EVEN TELL HIM THE MOST IMPORTANT THING OF ALL...
THIS IS GOODBYE?
THIS IS THE END?
NO...

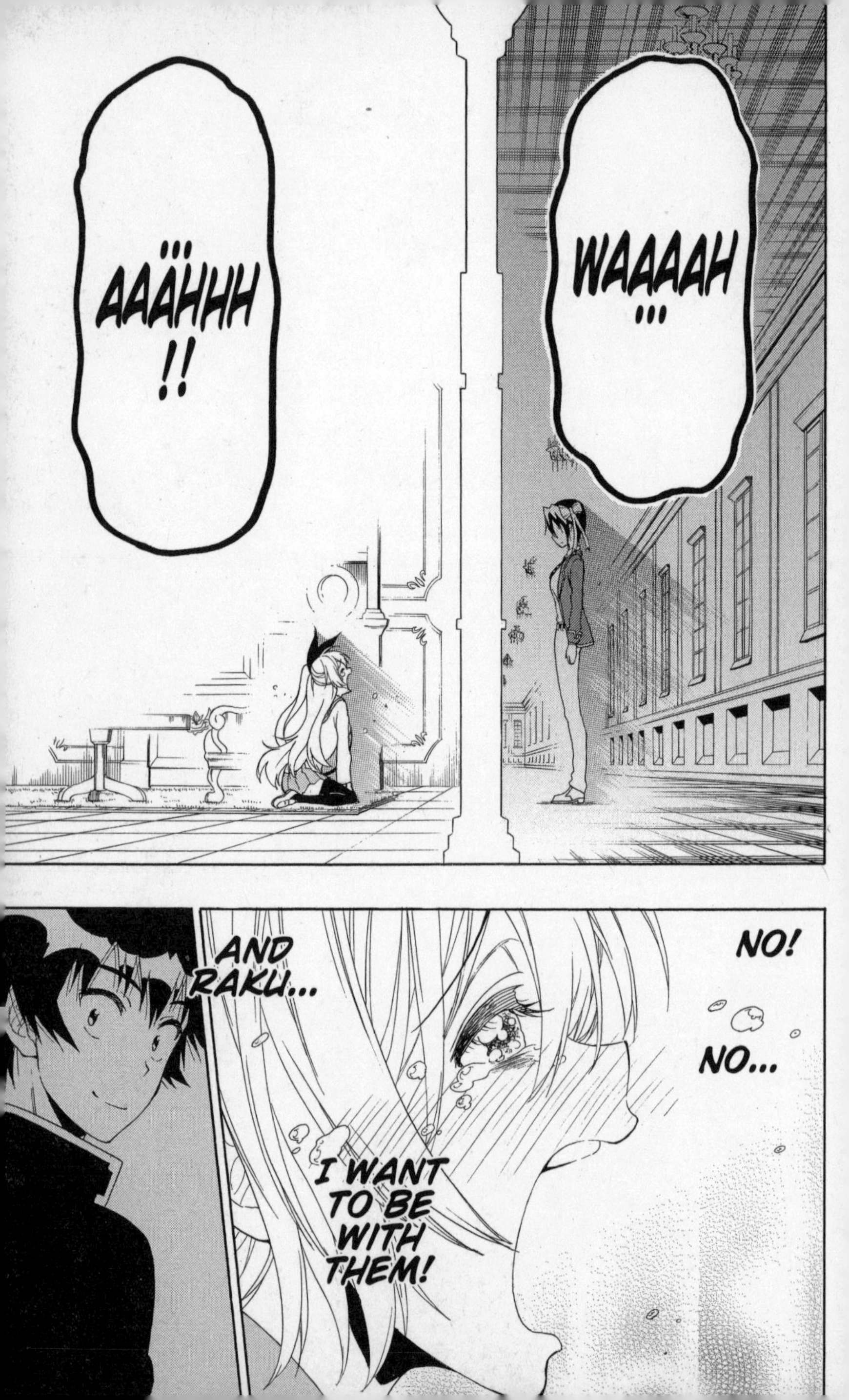
WAAAAH...
...AAAHHH!!
NO!
NO...
AND RAKU...
I WANT TO BE WITH THEM!

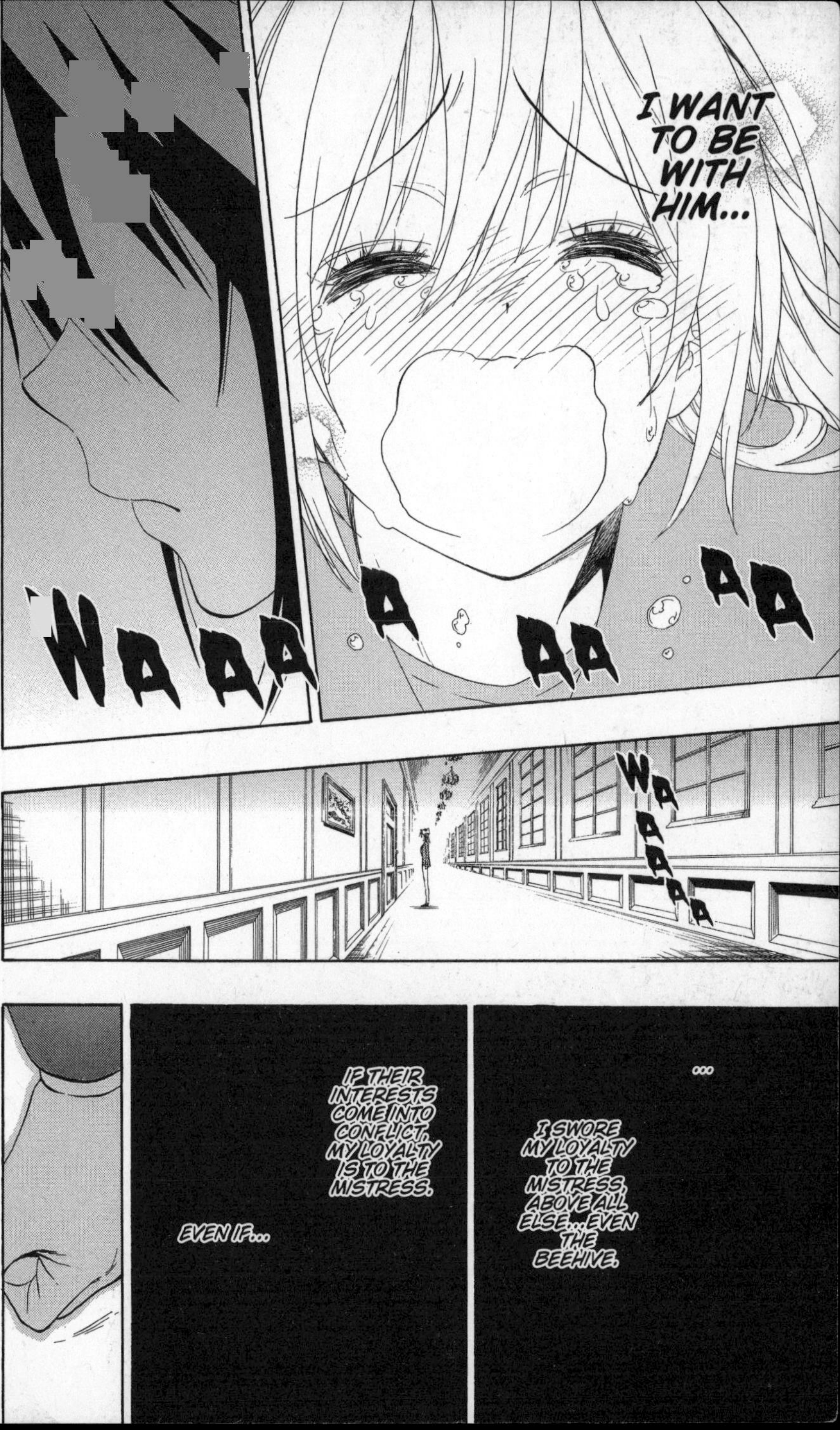
I WANT TO BE WITH HIM...
WAAAA A AA AA
WAAAAAA
...
I SWORE MY LOYALTY TO THE MISTRESS, ABOVE ALL ELSE... EVEN THE BEEHIVE.
IF THEIR INTERESTS COME INTO CONFLICT, MY LOYALTY IS TO THE MISTRESS.
EVEN IF...

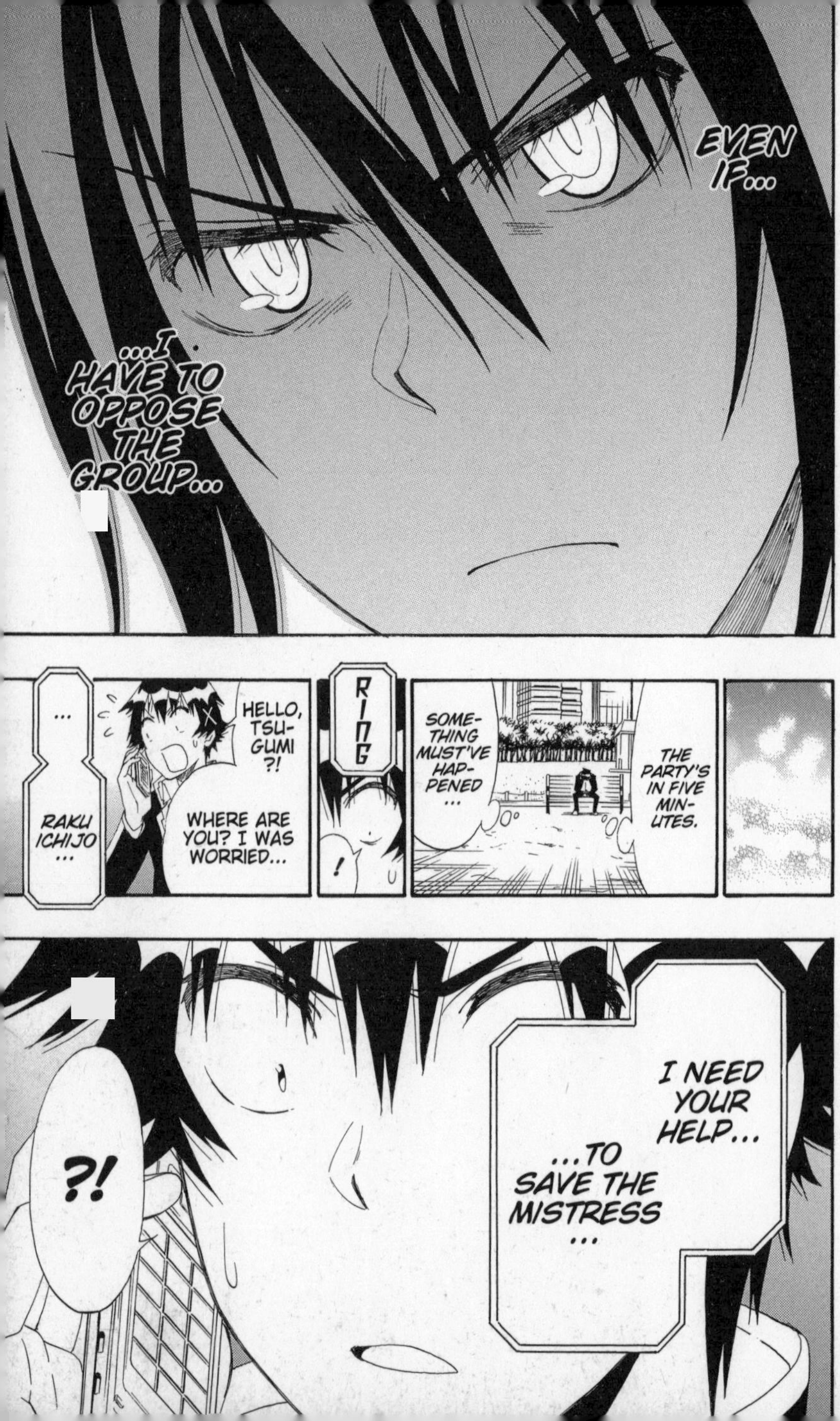
EVEN IF...
...I HAVE TO OPPOSE THE GROUP...
THE PARTY'S IN FIVE MINUTES.
SOMETHING MUST'VE HAPPENED...
RING
!
HELLO, TSUGUMI?!
WHERE ARE YOU? I WAS WORRIED...
... RAKU ICHIJO ...
I NEED YOUR HELP...
...TO SAVE THE MISTRESS...
?!

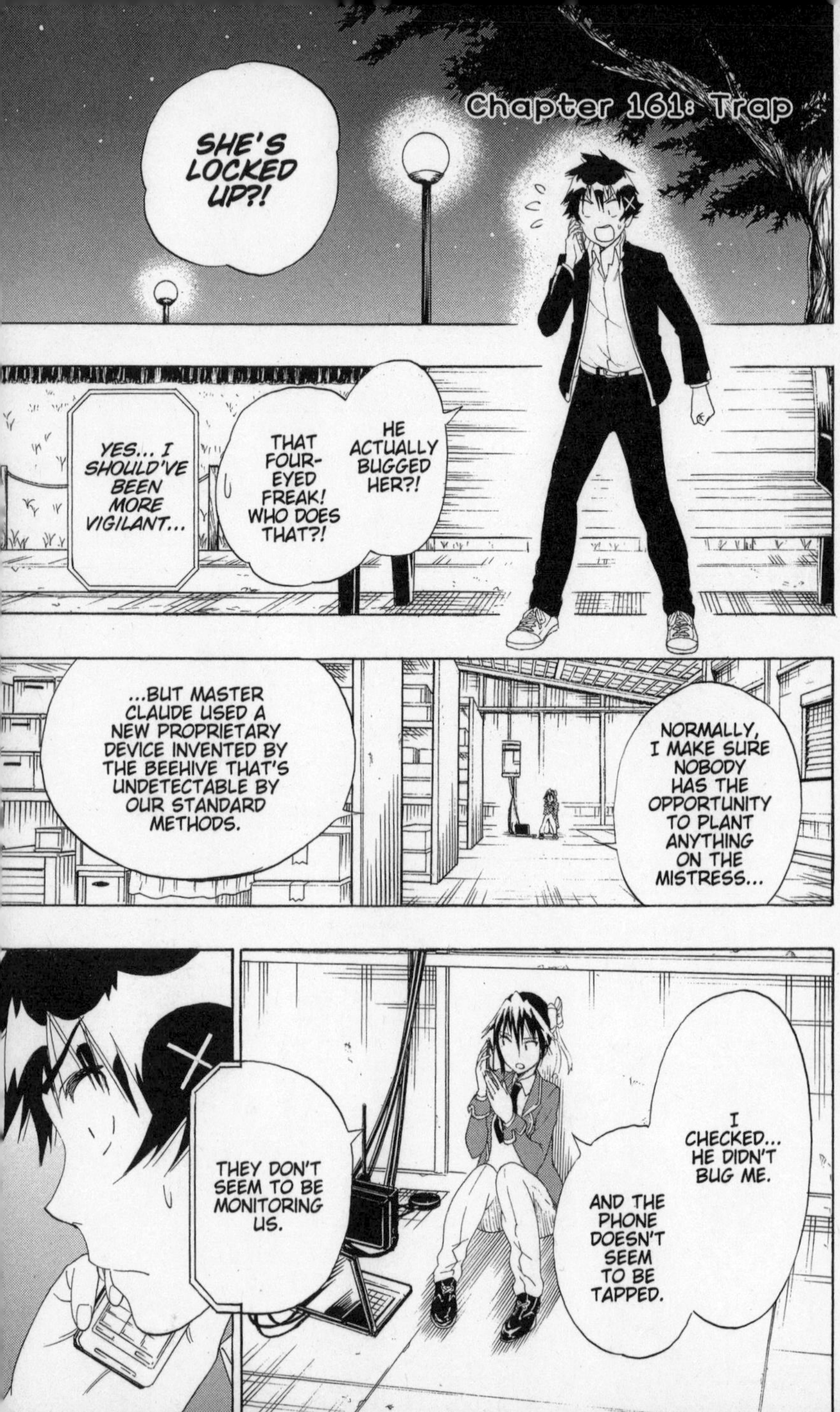
Chapter 161: Trap
SHE'S LOCKED UP?!
HE ACTUALLY BUGGED HER?!
THAT FOUR-EYED FREAK! WHO DOES THAT?!
YES... I SHOULD'VE BEEN MORE VIGILANT...
NORMALLY, I MAKE SURE NOBODY HAS THE OPPORTUNITY TO PLANT ANYTHING ON THE MISTRESS...
...BUT MASTER CLAUDE USED A NEW PROPRIETARY DEVICE INVENTED BY THE BEEHIVE THAT'S UNDETECTABLE BY OUR STANDARD METHODS.
I CHECKED... HE DIDN'T BUG ME.
AND THE PHONE DOESN'T SEEM TO BE TAPPED.
THEY DON'T SEEM TO BE MONITORING US.

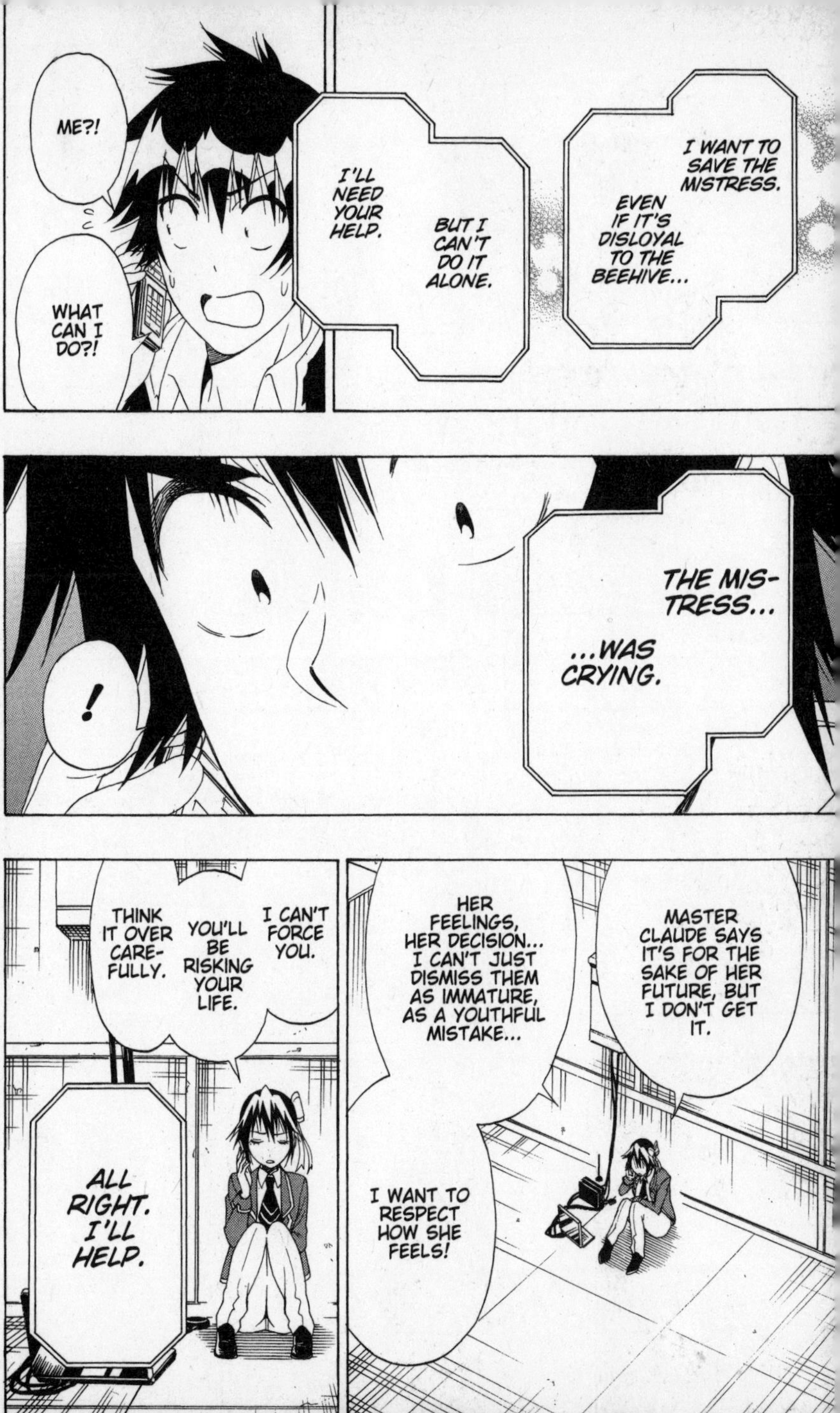
I WANT TO SAVE THE MISTRESS.
EVEN IF IT'S DISLOYAL TO THE BEEHIVE...
BUT I CAN'T DO IT ALONE.
I'LL NEED YOUR HELP.
ME?!
WHAT CAN I DO?!
THE MIS-TRESS...
...WAS CRYING.
!
MASTER CLAUDE SAYS IT'S FOR THE SAKE OF HER FUTURE, BUT I DON'T GET IT.
HER FEELINGS, HER DECISION... I CAN'T JUST DISMISS THEM AS IMMATURE, AS A YOUTHFUL MISTAKE...
I WANT TO RESPECT HOW SHE FEELS!
I CAN'T FORCE YOU.
YOU'LL BE RISKING YOUR LIFE.
THINK IT OVER CARE-FULLY.
ALL RIGHT. I'LL HELP.

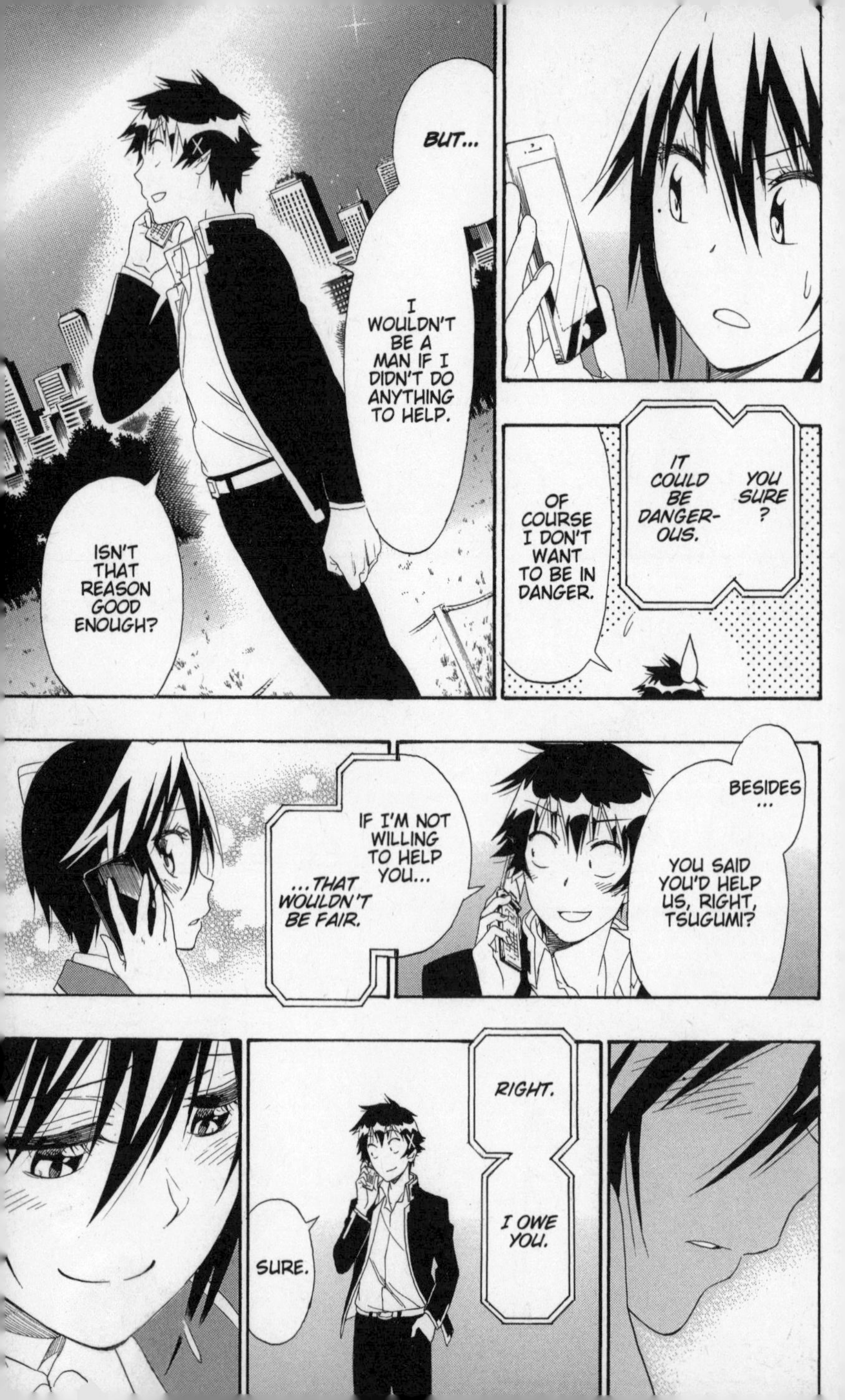
YOU SURE?
IT COULD BE DANGEROUS.
OF COURSE I DON'T WANT TO BE IN DANGER.
BUT...
I WOULDN'T BE A MAN IF I DIDN'T DO ANYTHING TO HELP.
ISN'T THAT REASON GOOD ENOUGH?
BESIDES...
YOU SAID YOU'D HELP US, RIGHT, TSUGUMI?
IF I'M NOT WILLING TO HELP YOU...
...THAT WOULDN'T BE FAIR.
RIGHT.
I OWE YOU.
SURE.

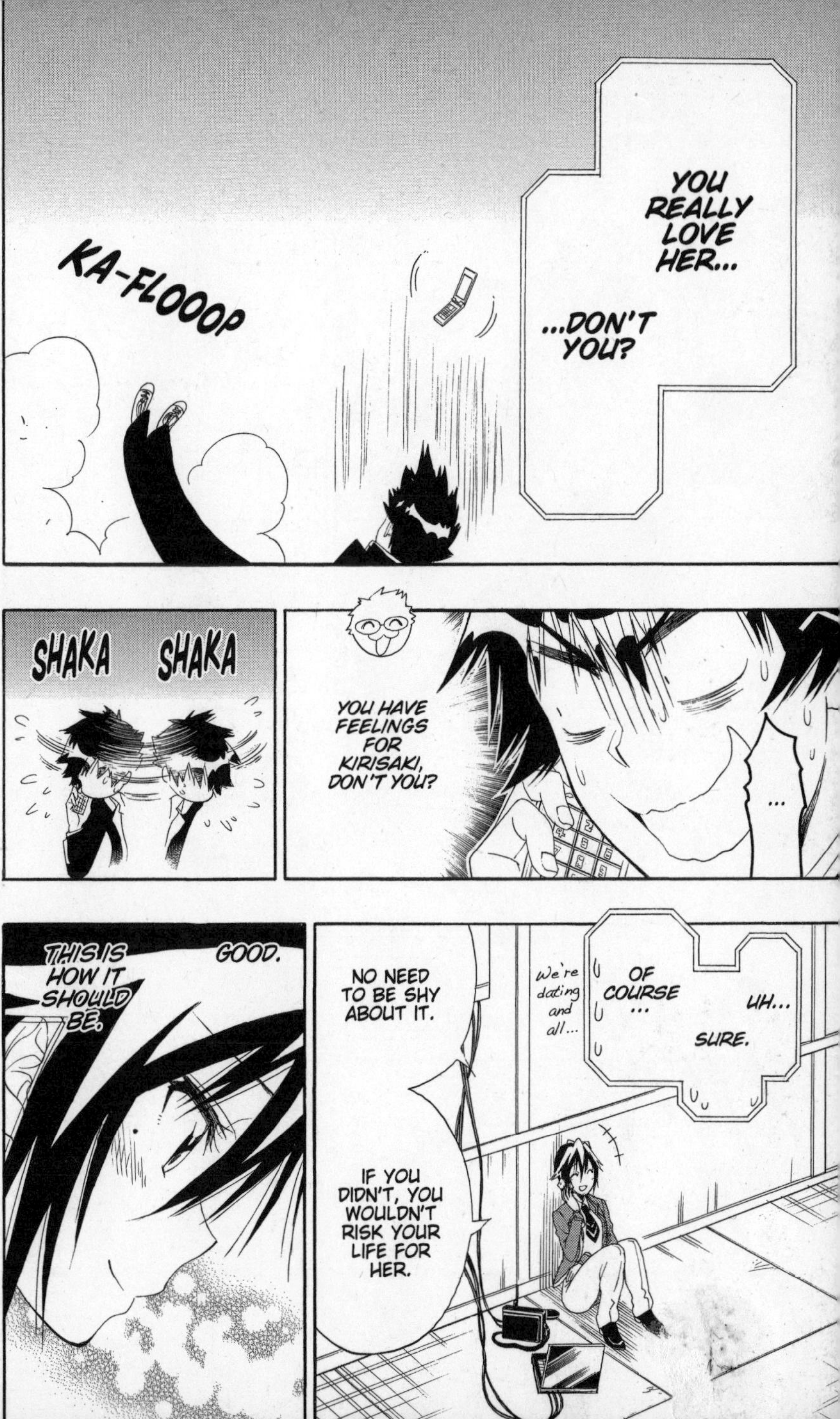
YOU REALLY LOVE HER...
...DON'T YOU?
KA-FLOOOP
YOU HAVE FEELINGS FOR KIRISAKI, DON'T YOU?
...
SHAKA SHAKA
UH... SURE.
OF COURSE...
We're dating and all...
NO NEED TO BE SHY ABOUT IT.
IF YOU DIDN'T, YOU WOULDN'T RISK YOUR LIFE FOR HER.
GOOD.
THIS IS HOW IT SHOULD BE.

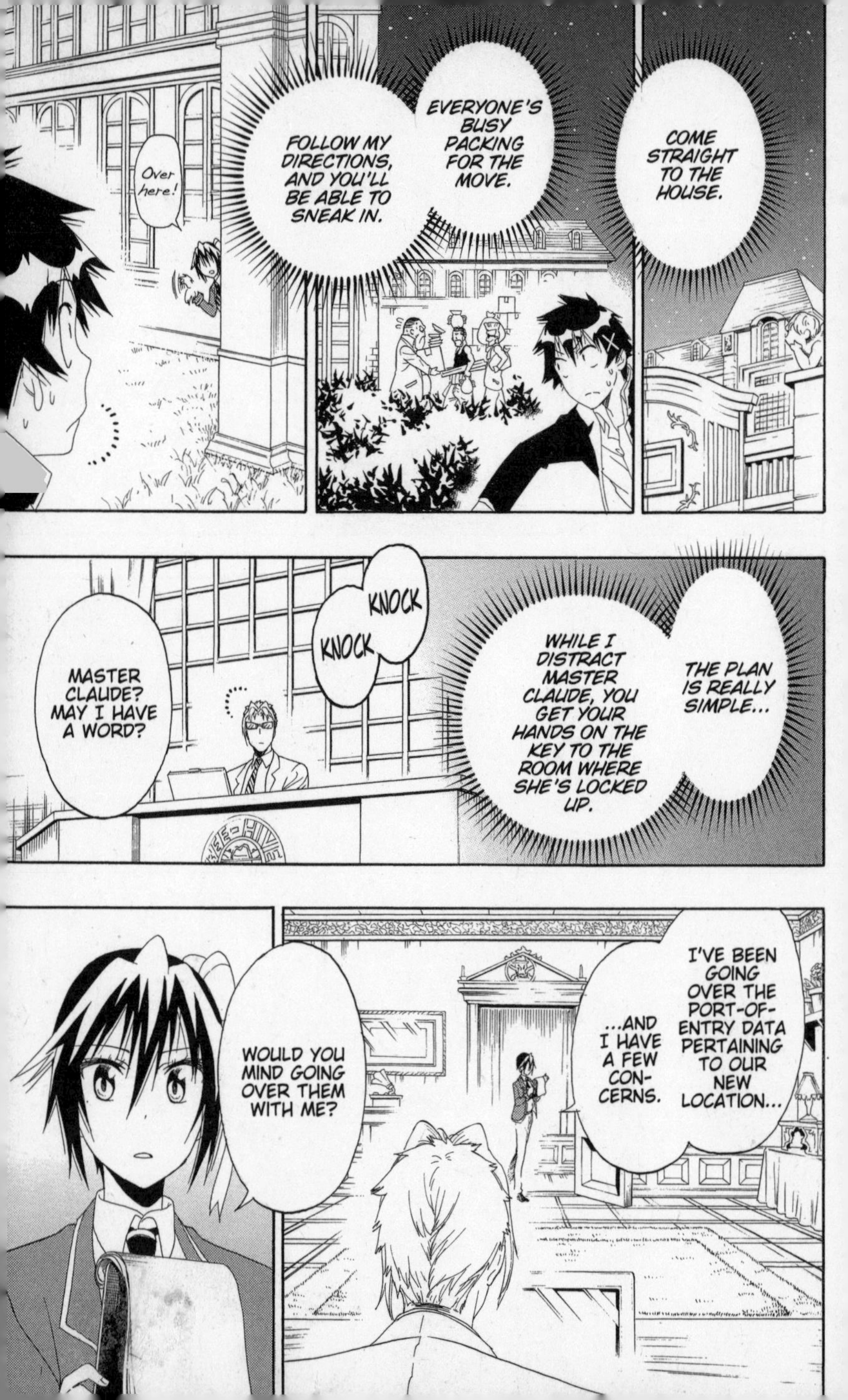
COME STRAIGHT TO THE HOUSE.
EVERYONE'S BUSY PACKING FOR THE MOVE.
FOLLOW MY DIRECTIONS, AND YOU'LL BE ABLE TO SNEAK IN.
Over here!
THE PLAN IS REALLY SIMPLE...
WHILE I DISTRACT MASTER CLAUDE, YOU GET YOUR HANDS ON THE KEY TO THE ROOM WHERE SHE'S LOCKED UP.
KNOCK
KNOCK
MASTER CLAUDE? MAY I HAVE A WORD?
I'VE BEEN GOING OVER THE PORT-OF-ENTRY DATA PERTAINING TO OUR NEW LOCATION...
...AND I HAVE A FEW CON-CERNS.
WOULD YOU MIND GOING OVER THEM WITH ME?

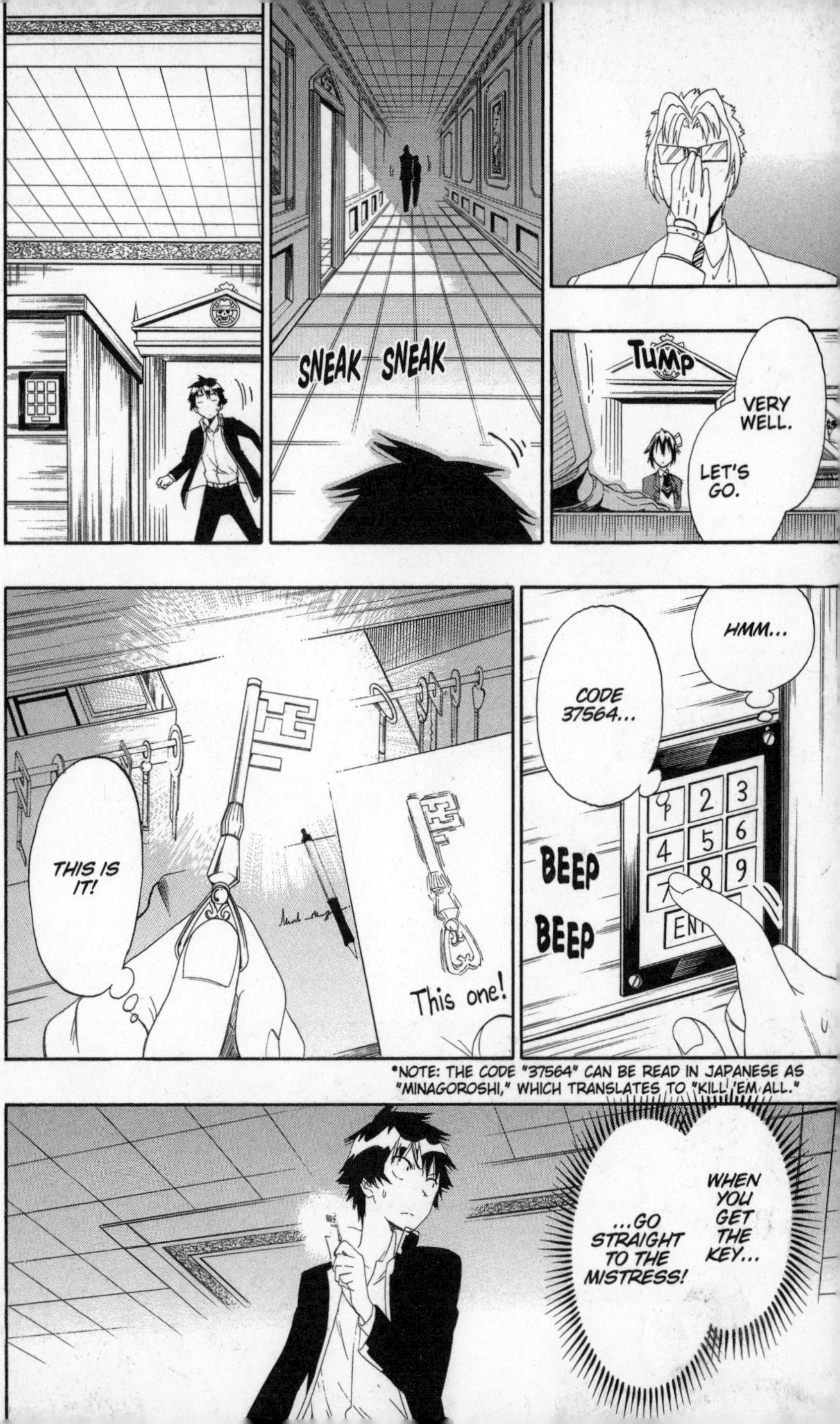
TUMP
VERY WELL.
LET'S GO.
SNEAK SNEAK
HMM...
CODE 37564...
BEEP
BEEP
THIS IS IT!
This one!
*NOTE: THE CODE "37564" CAN BE READ IN JAPANESE AS "MINAGOROSHI," WHICH TRANSLATES TO "KILL 'EM ALL."
WHEN YOU GET THE KEY...
...GO STRAIGHT TO THE MISTRESS!

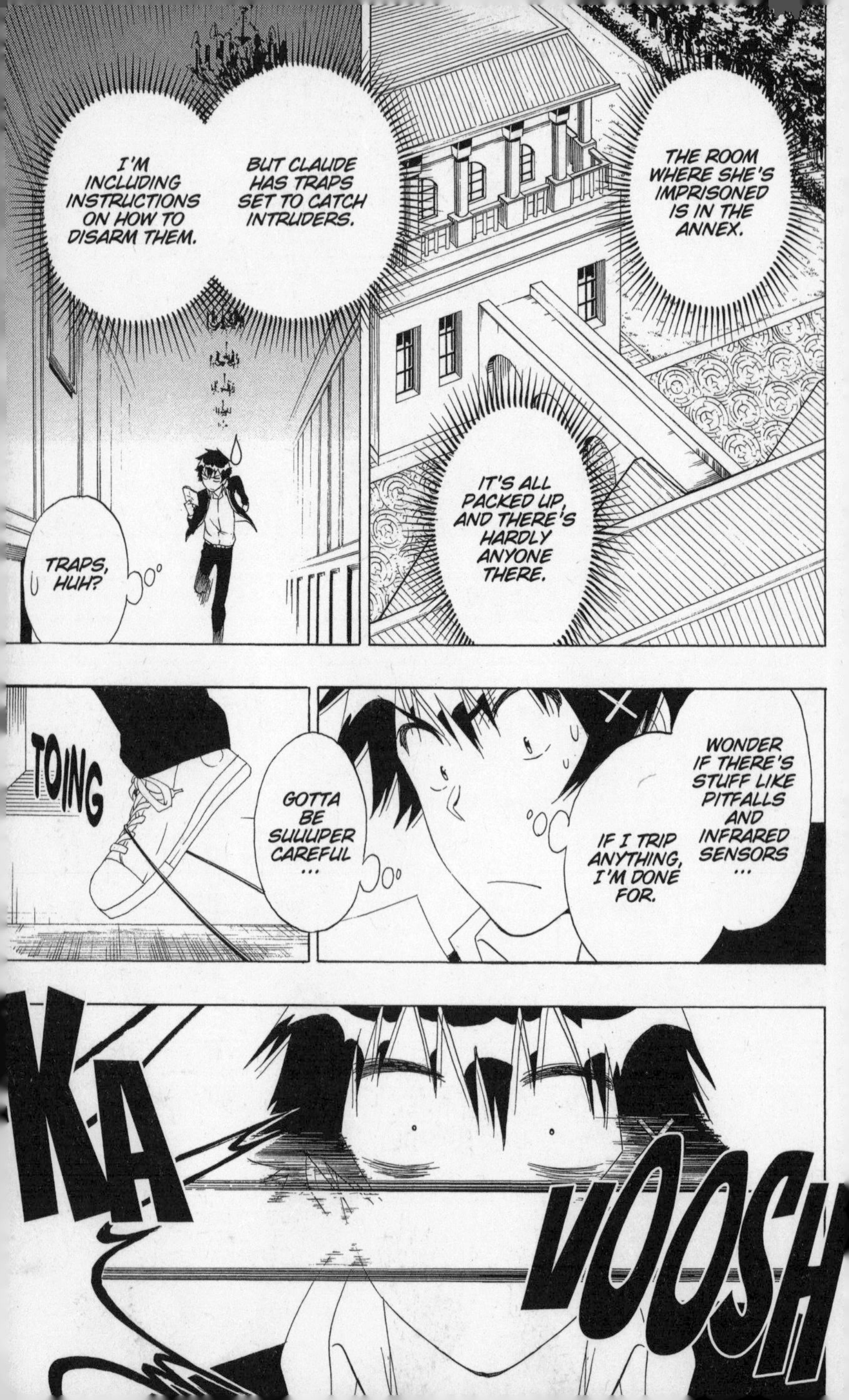
THE ROOM WHERE SHE'S IMPRISONED IS IN THE ANNEX.
IT'S ALL PACKED UP, AND THERE'S HARDLY ANYONE THERE.
BUT CLAUDE HAS TRAPS SET TO CATCH INTRUDERS.
I'M INCLUDING INSTRUCTIONS ON HOW TO DISARM THEM.
TRAPS, HUH?
WONDER IF THERE'S STUFF LIKE PITFALLS AND INFRARED SENSORS...
IF I TRIP ANYTHING, I'M DONE FOR.
GOTTA BE SUUUPER CAREFUL...
TOING
KA-
VOOSH

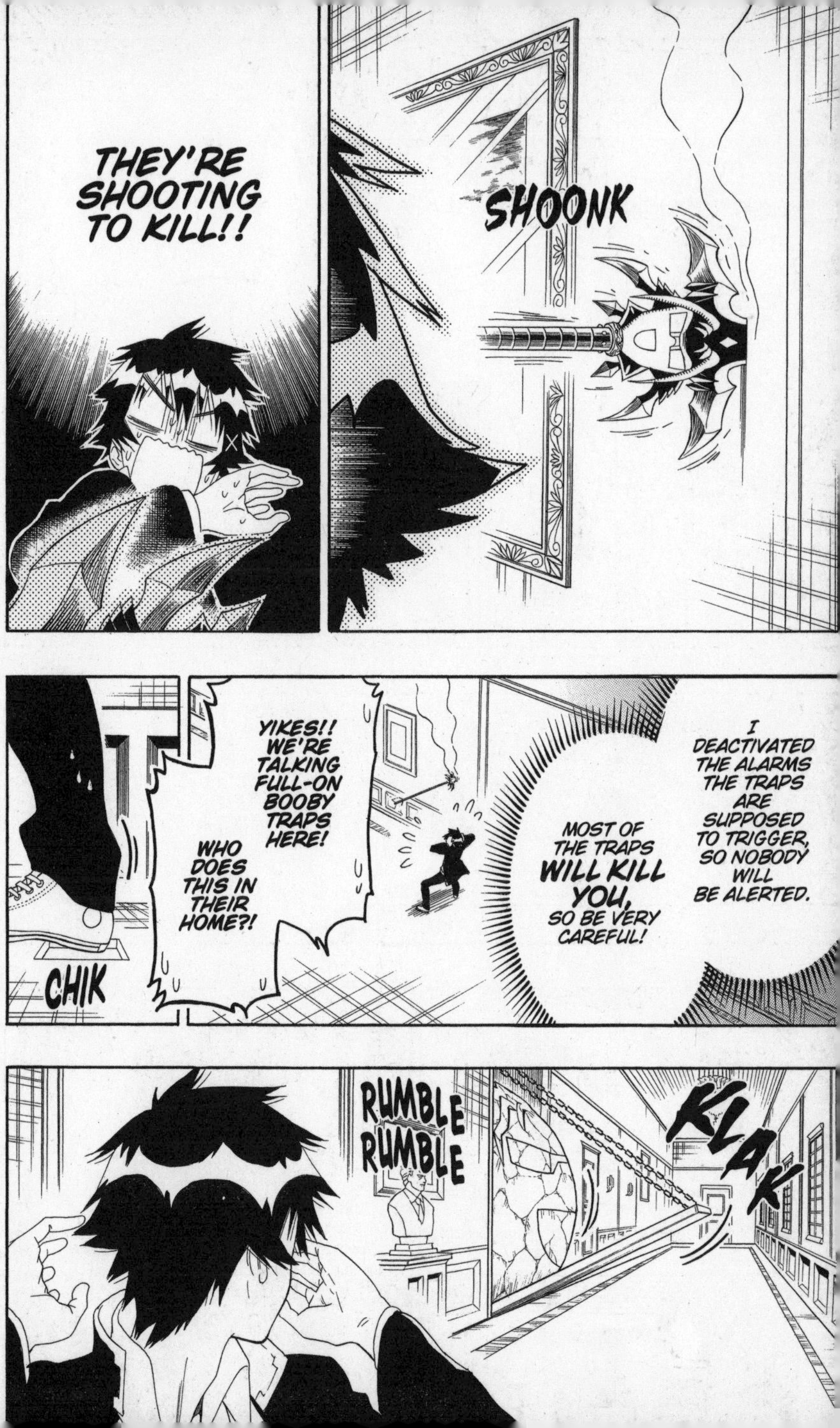
SHOONK
THEY'RE SHOOTING TO KILL!!
I DEACTIVATED THE ALARMS THE TRAPS ARE SUPPOSED TO TRIGGER, SO NOBODY WILL BE ALERTED.
MOST OF THE TRAPS WILL KILL YOU, SO BE VERY CAREFUL!
YIKES!! WE'RE TALKING FULL-ON BOOBY TRAPS HERE!
WHO DOES THIS IN THEIR HOME?!
CHIK
KLAK
RUMBLE RUMBLE

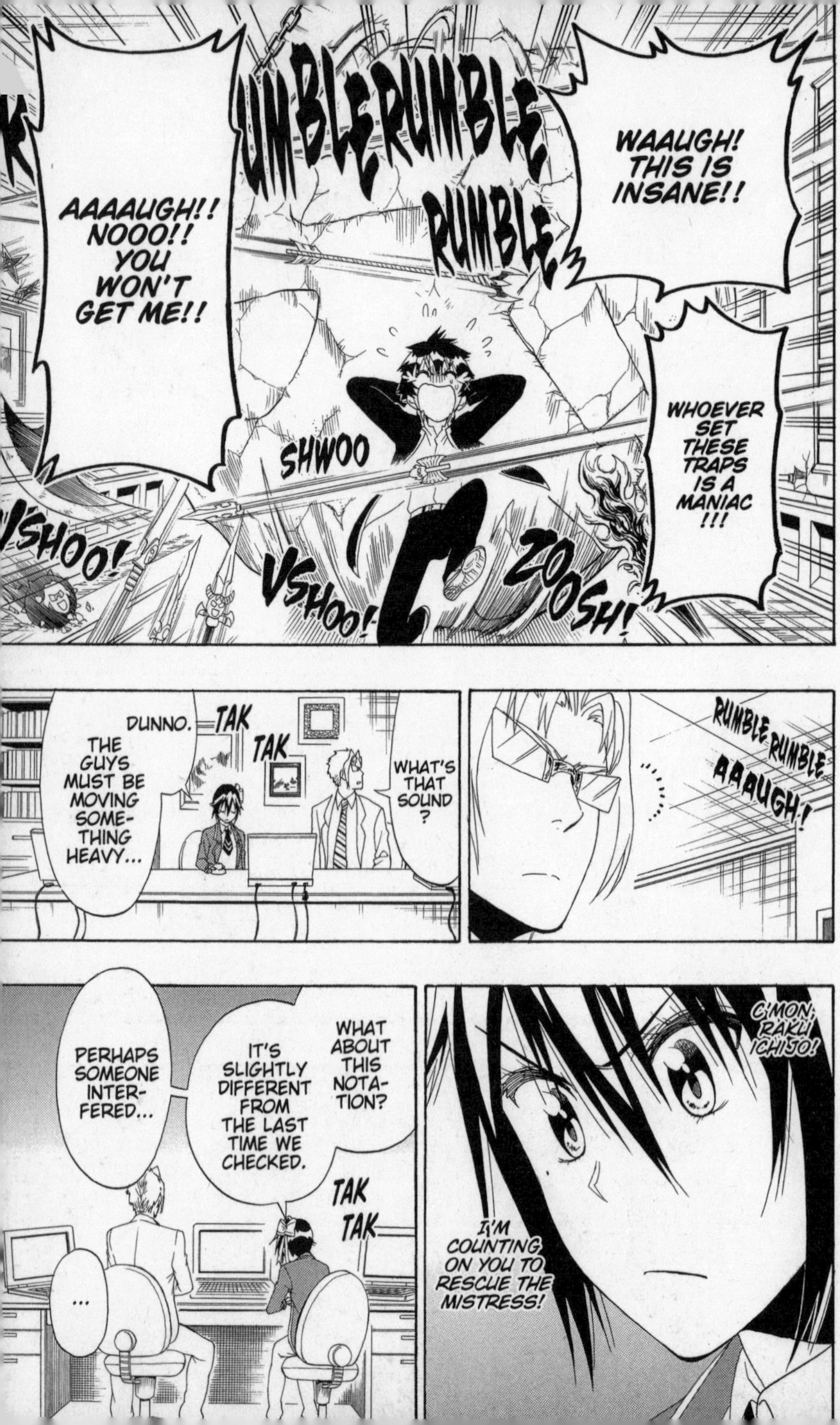
WAAUGH! THIS IS INSANE!!
WHOEVER SET THESE TRAPS IS A MANIAC!!!
UMBLE RUMBLE RUMBLE
AAAAUGH!! NOOO!! YOU WON'T GET ME!!
SHWOO
ZOOSH!
VSHOO!
VSHOO!
RUMBLE RUMBLE
AAAUGH!
...
WHAT'S THAT SOUND?
TAK
TAK
DUNNO. THE GUYS MUST BE MOVING SOME-THING HEAVY...
C'MON, RAKU ICHIJO!
I'M COUNTING ON YOU TO RESCUE THE MISTRESS!
WHAT ABOUT THIS NOTA-TION?
IT'S SLIGHTLY DIFFERENT FROM THE LAST TIME WE CHECKED.
TAK
TAK
PERHAPS SOMEONE INTER-FERED...
...

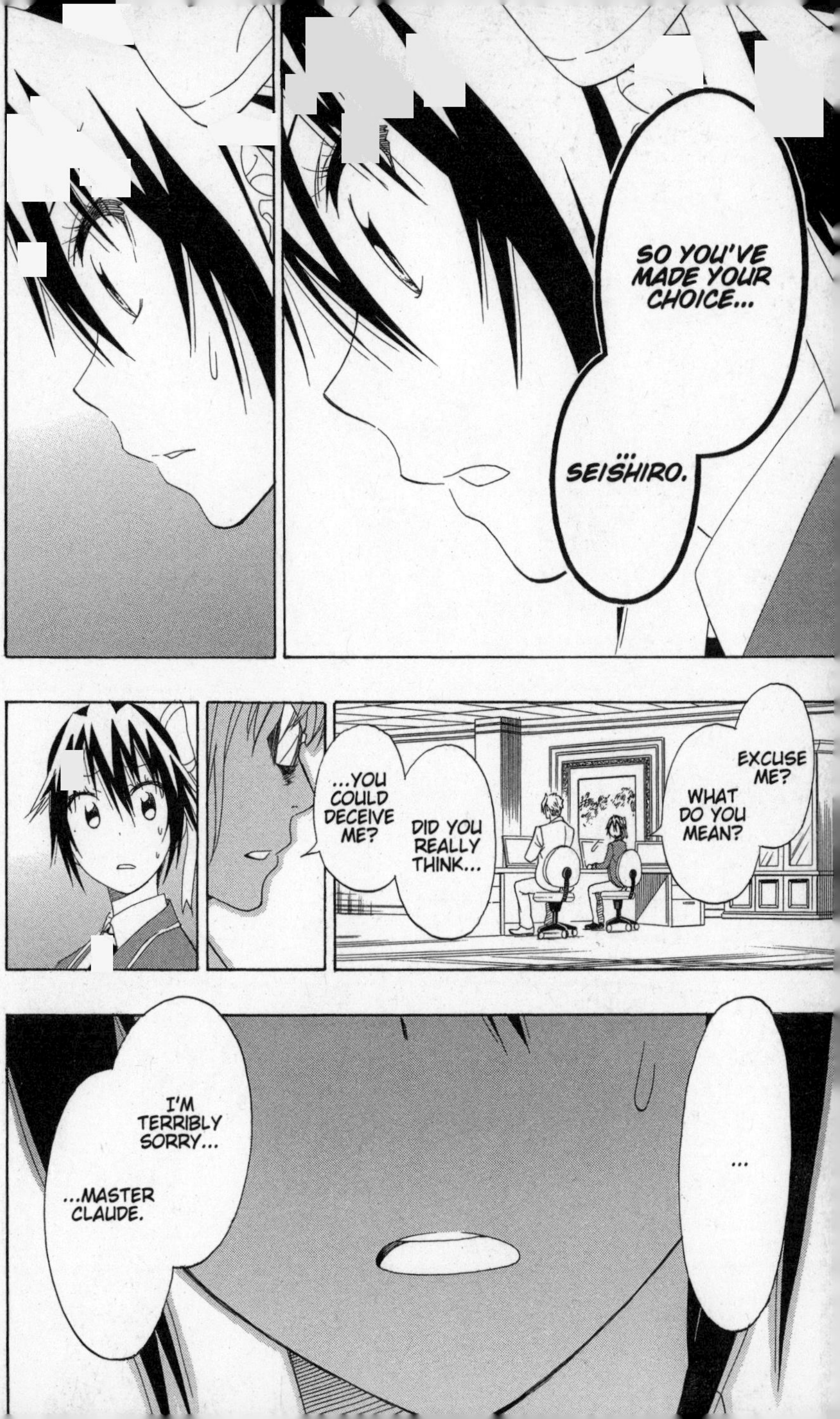
SO YOU'VE MADE YOUR CHOICE...
...SEISHIRO.
EXCUSE ME?
WHAT DO YOU MEAN?
DID YOU REALLY THINK...
...YOU COULD DECEIVE ME?
...
I'M TERRIBLY SORRY...
...MASTER CLAUDE.

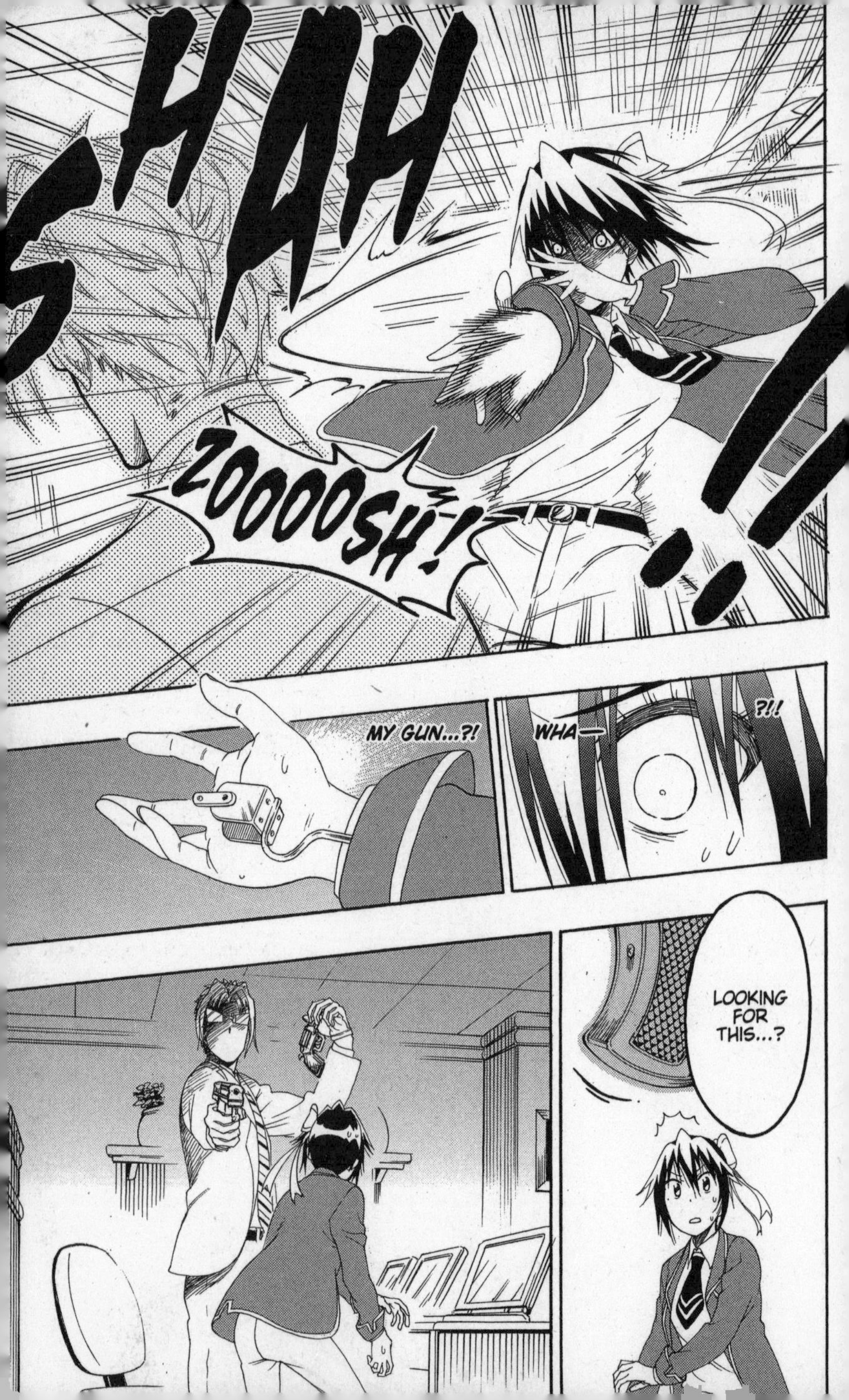
SHAH
!!
ZOOOOOSH!
WHA—
?!!
MY GUN...?!
LOOKING FOR THIS...?

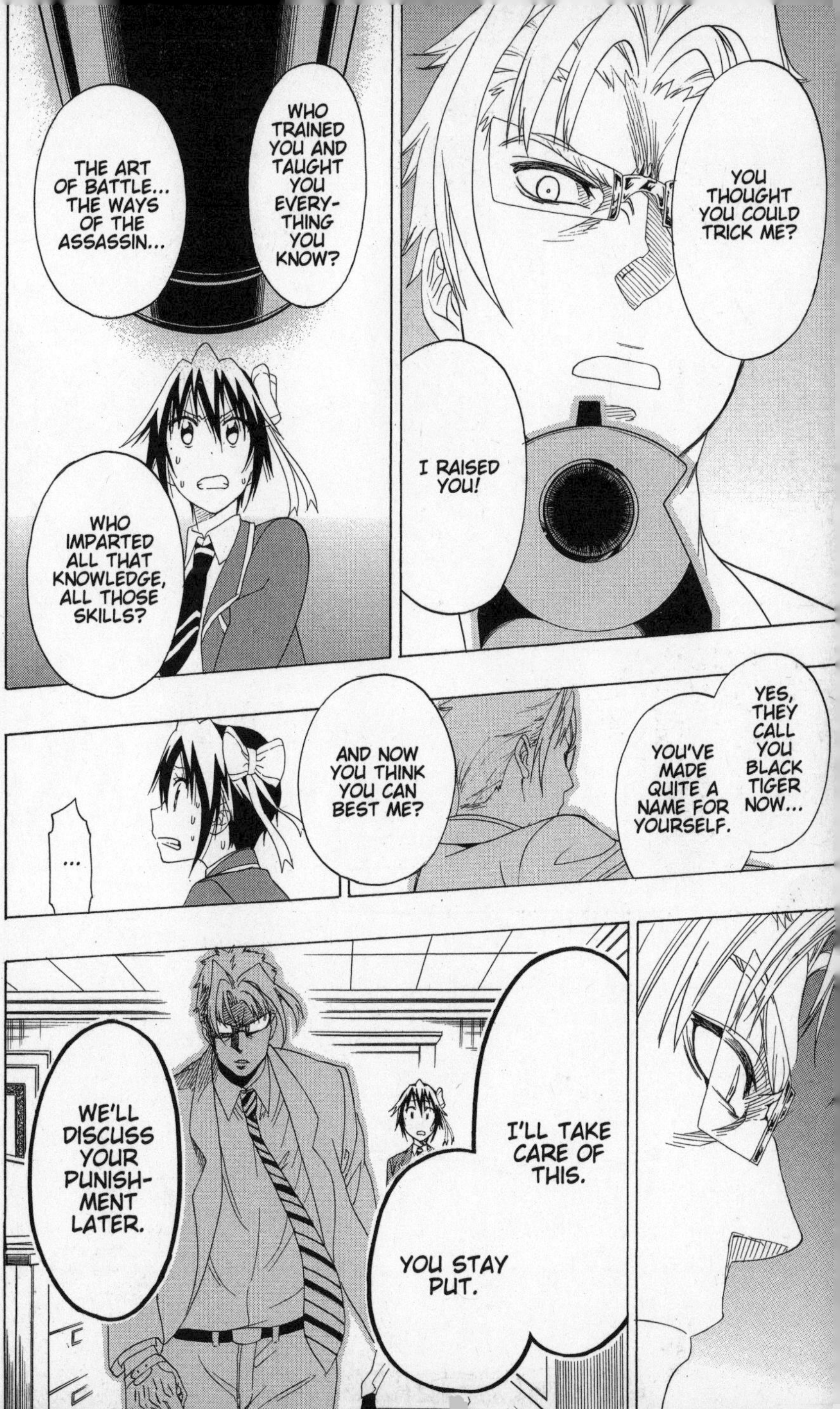
YOU THOUGHT YOU COULD TRICK ME?
I RAISED YOU!
WHO TRAINED YOU AND TAUGHT YOU EVERY-THING YOU KNOW?
THE ART OF BATTLE... THE WAYS OF THE ASSASSIN...
WHO IMPARTED ALL THAT KNOWLEDGE, ALL THOSE SKILLS?
YES, THEY CALL YOU BLACK TIGER NOW...
YOU'VE MADE QUITE A NAME FOR YOURSELF.
AND NOW YOU THINK YOU CAN BEST ME?
...
I'LL TAKE CARE OF THIS.
YOU STAY PUT.
WE'LL DISCUSS YOUR PUNISH-MENT LATER.

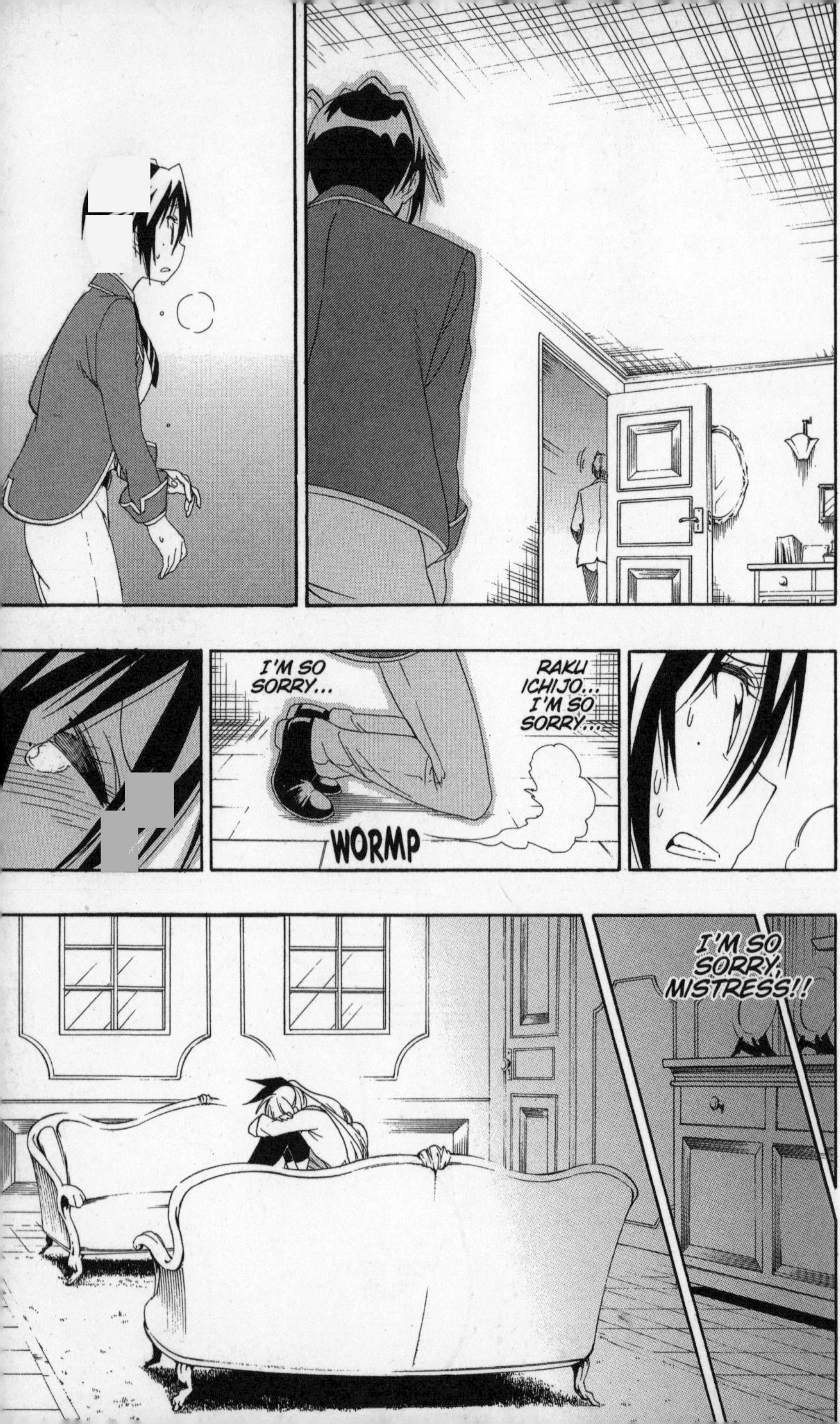
RAKU ICHIJO... I'M SO SORRY...
I'M SO SORRY...
WORMP
I'M SO SORRY, MISTRESS!!

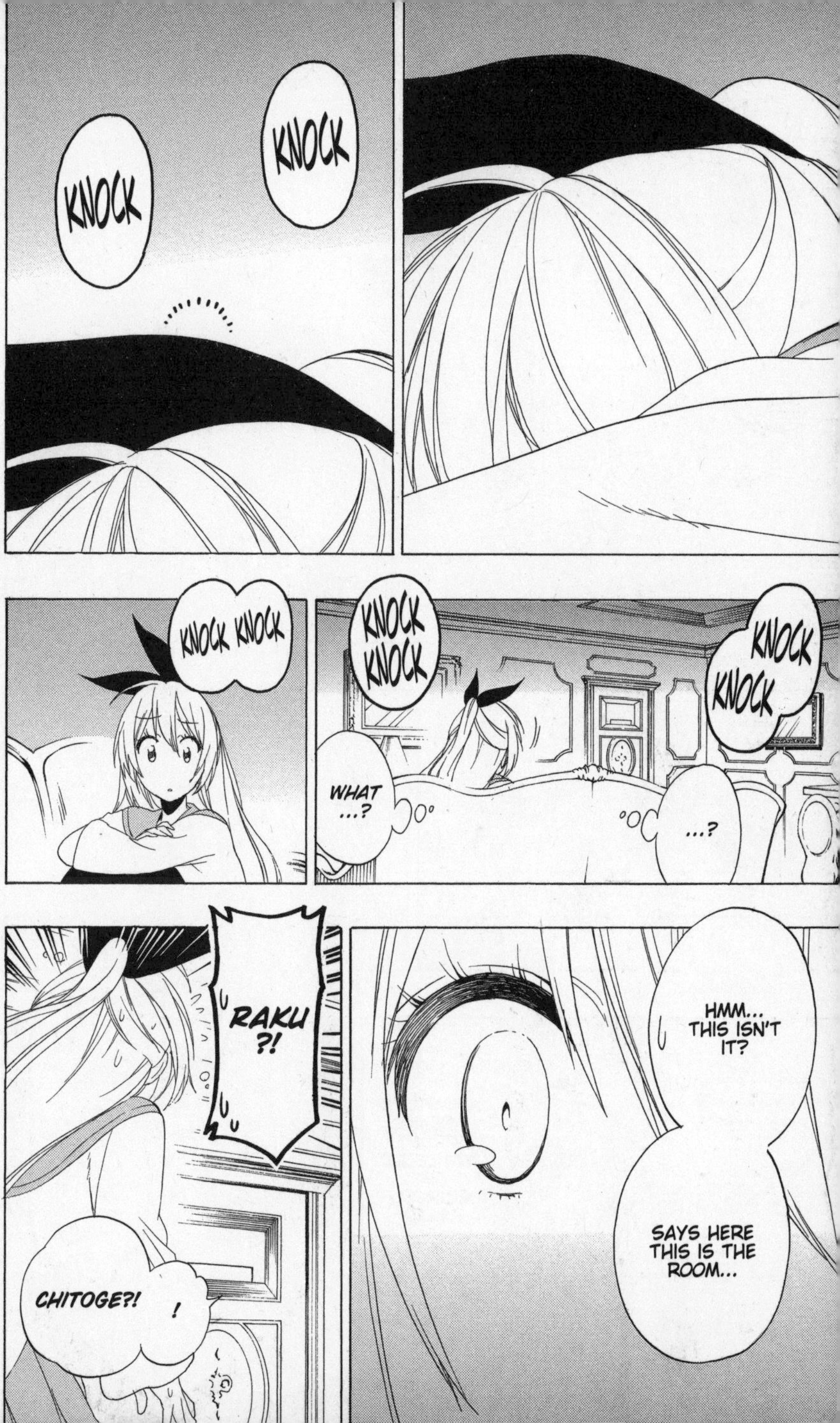
KNOCK
KNOCK
KNOCK KNOCK
KNOCK KNOCK
WHAT ...?
...?
KNOCK KNOCK
HMM... THIS ISN'T IT?
SAYS HERE THIS IS THE ROOM...
RAKU ?!
CHITOGE?!
!

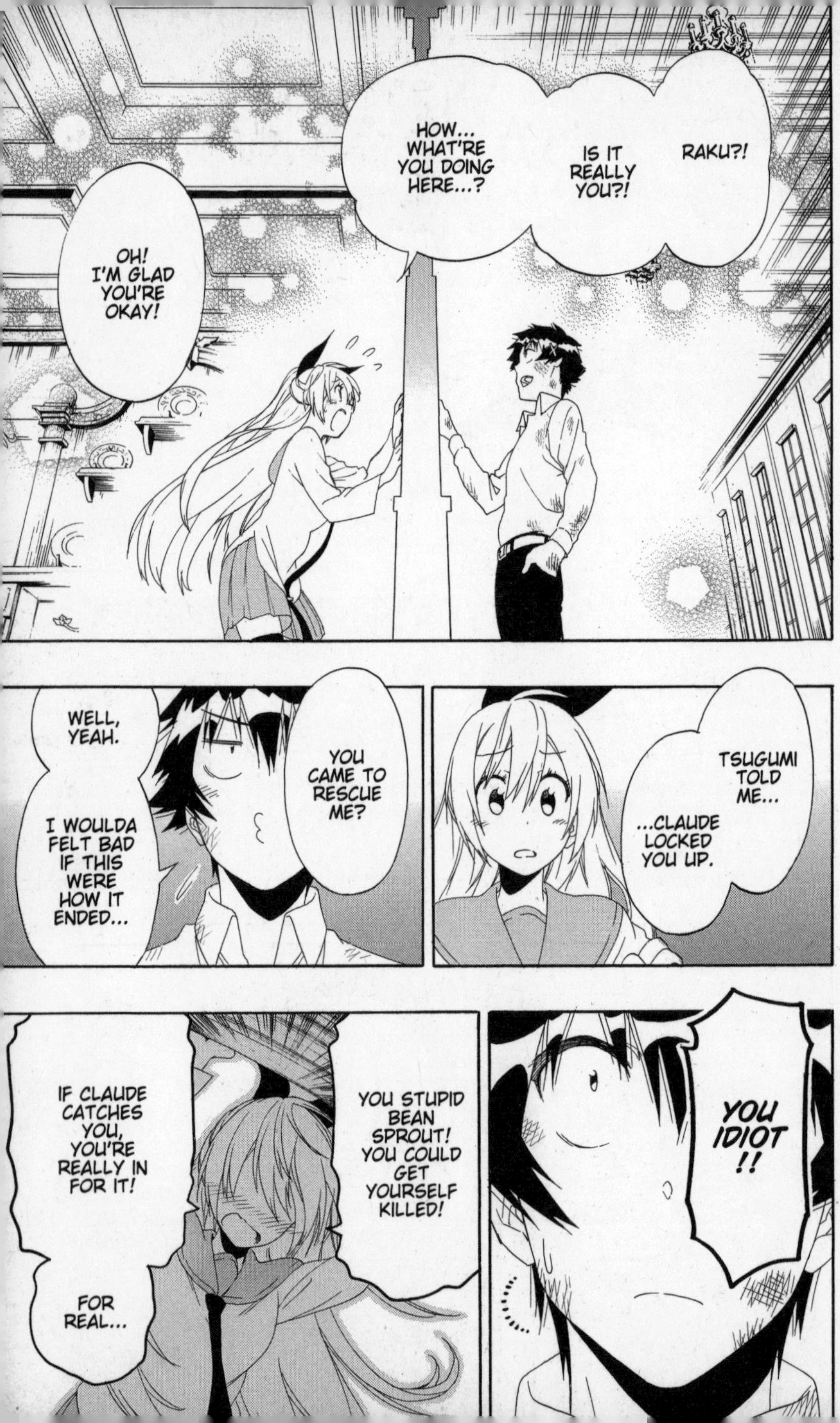
RAKU?!
IS IT REALLY YOU?!
HOW... WHAT'RE YOU DOING HERE...?
OH! I'M GLAD YOU'RE OKAY!
TSUGUMI TOLD ME...
...CLAUDE LOCKED YOU UP.
YOU CAME TO RESCUE ME?
WELL, YEAH.
I WOULDA FELT BAD IF THIS WERE HOW IT ENDED...
YOU IDIOT!!
YOU STUPID BEAN SPROUT! YOU COULD GET YOURSELF KILLED!
IF CLAUDE CATCHES YOU, YOU'RE REALLY IN FOR IT!
FOR REAL...

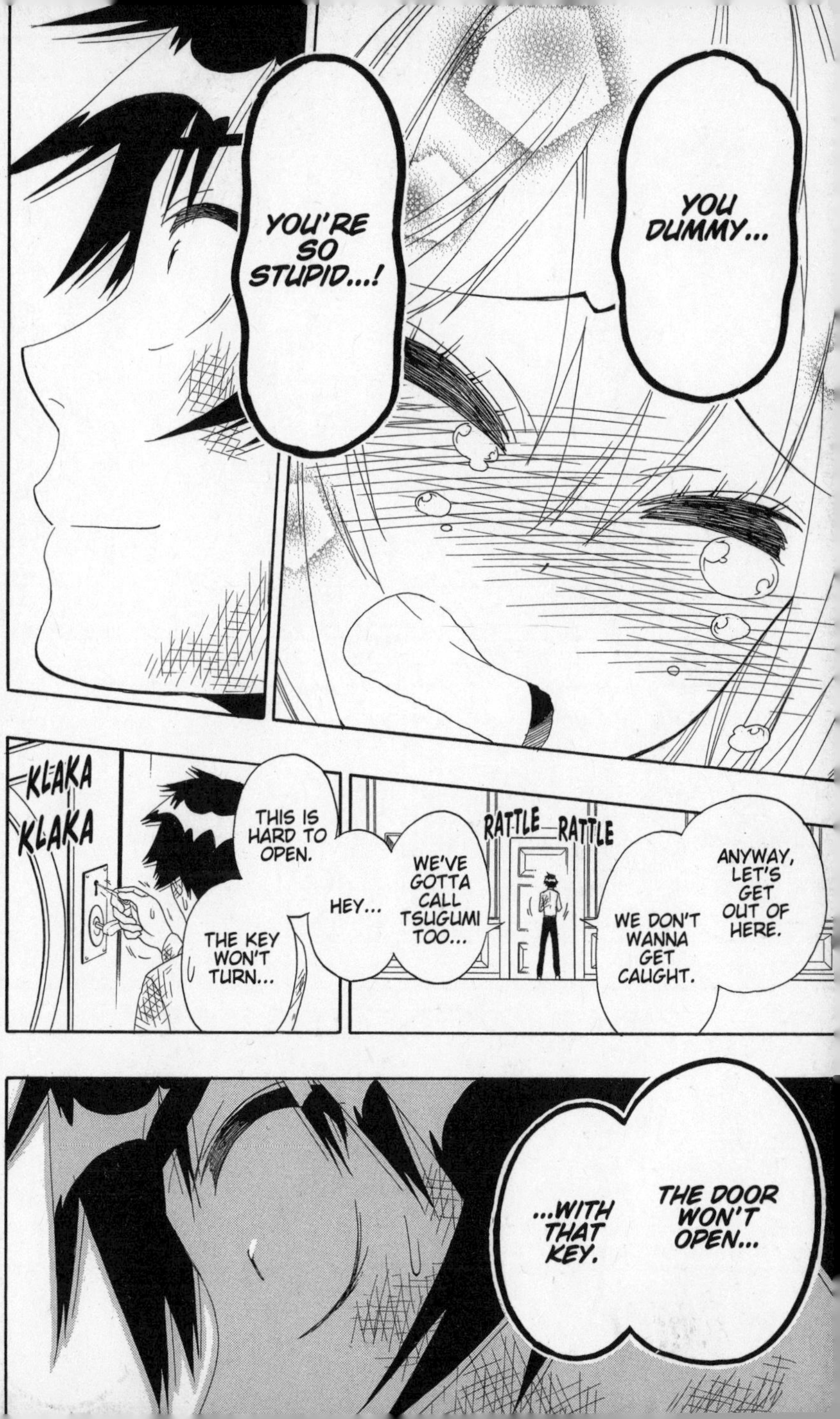
YOU DUMMY...
YOU'RE SO STUPID...!
ANYWAY, LET'S GET OUT OF HERE.
WE DON'T WANNA GET CAUGHT.
RATTLE RATTLE
WE'VE GOTTA CALL TSUGUMI TOO...
HEY...
THIS IS HARD TO OPEN.
THE KEY WON'T TURN...
KLAKA KLAKA
THE DOOR WON'T OPEN...
...WITH THAT KEY.

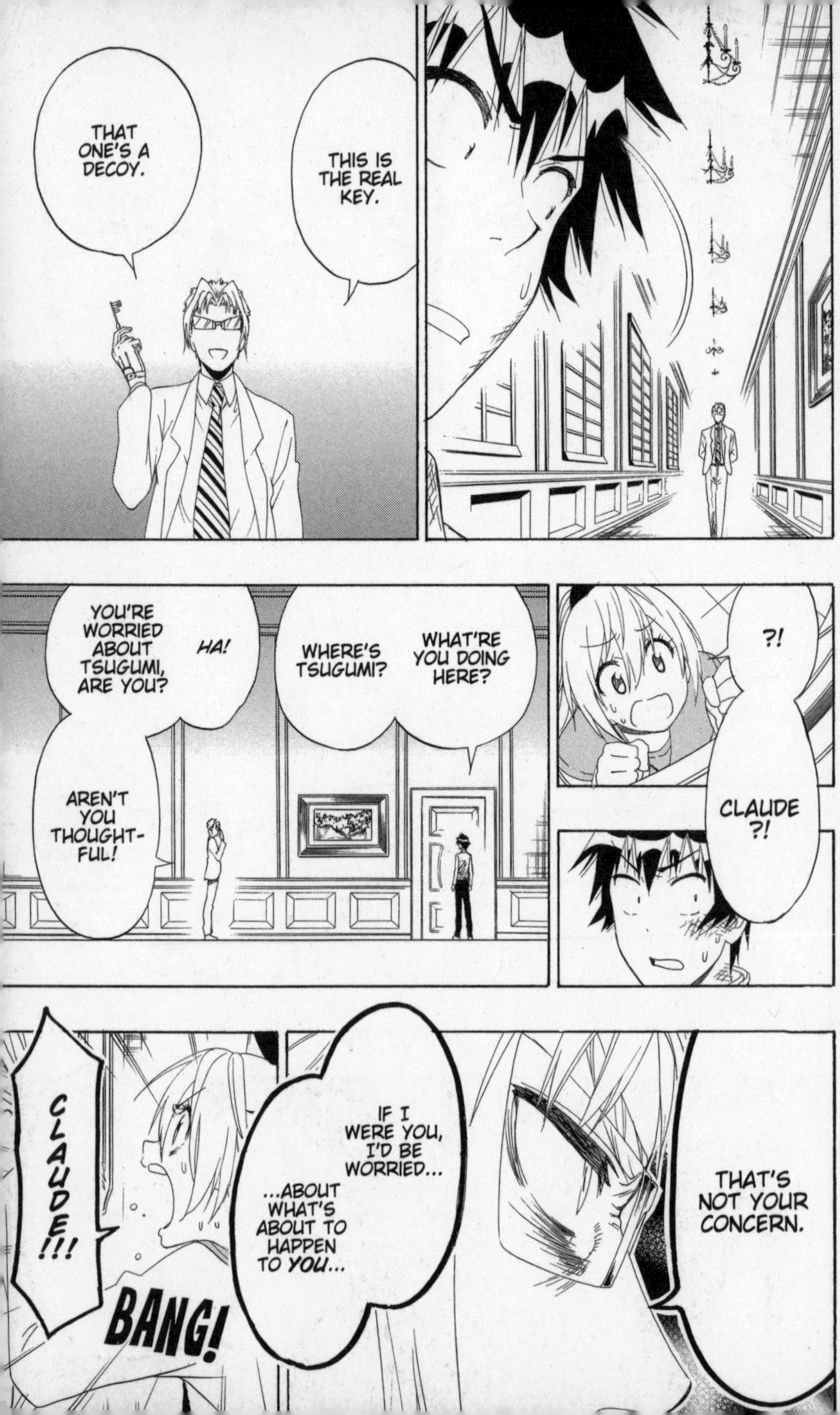
THIS IS THE REAL KEY.
THAT ONE'S A DECOY.
?!
CLAUDE?!
WHAT'RE YOU DOING HERE?
WHERE'S TSUGUMI?
HA!
YOU'RE WORRIED ABOUT TSUGUMI, ARE YOU?
AREN'T YOU THOUGHTFUL!
THAT'S NOT YOUR CONCERN.
IF I WERE YOU, I'D BE WORRIED...
...ABOUT WHAT'S ABOUT TO HAPPEN TO *YOU*...
CLAUDE!!!
BANG!

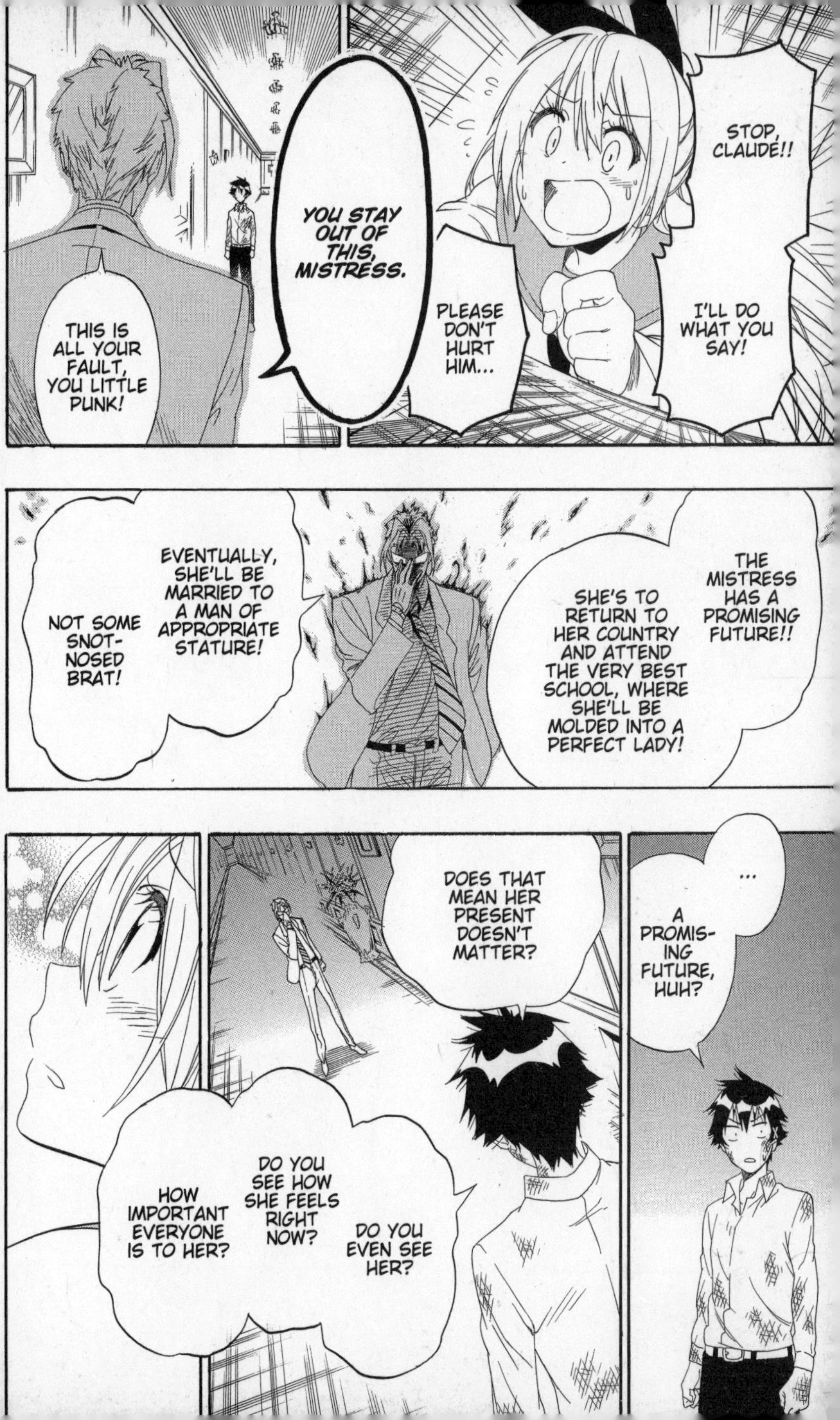
STOP, CLAUDE!!
I'LL DO WHAT YOU SAY!
PLEASE DON'T HURT HIM...
YOU STAY OUT OF THIS, MISTRESS.
THIS IS ALL YOUR FAULT, YOU LITTLE PUNK!
THE MISTRESS HAS A PROMISING FUTURE!!
SHE'S TO RETURN TO HER COUNTRY AND ATTEND THE VERY BEST SCHOOL, WHERE SHE'LL BE MOLDED INTO A PERFECT LADY!
EVENTUALLY, SHE'LL BE MARRIED TO A MAN OF APPROPRIATE STATURE!
NOT SOME SNOT-NOSED BRAT!
...
A PROMISING FUTURE, HUH?
DOES THAT MEAN HER PRESENT DOESN'T MATTER?
DO YOU EVEN SEE HER?
DO YOU SEE HOW SHE FEELS RIGHT NOW?
HOW IMPORTANT EVERYONE IS TO HER?

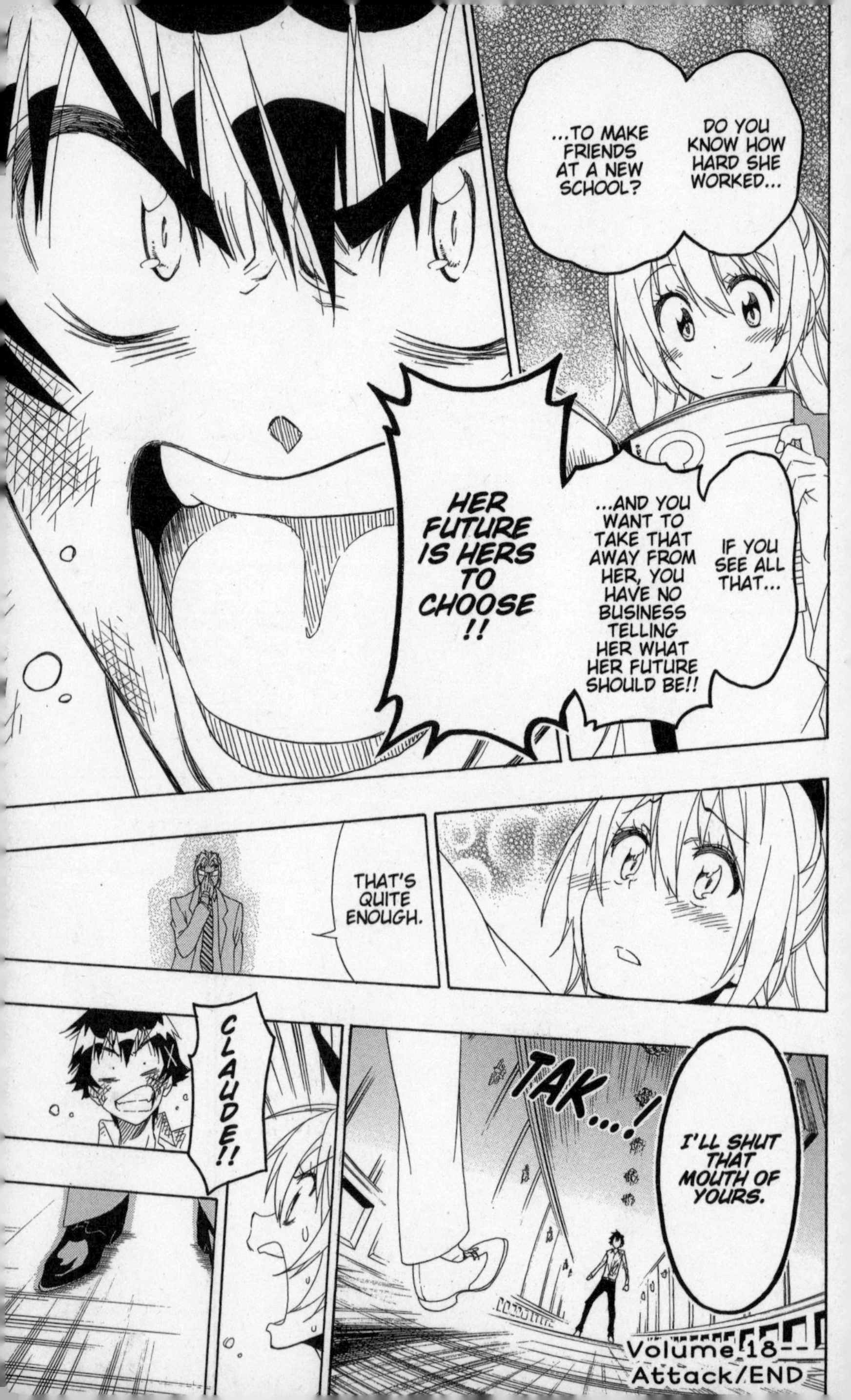
DO YOU KNOW HOW HARD SHE WORKED...
...TO MAKE FRIENDS AT A NEW SCHOOL?
IF YOU SEE ALL THAT...
...AND YOU WANT TO TAKE THAT AWAY FROM HER, YOU HAVE NO BUSINESS TELLING HER WHAT HER FUTURE SHOULD BE!!
HER FUTURE IS HERS TO CHOOSE!!
THAT'S QUITE ENOUGH.
TAK...!
I'LL SHUT THAT MOUTH OF YOURS.
CLAUDE!!

Volume 18 -- Attack/END

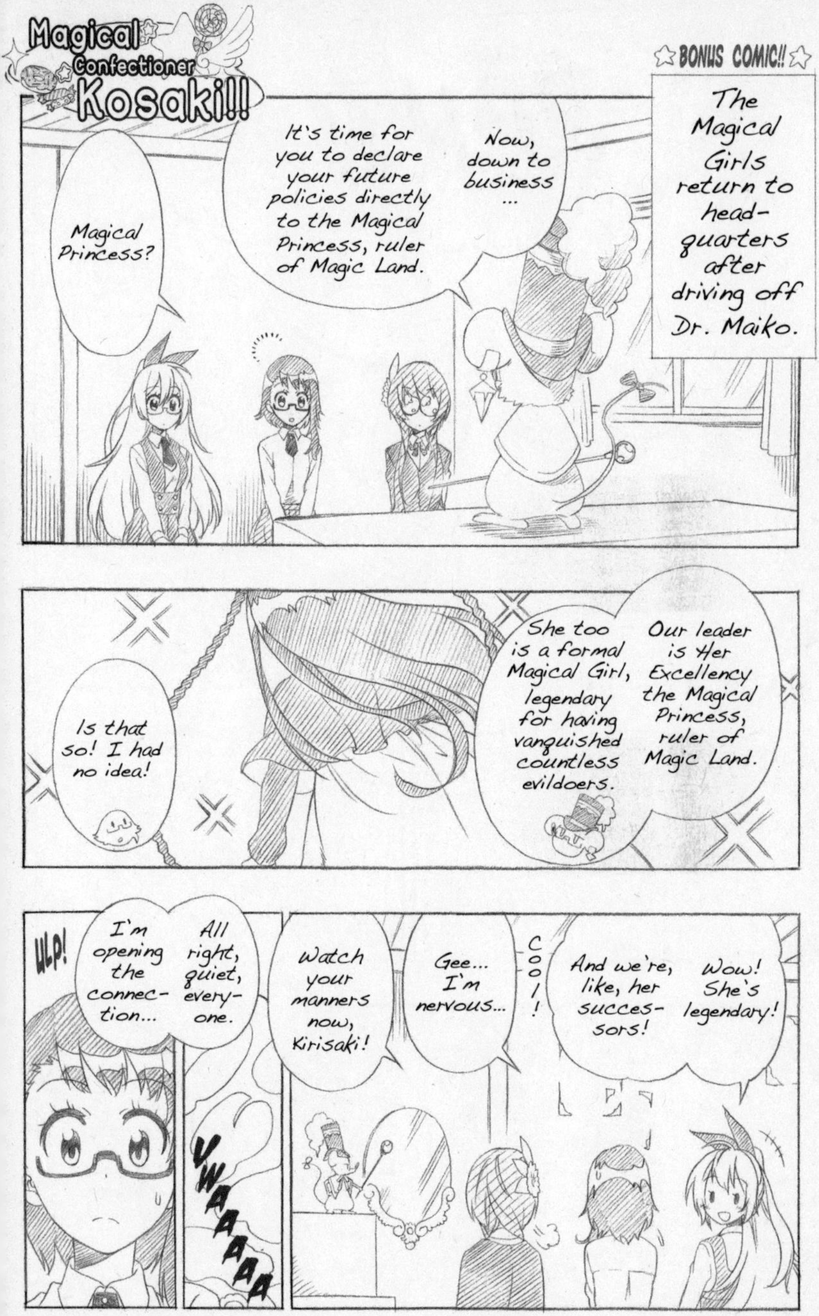
BONUS COMIC!!
Magical Confectioner Kosaki!!
The Magical Girls return to headquarters after driving off Dr. Maiko.
Now, down to business...
It's time for you to declare your future policies directly to the Magical Princess, ruler of Magic Land.
Magical Princess?
Our leader is Her Excellency the Magical Princess, ruler of Magic Land.
She too is a formal Magical Girl, legendary for having vanquished countless evildoers.
Is that so! I had no idea!
Wow! She's legendary!
And we're, like, her successors!
Cool!
Gee... I'm nervous...
Watch your manners now, Kirisaki!
All right, quiet, everyone.
I'm opening the connection...
ULP!
VWAAAAAA

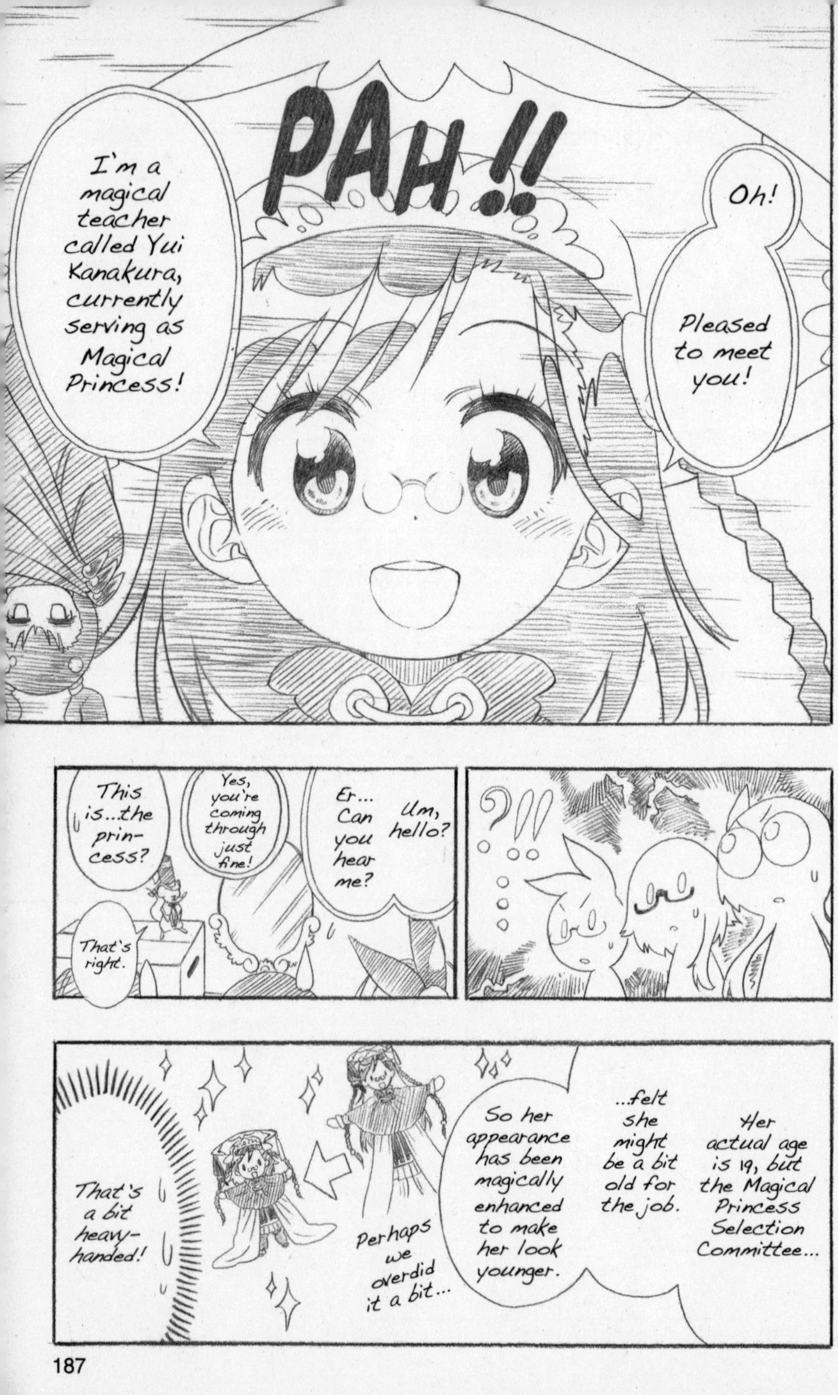
PAH!!
Oh!
Pleased to meet you!
I'm a magical teacher called Yui Kanakura, currently serving as Magical Princess!
?!!
Um, hello?
Er... Can you hear me?
Yes, you're coming through just fine!
This is...the princess?
That's right.
Her actual age is 19, but the Magical Princess Selection Committee...
...felt she might be a bit old for the job.
So her appearance has been magically enhanced to make her look younger.
Perhaps we overdid it a bit...
That's a bit heavy-handed!

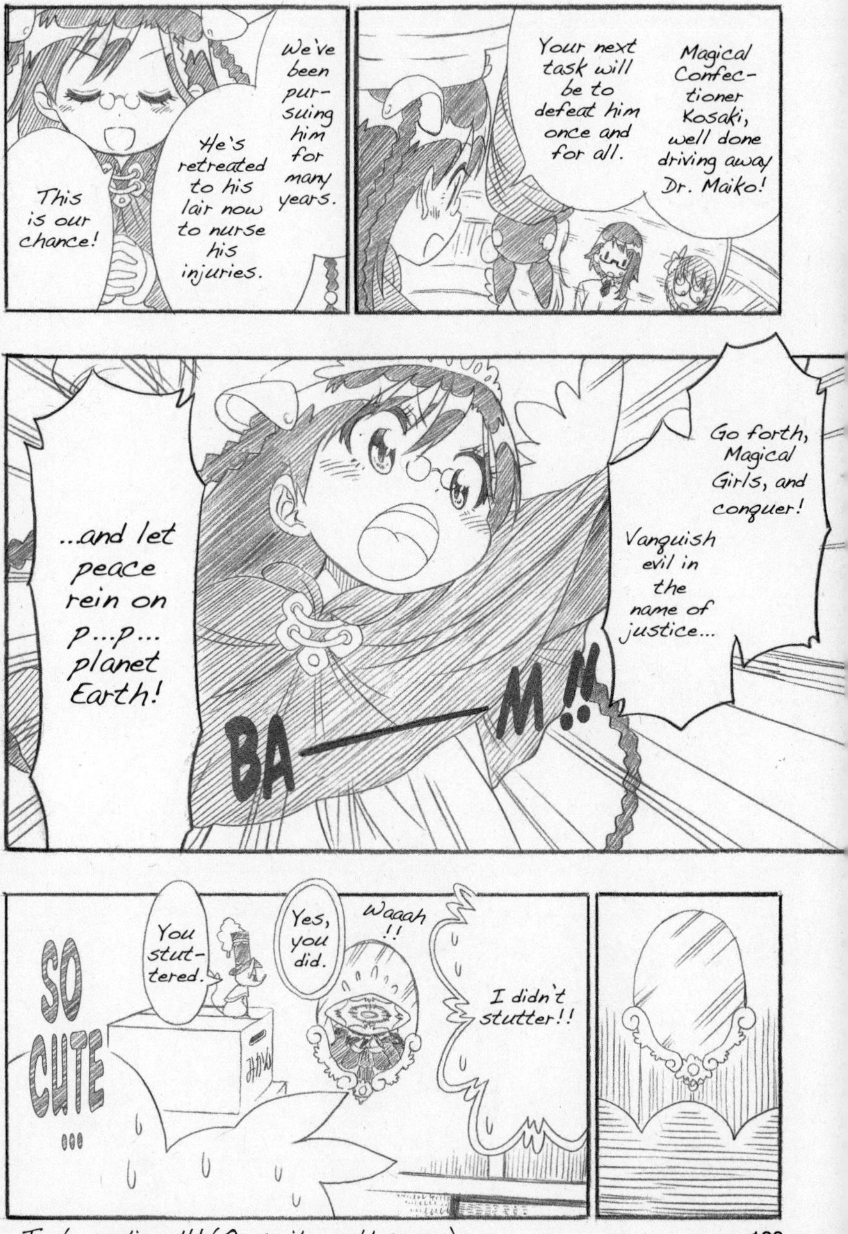
Magical Confectioner Kosaki, well done driving away Dr. Maiko!
Your next task will be to defeat him once and for all.
We've been pursuing him for many years.
He's retreated to his lair now to nurse his injuries.
This is our chance!
Go forth, Magical Girls, and conquer!
Vanquish evil in the name of justice...
...and let peace rein on p...p... planet Earth!
BA—M!!
I didn't stutter!!
Waaah!!
Yes, you did.
You stuttered.
SO CUTE...

To be continued!! (Or so it would seem...)

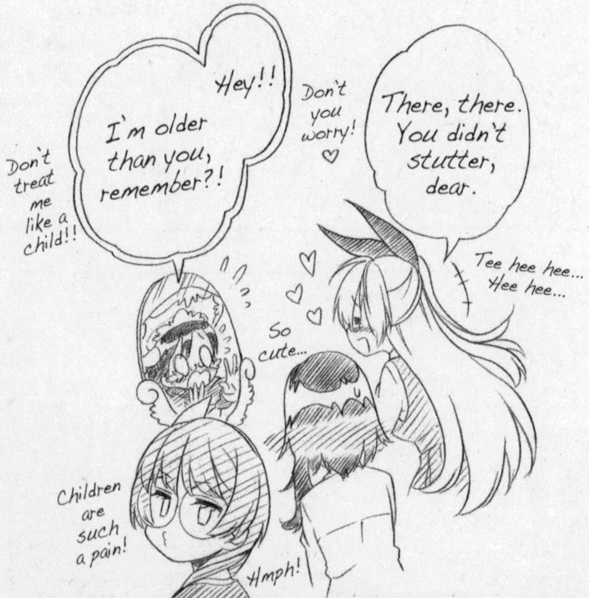
There, there. You didn't stutter, dear.
Don't you worry! ♡
Tee hee hee... Hee hee...
Hey!! I'm older than you, remember?!
Don't treat me like a child!!
So cute...
Hmph!
Children are such a pain!

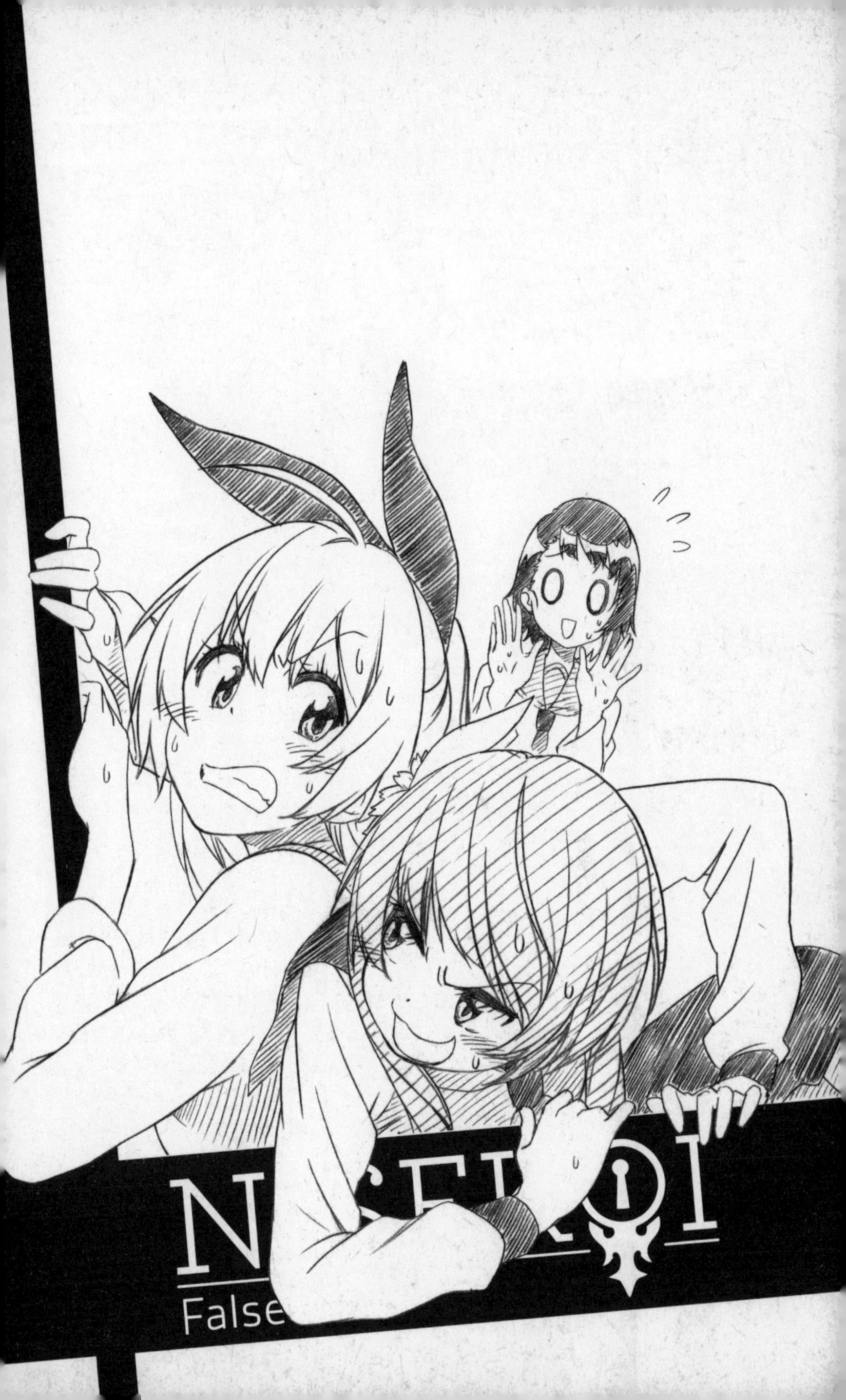
False

You're Reading the WRONG WAY!

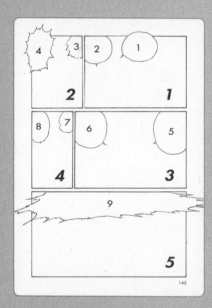

NISEKOI reads from right to left, starting in the upper-right corner. Japanese is read from right to left, meaning that action, sound effects, and word-balloon order are completely reversed from English order.

NISEKOI:
False Love
VOLUME 18
SHONEN JUMP Manga Edition

Story and Art by
NAOSHI KOMI

Translation ⟋ Camellia Nieh
Touch-Up Art & Lettering ⟋ Stephen Dutro
Design ⟋ Fawn Lau
Shonen Jump Series Editor ⟋ John Bae
Graphic Novel Editor ⟋ Amy Yu

Published by VIZ Media, LLC
P.O. Box 77010
San Francisco, CA 94107

10 9 8 7 6 5 4 3 2 1
First printing, November 2016

www.shonenjump.com   www.viz.com

When I look something up, I often wind up reading about stuff totally unrelated to my original question. The other day, I found myself reading about intestinal blockages and the compound armor on military tanks. What was I thinking?

Naoshi Komi

Got a problem with that?

Second Time

NAOSHI KOMI was born in Kochi Prefecture, Japan, on March 28, 1986. His first serialized work in *Weekly Shonen Jump* was the series *Double Arts*. His current series, *Nisekoi*, is serialized in *Weekly Shonen Jump*.